Educational Leadership

This Reader forms part of *Educational Leadership: context, strategy and collaboration*, (E856), a major new 60-point module in the Masters in Education programme, and one of the two modules forming the specialist Leadership and Management qualification in the programme.

The Open University Masters in Education

The Open University Masters in Education is now firmly established as the most popular postgraduate degree for education professionals in Europe, with over 3000 students registered each year. It is designed particularly for those with experience of teaching, the advisory service, educational administration or allied fields. Specialist lines in leadership and management, applied linguistics and special needs/inclusive education are available within the programme. Successful study on the MA entitles students to apply for entry into the Open University Doctorate in Education programme.

Details of this programme and other Open University modules can be obtained from the Student Registration and Enquiry Service, The Open University, PO Box 197, Milton Keynes MK7 6BJ, United Kingdom; telephone: +44 (0) 845 300 6090; e-mail: general-enquiries@open.ac.uk.

Alternatively, you may wish to visit the Open University website at www.open.ac.uk, where you can learn more about the wide range of modules and qualifications offered at all levels by The Open University.

Educational
Leadership

Context, Strategy and Collaboration

Margaret Preedy, Nigel Bennett and Christine Wise

The Open University

SAGE

Los Angeles | London | New Delhi
Singapore | Washington DC

First published 2012

The Open University
Walton Hall
Milton Keynes
MK7 6AA
United Kingdom
www.open.ac.uk

SAGE Publications Ltd
1 Oliver's Yard
55 City Road
London EC1Y 1SP

SAGE Publications Inc.
2455 Teller Road
Thousand Oaks, California 91320

SAGE Publications India Pvt Ltd
B 1/I 1 Mohan Cooperative Industrial Area
Mathura Road
New Delhi 110 044

SAGE Publications Asia-Pacific Pte Ltd
33 Pekin Street #02-01
Far East Square
Singapore 048763

Library of Congress Control Number: 2011920777

British Library Cataloguing in Publication data

A catalogue record for this book is available from the British Library

ISBN 978-1-4462-0163-3
ISBN 978-1-4462-0164-0 (pbk)

Typeset by C&M Digitals (P) Ltd, Chennai, India
Printed in Great Britain by TJ International Ltd, Padstow, Cornwall
Printed on paper from sustainable resources

Contents

Acknowledgements vii

About the Editors x

Introduction 1
Margaret Preedy, Nigel Bennett and Christine Wise

Part 1: Leadership theories and values **9**

1 An overview of the leadership discourses 11
 Simon Western

2 From successful school leadership towards
 distributed leadership 25
 Lejf Moos

3 Leading with moral purpose: the place of ethics 38
 Paul T. Begley

4 Emotional intelligence, emotional labour and
 affective leadership 52
 Sam Held and Judy McKimm

Part 2: Strategic leadership and managing change **65**

5 Concepts of leadership in organizational change 67
 Gill Robinson Hickman

6 The nature and dimensions of strategic leadership 83
 Brent Davies and Barbara J. Davies

7 The strategy lenses 96
 Gerry Johnson, Richard Whittington and Kevan Scholes

8 The practice of leadership in the messy world of organizations 115
 Jean-Louis Denis, Ann Langley and Linda Rouleau

Part 3:   Leadership in context   **129**

9   Reframing the role of organizations in policy implementation:
    resources *for* practice, *in* practice   131
    James P. Spillane, Louis M. Gomez and Leigh Mesler

10 Contextualizing leader dynamics: how public service leaders
    endeavour to build influence   145
    Mike Wallace and Michael Tomlinson

11 Stories of compliance and subversion in a prescriptive
    policy environment   159
    John MacBeath

12 Evaluation, accountability, and performance measurement in
    national education systems: trends, methods, and issues   173
    Katherine E. Ryan and Irwin Feller

13 'Blended leadership': employee perspectives on effective
    leadership in the UK Further Education sector   189
    David Collinson and Margaret Collinson

14 Leadership for diversity and inclusion   201
    Jacky Lumby

Part 4:   Partnerships and collaboration   **213**

15 Reconfiguring urban leadership: taking a perspective
    on community   215
    Kathryn A. Riley

16 Networks as power bases for school improvement   227
    Tessa A. Moore and Michael P. Kelly

17 Inter-professional work and expertise: new roles at the
    boundaries of schools   240
    Anne Edwards, Ingrid Lunt and Eleni Stamou

18 Approaches to system leadership: lessons learned
    and policy pointers   253
    Beatriz Pont and David Hopkins

Part 5:   Looking to the future   **267**

19 Leadership, participation and power in the school system   269
    Richard Hatcher

20 The fourth way   283
    Andy Hargreaves and Dennis Shirley

Index   289

Acknowledgements

Chapter 1

Western, S. (2008) 'An overview of the leadership discourses', chapters 12 and 13 in Western, S. *Leadership: a critical text*, London, Sage Publications Ltd. You may access the author's webpage at www.simonwestern.com

Chapter 2

Moos, L. (2010) 'From successful school leadership towards distributed leadership', chapter 6 in Huber, S. (ed.) *School Leadership: international perspectives*, Dordrecht, Springer.

Chapter 3

Begley, P. (2010) 'Leading with moral purpose: the place of ethics', in Bush, T., Bell, L. and Middlewood, D. (eds) *The Principles of Educational Leadership and Management*, 2nd edition, London, Sage Publications Ltd.

Chapter 4

Commissioned chapter by Held, S. and McKinn, J. 'Emotional intelligence, emotional labour and affective leadership' based on a reworking of 'Emotional intelligence, emotion and collaborative leadership', chapter 7 in McKimm, J. and Phillips, K. (eds) (2009) *Leadership and Management in Integrated Services*, Exeter, Learning Matters.

Chapter 5

Hickman, G. (2010) 'Concepts of leadership in organizational change', chapter 3 in Hickman, G. *Leading Change in Multiple Contexts*, Thousand Oaks, California, Sage Publications Inc.

Chapter 6

Davies, B. and Davies, B.J. (2010) 'The nature and dimensions of strategic leadership', in *International Studies in Educational Administration*, Vol. 38, no. 1, pp 5–21. Printed with the kind permission of the Commonwealth Council for Educational Administration and Management (CCEAM).

Chapter 7

Johnson, G., Whittington, R. and Scholes, K. (2011) 'The strategy lenses', in *Exploring Strategy*, 9th edition, Pearson.

Chapter 8
Denis, J-L. et al. (2010) 'The practice of leadership in the messy world of organizations', in *Leadership*, Vol. 6, no. 1, pp. 67–88. London, Sage Publications Ltd.

Chapter 9
Spillane, J. et al. (2009) 'Reframing the role of organizations in policy implementation', chapter 33 in Sykes, G. et al. (eds) *Handbook of Education Policy Research*, New York, Routledge (for the AERA). Reprinted by permission of the publisher (Taylor & Francis Ltd, http://www.informaworld.com).

Chapter 10
Wallace, M. and Tomlinson, M. (2010) 'Contextualizing leader dynamics: how public service leaders endeavour to build influence', in *Leadership*, Vol. 6, no. 1, pp. 21–45. London, Sage Publications Ltd.

Chapter 11
MacBeath, J. (2008) 'Stories of compliance and subversion in a prescriptive policy environment', in *Educational Management, Administration and Leadership*, Vol. 36, no. 1, pp.123–48. London, Sage Publications Ltd.

Chapter 12
Ryan, K. and Feller, I. (2009) 'Evaluation, accountability, and performance measurement in national education systems', chapter 10 in Ryan, K. and Cousins, J. (eds) *Sage International Handbook of Educational Evaluation*, Thousand Oaks, California, Sage Publications Inc.

Chapter 13
Collinson, D. and Collinson, M. (2009) '"Blended leadership": employee perspectives on effective leadership in the UK Further Education sector', in *Leadership,* Vol. 5, no. 3, pp. 365–80. London, Sage Publications Ltd.

Chapter 14
Lumby, J. (2010) 'Leadership for diversity and inclusion', chapter 12 in Bush, T., Bell, L. and Middlewood, D. (eds) *The Principles of Educational Leadership and Management*, 2nd edition, London, Sage Publications Ltd.

Chapter 15
Riley, K.A. (2009) 'Reconfiguring urban leadership: taking a perspective on community', in *School Leadership and Management*, Vol 29, no 1, pp. 51–63. Reprinted by permission of the publisher (Taylor & Francis Ltd, http://www.informaworld.com).

Chapter 16
Moore, T. and Kelly, M. (2009) 'Networks as power bases for school improvement', in *School Leadership and Management*, Vol. 29, no. 4, pp. 391–404. Reprinted by permission of the publisher (Taylor & Francis Ltd, http://www.informaworld.com).

Chapter 17
Edwards, A. et al. (2010) 'Inter-professional work and expertise: new roles at the boundaries of schools', in *British Educational Research Journal*, Vol. 36, no. 1, pp. 27–45. Reprinted by permission of the publisher (Taylor & Francis Ltd, http://www.informaworld.com).

Chapter 18
Pont, B. and Hopkins, D. (2008) 'Approaches to system leadership: lessons learned and policy pointers', chapter 9 in OECD, *Improving School Leadership: Volume 2: Case Studies on System Leadership*, OECD Publishing.

Chapter 19
Commissioned chapter by Hatcher, R. 'Leadership, participation and power in the school system', drawing on two of his published articles in (2005) *British Journal of Sociology of Education* and (2008) *Management in Education*, London, Routledge and Sage Publications Ltd.

Chapter 20
Hargreaves, A. and Shirley, D. (2009) 'The fourth way', chapter 4 in *The Fourth Way: the inspiring future for educational change*, Thousand Oaks, California, Corwin Press.

About the Editors

Dr Margaret Preedy is a Senior Lecturer in the Department of Education at The Open University. Her research interests include school improvement, implementing change, and student attitudes towards education.

Professor Nigel Bennett is Emeritus Professor of Leadership and Management in Education at The Open University.

Dr Christine Wise is a Senior Lecturer in the Department of Education at The Open University. Her research interests include the role of middle leaders in education and the development of professional identity.

Introduction

Margaret Preedy, Nigel Bennett and Christine Wise

There is widespread recognition that leadership is a key factor in successful educational organisations. At the same time, the demands on educational leaders have arguably never been greater. This volume explores current thinking and debate on the role of educational leaders and the strategic challenges they face. We do not seek to provide ready answers but rather to stimulate critical reflection and discussion.

The environment in which schools and colleges operate is characterised by increasing turbulence and uncertainty as a result of economic, social and political pressures. The globalisation of capital and labour and the impetus for nation states to compete in the international marketplace create policy pressures for educational organisations to produce a labour force with the skills needed for this marketplace, with schools and colleges held accountable for year-on-year improvements in student outcomes: 'Education is now seen as a crucial factor in ensuring economic productivity and competitiveness in the context of ... the pressures and requirements of globalisation' (Ball, 2008:1). Linked to these developments, the large-scale educational reforms that have taken place in the UK, USA and many other countries over recent decades mean that educational leaders face a complex range of competing pressures and challenges, including:

- increased autonomy for schools and colleges with respect to operational decisions accompanied by
- greater accountability for their performance and spending decisions to central/state governments
- market accountability pressures as a result of competition between educational organisations, driven by the linkage of funding to student enrolments, and parental choice, accompanied by
- policy and practical incentives to develop collaborative partnerships with other educational organisations
- severe budgetary constraints as a result of the impact of the global financial crisis on national spending on education and other areas of public sector provision
- tensions between the demands of external stakeholders and internal priorities and expectations, and between the standards agenda, focused on raising student academic achievement, and a broader and more holistic focus on the overall well-being and social development of children and young people

- increasing diversity and heterogeneity of students and parents, and their needs and expectations (Huber, 2010), giving rise to the challenge of celebrating diversity while at the same time building consensus on values and purposes across the organisation.

Recognition of growing environmental ambiguity and the intensification of the demands and expectations placed on head teachers and other educational leaders has led to the realisation that the traditional model of the solo heroic leader is no longer feasible. Post-heroic perspectives emphasise the situated and relational nature of educational leadership and a shift away from the individual leader to multiple sources of influence, as exemplified in notions of distributed, teacher and 'hybrid' leadership (Gronn, 2010).

There has also been increasing acknowledgment of the limits to the influence and authority of individual and collective leadership in the face of a rapidly changing and largely unpredictable environment and permeable organisational boundaries which mean that the 'external' context is no longer 'out there' as in the past, but is a central influence on organisational events. These perspectives highlight the uncertainty and impermanence of leadership, the less than rational aspects of policy making and practice, and the loosely coupled nature of structures and actions within educational organisations and across education systems more broadly. Another important trend in the literature has been the growing attention to the moral and ethical dimensions of leadership in terms of personal values and integrity and in fostering a shared commitment to the organisation's core purposes and values.

This book explores the challenges outlined above and their implications for how educational leadership is conceived and enacted. It draws on the work of many leading writers in the field from the UK and elsewhere. While much of the literature on educational leadership continues to be largely Anglo-centric in origin and approach (Walker and Dimmock, 2002), we have included a strong international perspective in the chapters included here, representing authors from a range of countries and work which takes a trans-national perspective in exploring themes and issues that are of widespread interest and concern in a global setting. We have also selected a range of studies set in specific national contexts, particularly England, to explore ideas that we believe are of wider relevance. The selection also seeks to represent a range of sectors and settings within and beyond education. The volume is based on the premise that it is illuminating for educational leaders to transcend national and sectoral boundaries in their thinking – there is much to be learned from reflecting on one's professional practice in the light of insights from other cultures and sectors. The chapters here also take a range of conceptual and methodological approaches: theoretical overviews, research studies, applications of conceptual frameworks to leadership practice, and case examples.

In exploring this complex landscape of educational leadership, the chapters in this book are organised around five broad themes. Part 1 examines conceptualisations of leadership, including the important role of values and moral purposes underpinning leadership integrity. Part 2 explores a key task for educational leaders: strategic leadership and managing change. Part 3 moves on to look at leadership in context and the influences of external and internal organisational factors on how leadership is enacted in practice. Part 4 then explores partnerships and collaboration, within and across educational organisations. Part 5 concludes with a look to the future, drawing on two contrasting perspectives – one proposing a relatively optimistic view of educational reform, while the other proposes a more critical approach, questioning the dominant paradigm within educational leadership. We outline briefly below the chapters comprising each part.

Part 1: leadership theories and values

In Chapter 1, Western presents a critical introduction to the development of leadership theory, identifying three broad discourses that group together the multiplicity of theoretical stances developed during the twentieth century. He then explores the possibility of a new developing discourse, eco-leadership, which will take account constructively of the developing moral and ecological issues resulting from globalisation. He argues that the discourses he identifies are not sequential but developmental, and that they co-exist both in organisations and, importantly, within individuals' thinking about leadership practice.

In Chapter 2, Moos pursues the arguments about the moral nature of leadership further, incorporating into the discussion issues of organisational effectiveness and the ideas of shared, distributed or dispersed leadership that have developed in education since the turn of the century, and in the wider general leadership literature in the 15 years before that. Moos locates his discussion in the context of the Danish educational system, with its relatively flat hierarchies and low power-differential between students and teachers.

Chapter 3 explores moral issues in more depth. Begley argues that educational leaders must keep in mind the core purposes of education and the values that are derived from them as the basis for moral leadership. He explores the multiple sources of our personal, professional and social values, and how educational leaders respond to the ethical dilemmas they encounter. The chapter identifies four key ethical paradigms and proposes how they might be used to guide leaders' moral analysis of particular problems and dilemmas, pointing to the critical importance of context in leading with moral purpose.

Chapter 4, by Held and McKimm, concludes this part of the volume. The authors move us away from the traditional rational perception of the context of leadership to discuss how leaders must both face and address their own emotional responses to circumstances and recognise those of their colleagues. In examining these themes, they explore the strengths and weaknesses of the popular concept of emotional intelligence as a means of understanding and developing sensitive responses to emotions in leadership and organisations more generally. In this, a key consideration for leaders is the extent to which they must 'perform' emotional labour in order to acknowledge and respond to their colleagues' needs.

Part 2: strategic leadership and managing change

It is essential for educational leaders to be able to manage multiple and ongoing changes, balancing externally initiated innovations with the organisation's own values, purposes and priorities. This entails a strategic overview, developing an agreed way forward which looks to the medium and longer-term direction of the organisation.

In Chapter 5, Hickman puts forward a range of concepts for understanding the leadership of change. She takes an international perspective, drawing on ideas from various cultures, to argue that leading change is a complex and collective process, so no one explanatory model or approach is adequate. Instead, she suggests that we need a compilation of leadership concepts to guide action and to take into account the differing challenges and concerns involved in externally and internally focused aspects of change. While leader-focused theories and authority structures tend to be dominant, successful innovation entails preparing and involving people throughout the organisation to take part in leading the change process.

The next chapter, by Davies and Davies, draws on the authors' research to look in more detail at the nature of strategic leadership and the activities that strategic leaders undertake. They identify three broad approaches to strategic development: the traditional planning model, emergent strategy which recognises ongoing external and internal change and evolution, and strategic intent, where leaders and their colleagues have a picture of the desired future position but the means of achieving this are not clear. In these circumstances, it is argued, it is necessary to engage organisational members in a learning and development phase to work towards achieving the defined intents. The authors go on to explore what strategic leaders do to develop a strategic approach across the organisation.

In Chapter 7, Johnson et al. develop the theme of the limitations of traditional planning approaches to strategy in proposing different lenses or perspectives on the strategy process, arguing that we need to draw on each of these to develop a rounded picture of the realities of how strategies are developed. They suggest that we need to question the conventional wisdom of strategy development as a logical process of analysis and decision making by taking alternative views: the role of people and their experiences, of new ideas and of discourse in shaping strategy.

In the final chapter in this part, Denis et al. also challenge rational models of organisational change, drawing on case examples from an empirical study of healthcare organisations in Canada. They point to the ambiguities and plurality of interests and values in large organisations and examine leadership as a practical activity within this context. The authors argue that leadership is dynamic, collective, situated and dialectic – leaders are embedded in settings and networks that they do not fully control and are subject to unpredictable forces for change, including the consequences of their actions and decisions.

Part 3: leadership in context

This part turns to look at the interrelationships between the external environment and internal contextual factors and how these impact on educational leadership.

In Chapter 9, Spillane et al. explore the important theme of how policy is implemented in educational organisations. Like Denis et al., Spillane and his colleagues focus on practice as it unfolds in the interactions between people in particular settings. They explore various organisational resources – human and social capital, technology and organisational routines – and how these enable and constrain policy implementation. The authors argue that we need to attend not just to what resources are available but to what organisational members working collectively do with them in particular places and at particular times.

Wallace and Tomlinson, in Chapter 10, draw on a qualitative study of senior public sector leaders to examine the evolutionary relationship between leader activity and their external and internal contextual settings. They portray leaders' interactions with their environment as a dynamic process where leaders can, to varying degrees, affect and 'manipulate' contextual factors to extend their scope for future influence. From this perspective, leadership is not just context-dependent but in many ways context-creating.

MacBeath also explores the nature of the relationship between leaders and their contexts, focusing on head teachers' interpretation of and response to the policy environment. His study contrasts with that of Wallace and Tomlinson in suggesting that educational leaders see little room to manoeuvre in influencing the external environment. Perspectives of the 12 head teachers in the study showed a wide range, from, at one extreme, seeing policy requirements as a positive force for improving learning and teaching, and, at the other extreme, perceiving government policy as imposing dysfunctional strategies which deskilled and disempowered heads and teachers. MacBeath argues that government policies have made a deep imprint on the practice and discourse of schools. While some heads expressed dissatisfaction with various aspects of external evaluation and assessment requirements, the perceived scope for challenging and resisting external authorities and policies was very limited – heads and their staff tended to 'play safe', complying, with varying degrees of willingness, to external mandates. As the author notes, the apparent lack of room for dissent is antithetical to notions of the learning organisation which engages in an ongoing process of challenging and reviewing its activities and thinking.

Ryan and Feller, in Chapter 12, take a transnational approach in exploring two key policy themes which impact on leaders in all educational organisations – national systems for evaluation and accountability. They argue that accountability and performance measurement have become intertwined; performance measurement is the increasingly preferred or mandated means through which schools, colleges and higher education institutions are held accountable. Their analysis highlights the importance of specific contexts in how national policies play out. Accountability and evaluation can have very different meanings and outcomes in different national contexts and different education sectors. The authors caution against the dangers of 'one size fits all' and technical–managerial approaches to educational accountability.

The next two chapters turn to focus more specifically on internal contextual influences on leadership, looking at the UK further education (FE) sector. Collinson and Collinson argue that studies of leadership effectiveness tend to take dichotomous approaches, focusing either on the individual qualities of 'hero' leaders or on the collective nature of 'post heroic' leadership. Their study of FE staff views found that these respondents value practices that combine elements of both models, a combination of delegation and direction, and internal and external engagement, which the authors term 'blended leadership'. They highlight the value of dialectical studies of leadership which explore the dynamic tensions between seemingly opposite approaches and practices, transcending the simplistic either/or assumptions found in much leadership literature.

Finally in this part, Lumby, in Chapter 14, examines leadership for diversity and inclusion, drawing together some key concepts and research and their implications for leadership action. She notes the multiple and contested definitions of both 'diversity' and 'inclusion', based on different literatures and research traditions, and looks at some of the major issues in identifying organisational goals and leadership preparation to develop inclusive educational organisations. While official policy documents espouse a commitment to increasing equality of opportunity and social justice, there continues to be a wide gulf between intention and actual practice – there is a long way to go in transcending issues of inequality and achieving truly inclusive educational organisations.

Part 4: partnerships and collaboration

Here we begin to look in a much more focused way outside the remit of the single leader or single institution. There is growing interest in the ways in which cooperation and collaboration can improve not only the educational experience of children and young people through raising standards, but also the life experience of children and young people through better integration of services and responses.

In the first chapter, Riley maps the key features of the community contexts in which a range of urban schools facing challenging circumstances are located, highlighting the community-related issues for school leaders. She suggests that it is necessary to reconfigure leadership to strengthen connections with the communities and to build trust for the benefit of children and young people.

In Chapter 16, entitled 'Networks as power bases for school improvement', Moore and Kelly critique assumptions about collaborative working arrangements as tools for school improvement. They look at two English primary school initiatives designed as a response to the national standards agenda and question the impact of power, authority and influence on the networks and their long-term working. They conclude by suggesting an 'ideal' model for networks that might improve their sustainability.

Chapter 17 looks at some of the issues facing workers at the boundaries of the – supposedly – more integrated schools in England. Edwards et al. draw on their own research into the new roles that have been created by the changes in teachers' contracts and the need to interface with the wider group of professionals in Children's Services. 'Inter-professional work and expertise: new roles at the boundaries of schools' examines these new roles and questions whether those occupying the new posts that have arisen have the expertise to do the work required without considerable development.

In Chapter 18, Pont and Hopkins look more widely across five OECD countries to consider the commonalities and differences in national approaches to introducing system leadership. The chapter, entitled 'Approaches to system leadership: lessons learned and policy pointers', considers the benefits and challenges of these collaborations. It proposes that there are benefits to this level of sharing of skills, expertise, experience and resources, but that there are system-level challenges that need to be addressed if the potential is to be fully realised.

Part 5: looking to the future

The volume concludes with two contrasting perspectives. Hatcher (Chapter 19) takes a critical stance in examining two key themes in leadership research and practice – distributed and systems leadership. He argues that the dominant academic and policy paradigm of educational leadership neglects questions of power within and over the education system – managerial power and state power – and how these limit authentic democracy and public participation in education. He suggests that within schools and school networks, there are contradictions between the benefits of participation claimed for distributed leadership and networks and the structural constraints of hierarchical management structures driven by state power. He argues that we need to continue to critique the dominant view and to develop credible alternatives based on authentic collective participation in decision making.

In Chapter 20, Hargreaves and Shirley propose an agenda for future educational reform which brings together government policy, professional development and public engagement into an interactive partnership around values of creativity and inclusiveness to promote learning, achievement and well-being. They argue that earlier approaches to educational reform have failed internationally and that a new approach is needed which promotes educational change through deepened and demanding learning, professional quality and engagement and invigorated community development. The authors put forward an appealing and optimistic vision of the way forward for education.

Finally, it should be noted that this selection of reading is partial and selective – it makes no claim to provide a comprehensive picture of the educational leadership field. Instead, it presents a range of perspectives on some key areas of the strategic and outward-facing aspects of educational leadership. In particular, it does not seek to cover key areas of leading learning and organisational improvement which are addressed elsewhere in Open University publications and in a planned companion volume to this one. We hope that this collection will contribute to critical thinking and debate among researchers, practitioners and students of educational leadership.

References

Ball, S. (2008) *The Education Debate*. Bristol: The Policy Press.

Gronn, P. (2010) 'Where to next for educational leadership?', in T. Bush, L. Bell and D. Middlewood (eds) *The Principles of Educational Leadership and Management*, 2nd edn. London: Sage.

Huber, S. (ed.) (2010) *School Leadership – International Perspectives*. Dordrecht: Springer.

Walker, A. and Dimmock, C. (eds) (2002) *School Leadership and Administration: Adopting a Cultural View*. London: Routledge-Falmer.

Part 1

Leadership Theories and Values

1

An Overview of the Leadership Discourses

Simon Western

Introduction

This chapter summarizes the leadership discourses, and show how they relate to each other and to leadership practice. It is important to highlight that while these discourses emerged at different social and economic periods, each are now familiar and have become normative. Each discourse dominated a historical period, in contemporary organizations, each one has its strengths and weaknesses. Each discourse may stand alone and dominate different sectors and organizations, but they also co-exist, within organizations and within individual leaders and leadership teams. However, one discourse is usually dominant in any given situation at any given time. In leadership practice, co-existence usually means one of two things:

1. a strategic leadership synthesis of skills and culture to maximize organizational efficiency and enhancement of member engagement;
2. competing cultures and visions of how to lead the organization.

I will now summarize each discourse.

Discourse 1: leader as controller

The first leadership discourse that emerged at the beginning of the twentieth century epitomized by Taylor's scientific management is the Leader as *Controller*. This character is very similar to MacIntyre's social 'manager' character, which he claims signifies the tension between manipulation and non-manipulation, and I would add between control and autonomy. The Controller leadership discourse is born from scientific rationalism and the industrial revolution, which, in the name of the Enlightenment and progress, relegated the worker to being a cog in a machine, mirroring standardization and mechanization within

---

Source – An edited version of Western, S. (2008) 'An overview of the leadership discourses'.

the mass production of the factory. The leader as Controller operates as a technocrat leader focusing on efficiency. In Etzioni's (1961) taxonomy of control, this leadership character is based on an overt system of coercive and utilitarian control, using reward and deprivation (transactional leadership). In the leadership discourse, covert control is applied from beyond the workplace. The political/economic and social leadership supports the drive for worker efficiency, leveraging worker productivity through class power relations and the threat of unemployment, poverty, healthcare and pension benefits. Political leadership always retains the leader as Controller discourse in the background alongside other leadership discourses, using the threat of job loss and welfare to work benefit links etc., as a social control mechanism (healthcare linked to paid employment is very important in the USA).

Discourse 2: leader as therapist

The second discourse is the leader as *Therapist*. [It] signifies the dominant therapeutic culture in contemporary Western society and highlights the tension between individualism and alienation, personal growth and workplace efficiency, well-being and mental/emotional health. [It] represents the subtlety of therapeutic governance as opposed to coercive control. This leadership reflects the wider social trends of atomization, self-concern, and the post-war individualistic expectations of being fulfilled, successful and happy (Rieff, 1966; Lasch, 1979; Furedi, 2003).

The Therapist leader emerged from within the Human Relations movement and encompasses the work of theorists such as Mayo, Lewin, Maslow, Frankl and Rogers. Their focus on individual personal growth and self-actualization was readily translated to the workplace, through techniques to motivate individuals and teams, through job re-design and job enhancement to make work more satisfying and to produce work-group cohesion. Employers and theorists believed that happier workers would be more productive than unhappy, coerced workers. This approach in essence was seen as more progressive and productive. It aimed to overcome the alienation created by the machine-like efficiency under the leader as Controller discourse. Work became a site for personal growth and achievement, a place to create meaning and identity. Under the leader as Therapist, people 'went to work to work on themselves' (Rose, 1990), embracing therapeutic culture in society at large.

Personnel departments were established, management consultants and new texts, theories and a huge training and development industry flourished. The leader as Therapist still flourishes, often alongside the later Messiah character; a common scenario is the HR Director acts as the Therapist character and the CEO as leader as the Messiah character. Recent examples of the therapist discourse are the interest in emotional intelligence and the huge growth of executive coaching. However, this discourse lost its potency in corporate life, as it could no longer deliver the economic benefits across global business.

Discourse 3: leader as messiah

The third discourse is the leader as Messiah. The term leader has been elevated in recent years, challenging the dominance of the term 'manager' and signifying more social change. Coming to the fore since the early 1980s and most clearly articulated within the

Transformation leadership literature, the *Messiah discourse* provides charismatic leadership and vision in the face of a turbulent and uncertain environment. The Messiah character signifies the tension between salvation and destruction, between the technocrat and the moral visionary, and between hope and despair. The Messiah discourse appeals to individuals and society, promising salvation from the chaotic world in which a lack of control is experienced and where traditional community is diminished. As the workplace rises in importance as a site of community, replacing institutions such as the church and family, so the manager/leader replaces the priesthood as a social character of influence.

The Messiah character leads through their signifying capacity, symbolism, ritual, myth and language. Their focus is to act on culture change and the Messiah leadership discourse relies on 'normative control', which is self- and peer-control through surveillance and internalization, emotionalism and cultural norms. Followers of the Messiah character work hard because of an internalized belief system aligned to the leader's vision and values.

The earnings of leaders graphically represent the new values and expectations on leaders since the Messiah discourse arrived. In the 1980s, in the USA, CEOs earned 40 times the average wage (as the Therapist character), in 2000 (as the Messiah character) they earn over 475 times (*Business Week*, 'Executive compensation scoreboard', 17 April 2000).

Table 1.1, at the end of the chapter, shows an overview of the signifying qualities of each discourse, clearly demonstrating the differences between them and how they impact on leadership practice. It also includes an overview of a fourth discourse – eco leadership – that is discussed later in the chapter. It is an interesting exercise to be playful with the discourses we have discussed, to observe leadership and the language leaders use, seeing if they fit into one or more of these discourses. Also look at vision statements, company websites, newspaper articles, and try to identify these discourses. When you have identified a leadership discourse, look for any patterns and the context in which they occur. Practising this alerts you to the underlying discourses in any leadership situation, which then enables you to take a critical stance, and ask why a certain discourse is favoured, and what implications this has for the employees and the organization.

The leadership discourses in practice

The embodiment of the leadership discourse by a leader character brings the concept of a discourse into the lived workplace. It provides a tangible and observable leadership practice to engage and negotiate with. It reveals to those who take a critical perspective how a discourse impacts and influences organizations, managers and employees. It reveals the constantly changing tensions and desires within the social realm and how this impacts on leadership at work. There is a dynamic interaction between the character (the discourse-filled role) and the actor inhabiting the character. The interaction extends also to those interacting with the leader or leadership team.

Discourses preference

Individual leaders, leadership teams and organizations rarely consciously choose their preferred leadership discourse as these are hidden within normative behaviours and expectations. However, they are drawn to discourses for various reasons.

Sometimes leaders and organizations are 'trapped' within a discourse; others change between leadership discourses under certain conditions. Individuals and groups can be attracted to different discourses depending on their personal social location and how they perceive the world from this location.

Often individuals have an internalized 'idealized' leadership stance, which relates to their social location, and their personal experience of leadership, beginning from their parenting. If a person has a very strict mother or father, or they are brought up in a strict religious culture or a harsh boarding school, this may influence the leader they identify with later in life. They may assume that all leaders should be in the Controller discourse, as this is the norm to them. Alternatively they may internalize a view that this early experience was damaging to them and they may seek a reparative leadership model that would situate them in the 'therapy discourse'. Individuals who doted on their parents or another early leadership role model may identify with the Messiah discourse, relating to the special leader who presents as a saviour.

Changes in leadership discourses often arise due to external pressures. An individual leader can be pulled by competing discourses. As British Prime Minister, Tony Blair embodied the Messiah discourse, talking passionately, with vision, with persuasion, attempting to modernize and change the culture of his political party, the country and beyond, but every so often he reverted to the Controller leadership discourse. His desire seems to be visionary, but his instincts seem to be the controller, the interventionist leader, setting a target and audit culture of micromanagement in the public sector.

Anxiety over performance often distorts a leadership team who favour the Messiah discourse, and all the company rhetoric supports transformational leadership, but then return instinctively to the controller discourse, when they receive poor output figures or share prices drop.

Understanding the leadership discourses makes it easier for leaders in practice to recognize these processes. When they are recognized, leaders can act to ensure that reactivity to short-term pressure doesn't alter their strategic course.

Different geographical, historical and socio-cultural contexts will also favour different leadership discourses. It appears that in the USA leadership seems more generically accepted than in Europe where it seems more distrusted. The Messiah discourse is therefore more likely in the USA, and the Therapist discourse more likely in Europe as it has less of an overt leadership feel to it.

The British National Health Service (NHS) is an interesting example of a large public sector institution which has experienced all three discourses. It was dominated by hierarchy and control in the early years and until the 1970s was led by the leader as Controller discourse with severe matrons, rigid role definitions, a bureaucratic structure and medical personnel acting with omnipotent power. This shifted towards the leadership as Therapist discourse as new management/leadership techniques filtered in from the private sector, and it was realized that leadership and motivation were key issues as employee morale waned in an under-resourced and underpaid service. In the late 1980s, greater reforms began to take place and again, following the corporate lead, the leader as Messiah discourse became prominent, with the aims of modernizing the NHS and changing the culture to enable flexible and adaptive working. Huge sums were spent on leadership development using competency frameworks designed to support the change using the Messiah discourse. Symbolic culture changes took place, which were/are hotly contested, for example, to make patients into customers with choices and create an internal market. Interestingly, while the espoused leadership was the Messiah discourse and CEOs have been given more positional power to change culture, the reality on the ground has been one of competing discourses. The health workers' favoured discourse is the Therapist discourse, which relates closely to their clinical roles and vocations, and that is what clinical leaders attempt to provide. The senior management attempts to create culture change through the Messiah discourse, but complain that the government is so anxious about its modernizing reforms that it reverts to the leader as Controller discourse, micro-managing CEOs' performance. This is due to the government anxiety that if the reforms fail they would themselves lose office. This anxiety is passed down throughout the institution and the experienced leadership is the Controller discourse. An ex-colleague of mine spoke of her experience as a clinical leader:

> My job used to be caring for people, now I feel like I am running a production line, all we are concerned about is getting the waiting times down, if we don't, our funding is reduced. The leadership here talks about creating a culture of trust, empowering us to do our jobs, but in reality they are the most controlling leaders we have had in my 24 years of service. (Ward Charge Nurse, NHS hospital, September 2005: Anonymous)

The result of an espoused Messiah leadership discourse colliding with the experience of a Controller discourse creates cynicism and distrust, resulting in low morale.

Positions within hierarchies, and location in functions and departments, also impact on the leadership discourse. The Messiah leadership discourse is more favoured, the higher in the organization one climbs. The Therapist leader has become favoured in the realms of aspiring middle managers, HR departments and the public sector. Human Resource departments often fluctuate between the Controller discourse, when operating on transactional and contractual concerns, and the Therapist discourse, when dealing with leadership development. This split is unhelpful. They can be perceived as Controlling characters from below, and as Therapist characters from above. Structurally within companies the HR leadership becomes split between discourses, which is unhelpful as they are in a vital influencing position and should be working towards the company's strategic leadership vision.

Leadership development, often instigated through the HR function, is a very risk-averse process, because the deliverers worry about having safe and measurable outcomes to justify their work. Also when working with senior personnel, the risk is increased because of the power held by these executives. This often influences choices and the deliverers revert to individualist, reductionist and formulaic solutions: competency frameworks setting universal leadership goals, followed by individual 'tests' to 'scientifically' measure skills and identify gaps. The weakest part of this process is usually the follow-up. Sometimes it is missing altogether or the individual is given token leadership development. This approach is situated in the Therapist discourse, attempting to change individual behaviour through modification using a technician-rational approach. What is missing is a coherent systemic approach with an organizational development and strategic vision.

Leadership discourses can be used heuristically to help understand an organizations' individual leadership assumptions. If an HR leader can understand the tensions in their roles, they can resist the pull to the Therapist discourse and take a more strategic view alongside the individualist rational approach.

To make progress in the emancipatory role of leadership in organizational life, the discourses help identify normative assumptions, social relations and beneath-the-surface structural dynamics. They also help to reveal how power, authority, control and influence are exerted. The leader is as ensnared in the dominant discourse as are the followers; nobody is acting as a free agent unless they are aware of the dominant discourses which create the boundaries and norms in which we all act.

Working with leadership discourses

Each discourse has its merits and its weaknesses. Once aware of the discourse, we can make some judgement and assessment as to how each discourse affects leadership and organizational culture. While we are all in a sense captured by a particular discourse, we are also able to negotiate, individually and collectively, to change the discourse and our relationship to it. Collectively, the discourse can be transformed, and with it the power and social relations that emanate from it. It is through this social construction (of which we are all active agents) that negotiation takes place and social change occurs.

Boxes 1.1, 1.2 and 1.3 offer examples of how each leadership discourse might impact within different work situations (which often reflects how they emerged). These boxes are there to open dialogue as to which leadership discourses, and the accompanying assumptions, fit to different situations and contexts. As stated previously, discourses can and often do co-exist within organizations and sectors, but one is usually dominant.

Box 1.1   Controller leader discourse

Strengths	Weaknesses
Focus on output and task	Creates employee alienation, resentment and resistance
Results driven	
Improves efficiency	Poor use of human resource: does not utilize employees' knowledge, skills and creativity
Empirical and measurable targets	
Decisive leadership in a crisis	Creates inflexible and rigid 'them and us' workforce relations
Creates clear boundaries between work and home identity	Often leads to disputes
Useful settings	**Less useful settings**
Production line, old manufacturing	Post-industrial workplaces
Workplaces where efficiency and control are vital	Knowledge-led industries
Nuclear industry, projects which require high security, and high levels of checking	Education sector
	Entrepreneurial business
Accounting departments	Innovation and creative sector
Construction industry	Senior strategic leadership
Task-focused project management	
First line leadership	

Box 1.2   Therapist leader discourse

Strengths	Weaknesses
Individual and team focus	Lacks big picture, strategic focus
Emotional awareness	Lacks dynamism and energy
Builds trust	Doesn't build strong cultures
Empowers through engaging individual and team through building rapport, listening and finding ways to offer personal growth and development opportunities	Individual focus rather than systems focus
	Organization can become introverted and narcissistic, focusing on employee needs rather than an external focus
Useful settings	**Less useful settings**
Steady state organizations	Fast changing organizations
Education, health, public and not-for-profit sectors	Multinationals with complex structures, requiring more of a systemic and culture-led approach
Value focuses in organizations with an ethos of human development	Manufacturing sector, building industry which require robust, task focus
Middle management-leadership roles, supporting individuals and teams	Senior leadership requiring strategic focus
Human Resource function	Asian cultures which are less culturally embedded in therapy culture than Western cultures

Box 1.3   Messiah leader discourse

Strengths	Weaknesses
Builds strong aligned companies	Unsustainable over long periods totalizing-fundamentalist cultures
Dynamic energized cultures	
Innovative, dispersed leadership	Leaders can become omnipotent, dependency then becomes an issue
Builds in dispersed leadership and autonomous teams	Conformist homogeneous cultures can stifle innovation and creativity
Strategic and visionary	
Useful settings	**Less useful settings**
Post-industrial companies	Steady state organizations
Knowledge-based companies	Industrial, manufacturing sector
Global multinationals, large corporations	Organizations reliant on continuity rather than transformation, e.g. health-care, banking
Senior strategic leadership	Middle management/leadership
	Organizations with resistance to 'leadership cultures' (public sector organizations)

When thinking about leadership in one's own workplace, or when visiting another organization, these boxes can highlight a few of the relevant issues to consider. If a discourse exists in the wrong context, there will be increased tension, and the leader character will experience the full effects of this tension. If as a leader, you experience such tensions, then look at conflicts in discourses as a potential way of understanding and getting to the source of the problem.

[…]

An emergent discourse: the eco-leader

Post-heroic leaders

The Messiah discourse is not the final word, but it remains the contemporary dominant discourse in the mainstream literature and practising leaders' mindset. However, there has been a small but growing backlash against the Transformational and hero leader.

[…]

Badarraco (2001: 121) makes the case for quiet moral leadership: 'modesty and restraint are in large measure responsible for their extraordinary achievement'. […] [This] is the post-heroic leader, but under examination we find regurgitated leadership approaches, taken directly from the Therapist leader discourse.

[…]

The leader is toned down, forceful but with humility and quiet but focused influence […]

[S/he] needs to be authentic, emotionally intelligent, sensitive and less rational, privileging the emotional and internal self. Binney et al. (2004) describe the post-heroic leader as relational, as about people, the classic 'leader as Therapist' discourse. The post-heroic leadership literature also includes the recent idea of leader-coaches, the archetype leader-therapist. Much of this literature represents ideas from democratic and the Human Relations movement; it is particularly close to Greenleaf's 'servant leader' (1977) which pioneered post-heroic leadership under a different name, over 30 years before. […]

The post-heroic leader literature also calls for dispersed leadership, networking and matrix organizations and advocates greater collaboration, in line with much of what the Transformational leader set out to achieve.

Attempts have been made to harness the Therapeutic character to serve the interests of the Messiah discourse. For example, Jim Collins' (2001) 'Level 5 leader' retains the heroism but inverts it. […]

Leadership spirit/spiritual leadership

Leadership spirit implies that leaders act with spirit, or there is a spirit of leadership. […]

It matters little what informs or underpins the leadership spirit, however, the spirit must support the joy, creativity, the positive life-force and the underlying ethics and holistic approach of the Eco-leader discourse. Practising how to leverage this leadership spirit is more important than finding its source.

[...]

The spiritual leadership literature (e.g. Mitroff and Denton [1999]) blends the Christian-Judaeo tradition finding that spirituality is individual and transcendent, with the Eastern and perhaps indigenous Native American tradition, focusing on the ecological ideas that 'We are all interconnected. Everything affects everything else'. [...]

The language used to describe the post-heroic leaders creates an image of a Therapist leader with spiritual and moral intent. These post-heroic leaders, however, are often more idealized, more of a fantasy, than charismatic leaders of the past.

Spirituality is now entering the leadership literature and practice: 'For at least a decade the press has reported company leaders speaking about spirituality and business, while multiple publications have advocated links between corporate success and issues of the soul' (Calas and Smircich, 2003: 329).

According to May (2000), spirituality is the most important influence in leadership. But as Tourish and Pinnington point out, 'Ironically, this effort is often driven by a very non-spiritual concern – the desire to increase profits' (2002: 165).

[...]

The Eco-leader discourse

[...]

The Eco-leadership discourse is about a new paradigm of leadership which takes an ecological perspective. This is a perspective which understands: that solutions in one area of business may create problems in another; that growth in one industry causes decline in another, with social consequences; that short-term gains may have immediate benefits, but may have longer-term consequences which may damage the business and the environment. Eco-leadership recognizes that within an organization there are inter-dependent parts which make up a whole; this goes for all stakeholder relationships, and in ever-widening circles that eventually reach the air that we breathe. It is about con-nectivity, interdependence and sustainability underpinned by an ethical, socially respon-sible stance. The Eco-leadership discourse takes ethics beyond business ethics into social concerns; it takes ethics beyond human concerns and recognizes a responsibility and relationship to the natural world. It also focuses the connectedness within each of us, and between each of us. The Eco-leadership discourse is fuelled by the human spirit. For some, this is underpinned by spirituality, for others not. Either way, the Eco-leadership discourse is a spirit-filled leadership, and a connected leadership. [...] As globalization and new technologies make the world 'smaller', our connections seem more important, and our vulnerability and reliance on each other and on safeguarding the natural world are rising concerns.

[...]

There is an ever-growing complexity of connected networks of organizations, suppliers, producers and consumers, forming webs of interaction with no single leadership, no planned strategy, set in a constantly emerging and changing political and social environment. From this arises new organizational forms and leadership approaches. [...]

Leaders of multinational corporations are also finding that they have to find ways to increase the emergent capabilities within their companies to have any chance of keeping pace with change and the de-centralized forces impacting on them.

[...]

If one looks at the Messiah discourse through an open-systems perspective (von Bertalanffy, 1968), one can account for the un-sustainability of this leadership as the organizational boundaries are ever-closing and become increasingly rigid. When an organism's (or organization's) boundaries get too closed and don't allow inputs and outputs to flow (in human systems this includes communications), the organism starts to atrophy and will die. [...]

Open-systems thinking teaches us that we have to interact with the environment, and to achieve this successfully requires adaptive- and self-regulation. In terms of leadership, self-regulation and adaptive practice can only occur when there is dispersed leadership able to act and react to local change.

[...]

Eco-leadership is a discourse which creates self-organizing and emergent properties arising from dispersed leadership, which build into organizations the ability to be adaptive to fluctuations and constant change.

One of the focuses of Eco-leadership is to find ways to harness the human spirit, and our intuition, connectedness to each other, to nature, and our non-rational ways [of] knowing.

Holism is vital to this discourse – leadership is always conceptualized as fluid and dispersed throughout an organization. Leadership may emerge from surprising places given the right conditions. It is about acknowledging diversity and connectiveness rather than attempting to homogenize company cultures. It is about a leadership which looks for patterns, emerging in and outside of the company, and creates an adaptive culture and a localized and dispersed leadership which can both react more quickly and notice the changes occurring at grassroots level.

Ethics and Eco-leadership

If the purpose of ethics is to inform moral conduct, then two clear questions arise when thinking about contemporary leadership. The first is well rehearsed: how can ethics inform the moral conduct of leaders, as individuals and as collective groups such as corporate boards? [This focuses on] our actions which affect others near to us, those we are in contact with or those we are responsible for.

The second question is less well rehearsed. This ethical responsibility goes beyond being responsible only for what is directly in your control, and takes ethics to mean that we all share a responsibility for the planet, and for the indirect consequences of our individual and collective actions.

[…]

The Eco-leader discourse is beginning to recognize that leadership now means re-negotiating what success means for an organization or company. There is a need to look awry at this question, and not take the macro-economic and neo-liberal agenda for granted. Delivering growth and short-term shareholder value is no longer acceptable as the sole measurement of success if we are to act ethically and responsibly. […]

Leadership success will be to harness technological advancement, knowledge, and our global trading platforms, to 'provide' for a better quality of life, and a sustainable future.

Ethical leadership is to take a critical stance, to look awry, to think holistically, to be accountable for your own actions and for the systems and networks you inhabit, both locally and globally. It places social justice and the environment first.

[…]

Conclusion

This new Eco-leadership discourse is an emergent discourse that has both continuity and discontinuity with the previous discourses, and is aligned to other leadership approaches.

[It] has three key qualities:

1. *Connectivity (holism)*: It is founded on connectivity; how we relate and interrelate with the ecologies in which we work and live.
2. *Eco-ethics*: It is concerned with acting ethically in the human realm *and* with respect and responsibility for the natural environment.
3. *Leadership spirit*: It acknowledges the human spirit, the non-rational, creativity, imagination and human relationships.

The Eco-leadership discourse moves away from control and towards understanding emergence, connectivity and organic sustainable growth. The leader character exemplifies tension between central regulation and self-regulation, between emergence and direction, organic growth and strategic planning. For the highly rational management world, many of these ideas are challenging and truly create a new paradigm. How do you invest in a business whose leadership talks about not-knowing and *emergence as strategy*?

Leaders are realizing that inter-connectivity is a reality and feedback systems affect them and their business as well as the rest of the planet. Training leaders to think in this way, to understand ideas of self-regulating and self-managing systems, and emergence rather than planning, then linking these to the human skills from the therapeutic discourse might support a powerful new discourse.

Table 1.1 The four discourses of leadership

Discourse	Controller	Therapist	Messiah	Eco-Leadership
Vision Aims	**Iron Cage** Maximizes production through transactional exchange, control and coercion.	**Motivate to Produce** Maximizes production through increased motivation, personal growth and teamwork.	**Culture Control** Maximizes production through identifying with the brand's strong culture, and leader's values and vision. Meaning and salvation come through active followership and being part of a believing community.	**Holistic and Sustainable** Success is redefined in this new paradigm. Quality, sustainability and social responsibility are connected; therefore company success is measured differently from short term profit.
Source of Authority	**From Above: *Science*** The Boss/owner passes authority down the pyramid (position power) and management control gains authority from scientific rationalism.	**From Within: *Humanism*** Drawing on personal internalized authority and the power gained through self-actualisation and collaborative teamwork.	**From Beyond: *Charisma*** The leader embodies the values, vision and culture from which they gain authority.	**From the Eco-system: *Inter-dependence*** Eco-leaders draw authority from nature, networks and belief in inter-dependence and connectivity.
Perceptions of Employees	**Robots** Employees are seen as human assets, working as unthinking robotic machines, with little personal identity or autonomy.	**Clients** Are healed and made whole through reparation and creativity at work.	**Disciples** Following the leader and learning to be more like them. Creating an identity within a community of believers.	**Actors within a Network** Employees are part of a network, with agency and with autonomy, yet also part of an inter-dependent connected greater whole.

(Continued)

Table 1.1 (Continued)

Discourse	Controller	Therapist	Messiah	Eco-Leadership
Leads What?	**Body** Controller focuses on the body to maximize efficient production, via incentives and coercion (e.g. piece work and discipline).	**Psyche** Therapist focuses on the psyche to understand motivation, designs job enrichment, creates spaces for self-actualizing behaviours.	**Soul** Messiah works with the soul. Followers align themselves to the vision, a cause greater than the self (the company). The Messiah is role model, linking success with personal salvation.	**System** Eco-leaders lead through paradox, by distributing leadership throughout the system. They make spaces for leadership to flourish.
Organisational Metaphor	**Machine** Takes technical and rational view of world, thinks in closed systems, tries to control internal environment to maximize efficiency.	**Human Organism** Creates the conditions for personal and team growth, linking this to organizational growth and success.	**Community** The Messiah leads a community (sometimes a cult). The emphasis is on strong cultures, the brand before the individual.	**Eco-System** Leads through connections and linking the network. Organization is seen as a network of dispersed leadership held together by strong cultures.
Control (Axtell Ray, 1986)	**Bureaucratic** Control via manipulation and strict policing.	**Humanistic** Control by emotional management and therapeutic governance. Paternalistic benevolence.	**Culture** Culture control. Workers internalize the cultural norms which become an internalized organizational ideal. Policing is via self and peers. Open plan offices, lack of privacy and peer surveillance are techniques of control.	**Self-regulating Systems** Control from an Eco-leadership perspective resides in the system itself. The eco-system then needs nurturing to self regulate. However it can be damaged, if resources are over-used for example; or it can be supported if diverse actors are connected and their inter-dependence understood and cherished.

References

Axtell Ray, C. (1986) 'Corporate culture: the last frontier of control', *Journal of Management Studies*, 23(3): 286–95.

Badarraco, J. (2001) 'We don't need another hero', *Harvard Business Review*, 79(8): 120–6.

Binney, G., Wilke, G. and Williams, C. (2004) *Living Leadership: A Practical Guide for Ordinary Heroes*. London: Pearson Books.

Calas, M.B. and Smircich, L. (2003) 'To be done with progress and other heretical thoughts for organization and management studies', in E. Locke (ed.), *Postmodernism and Management: Pros, Cons, and the Alternative*, Research in the Sociology of Organizations, Vol. 21. Amsterdam: JAI.

Collins, J. (2001) 'Level 5 leadership', *Harvard Business Review*, January: 67–76.

Etzioni, A. (1961) *Complex Organizations*. New York: Holt, Rinehart and Winston.

Furedi, F. (2003) *Therapy Culture*. London: Routledge.

Greenleaf, R. (1977) *Servant Leadership*. Mahwah, NJ: Paulist Press.

Lasch, C. (1979) *The Culture of Narcissism: American Life in the Age of Diminishing Expectations*. New York: Warner Books.

May, A. (2000) 'Leadership and spirit: breathing new vitality and energy into individuals and organizations', *The Academy of Management Executive*, 14(2): 128–30.

Mitroff, J.I. and Denton, E.A. (1999) *A Spiritual Audit of Corporate America*, San Francisco: Jossey-Bass.

Rieff, P. (1966) *The Triumph of the Therapeutic: Uses of Faith after Freud*. London: Chatto and Windus.

Rose, N. (1990) *Governing the Soul*. London: Routledge.

Tourish, D. and Pinnington, A. (2002) 'Transformational leadership, corporate cultism and the spirituality paradigm: an unholy trinity in the workplace?', *Human Relations*, 55(2): 147–72.

Von Bertalanffy, L. (1968) *General Systems Theory: Foundations, Development, Application*. London: Allen Lane.

2

From Successful School Leadership Towards Distributed Leadership

Lejf Moos

Why the increased focus on leadership in schools today?

In contemporary societies, leaders are needed because authorities want a person that can be held responsible/accountable and also because changes in society make it important for communities like schools to be able to construct their identities in negotiating meaning and reducing complexity and in changing themselves. In this transformation of society and institutions, leadership becomes pivotal.

Leadership makes a difference

Empirical research within educational contexts has served to reinforce the importance of school leadership or principalship (Hallinger, 2003). Leithwood and colleagues in Canada, Hallinger and Heck in the United States and numerous studies of school effectiveness arrive at a consistent conclusion that 'strong' or 'firm' leadership is a key variable, generally referring to school leaders who exhibit a range of qualities which support the notion

Source – An edited version of Moos, L. (2010) 'From successful school leadership towards distributed leadership'.

of turnaround, leading governments to appoint 'superheads' and charismatic leaders (MacBeath and Moos, 2004).

Early effectiveness research (cf. the analysis of Hallinger, 2003) identified '*strong, directive leadership focused on curriculum and instruction from the principal*' as a characteristic of effective school leaders. Subsequent research by Reynolds (no year), Leithwood et al. (1994) and Southworth (2003), and reviews of research on how leadership can influence student learning in schools in challenging circumstances (Leithwood and Riehl, 2003; Leithwood et al., 2004) have developed these ideas.

Another account of the distinctive nature of school leadership is given in Goldring and Greenfield (2002). They describe four dimensions in school leadership:

- Moral dimension
- Stewardship
- Complexity
- Normative and people-intensive

There are some similarities between the findings: they all point to leaders setting directions and making sense or having a sense of mission that has to do with learning and teaching. They point to the fact that in the practice of schools there is not only one leader; leadership needs to be distributed and therefore people need to be developed and empowered so they can accept and carry out leadership functions at different levels. Furthermore, all reviews point to the fact that leadership takes place in organizations and the organizations must be redesigned in order to accommodate new functions and practices.

[...]

Mulford (2005) suggests, on the basis of findings from a large Australian school leadership research project, that reforms should be related to four factors:

1. *Distributed leadership* – Teachers should be involved in leadership in order to feel cared for and valued and be given opportunities to learn from each other and to be involved in decision-making.
2. *Development and learning* – A unifying focus and shared insights into what the school is doing and why it is doing it provides the basis for learning and development.
3. *Context* – Socio-economic status, home background and school size have a clear interactive effect on leadership.
4. *A broader understanding of student outcomes* – What counts as school effects are not only academic achievements, but also, for example, self-confidence.

However, one cannot discuss strategies for school leadership without discussing the following question: What is the core purpose of the institution that is to be led? What is a successful school? and What is the core purpose of schooling?

Core purpose of schooling

Many points about the core purpose of schools are presented by Basil Bernstein (Bernstein, 2000, quoted in Arnot, 2004). [These can be summarized as follows:]

The main purpose of school leadership is to empower and to enable staff and students to assume responsibility for learning, acting and collaborating in school and outside school.

School is an important cultural institution in every society with a special purpose to contribute to the education of the next generation to become active, knowledgeable and caring citizens of their societies. Therefore the purpose of schools is to provide a comprehensive, liberal education with a responsibility to community – education for democratic citizenship – and learning (also called 'Bildung'), so the students can grow or develop into being independent and enlightened adults who are concerned with equity and social justice. In the Danish discussion this has been called 'action competence': the individual is able and willing to be a qualified participant (Jensen and Schnack, 1994).

We know from experience that children are not able to take care of themselves. They must be educated. Parents educate children and they leave it to schools and other institutions to educate on behalf of themselves. Education is at any rate an external influence (Moos, 2003b). Second, it is a main purpose because the activities of schooling take place in schools and classrooms (and in other communities), which makes it necessary for people to behave and to feel like members of communities. And third, school acts according to the goals and aims set by the society at large and is therefore accountable to society.

That leads to a short discussion of democracy, democratic schools and democratic leadership. These notions are in many countries considered to be pivotal societal values. But while most people agree that democratic schools and democratic leadership is good for schools, they do not agree on what that means. For Dewey (1916), who has been a great inspiration for many theorists as well as practitioners, democratic leadership meant that democracy was lived through participation in the everyday practice of school life. [He] saw 'deep' democracy as involving respect for the dignity of individuals and their cultural traditions, reverence for and proactive facilitation of free and open inquiry and critique, recognition of interdependence in working for the common good, the responsibility for individuals to participate in free and open inquiry, and the importance of collective choices and actions in the interest of the common good.

Before we continue looking at democratic leadership it is useful to position the view of democracy that is used by this author: the concept of participatory democracy, which is the most appropriate and useful concept in regard to schools and education. Everybody – almost – can agree that democracy is based on positive principles but have different opinions on what it means. Karen Seashore Louis (2003) has given us a tool to distinguish between three basic forms of democracy:

- *Liberal Democracy* – The purpose of society is to support the individual in becoming autonomous, [resolving the] tension between perceived societal needs and individual freedom. So Liberal democracy argues that educational goals should be determined by the will of the majority.

- *Social Democracy* – [In its emphasis on] social rights and equality, group cohesiveness and [the] redistribution of social good including education, equalizing educational attainment and opportunity, social democracy argues that protecting vulnerable classes of students – that is, students of linguistic, religious and racial minorities – requires stable state control over goals.
- *Participatory Democracy* – Based on the Greek ideal of citizenship, participation and ownership, congregations debate and determine key issues, schools belong to a local community [and must demonstrate] local responsiveness, so participatory democracy agues that participants in the educational project are best able to determine goals. (p. 101)

Closely linked to the concept of participatory democracy is the ideal of the 'better argument'. The rational ideal calls on the participants to strive to build communication on the ideal of the better argument that prevails without the use of coercion (Habermas, 1984, 1987).

Another account of the view is given in a series of portraits of school leaders striving to become democratic leaders where the following orientations were shared (Blase et al., 1995):

- They all tried to encourage teachers' involvement in decision-making about instruction and were committed to the principle of sharing power with others.
- They were all child centred and strongly committed toward improving teaching and learning and supporting teachers.
- They all had trust in teachers' motives.
- They all had the ability to listen and to communicate openly.

Teaching and leading in communities

Classrooms and schools are social fields and education and learning take place in those social fields. Loyalty and commitment to the organization are not by any means an automatic starting position for any institution; so building and deepening it is a leadership duty and mission. If staff and students are to behave loyally to their organization, leaders should make an effort to transform the organization, which is characterized only by a formal structure, into a community, which is characterized by all members being sufficiently committed to the ethos of the community. A prerequisite for this transformation is to focus on the integrity of the organization: the ability to be both a convincing internal work- and life-frame and the ability to appear reliable in the eyes of all stakeholders.

[...]

Sergiovanni (1995) points to differences between communities and organizations. The Gemeinschaft–Gesellschaft continuum illustrates these differences. In a community, the decisions represent a pattern of relationships that are listed on the left-hand side of the hyphens: affective-effective neutrality; collective orientation-self-orientation; particularism-universalism; ascription-achievement; diffuseness-specificity (p. 22).

We can find different kinds of communities in schools: the classroom as a democratic community, a professional community, a community of learners and a 'community of leaders'. This last type of community is based on the notion of shared leadership: 'In communities, leadership as power over events and people is redefined to become leadership as the power to accomplish shared goals' (p. 170).

This leads to the concept of leaders and followers: 'Subordinates comply with management rules and procedures and with the leader's directives; the job gets done. Followers, however, respond to ideas, ideals, values, and purpose; as a result, the job gets done well' (Sergiovanni, 1995, p. 131). [...]

Power and trust

When describing schools and classrooms as communities one should not forget that they are at the same time social fields (Bourdieu, 1977, 1990) with struggles for positions as a key feature. It is then also about concepts like power and trust. [...]

Power is described as 'The capacity – in persons and institutions – that makes people do things, they (probably) would not do otherwise' (Sørhaug, 1996). [It] is likened to energy. Trust can be likened to energy too. It creates the conditions and mobilizes people to action and collaboration. Trust is dependent on the will and goodwill of people when new issues are being addressed.

The two forces threaten each other and they presuppose each other: power without trust eats up its own basis, and trust without power cannot survive, because there will always be a portion of violence in a group/a field. Agents participating in a field have different interests that sometimes are contrary to the communal norm. There is need for a leader who is endowed with appropriate means of power, who can restore the trust through trustworthy use of power. This someone is more often than not the principal.

A very crucial leadership task is to restore the limits of the community. This is the pivotal point for the trust–power interplay, but external pressure begins to alter internal power relations in school communities with consequences for trust. This discussion points to the need for leaders to set the agenda for the professional discussions in schools: what is interesting for our community and how we are going to resolve those problems.

Leadership communication and interaction

[T]here is almost consensus on the need for distributed leadership. There is a sense, based on evidence, that the principal cannot be sufficiently informed to make all decisions in a school, nor can she/he be present in all places and situations where decisions need to be made. This is eminently the case in classrooms, where teachers have to interpret demands, goals and situations and make decisions many times every lesson. And it is the case in teacher teams that meet to plan, evaluate their instruction or engage in professional development. If the principal is not present, she/he is excluded from making decisions (of course she/he can construct the frames within which teams can manoeuvre).

However, as Spillane and Orlana (Spillane and Orlina, 2005) write, distributed leadership can take many forms. At the core of their concept of leadership is the notion that leadership is not the actions of the leaders per se but the *interactions* between leaders and other agents. Leadership is therefore 'an influencing relation' between leaders and followers that takes place in situations (that can be described by their tools, routines and structures).

From another theoretical perspective, a systems theory or social constructivist perspective (Thyssen, 2003a, b), leadership can be understood as 'the goal-oriented and specialized communication that aims at stimulating learning at all levels in schools' (Moos, 2003c). This communication concept is parallel to Spillane and Orlana's interaction concept because both focus on the relations between leaders and teachers. The actions of the leader are only interesting if they are understood as leadership actions by the followers or co-leaders.

[...]

The interactions can be described (Spillane and Orlina, 2005) as: *collaborated distribution* – leaders work together in place and time to execute the same leadership routine; *collective distribution* – leaders work separately but interdependently (like in a game of sport where each player performs separate functions in the same game); or *coordinated distribution* – leadership activities are performed in a particular sequence (like in a relay race).

These categories are descriptive only and cannot be used in themselves to find out how the power relations between the leader and the followers are; they should therefore be supplemented with a concept of practice and action processes in the form of a model of practice processes.

A model of processes of practice:

1. Identification of problem/interpretation of demand
2. Setting of goal/describing the desired difference
3. Planning for/organizing the action to be taken
4. Action/implementation of development
5. Monitoring and evaluating the process and outcomes.

The interesting questions can now be posed: *who* is active or in command in each of the phases? Is the principal the only agent in phases 1, 2, 3 and 5? Are other agents involved in more phases – and how are they involved?

In the literature we often see that a manager is defined as 'someone who is in a role in which he (sic) is authorized to get work done through employed subordinates for whose work he is held accountable' (Gronn, 2002, p. 659). The means by which she/he can manage range from coercion, force and manipulation through to leadership. Leadership and management practices are interrelated and are aspects of the same processes of maintaining and developing schools. Leadership is about pointing out a difference (between what is and what should be) and management is about minimizing the difference (between reality and vision).

At this stage it is also possible to distinguish between different forms of distributed leadership, like democratic leadership, 'concertive action' or 'spontaneous collaboration' (Gronn, 2002), and to describe in more depth the differences and similarities between principalship and leadership.

Empirical evidence

In the Danish part of the 'International Successful Principal Project' we were interested in investigating how leadership (including principalship) influenced students' democratic 'Bildung' (enlightenment and action competencies) and communicative competencies. Our understanding of the schools as organizations was that they were communities that were organized and managed on the basis of communications in the form of leadership decisions. Leadership decisions are made in order to reduce complexity in some situations (in that they choose or do not choose possibilities/options) or create complexity in other situations (by opening up for choices). When decisions are made, they form the premises for other decisions. Decisions need to be relevant, acceptable and legitimate (Thyssen, 2003a).

When we observed practice, be it in meetings or instruction, we looked for aspects of the communication like positions of agents (symmetrical, hierarchical), means of communication (spoken, non-verbal, writing, images), and types of communication (dialogue, discussion, information, counselling, ordering, feedback, questions, statements, confirmation, interpretation, analysis, circular questions or linear questions). We also look for the positioning of agents: including or excluding from community (membership), signs of trust and of cultural sensibility.

Leadership in webs

It has been a major intention of the Danish educational system to further the democratic education for citizenship for many years.

One consequence of this endeavour is that the relations between leaders and staff and between adults and students shall be based on collaboration, participation and dialogue. Thus schools experiment with different forms of relations between staff and leadership. In the project schools we see webs of groups and teams (Gronn, 2002, p. 659). Another form is the establishment of stable teams of leaders and of teachers. A third form is the development of project work with students. Those three trends shall be presented and discussed next.

In the six Danish schools we see an intricate pattern of meetings and committees/teams/ groups. The constructions are not identical from one school to the other, but the pattern is the same: the decentralization from state to school district to schools is being extended into schools, but at the same time the principals function as the spiders in a web: nothing much can happen in a school without the principal having initiated it, having accepted it or at least having known about it.

It is therefore interesting to look at the content, the forms and the interactions of the meetings, as will be done hereafter.

The content

In all schools there is emphasis on the conditions for students' learning, which principals mostly influence in indirect ways, rather than on students' attainment and results. Results are discussed more in some schools rather than others. The reason for that could well be that some schools are situated in affluent areas where parents give more support to their children and are more ambitious on their behalf than parents in the less fortunate school districts. It could also be an effect of the very strong influence that some local educational authorities have on schools.

The content of meetings in self-governing teams is often focused on planning for the next week or month. Very often teams use a considerable part of their meeting time to discuss students with special needs or with behaviour problems. When principals meet with teams, deliberations about students with difficulties often take up much time, too. Danish principals are the pivotal point when it comes to students at risk: they often take over the communication with parents and authorities, and they manage the resources for special needs education. In some schools, those resources have been relocated to the self-managing teams.

Principals attend many meetings with a technical or householding orientation. Meetings in developmental committees often function as forums where principals can test ideas before putting them to the whole staff. They also function as forums for dissemination.

The forms and interactions

In the Danish schools we find robust signs of what James A. Beane and Michael Apple have labelled participatory democratic communities (Furman and Starrat, 2002): the open flow of ideas, critical reflection and analysis, concern for the welfare of others and the 'common good' as well as concern for the dignity and rights of individuals and minorities. In many ways we see schools that are striving to be good communities for the broad and comprehensive development of students' cognitive, personal and social competencies.

The schools and their leaders have different interpretations of how to lead in a democratic way (Blase et al., 1995), but they can all be said to encourage teachers' involvement in decision-making. Teachers on their part encourage students to involve themselves in decision-making at the classroom level. Leaders are all child centred and committed towards improving teaching and learning. They all have trust in teachers' motives, and they are all able to listen and to communicate openly.

[…]

In a meeting of the developmental committee we observed how the principal was able to signal the direction she wanted the school to follow: 'I want to say that it is not helping us if we cannot respond to questions from the outer world.' The school must be more open and transparent to the local community, said the principal. At the same meeting she was able to communicate when behaviour or ideas were not complying with the norms (Bourdieu, 1998) of the school community: 'As a teacher you are obliged continuously to assess the students' attainment and to set new goals.' This signal tells teachers that if they do not assess students they are not complying with the norms the way the principal sees them and they are therefore jeopardizing their membership of the community. The members of the developmental committee of course knew that and they openly agreed to this expectation.

In this meeting the principal was able to function as the school leader, who sets directions, and at the same time as the school manager, who tries to move the school in the right direction.

Intricate patterns of meetings

In another school in this project, the interplay between different levels in the school – the school as a whole, blocks and class and grade teams – is intricate and builds on a web of meetings. There are meetings in the blocks (which department leaders participate in because they are attached to blocks), regular meetings of teams of teachers of the same grade, meetings between the chairs of blocks (elected chairs meet every Wednesday with the SMT) and 'in-tray meetings' (the SMT meets every Monday).

At the 'in-tray meeting' that we observed, there was a mix of information and agreements. Heads of departments and the principal made strategies for dealing with external stakeholders. The heads of department talked and nodded. One item was an agreement or strategy on how to react to the advice that the Pedagogical Committee (which is advisory to the principalship) was going to give on next year's work plan. What kind of advice would the SMT accept? The SMT group needed to be unanimous, said the principal. Heads of departments describe the role of the principal as a sounding board who influences processes through dialogue – in this case with the rest of the SMT. [...]

The principal tells us that often heads of departments and teachers approach him and present ideas of their own in order to get his acceptance and have him give feedback. He sometimes wonders why they have to get this reassurance, because they could have made the decisions themselves. This seems to be a kind of reaffirming mechanism for them: they want to have a 'father's nod' for their ideas before they proceed to realize them. He describes his role in creating meaning in the school in this way:

> I fertilize the ground or plant an idea in the right spot and let it grow and mature until the person with whom the idea was shared at one point sees it as his/her own idea. I then encourage him/her to follow up on it. Often I give the idea to the heads of departments to spread. In this way they seem even more genuine.

> Teachers are used to being masters in their own right. They are very autonomous, and they must be so when they teach classes, so you cannot lead them like employees in a private enterprise. My basic attitude is that if you give people room to manoeuvre they will fill it out and increase their competencies.

There are many meetings in different groupings every week.

> *Head of Department*: 'It is about keeping the creation of myths and gossip at a minimum and proceedings at a maximum. ... We are responsible for different functions and tasks and therefore we need to communicate and keep one another

up to date with what is happening so that all members of the SMT know about everything.'

[T]he shadowing of a teacher and a student and the subsequent interviews with them showed that they agree with the leaders that they have room to make decisions and choices of their own and that the communication between stakeholders is very similar to what we saw and what was reported to us.

Leadership in teams

In a review of literature on teacher leadership Alma Harris (2005) describes the development of teacher leadership in the Anglo-American literature [as moving] from a top-down towards a more participative approach and from a more formal structural towards a more community-based approach.

In the Danish context the development has been different and based on a number of diverse tendencies. Until 15 years ago there was a very flat structure where the principal was considered to be 'the first among equals'. He/she acted as an administrator who gave teachers great autonomy in planning for and carrying through instruction in classrooms. Over the past 15 years principals have been given more formal power and they have had to fight to be acknowledged as leaders and managers.

From the beginning of the 1990s much administrative and financial power has been devolved from state to the municipal (school district) level and from there on to school level. Five years ago the next level of decentralization was implemented as 'self-managing teams' of teachers were made an option to schools. These teams consist of all teachers in a section of the school. The schools themselves decide which areas they want to devolve to the teams, except for salaries and appointments and dismissals of teachers. The teams are often considered to be small schools-in-schools. The reasons for this option were on the one hand, a wish to devolve the finances to the people who were responsible for the work and on the other hand, an understanding that this transformation would contribute to better working conditions and more commitment.

Several studies show that leadership gives teachers more self-esteem and work satisfaction and in indirect ways better instruction, although interpersonal factors are crucial (Harris, 2005). To a great extent those interpersonal factors are the same as the interpersonal factors at school level where principals act.

This transformation is a fundamental change in school life and it is therefore not close to being implemented yet. Traditional teacher roles and collaboration conceptions are difficult to change. As an illustration, the leaders of the self-managing teams are not called leaders but coordinators. It is an impression from the schools in the project that teachers are beginning to change the traditional private, isolated teachers' autonomy into a more shared responsibility for the entire life and education of their grades in collaboration with principals and other members of the SMT, but there is a need for more research into this.

Project work

There is a [Danish] tradition that teachers involve students in decisions on what and how they should learn. This effort to involve students in several or most of the phases in teaching and learning processes (see the model of processes of practice) has over the past 15–20 years been institutionalized in the demand in the act on schools to have students complete a project assignment as one of the school leaving tests.

The teachers formulate in collaboration with students an overarching theme and groups of students decide on the problem they want to investigate; they plan their work, collect data and write the assignment within a week. They can choose to present their findings and deliberations through other forms of expression. This project work demands collaborative competences of students as well as subject knowledge and cross-disciplinary knowledge. It also demands a high level of independence and communicative competences.

Discussion

One aspect of democratic or shared leadership in these schools is making sure that the people who are to make decisions are able to do so in a competent way. The principals and the rest of the leadership teams show great trust in teachers' teaching competences, and the principals show great trust in the competence and commitment of deputy and department leaders. In one instance [the principal] said that when heads of departments have learned to make the right decisions in the same way as he does, then they are competent to assume responsibility for those decisions.

Another aspect that we observed and heard of is that many teachers and heads of departments asked for the principal's advice or acceptance of their ideas. They often wanted a 'father's or mother's nod' before they carried their ideas out in practice. It was often ideas or actions that they themselves were authorized to carry out on their own and therefore the request for acceptance can be seen as feedback to the principal, asking for acceptance of the action being within the norms of the professional community. The communication in these situations was often clear, transparent and elaborated, so both parties knew what was agreed on and on what premises. On the other hand, there seemed to be a tendency for teachers and department leaders to ask for acceptance from the principal as an authority and at the same time for reassurance from the principal as a person.

The observations made in these schools led us to ask whether there is a trend towards building relations in schools on affective rather than on cognitive sources (Moos, 2003c; Warren, 1999). If this trend increases one could ask whether it eventually is going to undermine the rational community and the democratic relations and leave (too?) much power in the hands of a charismatic leader?

More generally there seems to be a tendency for empowered employees to seek reassurance and acceptance from their leaders. Poul Poder (Mehlsen, 2005) has found in a research project that many employees have also grown dependent on the emotional support of their leaders. The trend is a result of the decentralization of power within value-led enterprises and institutions that rely heavily on the commitment of employees' willingness to work according to the values of the institutions and not according to rules. The case schools are in many ways examples of value-led institutions or communities and the principals are seen as, on the one hand, good rational communicators of insights and ideas, but on the other hand as beginning to grow into 'paternalistic/maternalistic dependency leaders' because the teachers and department leaders draw them into that position.

This could lead to the question of 'How can staff be led and empowered in ways that enable them to become autonomous professionals and co-leaders?' (Moos, 2003a; Moos et al., 2005).

References

Arnot, M. (2004). *Educating learner-citizens for social change: a gendered approach to citizenship education in contemporary societies.* Paper presented at the Nordic Educational Research Association 32nd Conference in Reykjavik, Reykjavik, March 2004.

Bernstein, B. (2000). *Pedagogy, symbolic control and identity: theory, research and critique.* Lanham: Rowman and Littlefield.

Blase, J., Blase, J., Anderson, G.L. & Dungan, S. (1995). *Democratic principals in action. Eight pioneers.* Thousand Oaks: Corwin Press.

Bourdieu, P. (1977). *Outline of a theory of practice.* Cambridge: Cambridge University Press.

Bourdieu, P. (1990). *The logic of practice.* Stanford: Stanford University Press.

Bourdieu, P. (1998). *Af praktiske grunde.* København: Hans Reitzel.

Dewey, J. (1916). *Democracy in education.* New York: Macmillan.

Furman, G.C. & Starratt, R.J. (2002). Leadership for democratic community in schools. In J. Murphy (Ed.). *The educational leadership challenge.* Chicago: Chicago University Press.

Goldring, E. & Greenfield, W. (2002). Building the foundation for understanding and action. In J. Murphy (Ed.). *The educational leadership challenge* (pp. 1–19). Chicago: The University of Chicago Press.

Gronn, P. (2002). Distributed leadership. In K. Leithwood & P. Hallinger (Eds.). *Second international handbook of educational leadership and administration* (pp. 653–696). Dordrecht: Kluwer Academic Publishers.

Habermas, J. (1984). *The theory of communicative action – reason and the rationalization of society* (Vol. 1). Boston: Beacon Press.

Habermas, J. (1987). *The theory of communicative action – lifeworld and system: a critique of functionalist reason.* Boston: Beacon Press.

Hallinger, P. (2003). Leading educational change: Reflections on the practice of instructional and transformational leadership. *Cambridge Journal of Education,* 33(3), pp. 329–352.

Harris, A. (2005). *Teacher leadership: more than just a feel good factor?* Paper presented at the AERA Annual Meeting, Montreal.

Jensen, B.B. & Schnack, K. (1994). (Didaktiske studier. Studies in Educational Theory and Curriculum: nr. 12). In Jensen, B.B., Action and action competence as key concepts in critical pedagogy (pp. 5–18). Copenhagen: Danmarks Lærerhøjskole.

Leithwood, K., Begley, P. & Cousins, J.B. (1994). *Developing expert leadership for future schools.* London: Falmer Press.

Leithwood, K., Louis, K.S., Anderson, S. & Wahlstrom, K. (2004). *Review of research: how leadership influences student learning.* Toronto: University of Minnesota. University of Toronto, The Wallace Foundation.

Leithwood, K.A. & Riehl, C. (2003). *What do we already know about successful school leadership?* Toronto: OISE.

Louis, K.S. (2003). Democratic schools, democratic communities. *Leadership and Policy in Schools*, 2(2), pp. 93–108.

MacBeath, J. & Moos, L. (2004). *Leadership for learning*. Paper presented at the ICSEI Rotterdam 2004, January 6–9, Rotterdam.

Mehlsen, C. (2005). Empowerment som frihedsgode. *Astrix*. February 2005, No. 21, pp. 25–26.

Moos, L. (2003a). Educational leadership: leading for/as 'dannelse'? *International Journal of Leadership in Education*, 6(1), pp. 19–33.

Moos, L. (2003b). Leadership for/as 'dannelse'? In L. Moos (Ed.). *Educational leadership*. Copenhagen: Danish University of Education Press.

Moos, L. (2003c). *Pædagogisk ledelse – om ledelsesopgaven og relationerne i uddannelsesinstitutioner*. København: Børsens Forlag.

Moos, L., Krejsler, J., Kofod, K. & Jensen, B.B. (2005). Successful school principalship in Danish schools. *Journal of Educational Administration*, 43(6), pp. 563–572.

Mulford, B. (2005). *Leadership for school and student learning – what do we know?* Nottingham: NCSL.

Reynolds, D. (no year). *Effective school leadership: the contribution of school effectiveness research*. Nottingham: National College for School Leadership.

Sergiovanni, T.J. (1995). *The principalship. A reflective practice perspective*. Boston: Allyn and Bacon.

Sørhaug, T. (1996). *Om ledelse. Magt og tillid i moderne organisering*. Oslo: Universitetsforlaget.

Southworth, G. (2003). Learning-centred leadership in schools. In L. Moos (Ed.). *Educational leadership*, pp. 33–52. Copenhagen: Danish University of Education Press.

Spillane, J.P. & Orlina, E.C. (2005). *Investigating leadership practice: exploring the entailments of taking a distributed perspective*. Paper presented at the AERA Annual Meeting, Montreal.

Thyssen, O. (2003a). Luhman og ledelsen. In H. Højlund & M. Knudsen (Eds.). *Organiseret kommunikation – systemteoretiske analyser*. Frederiksberg: Samfundslitteratur.

Thyssen, O. (2003b). *Organisationens usynlighed*. Paper presented at the Professor tiltrædelse, CBS, Handelshøjskolen, Kobenhavn.

Warren, M.E. (1999). Democratic theory and trust. In M.E. Warren (Ed.). *Democracy & trust*. Cambridge: Cambridge University Press.

3

Leading with Moral Purpose: the Place of Ethics[1]

Paul T. Begley

In recent years there has been a dramatic increase in the amount of attention directed to the consideration of ethics as an influence on educational leadership and management, by both academics and educational practitioners. This trend appears to be driven by a number of forces, but most notably the increasing diversity of our communities. One of the most obvious outcomes of increasing cultural diversity in our communities is a broader range of social values, some of which are not compatible with each other, and a subsequent increase in the frequency of culturally based value conflicts that require attention. A second social condition that has highlighted the need to consider ethics is the revolutionising effects of several technological innovations. The Internet has radically changed our access to and use of information. Economic forces associated with globalisation have also become associated with a number of persistent and troubling challenges to the well-being and survival of our society that can be at least partly explained as the outcomes of unethical actions.

[...]

Leading with moral purpose

School leaders in many countries currently confront as a normal condition of their work a veritable quagmire of reform initiatives, curricular innovations and policy dictates. This has become a defining characteristic of educational leadership in many sectors of the world. Given the dynamics of these multiple social and professional expectations for schools, it has become more necessary than ever for school administrators to fall back on basic principles and the fundamental purposes of education – as they exist traditionally and

Source – An edited version of Begley, P. (2010) 'Leading with moral purpose: the place of ethics'.

as they are currently interpreted in locally relevant contextual settings. Using these ethical postures as guidelines is probably the soundest way for school leaders to critically deconstruct the edu-babble they regularly encounter, respond effectively to trendy initiatives and perhaps even help to defuse those assaults on the teaching profession that have become so common to education.

Unfortunately, this clearly good advice for leaders is often ignored. When educational administrators carry out their roles without explicit reference to educational purposes, they run the risk of directing their energy to inappropriate or wasteful tasks, and become more vulnerable to manipulation and exploitation by individuals, organisations and special interest groups bent on pursuing their self-interests. Indeed, one of the most common failings observable among educational leaders today is a failure to adequately distinguish between means and ends. Are standardised test scores best thought of as a means or an end? When leaders manage the operation of educational programmes in their schools – a traditional notion of instructional leadership in many countries – is this attending to a means or an end? Even venerable and seemingly inviolate notions like child-centred or learner-centred education might be best thought of as a means to an educational end rather than some sort of absolute objective, particularly if the educational focus is on the individual child rather than children in the more global sense. Moreover, in the practitioner world it often seems that every educational innovation that comes along is touted as some sort of unquestioned end of education. Obviously, they cannot all be that important, and one of the best ways for educational leaders to navigate these perennial challenges is to keep their professional goals and purposes at the forefront of their administrative practices.

The purposes of education

Hodgkinson (1991) provides an insightful and comprehensive exploration of the special purposes of education. He does so by examining the historical roots of each category of educational purpose that he proposes. He traces aesthetic purposes back to the humanistic traditions of Greece – a focus on the formation of character and the subsequent notions of a classic liberal education. Applied to modern education practices in many countries in recent decades, a concern with aesthetic purposes has become associated with progressive education and focused by notions like student self-esteem, personal fulfilment of the individual, and lifelong learning. There is also a curricular tradition that most clearly associates with aesthetic purposes. It is that of transformational learning with its emphasis on synthesis and reapplication of learning and personal transcendence (Miller and Seller, 1985).

The economic purposes of education, according to Hodgkinson (1991), can be traced back to the influence of the Romans. Learning to earn is a simple but accurate way to conceptualise the economic purposes in education. The Romans were apparently the first to promote the notion of professional accreditation in the sense that has become so common to our societies today. For example, a centurion might have been expected to successfully complete particular training to become qualified for that military role in the same way we do today with aircraft pilots, doctors, lawyers, yoga instructors and perhaps even kindergarten graduates. The curricular tradition that aligns best with the economic purposes of education is a transactional orientation to learning. If it is accurate to say that teachers have a bias towards the aesthetic purposes of education, then it is parents, the media and business leaders that tend to champion the primacy of economic purposes in education today. Yet economic purposes, as much as aesthetic purposes, remain an important priority for school leadership.

The ideological or socialisation functions of education represent perhaps the most basic of educational purposes. This third broad purpose is normally associated with notions of citizenship and social skills. During the early days of North American settlement, or any newly developing region of the world, it is not hard to imagine parents being highly motivated to quickly establish schools so their children can learn what they need to know to function in society, comply with the norms of society, and contribute to the well-being of their communities. Moreover, this is one of the most powerful ways for a society to pass on its norms and standards of conduct to succeeding generations of citizens. Other smaller-scale manifestations of ideological purposes in modern schooling might include an anti-racism curriculum, the promotion of tolerance for cultural diversity, and notions of environmental responsibility. The curricular tradition that most closely aligns with ideological purposes of education is the transmission mode of curriculum – the direct transfer of knowledge and skill to the learner, the filling of the empty vessel.

Examining the educational mission statements produced by many school districts typically reveals the implicit if not explicit presence of all three of these purposes of education, albeit with the usual culturally driven ebb and flow of emphasis from district to district and region to region across time. To this extent the purposes of educational leadership can become codified and made accessible to professional educators as a mandate. However, a balanced education can be defined in terms of how well all three purposes have been accommodated as part of the educational experience of each child. Too much emphasis on one purpose can compromise the overall educational experience of learners. In particular, the arts have been discounted in favour of the sciences. This illustrates a disturbing trend in a diverse range of countries towards an overemphasis on economic purposes and transactional curriculum at the expense of the more transformational agendas of aesthetic learning, and the social interaction skills associated with ideological literacy. Nevertheless, even at the best of times, the purposes of education are somewhat fluid and dynamic, the emphasis and balance shifting with time and circumstances. Yet, they require a balanced presence. Otherwise educational purposes can be skewed by loud, persistent or powerful voices as the emphasis among purposes cycles through alternating periods of conservatism and liberalism.

Sorting out terminology: morals, values and ethics

Before getting into a full-blown discussion of leadership with moral purpose, it is important to sort out a few terms. Depending on the country and scholarly context, terms like 'morals', 'values' and 'ethics' are often used interchangeably – to the chagrin of classically trained philosophers and the confusion of graduate students and practitioners. For the purposes of this chapter the terms will be defined and differentiated from each other.

The term 'values' can be thought of as the umbrella term within which other specialised forms of values can be subsumed. Values can be formally defined as conceptions of the desirable with motivating force characteristic of individuals, groups, organisations and societies'that influence choices made from available resources and means (Hodgkinson, 1978). Begley (2006) describes the influence of values within individuals as the internal psychological reflections of more distilled levels of motivation (for example, a concern for personal interests, consequences or consensus) that become tangible to an observer in the form of attitudes, speech and actions. Thus, values in their various forms, including ethics, can be thought of as conscious or unconscious influences on attitudes, actions and speech. However, it is important to note that valuation processes can involve more than ethics. Values can take different forms and can be best categorised according to their motivational grounding.

Ethics, as a particular form of values, as opposed to the study of ethics as a scholarly discipline, are normative social ideals or codes of conduct usually grounded in the cultural experience of particular societies. In that sense they are a sort of *uber* form of social consensus. For example, many societies have core ethics equivalent to the American notions of democracy, freedom of speech and the priority of individual rights. Those of us steeped in the traditions of such classic Western philosophical thought can easily make the mistake of assuming that our most cherished ethical postures, such as democracy, are universal. However, they seldom are, especially as interpreted from culture to culture. Ethics in their purest forms tend to be expressed in a relatively context-stripped form that conveys only the essence of the normative behaviour. Indeed, in some forms and social applications they can be, and often are, treated as absolute values. This inclination to view ethics as some sort of absolute value is sometimes inappropriately enabled by evidence of consensus across cultures on certain ethical postures like respect for human rights, honesty and democracy. And, indeed, there are probably some ethics of the human condition that approach a condition of universal relevance. However, the devil is literally in the details when it comes to ethical postures. The interpretation of meaning associated with an ethic can vary greatly from society to society. Simply pondering the contrasting notions of what constitutes democracy in countries like Sweden, the USA and China illustrates this point. Except perhaps in the most culturally homogeneous of contexts, using ethical postures as a basis for making social choices requires the inclusion of a dialogic component. This is not to argue against the relevance and importance of ethics to leadership actions. It is more a caveat to their proper use.

There are other issues when it comes to ethics and their relevance to educational leadership processes. Human behaviour involves a range of motivational bases, only a few of which can be associated with ethical postures. These other motivational bases can range from self-interest to a concern for rationalised positions grounded in consensus or consequences, not just the trans-rational groundings of ethical postures (Begley, 2006; Hodgkinson, 1978). The point is that because ethical postures are usually associated with ideal states, they do not necessarily accommodate the full range of motivations for human behaviour. This circumstance is critically important to individuals in leadership positions seeking to understand their own motivational bases as well as those of others. It hardly needs to be said that not all individuals encountered in organisational settings act in ethical ways. Ethics-based postures are highly relevant for guiding appropriate responses to complex organisational situations, but they may not be sufficient in themselves for a comprehensive analysis and understanding of human motivations.

For the purposes of this chapter, the term 'ethics' is used to signify a specific category of values – those that are trans-rational in nature, usually normatively grounded in a particular cultural context and taking the form of statements of basic principle expressed in abstract and context-stripped forms. A final key term is 'moral'. This term is properly associated with a situated or context-specific form of values. Moral actions are values-justified actions. Moral actions usually occur in a specific context. Morals are values in an applied form.

[…]

Alternate ethical paradigms: critique, care, justice, profession and community

The complexity of social and administrative situations makes it attractive for school leaders to employ processes to aid their interpretation and structuring of situations, but this must be done in socially and culturally sensitive ways. For example, Shapiro and Stefkovich (2005) espouse the application of a multi-ethical analytical approach to the interpretation of ethical dilemmas as a way to improve or ensure the quality of decision-making. The key ethical orientations suggested by these scholars include the ethic of justice, the ethic of critique, the ethic of care and a hybrid multi-dimensional model, the ethic of profession.

[…]

Begley (2006) argues that in the *professional context* of school leadership, where the individual is essentially an agent of society, there is probably an implied sequence for the appropriate application of these classic Western ethical lenses. Begley argues that there is a professionally appropriate sequence for the application of these ethical lenses in a school leadership situation. Beginning with the ethic of critique is justified in order to name and understand as much as possible the alternate perspectives applicable to a situation, especially those of minorities and individuals otherwise without voice or representation. To do otherwise is to risk gravitation to the preferred cultural orientations of the leader or the mainstream orientations of a given cultural group. The ethic of care can naturally follow in the sequence as a way to keep the focus of the process on people and their best interests rather than an overly quick gravitation towards organisational imperatives or policies. Using the ethic of care, one can assess the capacity and responsibility of stakeholders to a situation in a humane way. Finally, once the ethics of critique and care have been used to carefully interpret a situation, the ethic of justice can be applied as a basis for deciding on actions that will maximise benefits for all while respecting the rights of individuals. This is not to suggest a dogmatic adherence to a prescriptive sequence of application for these classic ethics of Western philosophy. In all cases, the sequencing and application of ethical perspectives needs to be very fluid and dynamic as an initial organiser, not a recipe, and as a stimulus for reflection or dialogue, not a prescription. However, the application of any lens to a situation, including ethics, begins the process of highlighting some information as relevant and diminishing or veiling the relevance of other information. School leaders accountable to their communities must take care to interpret situations in a sensitive way.

[...]

Arenas of leadership as sources of influence, conflicts and identity

In recent decades, school leaders have learned how important it is to lead and manage with proper reference to the broader environmental context of their community. The influences on leadership, decision-making, and education in general can be thought of as coming from multiple social sources. Some of these influences can take on the status of values when they are perceived as conceptions of the desirable with motivating force (Hodgkinson, 1991). Unfortunately, our personal values as well of those of the profession, organisation, community and society are not necessarily consistent or compatible with each other. As a result, these influences and values derived from the various arenas of our environment can generate inconsistencies and conflicts. An onion figure (see Figure 3.1) is used to illustrate these distinctions. These are the interactive environments within which valuation processes and administration occur. They are also the source of personal, professional and social values, as well as the source of many of the conflicts people encounter in life.

Within Figure 3.1, the individual is represented within the centre ring and extending through all the rings. His or her character is the outcome of many transient influences as well as relatively more enduring values acquired from multiple arenas.

The second ring from the centre represents the arena of groups, and other collective entities including family, peers, friends and acquaintances. The third ring, profession, represents a more formal arena of administration that is closely related to the second ring, but is given special emphasis here because of its relevance to the professional context that is the focus of this chapter.

The fourth ring represents the arena traditionally of most concern to academics and practitioners in the field of educational administration, the organisation. Much of the literature of educational administration and most of the corporate literature are grounded within the organisational perspective, adopting it as a primary reference point for administrative activity.

Moving further outwards in the figure, one encounters the arenas representing the greater community, society, and culture. Within recent decades, school administrators have learned that it is necessary to pay a lot more attention to the community as a relevant administrative arena and source of influence on school leadership (Leithwood et al., 1992). The increasing diversity of our societies and a general trend towards globalisation has highlighted society and culture as relevant arenas of administrative activity.

A final, sixth ring is included to accommodate notions of the transcendental – God, faith, spirituality, even extra-sensory perception. Spirituality is of considerable importance to many individuals, and has begun to attract the attention of more scholars as an important

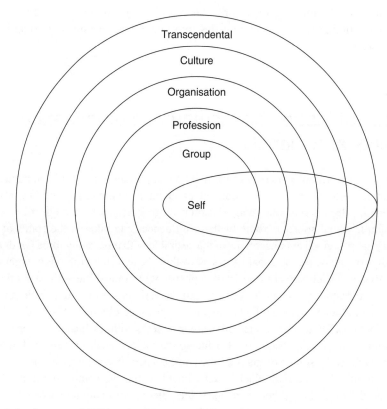

Figure 3.1   Arenas of influence (Begley, 2004)

influence on educational leadership. Even administrators who do not subscribe to a spiritual dimension as a source of influence in their own daily lives are well advised to keep this arena in mind, if only because at least some individuals associated with their professional role do. A leader who wants to understand the motivations of those they are supposed to lead will be sensitive to all potentially significant categories of influence.

Practitioner perspectives on leading with moral purpose

Perhaps the most fundamental way in which morals, values and ethics relate to leadership is as an influence on the cognitive processes of individuals and groups of individuals. It is essential for those in leadership roles to understand how values reflect underlying human motivations and shape the subsequent attitudes, speech, and actions of personnel (Begley, 2006; Hodgkinson, 1978; Kohlberg and Turiel, 1971). Begley's conception of authentic forms of leadership (2006) emphasises this capacity as something that begins with self-knowledge and then becomes extended to sensitivity to the perspectives of others. In that context it is argued that leaders should know their own values and ethical predispositions, as well as be sensitive to the value orientations of others. Branson (2006) has developed a very effective instructional strategy, called the deeply structured reflection process, that can be used as a support for developing this kind of knowledge and self-awareness. It involves the identification by individuals of critical incidents that have contributed to their personal or professional formation. Through deconstruction of, and reflection on, personal narratives of critical incidents, individuals develop an awareness of how their motivations, values and attitudes are derived and become predictive indicators of their actions in response to situations they will encounter in the future.

[…]

A second way in which valuation processes relate to moral leadership practices is as a guide to action, particularly as supports to making decisions and resolving ethical dilemmas. Ethics and valuation models are highly relevant to school leadership as rubrics, benchmarks, socially justified standards of practice and templates for moral action. These may be used by the individual leader or in more collective ways by groups of people. […] Scholars have developed well documented processes for the analysis of dilemma situations and development of ethical responses. One of these processes is outlined and discussed in some detail at the conclusion of this chapter and presented as a resource in support of leading with moral purpose.

However, there is a third and more strategic and collective application for ethics in moral leadership processes. It is common in a school or school district setting for ethical postures to be adopted with a strategic organisational intent – for example, as a focus for building consensus around a shared social or organisational objective. To illustrate, a school district superintendent might choose 'ethic of community' (Furman, 2003) as a rallying meta-value to focus the energies of personnel on collective action. Or, ethical notions such as 'due process' (Strike et al., 1998) or 'social justice' (Shapiro and Stefkovich, 2005) might be used as the objective for focusing the reform of school district processes in support of students with special needs. These more collective and strategic applications of ethics may very well be the more common manifestation of this value type in the administration of schools and school districts, at the government level, as well as in the corporate sector. In this sense leaders literally use ethics as leadership tools to support actions taken, model ideal practice, and/or promote particular kinds of organisational or societal activity. However, as will be argued, these strategic adoptions of ethical postures may or may not be ethical.

Using ethics versus being ethical

Research findings (for example, Begley and Johansson, 1998) confirm that the relevance of principles or ethics to administrative situations seems to be prompted in the minds of school administrators by particular circumstances. These circumstances include: situations where an ethical posture is socially appropriate (for example, the role of the arts); situations where consensus is perceived as difficult or impossible to achieve (for example, an issue involving ethnic bias); or situations when high stakes and urgency require decisive action (for example, student safety). There is also some evidence to suggest that school leaders use ethics in strategic applications as ways to develop group consensus, and a basis for promoting compliance with minimum need for justifying proof of effects (Langlois, 2004). These are all examples of *ethically sound* – meaning socially justifiable – applications of ethics to situations.

One has only to survey the newspaper or work in an organisation or live in a community for a few years to readily detect situations where ethics-based postures can be unethical and socially unjust. Ethical postures may be *unethical* under a number of circumstances: for example, when a cultural ethic is imposed on others, when an ethic is used to justify otherwise reprehensible action, an ethical posture veils a less defensible value or when an ethic is used to trump a basic human right. When unexamined values are applied in arbitrary ways, they can be anything but ethical. The essential, and often absent, component that makes adherence to a value genuinely ethical is dialogue. For these reasons, unexamined ethics applied in instrumental ways, or values accepted at face value without prior deliberation of meaning, represent a particular category of action that may not be consistent with moral leadership processes. It should be apparent that in order to cultivate the ability to distinguish the difference between using ethics and being ethical, we need the capacity to discriminate actual intentions within ourselves and among others. This is not an argument for moral relativism, nor is it value absolutism, it is an argument for the critical thinking necessary for leading with moral purpose.

How leaders respond to moral dilemmas

Dilemma situations have become common to educational leadership processes in most countries, but especially those communities experiencing increased cultural diversity among their population. The achievement of consensus on educational issues among even traditional educational stakeholders within a single community has become more difficult in many sectors. School administrators increasingly encounter dilemmas or value conflict situations where consensus cannot be achieved, rendering obsolete the traditional rational notions of problem-*solving*. Administrators must now often be satisfied with *responding* to a situation since there may be no solution possible that will satisfy all. Such dilemmas can occur within a single arena of administration or among two or more arenas. The most difficult dilemmas occur when one ethic literally trumps another.

A pilot study conducted during 2004 examined principals' perceptions of, and responses to, the moral dilemmas encountered in the professional context of their roles (Begley, 2005). […] The findings from this research provides insights into how school leaders respond to the ethical dilemmas encountered in their professional work.

[…]

Sources of dilemma

Begley's (2004) graphic portrayal of the arenas or domains (see Figure 3.1) of administration was employed as a guide to determining the source or sources of the dilemmas presented by the participants. Many of the dilemmas reported by the participants could be readily connected to organisational policies (for example, zero tolerance policies, required reporting of alleged abuse) that reduced the professional discretion of the administrator to make decisions in the best interest of students or the school. The most difficult of situations was perceived to be when the policies are seen as inappropriately punitive or when the student in question had no intention to break a rule or violate policy. Several school leaders also reported dilemmas that clearly revealed conflicts between personal moral positions and those of the profession, school district or community (that is, persistent racial discrimination by administrative colleagues).

Interpersonal versus intrapersonal dilemmas

The notion of arenas as a guide for identifying the source of the dilemmas was also useful for assessing whether the dilemmas were interpersonal or intrapersonal; that is, whether the dilemma explicitly involved more than one person or was an essentially internal struggle experienced by one person. In a surprising number of cases, clear evidence suggests that the dilemmas were intrapersonal. School administrators seem much inclined to sort out professional dilemmas on their own, without seeking the opinions and support of others. For the school administrators participating in this study, the dilemmas of practice seem to be viewed as private and personal challenges. Only one principal made reference to actively involving other staff or colleagues in the moral deliberation of the dilemmas encountered in the school.

Guiding meta-values

Most educational leadership literature highlights accountability as a significant influence on school administrators' assessment and interpretation of situations. This apparently quite consistent pattern of response has also been associated with an inclination for school administrators to gravitate towards the rational motivational bases of consequences and consensus. This phenomenon has also been used to explain in part why school administrators often avoid ethics as an explicit guide to decision-making, in preference to more rationally defensible decision processes grounded in consequences or consensus.

The data collected in support of this study about administrative responses to dilemmas both confirm and challenge the pre-eminence of accountability as a meta-value for school principals. Many of the dilemmas cases submitted by the participants do indeed make explicit and/or implicit reference to accountability as an overriding concern. However, there is another equally strong and frequently articulated meta-value that becomes apparent, and that is 'doing what is best for kids' or 'the best interests of students'. As much as accountability may be a primary influence on the general decision-making processes of school administrators, when situations are perceived by administrators to be dilemmas, there appears to be an equally strong inclination to adopt 'students' best interests' as the meta-value of choice.

Strategies for interpretation

The strategies employed by the participants to interpret and respond to the dilemmas of practice they perceived conform fairly well to the findings of research conducted by Roche (1999) based on the practices of principals in Queensland, Australia. His inquiry focused on how school administrators actually respond to moral and ethical dilemmas. He identified four primary ways in which principals respond to moral dilemmas. Predictably, he found that the press for accountability appears to heavily influence such processes. Listed in order of frequency of use by the administrators in Roche's study, the strategies principals used in response to the professional dilemmas they encounter are avoidance, suspended morality, creative insubordination and taking a personal moral stand. Avoidance (reinterpreting the situation so it no longer involves an ethical dimension) is the most frequently employed response among the administrators in the Roche (1999) study. Suspended morality, the second most common strategy, illustrates the ability of administrators to set aside some of their personal value orientations, and consciously respond to situations from a professional or organisational perspective. The third category of response identified by Roche is creative insubordination. As a strategy it is an opposite response to suspended morality. In this case organisational dictates are set aside, or creative approaches to compliance are found, that favour more humane concerns. The taking of a personal moral stand was the least frequently employed response, usually adopted only when the administrator assessed a high likelihood of successfully challenging the competing demands of the profession, organisation or society.

There is evidence of all four of Roche's identified strategies also being used by the respondents in the Begley (2005) study. Appeals to policy as a basis for responding to a situation equate with the avoidance strategy. Many of the dilemmas submitted by the principals conveyed the angst encountered when they felt compelled to suspend their own morality in favour of a professional or organisational position. A few of the reported dilemmas reveal the intent of the principal to take a public moral stand.

The value audit process: a resource for leading with moral purpose

In an effort to help school leaders develop their capacity to make ethically sound and professionally effective decisions, Begley has developed several versions of a value audit guide that can be used as a resource in support of leadership for moral purpose (see Figure 3.2). Originally based on a series of value audit questions proposed by Hodgkinson (1991), this resource document has gone through several evolutions and refinements as a result of being used with a succession of groups of school leaders in several countries over several years.

An examination of the version included here will reveal that it incorporates many of the key concepts introduced and discussed in this chapter, including: a sequenced application of the ethics of critique, care and justice; a bias towards careful interpretation before moving to action; and the four motivational bases of valuation by individuals. Begley has used this activity with some success in several countries as a component of graduate-level courses and also as a workshop activity in support of the professional development of principals.

Questions to Guide the Moral Analysis of a Situation, Problem or Decision

These questions may be helpful as guides, to be used by individuals or groups interested in analysing and responding ethically to critical incidents or dilemmas of practice encountered in school leadership situations.

Step 1: Interpretation of the Problem (ethic of critique)

- Who are the **stakeholders?** Are any unrecognised or without voice?
- What **arenas of practice** (self, profession, organisation, community, culture) are relevant?
- Does the conflict exist **within an arena or between two or more?** (for example, personal vs organisational)
- Can the **values in conflict** be named?
- How much **turbulence** are the values in conflict creating? (Degree of risk for structural damage to people, organisations, or community)

Step 2: Towards a Humane Response (ethic of care)

- What **motivations and degrees of commitment** are apparent among the stakeholders?

Four levels of motivation:

- concerned with self, personal preference, habitual, comfort (sub-rational values grounded in preference)
- concerned with desired outcomes, avoidance of undesirable (rational values grounded in consequences)
- concerned with perceptions of others, consultation, expert opinion (rational values grounded in consensus)
- concerned with ethical postures, first principles, will or faith (trans-rational, no need for rational justification)

- Is the conflict **interpersonal** (among individuals) or **intrapersonal** (within an individual)?
- What are the **human needs**, as opposed to organisational or philosophical standards?

Step 3: Ethical Action (ethic of justice)

- What actions or response would **maximise benefits** for all stakeholders?
- What actions or response would **respect individual rights?**
- Are desired '**ends**' or purposes interfering with the selection of a '**means**' or solution?
- If an ethical **dilemma** exists (a choice between equally unsatisfactory alternatives), how will you resolve it? (Avoidance, Suspended Morality, Creative Insubordination, Taking a Moral Stand)

Figure 3.2   Value audit guidelines (Begley, 2005)

Conclusion: leadership with moral purpose

Complexity, human interaction, and the dynamics of continually evolving social expectations are characteristic of the educational leadership role. Leadership involves management, but management skills are not sufficient. The mediation of competing interests and the fair allocation of scarce resources in support of an increasingly complex educational process necessitates that educational leaders have a clear set of educational purposes and a strong sense of moral purpose. They need to be able to lead, to navigate through multiple and competing interests.

As argued in this chapter, there are historically clear purposes of education. They are multifaceted and therefore complex to manage, but they are nevertheless the socially justified objectives of education in our societies. The mandate is clear and it is an educational one, not a corporate agenda or an economic agenda. The challenge for educational leaders is to keep the aesthetic, economic and ideological purposes of education in the forefront as guides to decision-making and strategic planning. They are the meta-values of the profession. This is nothing less than a purpose-driven approach to morally defensible educational leadership.

Four other key points are made in this chapter. One is that the purposes of educational leadership are the dynamic outcome of influences from several arenas or social domains, not just educational organisations. Secondly, authentic forms of leadership are defined as the outcome of self-knowledge, sensitivity to the perspectives of others, and the technical skills of organisation management and personnel leadership. Thirdly, leading for moral purpose requires a focus on leadership intentions and a commitment to reflective practice, not just the description or emulation of the practices of others. Finally, the increased diversity of society makes necessary an increased awareness of intercultural variations in perceptions and interpretation of leadership purposes. Context makes a big difference. These are the specialised purposes and nature of leadership with moral purpose.

Note

1. Portions of this chapter are based on material taken with the permission of the publishers from three previously published sources. These sources are: Begley, P.T. and Stefkovich, J.T. (2007) 'Integrating values and ethics into postsecondary teaching for leadership development: principles, concepts, and strategies', *Journal of Educational Administration*, 45(4): 398–412; Begley, P.T. (2006) 'Self-knowledge, capacity and sensitivity: prerequisites to authentic leadership by school principals', *Journal of Educational Administration*, 44(6): 570–89; and Begley, P.T. (ed.) (2008) *School Leadership in Canada*, 4th edn. Mt St Louis: Paul Begley and Associates.

References

Begley, P.T. (2001) 'In pursuit of authentic school leadership practices', *International Journal of Leadership in Education*, 4(4): 353–66.

Begley, P.T. (2003) 'In pursuit of authentic school leadership practices', in P.T. Begley and O. Johansson (eds), *The Ethical Dimensions of School Leadership*. Dordrecht: Kluwer Academic. pp. 1–12.

Begley, P.T. (2004) 'Understanding valuation processes: exploring the linkage between motivation and action', *International Studies in Educational Administration*, 32(2): 4–17.

Begley, P.T. (2005) 'The dilemmas of leadership: perspectives on the moral literacy of principals from Ontario and Pennsylvania', paper delivered at the Annual Meeting of the American Educational Research Association, Montreal, Quebec, April.

Begley, P.T. (2006) 'Self-knowledge, capacity and sensitivity: prerequisites to authentic leadership by school principals', *Journal of Educational Administration*, 44(6): 570–89.

Begley, P.T. and Johansson, O. (1998) 'The values of school administration: preferences, ethics and conflicts', *The Journal of School Leadership*, 8(4): 399–422.

Branson, C. (2006) 'Effects of structured self-reflection on the development of authentic leadership practices among Queensland primary school principals', *Educational Management Administration and Leadership*, 35(2): 227–48.

Furman, G. (2003) 'Moral leadership and the ethic of community', *Values and Ethics in Educational Administration*, 2(1): 1–8.

Hodgkinson, C. (1978) *Towards a Philosophy of Administration.* Oxford: Basil Blackwell.

Hodgkinson, C. (1991) *Educational Leadership: The Moral Art.* Albany, NY: SUNY Press.

Kohlberg, L. and Turiel, E. (1971) 'Moral development and moral education', in G. Lesser (ed.), *Psychology and Educational Practice*. New York: Scott Foresman pp. 530–50.

Langlois, L. (2004) 'Making the tough calls: complex decision-making in light of ethical considerations', *International Studies in Educational Administration*, 32(2): 78–93.

Leithwood, K.A., Begley, P.T. and Cousins, J.B. (1992) *Developing Expert Leadership for Future Schools*. London: Falmer Press.

Miller, J. and Seller, W. (1985) *Curriculum: Perspectives and Practice*. New York: Longman.

Roche, K. (1999) 'Moral and ethical dilemmas in Catholic school settings', in P.T. Begley (ed.), *Values and Educational Leadership*. Albany. NY: SUNY Press. pp. 255–72.

Shapiro, J. and Stefkovich, J.A. (2005) *Ethical Leadership and Decision Making in Education*, 2nd edn. Mahwah, NJ: Lawrence Erlbaum Associates.

Strike, K.A., Haller, E.J. and Soltis, J.F. (1998) *The Ethics of School Administration*, 2nd edn. New York: Teachers College Press.

4

Emotional Intelligence, Emotional Labour and Affective Leadership

Sam Held and Judy McKimm

Introduction

Few terms from leadership and personal development training become familiar in everyday language. However *Emotional intelligence* (EI) is an exception, as Daniel Goleman (1995, 1998, 2000), author and former psychologist, has so popularised his theories that his books have become best-sellers.

EI is widely considered a template for success in the fields of strategic collaboration and integrated practice. Supporters claim that EI is more important in life than academic success, while opponents claim it is not an 'intelligence', and some dismiss it as 'pop psychology' (Mayer et al., 2008).

In this chapter, we present two main strands of EI theory and offer a critique drawing on some key literature sources. We explore how insights from EI can be used, applying them to the concept of emotional labour and discuss the 'science' and 'art' of leadership, focusing on 'affective leadership'.

The evolution of emotional intelligence

Before the 1920s, research on intelligence studied primarily cognitive skills and abilities. In 1920, Thorndike suggested that 'social intelligence' offered 'the ability to understand and manage men and women, boys and girls (and) act wisely in human relations'. Building on these concepts, in 1990, Salovey and Mayer defined 'emotional intelligence' as 'the ability to perceive emotion, integrate emotion to facilitate

This chapter was commissioned especially for this volume.

thought, understand emotions and to regulate emotions to promote personal growth' (Mayer and Salovey, 1997, 31). Goleman became widely associated with EI after publishing *Emotional Intelligence: Why It Can Matter More Than IQ* in 1995. In a series of popular books, he expands one premise of Salovey and Mayer's work, that a high IQ is not necessarily a prerequisite for success. Three models of EI have since evolved:

- the Mixed model (The Goleman 'school')
- the Ability model (Mayer and Salovey)
- the Trait model (Petrides and Furnham, 2003).

We will discuss the two main models: the Mixed and Ability models.

The Mixed model

Goleman writes for a general readership, and his meta-message, that one doesn't need a high IQ to be successful, is powerfully appealing. The concept is illustrated by anecdotes about brilliant people who were unsuccessful in corporate life, others who were academically undistinguished, but successful in business or public life, and dramatic, shocking or violent vignettes to illustrate the alleged effects of a lack of EI.

Goleman defines EI as 'a capacity for recognising our own and others' feelings, for motivating ourselves, and for managing our emotions, both within ourselves and in our relationships' (1998: 317). He identifies 25 EI competencies or behaviours (1998: 26–7), claiming that a high level of EI can make the difference between business or public success and failure, grouping the competencies into five domains:

- **Self-awareness**: how emotions affect performance
- **Self-regulation**: controlling temper and stress
- **Motivation**: enjoying challenge and seeking achievement
- **Empathy**: the ability to understand others' realities
- **Social skills**: influencing skills and the ability to deal with others' emotions.

In later works, the domains are reduced to four:

- Self-awareness
- Self-management
- Social awareness
- Relationship management.

Goleman implies that these competencies were derived from 'analyses done by dozens of experts in close to five hundred corporations' (1998: 5) but fails to present any empirical evidence to support his claims. His journalistic style may contribute to the books' popular appeal but his theory of EI is not validated by research evidence.

Goleman's key theories

Goleman proposes that behavioural responses to emotional stimuli are indicators of emotional intelligence. Emotions, from basic 'fight or flight' responses to more complex emotions like anger, frustration and pleasure, are deemed to originate in more primitive areas of the brain than the 'higher' centres where reasoning occurs. Emotional centres thus receive stimuli before the thinking centres. When basic emotions like fear or anger are triggered, people can respond from the emotion centres, without the mediating effects of reason. While 'fight or flight' reactions are still important, they are rarely appropriate in the modern workplace. Goleman suggests EI is about controlling emotional reactions in oneself, while using reason to anticipate and control them in others.

In a later work, *The New Leaders* (2002) Goleman et al. apply EI to leadership rather than individual success. The authors return to the theme of *emotionally intelligent domains* and their *associated competencies* which they claim can be observed in success-ful leaders' behaviours. Drawing on an earlier Goleman study (2000) of leadership styles, they suggest that emotionally intelligent leaders select from six different styles depending on circumstances. Fullan (2004: 44) further developed the concepts, identifying messages for each style related to the education leadership context.

Fullan also maintains that effective leaders need to employ different styles at different times and the more styles a leader can draw from, the more successful they will be. In an emergency, you need a coercive or authoritative leader. Conversely, when organisational change is required, people need coaching and affiliative leadership: the affiliative leader focuses on building emotional bonds, builds relationships (Fullan, 2004: 51). Goleman also claims that leaders can learn to be more emotionally intelligent and override basic emotional responses.

The Ability model

Salovey and Mayer (1990) attempt to define EI within accepted psychological criteria for intelligence: a property of the mind, including capacity for abstract thought, reasoning, learning from past experiences and problem solving.

The ability-based model considers emotions as sources of information which help indi-viduals respond appropriately to the social context, suggesting people vary in their ability to process emotional input and relate emotion to cognition. These differences manifest themselves in adaptive behaviours. The model claims that EI includes four abilities:

1. Perceiving emotions – the ability to detect and read emotions in self, in faces, pictures, voices, etc. This is fundamental to EI.
2. Using emotions – the ability to harness emotions in thinking and problem solving.
3. Understanding emotions – the ability to comprehend emotion in language, perceive nuance and track emotions over time.
4. Managing emotions – the ability to regulate emotions in self and in others.

In terms of the contemporary leadership challenges in education, community work, social work, health and related fields, this definition seems more relevant.

The fundamental difference between Salovey and Mayer's (1990) construct and the 'Goleman School' is that the former retains the boundaries of EI within criteria of intelligence, used to influence practice outcomes and relationships, in contrast to a list of desirable personal characteristics and traits that influence business success.

A number of instruments for measuring EI have been developed, differing according to the EI model. The most well known are, for the Mixed model, the Emotional and Social Competency Inventory (ESCI) and the Emotional Intelligence Appraisal, and for the Ability model the Mayer–Salovey–Caruso Emotional Intelligence Test (MSCEIT).

The various approaches to measuring EI are not explored here, partly because they have already been subject to considerable scrutiny (see, for example, MacCann et al., 1993; Lewis et al., 2005), and partly because we will discuss below the relevance of quantitative measurement of EI (or indeed emotions) in the context of 'people-oriented work'.

Critical concerns about emotional intelligence

Among the critiques of EI theory, Goleman's models attract particular scrutiny. However, despite academic concerns, in contexts where success is measured in terms of productivity and profits, considerable anecdotal evidence and endorsements at the highest levels attest to the efficacy of Goleman-based EI practices.

The idea that success depends on interpersonal skills is not new. Early work on leadership focused on personality traits, and psychologists identified leadership traits such as emotional stability, conscientiousness, intuitiveness and empathy as key to leadership effectiveness (e.g. Cattell and Stice, 1954). In 1973, Mintzberg identified that leadership success was based on the ability to establish social networks and work effectively with subordinates and the facility to empathise, all key skills for collaborative leaders.

Goleman has been critiqued for taking others' ideas and repackaging them and for adding loose, undefined assertions unsupported by research. In his first book, he uses a range of different terms, including 'emotional literacy', 'emotional competence', 'emotional skills' and 'emotional malaise' to support his propositions without defining them or explaining their relationship to EI. Happiness and well-being as outcomes are rarely mentioned in Goleman's books. Locke (2005) contends that the (Goleman) EI construct is invalid on the grounds that it is not an intelligence as such, but a collection of skills or habits (2005: 428) and Lewis et al. (2005: 349) question whether it is even possible to integrate emotion and intelligence in a single construct, commenting that Goleman conflates *capability* and *competence*, two qualitatively different concepts. Woodruffe (2001) points out that emotional intelligence is described as both inherent and biologically based yet can be learned and developed, and that EI competencies are not new and are commonly associated with high achievement levels.

In later work, Goleman proposes that leaders should promote 'EI organisations' in order to lead better, however this circular argument has undertones of emotional control. Goleman's work is primarily aimed at the private sector, where the Weberian idea persists that control of (especially disruptive) emotions is desirable, whereas in education and related fields, staff are routinely exposed to elevated affect, are likely to encounter uncontrolled emotions and need more subtle skills to handle emotion than *control* implies. In highly emotionally charged contexts such as a staff meeting to discuss a round of budget cuts with possible redundancies, or a belligerent father demanding to know why his child has been excluded from school, leaders must be able to regulate their emotions according to the needs of their immediate environment.

Controlling disruptive emotions is a persistent theme in Goleman's work (Goleman et al., 2002, Appendix B). It could be argued that controlling emotions and *regulating* (Salovey and Mayer, 1990) or *managing* emotions (Waddington and Copperman, 2006) are the same. However, authenticity and congruence are valued attributes of leaders in complex professional fields such as education, whereas suppressing feelings and excessive emotional control may appear incongruous to colleagues and students alike. As Iszatt-White (2009: 450) points out: 'The need for emotional displays – the proactive use of emotions-based work in the accomplishment of leadership work – is the extra step which EI fails to take'. Goleman's EI is an individualistic concept, whereas effective leadership in fields that deal with vulnerable people, though partly resting on individual qualities, is equally part of a collective and collaborative endeavour (Fullan, 2004).

In Goleman's later works, *value-guided decision making* is omitted. Lewis et al. (2005: 349) cite Saarni's concern (2000) about the lack of a moral dimension to EI, suggesting that anyone who can understand and manage emotions in self and others could use this to manipulate others. EI concepts of emotional competence and self-awareness also need to be defined carefully in professions with higher than average emotional 'loads': professions where the potential for overt raised emotion displays among students (or clients, patients, etc.) and colleagues is high. Heron (1992) and MacCulloch (2001) each warn of the dangers of promoting emotional competence in organisations without ensuring that practitioners have opportunities to address their own emotional vulnerabilities.

Some critics of EI identify fundamental problems at the heart of the EI theory. Fineman asserts the impossibility (or futility?) of attempting to measure and tabulate emotions into a 'format that is convenient and politically defensible to a positivist research community' (2004: 731). Emotions are volatile and notoriously inconsistent, and measuring them through quantitative methodologies exposes the limitations of the proposition that EI is an intelligence. Fineman (2004) warns of the dangers of attempting to *box* emotions through psychometric measurement, and of the consequent empowerment of those who do the measuring, offering alternative qualitative approaches to studying and measuring emotion. This is particularly important where EI measures are used to inform management decisions about promotion and leadership potential, 'fast tracking' those who score highly and prejudicing those who don't.

EI, strategic and collaborative leadership development

In the first decade of this century, the UK government implemented a raft of strategic initiatives aimed at radically changing the way major public services worked together.

Table 4.1   Six styles of leadership

Leadership style	Key feature	Message	Impact on climate and performance
Coercive	Leader demands compliance	'Do what I tell you'	Negative impact – people resent and resist
Authoritative	Leader mobilises people towards a vision	'Come with me'	Positive impact
Affiliative	Leader creates harmony and builds emotional bonds	'People come first'	Positive impact
Democratic	Leader forges consensus through participation	'What do you think?'	Positive impact
Pace-setting	Leader sets high standards for performance	'Do as I do, now'	Negative impact – people get overwhelmed and burn out
Coaching	Leader develops people for the future	'Try this'	Positive impact

Source: adapted from TTA (1998), pp. 56–64 reproduced from McKimm and Held (2009)

Several of the ministries responsible included EI in their planning. For example, the Department for Children Schools and Families (DCSF) stated clearly in its Guidance on the Early Years Foundation Stage (2007):

> What is needed to bring about this change is emotional intelligence: the ability to take into account how different professionals view their own roles and bring them together through a common purpose and shared value base.

Writing on the challenges for social services leadership in the changing environment, Morrison (2007) cites Wheatley (1995: 25) on organisational theory who maintains that 'in life the issue is not control, but dynamic connectedness'. Morrison goes on to suggest that EI competence is 'pivotal to gaining the co-operation of other colleagues and services … to achieve their outcomes' (2007: 24a). He argues that competence is not based on control but on awareness of the emotional dimension and the ability to use emotions positively. It is interesting that both the DCSF's and Morrison's interpretations of EI are collective ideals, essentially at odds with Goleman's EI, which is based on personal success and individualism.

Despite the criticisms of EI, it can have value to leaders working strategically in education and related fields. Mayer and Salovey's (1997) four-branch model describes desirable qualities of a leader, according with Evans and Cruse's proposition that 'emotions may in fact be vital to intelligent action' (2004: xii). Goleman's Leadership Skills Framework (see Table 4.1) is often used in leadership development programmes to introduce leadership styles and approaches. EI offers a useful skills 'toolbox' from which individuals can select appropriately according to context, or can be trained to apply in certain situations. This aligns with the concept of contingency or situational leadership (Hersey et al., 2007) in which effective leaders actively choose styles and behaviours appropriate to the situation.

UK ministries that invested in leadership development typically chose transformational leadership (Bass and Avolio, 1994; Bolden et al., 2003) as the paradigm, and EI as a key attribute for those identified as existing or potential leaders. Transformational leadership aims to bring about change in individuals and systems, creating positive change in followers and developing them into future leaders. Bass and Avolio (1994) describe the Four I's of transformational leadership as:

- idealised influence
- inspirational motivation
- individualised consideration
- intellectual stimulation.

All of these resonate with EI competencies. Iszatt-White (2009) refers to Yukl's (2002) proposition that most contemporary leadership theories involve a process of social influence, and therefore call for components of EI. EI attributes are among the key characteristics of the authentic leader, according to Avolio et al. (2004) who contend that authentic transformational leaders are able to instil hope, trust and positive affectivity in their followers via personal and social identification, and George (2000: 1028) concludes that: 'emotional intelligence contributes to effective leadership as leaders must be able to anticipate how followers will react to different circumstances and effectively manage these reactions'.

It is difficult to determine what EI adds to the body of knowledge about leadership in strategic, complex, collaborative educational contexts. Empirical research carried out in this specific context is inconclusive and generally dated. This reflects a shift in the way that leadership is being conceptualised around emergent change and shared leadership (Morrison, 2010). This shift acknowledges that individual personality traits (including emotion, integrity and empathy) are important but need to be contextualised within complex systems, networks and inter-disciplinary collaboration (Bolden et al., 2003). Most studies have also encountered difficulties with the validity of the psychometric testing instruments or the generalisability of the data. Studies have also tended to show that EI tests are unreliable or inconclusive predictors of leadership success (e.g. the Stephens and Hermond, 2009 MCSEIT study).

Perversely, most studies have concluded that, as a rule, having a lot of the EI competencies at one's disposal is 'a good thing'. This corresponds with the general anecdotal sense acquired from multiple sources as to the value of EI. However, EI needs to be seen as part of a range of concepts and theories that describe and explain effective leadership, not as the primary construct.

Emotional intelligence and emotional labour

It may be possible to narrow the conceptual gap that occurs as a result of the 'so-what' factor of EI (Iszatt-White, 2009: 450) by considering the construct of 'emotional labour' in leadership. Grandey (2000) proposes that EI is a key variable that influences the levels and types of emotional labour strategies leaders employ. Waddington and Copperman

(2006: 5) define emotional labour, drawing on Hochschild (1983: 7), as 'paid work that involves the expression and manipulation of emotions'. Crawford (2009) applies the concept to leadership in education, describing emotional labour as 'a requirement to produce emotional states in others *or* exercise a degree of control over the emotional activities of others'. Goleman's theories on controlling emotions have been questioned here; however Crawford refers to the ability of good leaders to create the conditions for the safe expression of emotion among staff or pupils.

Teachers, health workers and other professionals routinely perform emotional labour. Hochschild identifies two types of regulation:

- antecedent-focused regulation – modifying initial feelings by changing the situation or cognitions of the situation
- response-focused regulation – modifying behaviour once emotions are experienced by suppressing, faking or amplifying an emotional response.

Hochschild (1979, 1983) proposes that emotion regulation is achieved in two ways. When employees change their outward emotional expressions without feeling the emotions they are displaying, they are *surface acting*. In contrast, when they actually feel the emotions they display, they are *deep acting*. Ashforth and Humphrey (1993) argue that employees also perform emotional labour through spontaneous and genuine emotion and suggest that, under certain circumstances, surface acting and deep acting may have harmful psychological effects. This depends on the degree to which the actor identifies with the role and occupation: 'if emotional labor is consistent with a central, salient, and valued social and/or personal identity ... it will lead to enhanced psychological wellbeing' (1993: 100–1). Crawford (2009) and Iszatt-White's (2009) fieldwork case examples also suggest that (generally) the more congruent and authentic leaders' emotional displays are, the more at ease they are with their actions.

Howe (2008) captures the 'essence' of the people-oriented professions with a vision of EI that stretches the original concepts:

> The people-oriented professions inevitably find themselves working daily with people whose needs are pressing and whose emotions are disturbingly aroused ... It is critical that ... workers understand the part that emotions play in the lives and behaviour of those who use their services ... Practitioners need to understand how emotions affect them as they work with users and engage with colleagues. (2008: 1)

Howe suggests that practitioners should engage with EI in proactive ways in relation to their response to emotional displays and how they display their own emotions.

EI may inform the leader as to when and what type of emotional labour strategy is required but it is not clear whether it can influence performance. For example, two departmental heads could both perform a similar leadership task calling for emotional labour, but one might do it in a clumsy and ineffectual fashion, while the other may perform competently and sensitively. They share similar cognitive skills and similar levels of EI competence, but there is something more than knowledge and competencies behind their ability to exert influence on their followers. Humphrey et al. (2008) published 15 propositions that distinguish emotional labour performed by transformational leaders from other forms of emotional labour, some of which may suggest what the 'extra something' may be. For example:

> P8. Leaders who perform emotional labor will be more likely to be perceived as transformational leaders, and deep acting will be more effective than surface acting at increasing perceptions of transformational leadership. …

> P12. Leaders high on empathy will prefer to use genuine emotional expressions and deep acting instead of surface acting. (2008: 159, 161)

Leaders in the emotionally charged contexts of education and related fields, who can draw on deep acting or spontaneous and genuine emotion, may well be considered most effective and gain the respect of followers. Such leaders must weave together EI competencies, an understanding of their context and networks and a willingness to perform emotional labour. This requires congruence between the leader's personality, behaviours and understanding that appears consistently authentic in a range of situations. This idea is supported by studies in which followers typically rate consistency, integrity, courage, enabling and role modelling as key leadership characteristics (Kouzes and Posner, 2007).

Leadership: art or science?

The massive body of leadership and management theory is in a state of continuous adaptation and creation, and no single theory of leadership can adequately account for every possible eventuality and challenge. Western (2008) cynically suggests that leadership theories are generated as much by the need to promote individual prominence as by rigorous academic scholarship and empirical research. Leaders need to be aware of theoretical developments (the 'science' of leadership) and how these might be applied in practice. Leadership theorists have long disputed the issue of whether leaders are born (with a 'leadership gene') or made. However, some people appear more naturally inclined to be better leaders than others and leadership skills can also be learned. Most leadership development activities acknowledge that a balance is needed between theory, building on innate personality traits, and developing practical and interpersonal skills and competencies associated with effective leadership (Bolden et al., 2003; Kouzes and Posner, 2007).

It is, however, the skills and demonstrated behaviours that may be seen in, for example, the field observations of college leaders in action (Iszatt-White, 2009) or primary school heads (Crawford, 2009) that could be considered closer to leadership 'art' than science. Fineman (2004) refers to the recorded emotional narrative as a 'key subjective, biographical *production*, combining interpretation, embodiment and lived experience'. Hochschild coined the terms surface and deep acting, and it is usual to refer to *performing* emotional labour, and to discuss leadership *performance*. Denhardt and Denhardt used *the dance of leadership* (2006) as a metaphor for the artful use of affect (expressed emotion) in leadership. This is the use of emotional labour through carefully moderated emotional display that shows situational awareness, contextual sensitivity and recognition of an individual's needs. Newman et al. (2009), studying affective leadership and emotional labour in public administration, suggest that in such contexts, to be an effective leader requires skills in affective leadership. The 'affective leader' needs to be able to rapidly assess the affective state of the other, analyse her own affective state, and from this select the appropriate affect to display in order to achieve the desired (or best achievable) outcome. It is a transactional process in that the followers agree to play their 'role' as long as the 'dance' steps are followed. For the skilled leader, the process is one of rapid cognition. It happens intuitively and outside conscious awareness, since the speed at which the various observations and decisions are made is greater than that of conscious thought. Leaders and followers constantly balance the tensions between rational thought, emotion and intuition.

Denhardt and Denhardt's work sheds light on the motivations behind followership in complex strategic collaborations involving multiple organisations:

> Leadership is far more deeply rooted in the human psyche than we tend to acknowledge. We think that is because the world has focused excessively on the science of leadership, a topic that is amenable to the rational use of technique, and has vastly underestimated the art of leadership, which clearly is not. Recognizing the artistic dimension of leadership, however, compels us to acknowledge and give further thought to the inner resources required by the leader. (2006: 160–1)

Applying EI, emotional labour and affective leadership in collaborative practice

As integrated working and collaborative practice have increased in public sector working in the UK and elsewhere, the infrastructures remain populated by different professions and sub-cultures with competing codes and values which, though outwardly similar, often create or conceal divisions. If EI were the model of leadership, Saarni's concerns (2000) about the negative use of EI could predict manipulation by the emotionally competent at the expense of the genuine common good. This questions how the voice of the vulnerable or marginalized would be heard.

Stevenson (2007) questions whether the current integrated working orthodoxy addresses the impact of emotions on professionals. She asks: 'how can organizations … run on principles of order and rationality take into account the underlying emotional dynamics which profoundly affect the behaviour of their staff?' (2007: 100). Effective collaboration must create space to understand the emotions vested in the work. Crucially for discussing links between emotion and EI, Stevenson suggests that 'these emotions should not be viewed in solely negative terms; they are the drivers of positive and negative behaviours and they underpin purposeful behaviour' (2007: 100).

This statement resonates with Salovey and Mayer's (1990) concept rather than with Goleman, who emphasises control of 'disruptive' emotions. Goleman is not specific on what disruptive means, but implies a causal relationship between disruptive emotions and negative behaviours. The emotions that drive positive and negative behaviours are both drivers and constrainers within dynamic systems. Emotions may be positive or negative, depending on how they are handled. Strategic leaders in these contexts need to be comfortable with emotional labour and affective leadership, and able to tolerate ambiguity.

Most professional groups have systems that provide space for the emotions of its members. Social workers have formal supervision to address the emotional content of their work, whereas other professions may have less formal coping structures. These differences have not necessarily been translated into collaborative working or interprofessional practice. This could be, as Waddington and Copperman (2006: 5) suggest: 'because management of self and emotion are seen as implicit concepts of professional practice and education, which transfer seamlessly into an interprofessional practice context'. This assumption at organisational level denies the complexity of integrated practice and underestimates the role of emotional labour.

Leaders in integrated practice must adopt an emotionally appropriate approach to managing different professional attitudes, expectations and stereotypes. The approach must match the affective expectations of the (often unequal) professional workforce, moderate their own and others' stereotypes and calm fears about professional identity and lack of control. This requires leaders to artfully use affect to enable professionals to work in an atmosphere of connectedness, tolerate uncertainty and learn from positive and negative emotional experiences. This aligns broadly with the Salovey and Mayer (1990) 'version' of EI, the perspective most able to accommodate the vital understanding of both emotion and emotional labour.

Conclusion

Although Emotional Intelligence is secure in the Western corporate consciousness, its relevance to collaborative leadership in the public and not-for-profit sector is less prominent. However, the concepts underpinning EI fit with much of the leadership literature, particularly that which considers transformational leadership and followership. As one of a range of tools for leadership development, EI may be of significant benefit in building individual awareness of behaviours and the emotions that motivate them.

Some criticisms of EI have substance, and its major shortcoming is that while it may inform a leader of the need for some kind of emotional action and highlight desired competencies, it does not necessarily equip the leader with the skills required to lead effectively in a range of complex contexts. This is where emotional labour can guide those working in emotionally demanding 'people-oriented work' to provide artful, affective leadership and emotional support for those who work with them.

References

Ashforth, B.E. and Humphrey, R.H. (1993) Emotional labor in service roles: the influence of identity. *Academy of Management Review* 181: 88–115.

Avolio, B.J., Gardner, W.L., Walumbwa, F.O., Luthans, F. and May, D.R. (2004) Unlocking the mask: a look at the process by which authentic leaders impact follower attitudes and behaviors. *The Leadership Quarterly* 15: 801–23.

Bass, B. and Avolio, B. (1994) *Improving Organizational Effectiveness through Transformational Leadership*. Thousand Oaks, CA: Sage.

Bolden, R., Gosling, J., Marturano, A. and Dennison, P. (2003) *A Review of Leadership Theory and Competency Frameworks*. Exeter: Department of Leadership Studies, University of Exeter.

Cattell, R.B. and Stice, G.F. (1954) Four formulae for selecting leaders on the basis of personality. *Human Relations* 7: 493–507.

Crawford, M. (2009) *Getting to the Heart of Leadership: Emotion and the Educational Leader*. London: Sage.

Denhardt, B. and Denhardt, V. (2006) *The Dance of Leadership: The Art of Leading in Business, Government, and Society*. Armonk, NY: M.E. Sharpe.

Department for Children, Schools and Families (2007) Effective practice: multi-agency working. In *The Early Years Foundation Stage Guidance*. Available at: http://nationalstrategies.standards.dcsf.gov.uk/node/84340 (accessed 11 October 2010).

Evans, D. and Cruse, P. (eds) (2004) *Emotion, Evolution and Rationality*. Oxford: Oxford University Press.

Fineman, S. (2004) Getting the measure of emotion – and the cautionary tale of emotional intelligence. *Human Relations* 57(6): 719–40.

Fullan, M. (2004) *Leading in a Culture of Change: Personal Action Guide and Workbook*. San Francisco, CA: Jossey-Bass.

George, J.M. (2000) Emotions and leadership: the role of Emotional Intelligence. *Human Relations* 53(8): 1027–55.

Goleman, D. (1995) *Emotional Intelligence: Why It Can Matter More Than IQ*. London: Bloomsbury.

Goleman, D. (1998) *Working with Emotional Intelligence*. London: Bloomsbury.

Goleman, D. (2000) Leadership that gets results. *Harvard Business Review* 78(2): 78–90.

Goleman, D., Boyatzis, R. and McKee, A. (2002) *The New Leaders: Transforming the Art of Leadership into the Science of Results*. London: Little Brown.

Grandey, A.A. (2000) Emotion regulation in the workplace: a new way to conceptualize emotional labor. *Journal of Occupational Health Psychology* 5: 59–100.

Heron, J. (1992) *Feeling and Personhood: Psychology in Another Key*. London: Bloomsbury.

Hersey, P., Blanchard, K.H. and Johnson, D.E. (2007) *Management of Organizational Behaviour: Leading Human Resources*. Upper Saddle River, NJ: Prentice Hall.

Hochschild, A. (1979) Emotion work, feeling rules, and social structure. *American Journal of Sociology* 85: 551–75.

Hochschild, A. (1983) *The Managed Heart: Commercialization of Human Feeling*. Berkeley, CA: University of California Press.

Howe, D. (2008) *The Emotionally Intelligent Social Worker*. Basingstoke: Palgrave Macmillan.

Humphrey, R.H., Pollack, J.M. and Hawver, T. (2008) Leading with emotional labour. *Journal of Managerial Psychology* 23(2): 151–68.

Iszatt-White, M. (2009) Leadership as emotional labour: the effortful accomplishment of valuing practices. *Leadership* 5(4): 447–67.

Kouzes, J.M. and Posner, B.Z. (2007) *The Leadership Challenge,* 4th edn. San Francisco, CA: Jossey-Bass.

Lewis, N., Rees, C., Hudson, J. and Bleakley, A. (2005) Emotional intelligence in medical education: measuring the unmeasurable? *Advances in Health Sciences Education* 10: 339–55.

Locke, E.A. (2005) Why Emotional Intelligence is an invalid concept. *Journal of Organizational Behavior* 26: 425–31.

MacCann, C., Matthews, G., Zeidner, M.R. and Roberts, D. (1993) Psychological assessment of emotional intelligence: a review of self-report and performance-based testing. *International Journal of Organizational Analysis* 11(3): 247–74.

MacCulloch, T. (2001) Emotional competence: teaching and assessment issues in health professional education. Paper presented at the ANZAME conference, Wellington July.

Mayer, J. and Salovey, P. (1997) What is emotional intelligence? In P. Salovey and D. Sluyter (eds) *Emotional Development and Emotional Intelligence: Educational Applications.* New York: Basic Books.

Mayer, J., Roberts, R. and Barsade, S.G. (2008) Human abilities: emotional intelligence. *Annual Review of Psychology* 59: 507–36.

McKimm, J. and Held, S. (2009) The emergence of leadership: from the twentieth to the twenty-first century. In J. McKimm and K. Phillips (eds) *Leadership and Management in Integrated Services.* Exeter: Learning Matters.

Mintzberg, H. (1973) *The Nature of Managerial Work.* New York: Harper and Row.

Morrison, K. (2010) Complexity theory, school leadership and management: questions for theory and practice. *Educational Management Administration and Leadership* 38(3): 374–93.

Morrison, T. (2007) Emotional intelligence, emotion and social work: context, characteristics, complications and contribution. *British Journal of Social Work* 37(2): 245–63.

Newman, M.A., Guy, M.E. and Mastracci, S.H. (2009) Beyond cognition: affective leadership and emotional labour. *Public Administration Review* 69: 6–20.

Petrides, K.V. and Furnham, A. (2003) Trait emotional intelligence: behavioural validation in two studies of emotion recognition and reactivity to mood induction. *European Journal of Personality* 17: 39–75.

Saarni, C. (2000) Emotional competence: a development perspective. In R. Bar-On and J.D.A. Parker (eds) *The Handbook of Emotional Intelligence.* San Fancisco, CA: Jossey Bass.

Salovey, P. and Mayer, J. (1990) *Emotional Intelligence.* Amityville, NY: Baywood Publishing.

Stephens, T. and Hermond, D. (2009) The level of Emotional Intelligence in principals of recognized and acceptable schools. *Academic Leadership – The Online Journal* 7(3). Available at: www.academicleadership.org/issue/summer-2009 (accessed 11 October 2010).

Stevenson, O. (2007) *Neglected Children and their Families: Issues and Dilemmas.* London: Blackwell.

Teacher Training Agency (TTA) (1998) *Leadership Programme for Serving Headteacher Training Manual.* London: TTA.

Thorndike, E.L. (1920) Intelligence and its use. *Harper's Magazine* 140: 227–35.

Waddington, K. and Copperman, J. (2006) Emotions and interprofessional practice: reflections upon research, practice and an emerging research agenda. Submitted to *International Journal of Organisation and Emotion*, March.

Western, S. (2008) *Leadership: A Critical Text.* London: Sage.

Wheatley, M. (1995) *Leadership and the New Science: Discovering Order in a Chaotic World.* San Francisco, CA: Berrett-Koehler.

Woodruffe, C. (2001) Promotional intelligence. *People Management* 7(1): 26–9.

Yukl, G. (2002) *Leadership in Organizations,* 5th edn. Upper Saddle River, NJ: Prentice Hall.

Part 2

Strategic Leadership and Managing Change

5

Concepts of Leadership in Organizational Change

Gill Robinson Hickman

Collective/collaborative leadership

Reliance on the collective or collaborative capabilities of organizational members and teams provides a logical means for leading change in turbulent or dynamic environments. Still, leader-focused theories and authority structures make it difficult to benefit fully from the collective capabilities of groups or organizational members in a Western context. Effective use of collective capabilities relies on adaptive work, cultural proficiency, organizational learning, and a willingness to experiment.

[T]he underlying premise of leadership in complex organizations is that 'answers are to be found in community' in group-centered organizations where 'everyone can learn continually' (Allen et al., 1998, p. 47). *Collective or collaborative* leadership in this text refers to leadership that uses the talents and resources of all members, not simply a single leader or executive team, to bring about change or generate creative and adaptive solutions. As a result, followers are being transformed into partners, coleaders, lifelong learners, and collaborators, and adaptive leaders are undertaking new roles as creators and sustainers of contexts that allow people to lead themselves (Allen et al., 1998; Chaleff, 1995; Kouzes and Posner, 2002; Manz and Sims, 1993).

[...]

Though Tapscott and Williams (2006) described this new form of collaboration in a business context, all forms of organizations – nonprofit, government, and virtual – are a part of the collaborative phenomenon.

Source – An edited version of Hickman, G. (2010) 'Concepts of leadership in organizational change'.

Shared leadership

Shared leadership is 'a dynamic, interactive influence process among individuals in groups in which the objective is to lead one another to the achievement of group or organizational goals or both' (Pearce and Conger, 2003, p. 1). The process involves peer or lateral influence and can involve upward or downward hierarchical influence. It differs from traditional leadership in that shared leadership is broadly distributed among a set of individuals where the influence process involves more than downward influence on members of the organization.

Robert Kelley (1988, 1992) emphasized that both leaders and followers engage in leadership. Their work is interdependent, fosters the same leadership ends, and engages participants in the change process as coleaders. Kelley (1988) indicated that leadership and followership are 'equal but different' roles (p. 146). [...]

Schneider and Somers (2006) described a similar leadership role they identify as tags: 'As tags are associated with action and outcomes, not necessarily with individuals or positions, one might co-function as leader, sharing the role in tandem' (p. 356). Tags exercise considerable influence, which moves others to action through their facilitation of cooperation, interaction, and resonance among agents involved in change or adaptation processes.

[...]

Adaptive leadership

The term *adaptive leadership* is appearing with more frequency in literature on organizational change. [...] Scholars began to infer the components and processes of adaptive leadership as they described the requirements for organizational adaptability in response to turbulent environments. On the basis of these descriptions, it is probable that adaptive leadership generates and sustains a context where people develop and use their capacity to pursue new opportunities, meet unknown conditions or threats, and solve problems that emerge from a complex, dynamic environment. This form of leadership may require the adaptive behaviors shown in Figure 5.1, among others: setting the context, encouraging organizational members to function as tags, establishing ethical standards, engaging in adaptive work, developing cultural competency, and creating adaptive capability.

Setting the context entails creating an organizational climate or context for change and designing the learning experiences for participants in the process (Schneider and Somers, 2006, p. 356; Wheatley, 1992). Such climates should encourage organizational members to function as tags. Tags lead with or without authority, often in a temporary capacity, to influence people and the processes of meaning making, cooperation, and action taking (Schneider and Somers, 2006, p. 356).

One of the most important functions of formal and informal leadership involves establishing ethical standards of behavior for all organizational activities, including change. Al Gini (2004) indicated that as a communal exercise ethics is the attempt to

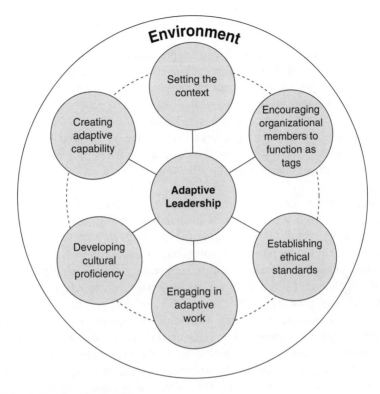

Figure 5.1   Adaptive leadership

work out the rights and obligations one has and shares with others (p. 28). Ethics requires people involved in organizational leadership and change to take into account the impact of their actions on others. Ethics is about the assessment and evaluation of *values*, defined as ideas and beliefs that influence and direct people's choices and actions. Values can form the centering mechanism and moral compass for organizations in dynamic environments.

Application of ethical standards and values in the process of leading change requires organizational members to engage in adaptive work. Ronald Heifetz (1994) described adaptive work as 'the learning required to address conflicts in the values people hold, or to diminish the gap between the values people stand for and the reality they face' (p. 22). The role of leadership in adaptive work is to orchestrate the conflict among competing value perspectives and hold people to the hard work of solving these problems together (p. 23).

Often, competing value perspectives originate from cultural differences among members and other stakeholders of the organization. A major function of adaptive leadership is to develop organizational contexts that intentionally attract, learn from, explore, struggle with, and experiment with different ideas, perspectives, and cultures embedded in diverse environments. Heifetz's (1994) concept of adaptive work, combined with a shared commitment among diverse members to advance the organization's well-being, can enhance the capacity of organizational members to lead change in a complex adaptive system.

Adaptive leadership in diverse environments requires organizational members to develop cultural proficiency, defined as a change in perspective or 'way of being' that enables people to respond to an environment shaped by diversity and allows them to deal with issues that emerge in such environments (Lindsey et al., 2003, p. 5). Acquiring cultural proficiency is a component of continuous learning that changes the way an organization functions by institutionalizing cultural knowledge in its policies, practices, and organizational culture. This adaptive work is no longer seen as external or supplemental to the 'real' work of the organization (Lindsey et al., 2003, p. 117) but as imperative for its thriving.

Cultural proficiency also includes understanding the organization's culture. Glover, Rainwater et al. (2002) warned against dismantling an organization's culture in the change process before fully understanding the meaning, content, and function that the culture provides. Culturally proficient individuals in leader roles who demonstrate their understanding of the organization's culture and respect for the people who cherish it increase the likelihood that members will respond positively to adaptive changes.

Creating adaptive capacity means that members of the organization are prepared to create and recreate fundamentally new structures and assume the new behaviors and responsibilities that accompany them (Glover, Friedman, and Jones, 2002, p. 21). Decisions about these and other substantive forms of change depend on the capability of organizational members to monitor the external environment – an ongoing process of scanning and interpreting events along with collecting and analyzing information about opportunities, threats, and trends that may affect the organization. Adaptive capacity requires people in direct contact with customers and other stakeholders of the organization to engage in monitoring and disseminating information about the external environment (Yukl and Lepsinger, 2004, p. 100). An organization's adaptive capacity can be constrained by limiting external monitoring solely to individuals in senior leadership roles.

[...]

Adaptive leadership requires increasingly more reliance on the collective or collaborative capabilities of organizational members to engage in monitoring the external environment, broadly disseminating information, and generating new structures, behaviors, services, and products.

Tao leadership

In the *Tao of Leadership*, Heider and Dao de Jing (1985) drew on the ancient wisdom of Lao Tzu's teachings from the *Tao Te Ching* (Lao Tsu et al., 1972) to provide insight for leading in a collective manner. Three examples from his writings illustrate the leader and group roles in collective work, the mindset and introspection that facilitate collective work, and the leadership processes that promote collective work.

In the first example, from the chapter 'Beyond Techniques,' Lao Tzu described the interconnectedness of leader and group roles:

The group members need the leader for guidance and facilitation. The leader needs people to work with, people to serve. If both do not recognize the mutual need to love and respect one another, each misses the point. They miss the creativity of the student–teacher polarity. They do not see how things happen. (Heider and Dao de Jing, 1985, p. 53)

In the second example, Lao Tzu posed several compelling questions in his teachings on unbiased leadership to guide the work of individuals in leader roles:

Can you mediate emotional issues without taking sides or picking favorites?

Can you breathe freely and remain relaxed even in the presence of passionate fears and desires?

Are your own conflicts clarified? Is your own house clean?

Can you be gentle with all factions and lead the group without dominating?

Can you remain open and receptive, no matter what issues arise?

Can you know what is emerging, yet keep your peace while others discover for themselves?

Learn to lead in a nourishing manner.

Learn to lead without being possessive.

Learn to be helpful without taking the credit.

Learn to lead without coercion.

You can do this if you remain unbiased, clear, and down-to-earth. (Heider, 1985, p. 19)

In the third example, from the chapter 'Being a Midwife,' Lao Tzu explained the leadership processes that support collective work:

Imagine that you are a midwife; you are assisting at someone else's birth. Do good without show or fuss. Facilitate what is happening rather than what you think ought to be happening. If you must take the lead, lead so that the mother is helped, yet still free and in charge. When the baby is born, the mother will rightly say: 'We did it ourselves!' (Heider and Dao de Jing, 1985, p. 33)

Current leadership structures, such as self-directed work teams, team leadership, and leader as coach, mentor, or trainer, use collective capacity to enhance the organization and its members. [...]

Ubuntu leadership

The philosophy of ubuntu leadership comes from traditional African concepts of leadership and life as a collective function. *Ubuntu* means 'a person can only be a person through others' (Mikgoro, 1998). It exists only in the interaction between people in groups and functions to sustain humanity and dignity. Ubuntu embodies the belief that an individual's most effective behavior occurs when he or she is working toward the common good of the group.

In organizations, leaders and members must integrate ubuntu into their processes, structure, policies, and practices to benefit from this philosophy. Organizational change occurs through interactive forums, collective value creation and clarification, self-accountability for decisions and actions consistent with group values, accountability to each other, and community problem solving (Boon, 1996, pp. 88–124).

According to Boon (1996), critical organizational discussions take place in interactive forums where members of all departments, sections, or teams work collectively to create the values that will govern the organization. The forums occur regularly and serve to build trust and meaningful relationships among participants. Members identify and develop consensus on the core values and work to narrow the gray areas in a manner similar to adaptive work. Participants consider the openness, interaction, and integrity of the process as important as the outcome.

The group's value consensus provides a basis for members to exercise self-accountability and accountability to each other. Members of the organization also handle serious matters, such as a lack of accountability or a values conflict, as a community rather than through a single leader. If it is impossible or impractical to hold an interactive forum, individuals can choose to have a group of elected elders act on their behalf to resolve the problem (Boon, 1996, pp. 117–118). Elders must examine each situation in relation to core values. They are accountable to their colleagues and can take any action they deem appropriate. Ultimately, the use of ubuntu in organizations results in a collective process of leadership and change that holds all members of the group responsible and accountable.

Invisible leadership

Sorenson and Hickman's (2002) concept of invisible leadership proposes a collective form of leadership that 'occurs when individuals, without regard for recognition or visibility, are motivated to take action by a passionate commitment to achieve a common purpose that is greater than the [group] members' individual self-interest and, in certain cases, even greater than the group's overall self-interest' (Hickman, 2004, p. 751). Sorenson and Hickman used the term *charisma of purpose* to refer to the dedication to a powerful purpose as the motivating force for people to take action and even give up personal needs or safety.

The researchers identify several interconnected components of invisible leadership:

- A compelling common purpose that draws people who have deep commitment to its intent. (This purpose does not appear magically but forms as the result of a cumulative set of events or ideas.)
- Individuals who are driven by their passionate commitment and ownership of the purpose and a willingness to take the necessary action to achieve it.
- An opportunity (event) or resource (human or intellectual capital) that makes collective action toward the purpose possible.

- The self-agency to act on behalf of the common purpose even in the face of sacrifice or fear.
- A readiness to use individual strengths in leader or follower roles with or without visible recognition.
- The willingness to rise above self-interest, when necessary, for the sake of the group's common purpose. (Hickman, 2004, p. 751)

[…]

Team and e-leadership

Contemporary organizations accomplish a great deal of their work, including leading change, in teams, a phenomenon known as team leadership. Forsyth (2006) indicated that teams have several basic qualities:

- *Interaction*: teams create, organize, and sustain group behavior. Teams focus primarily on task-oriented activity, because they are based in workplaces, and their members are paid to address work-related concerns. Teams also promote relationship-sustaining interactions.
- *Interdependence*: team members' interactions are cooperative and coordinated. Members work together, combining their individual inputs in a deliberate way.
- *Structure*: teams are structured groups. Group norms, members' specific roles in the group, and communication patterns are often explicitly stated.
- *Goals*: teams are goal oriented. Teammates' interdependence is based on the coordination of actions in pursuit of a common goal.
- *Cohesiveness*: teams are typically cohesive, particularly in the sense that their members are united in their efforts to pursue a common goal. (pp. 160–161)

[…]
Organizations that embrace group-centered leadership in teams transform the role of leader to consultant, teacher, coach, and facilitator because task, decision-making, control, and other functions are shared in the group. […]

Teams lead change as part of an organizational initiative or a team-generated initiative, or both, in alignment with organizational vision, mission, and values. In complex organizational settings, leading change in teams requires that organizations consistently develop adaptive capacity (as described earlier) throughout all their teams so that they can act individually and collectively to meet the challenges and opportunities of a dynamic external environment.

An underlying assumption of most mid- to late 20th century leadership theories is that leadership and change will occur in face-to-face (FTF) situations. In reality, organizational members use technology to varying degrees in their leadership interactions, a phenomenon known as e-leadership. *E-leadership* is defined as 'a social influence process mediated by AIT [advanced information technology] to produce a change in attitudes, feelings, thinking, behavior, and/or performance with individuals, groups, and/or organizations' (Avolio et al., 2000, p. 617).

Much of the research on e-leadership focuses on virtual teams. Virtual teams are geographically dispersed, often across time zones or countries, and may bring together members with diverse expertise, capabilities, and cultural backgrounds from one or more organizations or sections to work toward a common goal. Virtual or e-leadership facilitates collaborative work that generally would not be feasible or cost effective without information technology.

A small body of emerging research seems to indicate that e-leadership, by necessity, relies on the collective capabilities of team members to varying degrees and requires team members to be reasonably self-directed. Avolio and Kahai (2003) provided insights from various contributors to a special issue of *Organizational Dynamics* about the impact of a virtual medium and context on leadership. Several factors suggested by the contributors point to the possibility that e-leadership may have components that are unique to virtual versus FTF concepts of leadership:

- Virtual team leadership is expressed through the interplay of team members and technology and is not under the control of any one person.
- E-leadership requires virtual team leaders and members to project some level of 'telepresence.' This means that they must use the technology to convey a sense of themselves and a sense of 'being there' to members of the team. At the same time, certain technology often removes the influence that identifiable characteristics, such as age, ethnicity or race, physical appearance and abilities, and gender, may have on leaders and members.
- If 'information is power,' then e-leadership alters the power dynamics in the leader–follower or leader–team member relationship. E-leadership alters the patterns of how information is acquired, stored, interpreted, and disseminated, which broadens access to information and changes what people know, how people are influenced and by whom, and how decisions are made in organizations.
- There are certain leader behaviors that are likely to enhance a virtual team's ability to function together: virtual collaborative skills, virtual socialization skills, and virtual communication.
- The software employed by virtual groups, such as groupware (software that helps members of groups or teams in different locations to work collectively), can potentially take on roles in teams, including leadership roles. (Avolio and Kahai, 2003, pp. 327, 332–336)

Stace, Holtham, and Courtney (2001) view the e-revolution as a movement that 'appears to be pushing the boundaries of change *upward* to more collaborative and consultative approaches and *outward* to more transformative modes of change' (p. 414).

[...]

Strategic leadership

Strategic leadership adapts and changes the patterns, aims, behaviors, and capabilities of an organization as a whole so that it thrives in an increasingly turbulent and competitive environment (Boal, 2004, pp. 1498–1499). Strategic leaders are 'responsible for knowing the organization's environment, considering what it might be like in 5 or 10 years, and setting a direction for the future that everyone can believe in' (Daft and Lane, 2005, p. 510).

Strategic leadership seems most compatible with teleological and dialectical change. Participants involved in teleological change create their own goals (social construction) and reach consensus internally; however, this process often incorporates strategic analysis and goal setting due to the context of 21st century environments.

Strategic leadership can advance dialectical change through actions such as direct challenge to competitors through new-product innovation (e.g. Apple vs. IBM), elimination or absorption of competitors (buying or taking over other companies), or collaboration with other organizations in joint ventures. Effective use of strategic leadership during dialectical change requires that participants develop resilience, flexibility, and multiple strategies to handle outcomes (synthesis) from conflicting goals and perspectives in the external environment.

The concept of strategic leadership has gained rapid acceptance among organizational leaders and provides an engaging area of research for leadership scholars. Hunt (2004) suggested a need for more research on underlying explanatory factors in strategic leadership and more emphasis on several promising new research thrusts, including: absorptive capacity – the ability to learn by recognizing, assimilating, and applying new information; adaptive capacity – strategic flexibility and the ability to change in highly competitive and erratic conditions; and managerial wisdom – the ability to perceive variation in the environment, understand social actors and their relationships, and take the right action at a critical moment (pp. 40–41).

Transformational leadership

Transformational leadership motivates others to do more than they originally intended or thought possible (Bass and Riggio, 2006, p. 4). Leaders motivate followers 'by (1) making them more aware of the importance of task outcomes; (2) inducing them to transcend their own self-interest for the sake of the organization or team; (3) activating their higher-order needs' (Yukl, 2006, p. 262). Transformational leadership components, commonly known as the four I's, inspire participants to achieve high performance levels:

- *Idealized Influence* (II) – Followers see leaders as role models they admire, respect, and trust, and, consequently, want to emulate the leader's high standards and ethical behavior;
- *Inspirational Motivation* (IM) – Leaders involve followers in envisioning an attractive future state or compelling vision; they provide meaningful, challenging work and communicate clear expectations that encourage followers' commitment to the shared vision and goals (charisma);
- *Intellectual Stimulation* (IS) – Leaders stimulate followers to be innovative and creative by questioning assumptions, reframing problems, and approaching old situations in new ways; and

- *Individualized Consideration* (IC) – Leaders provide special attention, support, and encouragement to foster growth and achievement of followers through individualized mentoring and coaching. (Bass and Riggio, 2006, pp. 6–7)

[…]

Bass and Riggio (2006) cited research conducted by Nystrom and Starbuck that found in crisis situations, transformational leaders convert crises into challenges by questioning assumptions, identifying opportunities, and focusing on new ways of thinking and doing things (p. 77):

> It is important for the leaders themselves to believe they face a challenging problem rather than a crisis. They are more open to ideas and suggestions from their subordinates. More effective decisions are reached as a consequence. … [T]hose managers who thought they were in a challenging situation were most likely to explore and incorporate subordinates' views into their own. They were most likely to integrate their subordinates' opposing opinions into their own decisions, and they indicated most often the desire to hear more arguments. (pp. 78–79)

Irving Janis's (1982) well-known study of groupthink (when groups avoid or censor pertinent ideas and information in decision making to preserve group cohesiveness) substantiates the importance of the intellectual stimulation (IS) component of transformational leadership in decision making. […]

Charismatic leadership

Charisma is the inspirational motivation (IM) component of transformation leadership theory (Bass, 1985; Bass and Avolio, 1994; Bass and Riggio, 2006). Additionally, scholars study charismatic leadership as a distinct theory of leadership. They attribute charismatic leadership to individuals who, by the power of their person, have profound and extraordinary effects on their followers (Bass, 1985; Conger and Kanungo, 1988; House, 1977; Howell, 1990; Weber, 1947). It usually reflects perceptions by followers that the leader is endowed with exceptional qualities (Yukl, 2006, p. 252). Several characteristics distinguish charismatic leaders: 'their vision and values, rhetorical skills, ability to build a particular kind of image in the hearts and minds of their followers, and personalized style of leadership' (Hughes et al., 2006, p. 412).

Critics of transformational and charismatic leadership warn against the potential dark side of these theories wherein leaders become manipulative, self-serving, or authoritarian to exploit followers and fail to entrust followers with genuine power (empowerment). In response to these criticisms, Bass and Riggio (2006) distinguished between authentic and inauthentic transformational leadership. Authentic transformational leadership is morally uplifting and stimulates colleagues and followers to view their work from new perspectives; embrace the mission and vision of the team and organization; develop the ability and potential of others; and motivates individuals to look beyond their own interests to concerns that benefit the group. In contrast, inauthentic, or unethical, leadership is exploitative, self-concerned, self-aggrandizing, and power oriented (pp. 12–14).

Servant leadership

Servant leadership provides ongoing resources, support, and encouragement to individuals engaged in the change process. Robert Greenleaf (2002), a renowned AT&T executive, management consultant, and lecturer, believed that service to followers was the primary responsibility of leaders. Service includes nurturing, defending, and empowering followers by listening to them, learning about their needs and aspirations, and being willing to share in their pain and frustrations (Yukl, 2006, p. 420). Greenleaf (2002) provided certain criteria for successful servant leadership as follows:

> The best test … is this: Do those served grow as persons? Do they, *while being served*, become healthier, wiser, freer, more autonomous, more likely themselves to become servants? *And*, what is the effect on the least privileged in society? Will they benefit or at least not be further deprived? (p. 27)

Greenleaf (2002) insisted that businesses and other institutions that establish a servant-leadership ethic of 'people building' rather than 'people using' ultimately thrive as organizations and benefit society. Accordingly, servant leadership can apply to organizations with inherent life-cycle stages where individuals or teams need sustained resources and support to meet the challenges of an external approval process. The people-building focus of servant leadership may help organizations prevent the decline or extinction stages of life-cycle change. It can also support participants as they modify their organization's traits, structure, or functions in keeping with evolutionary change and development in organizational structure or behavior.

Transactional leadership

Transactional leadership 'occurs when one person takes the initiative in making contact with others for the purpose of an exchange of valued things' (Burns, 1978, p. 19). Leadership occurs through a social exchange process. The substance of this exchange may be economic, political, or psychological in nature and each participant is aware of the power resources and attitudes of the other.

Transactional leaders use either contingent rewards (CR) or management-by-exception (MBE) to encourage higher levels of performance from followers (Avolio, 1999, pp. 40–41, 49). [We can add to these] laissez-faire (LF), or inactive leadership, behaviors. CR consists of positive exchanges where followers anticipate rewards, such as performance bonuses, more autonomy over their work, a promotion, favor with senior managers, or teleworking privileges. Regarded as less effective than the use of contingent rewards, MBE is a corrective transaction wherein leaders step in and take corrective action when they discover that their followers have made mistakes. LF leadership is a passive style that demonstrates a lack of involvement or transaction with followers. Research findings indicate that LF is the most ineffective form of leadership, though it can apply in situations where the leader has no stake or reason to be involved with matters between followers (Bass and Riggio, 2006, p. 208). Avolio (1999) explained that in the full-range-of-leadership model, leaders exhibit each style to some degree, but leaders with more optimal profiles seldom use LF leadership (pp. 38–39).

Transactional leadership is more effective generally in relatively stable or incrementally changing environments that accompany life-cycle and evolutionary change, rather than in unstable or turbulent environments (Bass and Riggio, 2006, pp. 87–89). Burns (1978) contended that this form of leadership is effective when each person in the exchange is treated with respect as a person and gains his or her desired outcome (p. 19). Burns warned that the outcome of this reciprocal transaction will not bind leaders and followers together in the long-term pursuit of a higher purpose (p. 20), specifically because there is no strong commitment to a moral purpose.

Contingency theories of leadership

Contingency theory

Contingency theory 'maintains that leadership effectiveness is maximized when leaders correctly make their behaviors *contingent* on certain situational and follower characteristics' (Hughes et al., 2006, p. 361). Although there are several prominent contingency theories that may be applicable to leading change, this section of the chapter focuses on two – path-goal theory and task-relations-and-change theory.

Path-goal theory

The aim of leadership in path-goal theory (Evans, 1973; House and Mitchell, 1975; Vroom, 1964) is to influence the satisfaction, motivation, and performance of participants. Similar to transactional leadership, there is the promise of valued rewards (the goal) for followers who achieve the desired performance or objective. Path-goal theory adds a factor to transactional leadership given that leaders help followers find the best way (the path) to attain an objective. The theory identifies four leader behaviors for various situations:

- *Supportive leadership*: giving consideration to the needs of participants, displaying concern for their welfare, and creating a friendly climate in the work unit. Situation: when the task is stressful, boring, tedious, or dangerous.
- *Directive leadership*: letting participants know what they are expected to do, giving specific guidance, asking participants to follow rules and procedures, and scheduling

and coordinating the work. Situation: when the task is unstructured, participants are inexperienced, and there is little formalization of rules and procedures to guide the work.

- *Participative leadership*: consulting with participants and taking their opinions and suggestions into account, Situation: when the task is unstructured, this behavior increases role clarity.
- *Achievement-oriented leadership*: setting challenging goals, seeking performance improvements, emphasizing excellence in performance, and showing confidence that participants will attain high standards. Situation: when the task is unstructured (i.e., complex and non-repetitive), this behavior increases self-confidence and expectation of successfully accomplishing a task. (Hughes et al., 2006, pp. 378–385)

Contingency theories imply that there is one type of leadership for each situation, yet the complexity of change in contemporary organizations requires that leaders use several behaviors, often at the same time. In this environmental context, it makes sense to use the leadership behaviors in path-goal theory in an adaptable manner. Given the influx of knowledge workers and the use of teams in contemporary work settings, adaptive uses of path-goal leadership make joint endeavors between leaders and participants and participant-driven processes viable.

Task-relations-and-change theory

The task-relations-and-change model is a three-factor taxonomy of leadership effectiveness that adds change behaviors to the traditional contingency theories. The framework provides greater adaptability of leader behaviors in complex situations and departs from the 'one behavior for each situation' or mutually exclusive contingency approaches. Yukl, Gordon, and Taber (2002) identified three meta-categories of interrelated behaviors: task behaviors – short-term planning, clarifying responsibilities and performance objectives, monitoring operations and performance; relations behaviors – supporting, developing, recognizing, consulting, and empowering; and change behaviors – external monitoring, envisioning change, encouraging innovative thinking, and taking personal risks to implement change (Yukl et al., 2002, p. 18).

Yukl et al. (2002) incorporated definitions of change behaviors, along with well-established descriptions of task and relationship behaviors:

Envisioning change: presenting an appealing description of desirable outcomes that can be achieved by the unit, describing a proposed change with great enthusiasm and conviction.

Taking risks for change: taking personal risks and making sacrifices to encourage and promote desirable change in the organization.

Encouraging innovative thinking: challenging people to question their assumptions about the work and consider better ways to do it.

External monitoring: analyzing information about events, trends, and changes in the external environment to identify threats and opportunities for the organizational unit. (p. 25)

The inclusion of change behaviors in this taxonomy facilitates connections between concepts of change and concepts of leadership. [...]

Conclusion

The leadership component of change is a collective process in which no single form or concept of leadership will accomplish the change organizational members wish to achieve. Instead, a compilation of leadership concepts that guide action will better position organizations to deal with both external and internal requirements of change. Change that requires interaction between the organization and its external environment may require strategic, transactional, and charismatic leadership, whereas internal leadership may entail adaptive, ubuntu, team, and invisible leadership. Multiple combinations are possible in most change processes. The need for an ensemble of leadership approaches means that organizations must prepare and rely on people throughout the company, agency, or nongovernmental organization to assume leadership in the change process.

References

Allen, K. E., Bordas, J., Hickman, G. R., Matusak, L. R., Sorenson, G. J., & Whitmire, K. J. (1998). Leadership in the 21st century. In B. Kellerman (Ed.), *Rethinking leadership: Kellogg leadership studies project 1994–1997* (pp. 41–62). College Park, MD: James MacGregor Burns Academy of Leadership.

Avolio, B. J. (1999). *Full leadership development: Building the vital forces in organizations.* Thousand Oaks, CA: Sage.

Avolio, B. J., & Kahai, S. S. (2003). Adding the 'e' to leadership: How it may impact your leadership. *Organizational Dynamics*, 31, 325–338.

Avolio, B. J., Kahai, S. S., & Dodge, G. E. (2000). E-leadership: Implications for theory, research, and practice. *Leadership Quarterly*, 11, 615–668.

Bass, B. M. (1985). *Leadership and performance beyond expectations.* New York: Free Press.

Bass, B. M., & Avolio, B. J. (1994). *Improving organizational effectiveness through transformational leadership.* Thousand Oaks, CA: Sage.

Bass, B, M., & Riggio, R. E. (2006). *Transformational leadership* (2nd ed.) Mahwah, NJ: Lawrence Erlbaum.

Boal, K. B. (2004). Strategic leadership. In G. R. Goethals, J. M. Burns, & G. J. Sorenson (Eds.), *Encyclopedia of leadership* (pp. 1497–1504). Thousand Oaks, CA: Sage.

Boon, M. (1996). *The African way: The power of interactive leadership.* Cape Town, Africa: Zebra Press.

Burns, J. M. (1978). *Leadership.* New York: Harper & Row.

Chaleff, I. (1995). *The courageous follower: Standing up to and for our leaders.* San Francisco: Berrett-Koehler.

Conger, J. A., & Kanungo, R. N. (1988). *Charismatic leadership: The elusive factor in organizational effectiveness.* San Francisco: Jossey-Bass.

Daft, R. L., & Lane, P. G. (2005). *The leadership experience* (3rd ed.). Mason, OH: Thomson/ South-Western.

Evans, M. G. (1973). *Extensions to a path-goal theory of motivation*. Toronto: University of Toronto.

Forsyth, D. R. (2006). *Group dynamics* (4th ed.). Belmont, CA: Thomson/Wadsworth.

Gini, A. (2004). Moral leadership and business ethics. In J. B. Ciulla (Ed.), *Ethics: The heart of leadership* (2nd ed., pp. 25–43). Westport, CT: Praeger.

Glover, J., Friedman, H., & Jones, G. (2002). Adaptive leadership: When change is not enough (Part 1). *Organization Development Journal*, 20(2), 18–38.

Glover, J., Rainwater, K., Jones, G., & Friedman, H. (2002). Adaptive leadership (Part 2): Four principles for being adaptive. *Organization Development Journal*, 20(4), 18.

Greenleaf, R. K. (2002). *Servant leadership: A journey into the nature of legitimate power and greatness*. New York: Paulist Press.

Heider, J. L., & Dao de Jing. (1985). *The Tao of leadership: Lao Tzu's* Tao Te Ching *adapted for a new age*. Atlanta, GA: Humanics New Age.

Heifetz, R. A. (1994). *Leadership without easy answers*. Cambridge, MA: Belknap Press.

Hickman, G. (2004). Invisible leadership. In G. R. Goethals, J. M. Burns, & G. J. Sorenson (Eds.), *Encyclopedia of leadership* (pp. 750–754). Thousand Oaks, CA: Sage.

House, R. J. (1977). *A 1976 theory of charismatic leadership*. Toronto: Faculty of Management Studies, University of Toronto.

House, R. J., & Mitchell, T. R. (1975). *Path-goal theory of leadership*. Seattle: University of Washington.

Howell, J. M. (1990). *Charismatic leadership: A 1990 theory and seven empirical tests*. London: University of Western Ontario.

Hughes, R. L., Ginnet, R. C., & Curphy, G. J. (2006). *Leadership: Enhancing the lessons of experience* (5th ed.). Boston: McGraw-Hill/Irwin.

Hunt, J. G. (2004). What is leadership? In J. Antonakis, A. T. Cianciolo, R. J. Sternberg (Eds.), *The nature of leadership* (pp. 19–47). Thousand Oaks, CA: Sage.

Janis, J. (1982). *Groupthink* (2nd ed.). Boston: Houghton Mifflin.

Kelley, R. E. (1988). In praise of followers. *Harvard Business Review*, 66(6), 142–148.

Kelley, R. E. (1992). *The power of followership: How to create leaders people want to follow, and followers who lead themselves*. New York: Doubleday/Currency.

Kouzes, J. M., & Posner, B. Z. (2002). *The leadership challenge* (3rd ed.). San Francisco: Jossey-Bass.

Lao Tsu, Feng, G., & English, J. (1972). *Tao Te Ching*. New York: Vintage Books.

Lindsey, R. B., Robins, K. N., & Terrell, R. D. (2003) *Cultural proficiency: A manual for school leaders* (2nd ed.). Thousand Oaks, CA: Corwin.

Manz, C. C., & Sims, H. P. (1993). *Business without bosses: How self-managing teams are building high-performing companies*. New York: Wiley.

Mikgoro, J. Y. (1998). *Ubuntu and the law in South Africa*. Retrieved February 9, 2009, from http://epf.ecoport.org/appendix3.html

Pearce, C. L., & Conger, J. A. (2003). All those years ago: The historical underpinnings of shared leadership. In C. L. Pearce & J. A. Conger (Eds.), *Shared leadership: Reframing the hows and whys of leadership* (pp. 1–18). Thousand Oaks, CA: Sage.

Schneider, M., & Somers, M. (2006). Organizations as complex adaptive systems: Implications of complexity theory for leadership research. *Leadership Quarterly*, 17, 351–365.

Sorenson, G. J., & Hickman, G. R. (2002). Invisible leadership: Acting on behalf of a common purpose. In C. Cherrey & L. Matusak (Eds.), *Building leadership bridges* (pp. 7–24). College Park, MD: James MacGregor Burns Academy of Leadership.

Stace, D., Holtham, C., & Courtney, N. (2001). E-change: Charting a path towards sustainable e-strategies. *Strategic Change*, 10(7), 403–418.

Tapscott, D., & Williams, A. D. (2006). *Wikinomics: How mass collaboration changes everything*, New York: Portfolio.

Vroom, V. H. (1964). *Work and motivation*. New York: Wiley.

Weber, M. (1947). *The theory of social and economic organization*. New York: Oxford University Press.

Wheatley, M. J. (1992). *Leadership and the new science: Learning about organization from an orderly universe*. San Francisco: Berrett-Koehler.

Yukl, G. A. (2006). *Leadership in organizations* (6th ed.). Upper Saddle River, NJ: Prentice Hall.

Yukl, G., Gordon, A., & Taber, T. (2002). A hierarchical taxonomy of leadership behavior: Integrating a half century of behavior research. *Journal of Leadership and Organizational Studies*, 9(1), 15–32.

Yukl, G. A., & Lepsinger, R. (2004). *Flexible leadership: Creating value by balancing multiple challenges and choices*. San Francisco: Jossey-Bass.

6

The Nature and Dimensions of Strategic Leadership

Brent Davies and Barbara J. Davies

Introduction: what is strategy and strategic leadership?

One of the key challenges, when taking up a senior leadership position, is the move from an operational perspective to a strategic perspective. Strategic leadership, by definition, links the strategic function with the leadership function. School leaders articulate the definition of the organisation's moral purpose, which can be considered as 'why we do what we do'. The values that underpin this moral purpose are linked to the vision, considering 'where we want to be and what sort of organisation we want to be in the future'. Strategic leadership is the means of linking this broad activity to shorter-term operational planning, thereby imbuing the responses to immediate events with elements of the value system and the longer-term strategic direction. Strategic leadership is, therefore, defining the vision and moral purpose and translating them into action. It is a means of building the direction and the capacity for the organisation to achieve that directional shift or change. This translation requires a proactive transformational mind-set which strives for something better, rather than the maintenance approach of transactional leadership.

In attempting to define a strategic leadership perspective it is useful to build a broad understanding of strategy. Strategic leaders can use the following ideas to frame an initial understanding of strategy, which can be considered to encompass the following concepts:

- vision and direction setting;
- a broad organisational-wide perspective;
- a three- to five-year perspective;
- a template for short-term action;

Source – An edited version of Davies, B. and Davies, B.J. (2010) 'The nature and dimensions of strategic leadership'.

- considerable organisational change; and
- strategic thinking more than strategic planning.

In unpacking these ideas it can be seen that essentially strategic leadership is about creating a vision and setting the direction of the school over the medium to longer term. Where the school needs to be and what it needs to provide for its students should be the main focus for the strategic leader. Strategic leaders envisage what a desirable future for the school will be and create strategic conversations to build viable and exciting pathways to create the capacity to achieve that future.

A key shift in the mind-set of leaders who take on strategic roles is that they move away from the operational detailed view and develop a holistic and broad organisational perspective. This presents a challenge as staff often want a detailed step-by-step explanation of the plan for progression, but the necessary broad themes and capacity are only developed as the school moves forward.

The time frame of strategic leadership is notable. There is a danger in incremental approaches that take a detailed view of one year and similarly build an additional year of detail and then another year of detail on top of that. Strategic leadership takes a step back from that and looks three to five years ahead to identify major themes of building blocks to be achieved, then plans backwards from there, leaving the detail to the individual year planning. We would consider it possible for school development or improvement planning to be effective for a two- or three-year period and after that a broad strategic framework needs to be established for years three to five.

It is a mistake to think that operational and strategic perspectives are isolated from each other or that you do one first and then the other. A more useful perspective is to think that strategy provides the framework or template against which to set short-term activities. Strategy can be seen as providing a set of compass points and direction against which short-term activities can be set. The short term and long term should not be seen as sequential, with one done first and then the other; instead, they should be seen as parallel actions with one informing the other. Davies (2006) sees effective strategic leaders as being parallel leaders and not sequential leaders. Thus strategic leaders build a strategically focused school that can be defined thus:

> A strategically successful school is one that is educationally effective in the short-term but also has a clear framework and processes to translate core moral purpose and vision into excellent educational provision that is challenging and sustainable in the medium- to long-term. It has the leadership that enables short-term objectives to be met while concurrently building capability and capacity for the long-term. (Davies 2006: 11)

Strategic leaders are involved in taking their organisations from their current situation to a changed and improved state in the future. Change in both the structure and focus of schools is difficult, especially if it involves a change in the culture of the school. Thus strategic leaders are often 'change champions', building coalitions of staff to create conditions for change and embedding new ways of working. In personal terms this often involves leaders in managing conflict and living with the ambiguity of knowing what they want to achieve but not being able to move towards it as quickly as they would like.

Strategic leadership in context

This chapter argues that to understand the nature and dimensions of strategic leadership it is necessary to consider the strategic processes and the strategic approaches that leaders involve themselves in, and then the chapter will look at a taxonomy of what strategic leaders do. This is based on the perspective that a sustainable and successful school has to be strategically focused, as shown in Figure 6.1. This model was based on a major research project undertaken in England (see Davies et al. 2005).

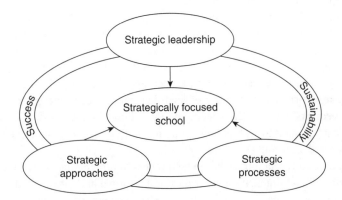

Figure 6.1   Model of a strategically focused school (Davies 2006)

Strategic leadership processes

The concept of how you do something is as important as what you do for successful strategic change, and underpins the need to give attention to strategic processes. Eacott (2008) sees strategic leadership moving through five stages: envisioning, engaging, articulating, implementing and monitoring. This is similar to the Davies et al. (2005) approach encapsulated in Davies (2006), which sees strategic leaders constructing a set of strategic processes which involve conceptualising, engaging, articulating and implementing, to which should be added monitoring and evaluating.

If strategy is to move beyond the strategic document that lies on the shelf in the principal's office and is instead a framework that guides current and future action, then how the strategic policy develops is of critical importance. First is the dimension of conceptualisation, which is how strategic leaders understand where they are and where they are going. This encompasses the stages of reflecting, strategic thinking and strategic analysis. Reflection answers the question of where we are now. It is about senior leaders attempting to understand where they are as leaders, where the school team is, and where the organisation is. Making time for reflection is difficult as short-term pressures may intervene.

This process of reflection moves on to a projection forward through the use of strategic thinking which answers the question 'Where could we be?'. Gratton (2000) talks about the capabilities that need to be established to enable this strategic thinking to take place: a visionary capability – school leaders needing to build rich and inclusive dialogues about the future; a scanning capability – leaders developing an understanding of what the future may bring by establishing a broad and shared understanding of educational and societal trends; and systemic capability – to see the school as a complex organisation and to see what it could become as a whole, not just focusing on part of its activities. These two processes of strategic reflection and thinking are supported by strategic analysis, which answers the question: 'What do we know?'.

Having worked through the conceptualisation processes, strategic leaders then have to focus on the key process in making strategy work – that of engaging the people in the school to be fully involved and committed. The key to the involvement of staff in the school is strategic leaders initiating strategic conversations. These can be structured discussions and conversations that are part of meetings, but they can also be powerful when they take place informally. A number of significant points can emerge from developing strategic conversations: establishing a common vocabulary, understanding how staff could make things happen, consensus building, outlining staff visions, building reflection, keeping everyone involved, carrying everyone forward.

These strategic conversations link into the process of articulating strategy, which can be in the form of oral communication, as witnessed by formal and informal strategic conversations. The articulation can be aided by how the leadership of the school organise strategic and operational meetings. It can be the simple measure of ensuring that, in meetings on the longer-term strategy, policy issues are separated out from shorter-term operational issues. Alternatively, this separation can take the form of a more radical approach so that different organisational structures encompass both the operational and the strategic dimensions of school life. Finally, articulation takes the form of the written plan.

Implementation is the most difficult part of the strategic process. Writing the plan and making something happen is not the same thing. Davies and Ellison (2003) used the phrase 'the thicker the plan the less it affects practice'. So the key element of implementation is focus and ensuring that strategy can be seen to be happening. Finally, the strategic processes need to be monitored and evaluated so a feedback loop can occur to improve and adjust the processes.

Moving the discussion forward requires an action and framework, and the next section of this chapter will consider three approaches that school leaders use to structure their strategic approaches.

Strategic leadership approaches

Strategic planning is a rational, linear approach which assumes that it is possible to define the desired outcomes and plan the stages necessary to get there. Strategic planning needs to be separated from short-term operational planning in that the latter deals with detail and a two-year time horizon while strategic planning has broader, medium-term objectives. Strategic planning would encapsulate a three-to five-year view of broader issues and not the detail of the operational plan, but would act as a template against which to align short-term activities.

In broad terms, a school can, for example, plan student numbers over a five-year period, plan projected income flows, and plan and manage a building project. School leaders can use this strategic planning approach in certain areas to great effect. However the mistake often made is to extend the detail of the operational plan in the belief that it can become strategic in future years. While school improvement plans may have some currency when extended into the third year, if the level of detail is extended to the fourth and fifth year the approach breaks down. Very often strategy has to be built or crafted as the school moves forward, and this will be considered next.

Emergent strategy assumes that schools often operate in an environment of change and turbulence and have a number of initiatives or events thrust upon them. In such an environment schools do not always have the time to fully understand a new initiative before they have to introduce it. The learning process is through 'learning by doing'. It could be considered a trial-and-error process where the school tries new things, but occasionally finds that some of them do not work so well. With a number of new activities undertaken by the school how can it learn by its experience? It has to set time aside to reflect on its actions; it can see that some actions were successful while others were less so. If a school can analyse experiences, it can determine which actions to repeat in the future (the successful ones) and which actions to abandon (the less successful ones). A pattern of successful behaviour emerges by building up a number of experiences and reflecting on them. By using that pattern of behaviour and actions, the strategy emerges through a reactive approach, which starts to become proactive if schools learn from that experience, and use it to set a framework for the future.

Mintzberg (2003) sees leaders less involved in planning strategy and more involved in crafting strategy. The key to a successful emergent approach is that leaders work to shape and create the future by constantly scanning the environment and analysing their own responses to it. Such an approach is needed because constant initiatives demand constant reappraisal and testing but, at the same time, leaders need to set these activities against a backdrop of futures thinking. As such, emergent strategy has a closer relationship to reality than an approach where strategy is only reconsidered at fixed time intervals.

Strategic intent is used when 'we know what major change we want, but do not yet know how to achieve it – but we will!'. It is a process of setting defined intents or objectives and committing the organisation to a learning and development phase to achieve them. It is a framework for attacking difficult organisational change by energising the organisation into learning how to reach for new and challenging goals.

This form of strategy is very useful in a period of considerable change or turbulence. The planning framework is one in which the senior leadership team, although it is able to articulate what major strategic shifts or changes it wishes to make, is unsure of how to operationalise these ideas. In brief, it knows where it wants to go but not how to get there. Determining the intent may be dependent on leadership intuition as well as leadership analysis. The key to deploying this form of strategic approach is to set targets in the form of strategic intents that stretch the organisation to perform in significantly different or increased levels. The school then engages in a series of capability- and capacity-building measures to 'leverage up' the organisation to produce at the higher level. The 'intent' is the glue that binds the organisation together as it focuses on how to achieve this new strategic outcome. Work by Hamel and Prahalad (1994) and Davies (2006) illustrates the significance of this approach.

When considering these three types of strategic approach it is a mistake to think that school leaders use one strategic approach to the exclusion of all others. In practice school leaders used a combination of strategic approaches in differing circumstances. Strategic planning may be the preferred approach when there is full knowledge and a time frame that facilitates it. However, given a need to implement a significant change at short notice with little prior knowledge of the area, then an emergent strategy approach would be evident. When the school is attempting to build a major cultural and organisational change by developing the capacity to achieve a significant shift in performance, it would build a series of strategic intents. All these approaches could be used concurrently in response to the challenges and possibilities which face schools, so deploying a portfolio of strategic approaches would be the appropriate response.

[...]

The chapter will now consider what strategic leaders do.

What strategic leaders do

This section will consider the nature and dimensions of strategic leadership by examining what strategic leaders do to promote a strategic approach. Davies (2003: 303) has identified the problem in isolating essential characteristics of effective strategic leaders:

> The difficulty in reviewing the literature, or interpreting the results of my current research, is that it is not always easy to distinguish the characteristics of 'good leadership' from those of strategic leadership.

In an attempt to resolve this difficulty it is possible to use the work of Boal and Hooijberg (2001), Bolman and Deal (1991), Sergiovanni (1984), Cheng (2002: 56–57), and Davies and Davies (2010) to establish a useful synthesis of what strategic leaders do:

a. Strategic leaders create the vision and future direction of the school.
b. Strategic leaders exert strategic influence.
c. Strategic leaders are strategic talent developers.
d. Strategic leaders balance the strategic and the operational.
e. Strategic leaders deliver strategic action.
f. Strategic leaders define strategic measures of success.

Strategic leaders create the vision and future direction of the school

A valuable and useful definition of vision is provided by Nanus (1992: 8): 'a vision is a realistic, credible, attractive future for your organisation'. This is supported by writers such as Westley and Mintzberg (1989: 17), who see vision as a 'desired future organisational state'. Put simply, vision is where you want to be in the future, what your school will look like, how it will feel to be there, what aspirations it will have and what values it will operate by. Nanus (1992: 16–18) articulates the advantage of having a vision for the organisation:

- The right vision attracts commitment and energises people.
- The right vision creates meaning in people's lives.
- The right vision establishes a standard of excellence.
- The right vision bridges the present and the future.

Gratton (2000: 13) uses powerful images to set the past, present and future in context:

> in the memories and commitments of the past, in the excitement of the present, and in the dreams and hopes of the future … Our memory of the past is balanced by a 'memory of the future', captured in our daydreams and the vignettes we paint to think through our options and the way we would like to see our life develop.

This idea highlights one of the key elements of a vision: it creates a sense of meaning and purpose for individuals within the school, and is something to which they can commit.

Baum, Locke and Kirkpatrick (1998) report that what makes a difference to organisational performance is a vision which is brief, clear and desirable, contains relevant imagery, and is communicated and implemented by personal commitment. […]

The overall vision for the school should be a unifying concept, but to make it an ethical or moral vision it needs to be based on a set of values and beliefs.

Strategic leaders exert strategic influence

Strategic influence is based on how leaders gain commitment to the vision and direction of the school from those who work and learn in the organisation. If the school is not only to achieve improved outcomes and outputs but to do so in a sustainable way, then involving others and getting them on board is critical to its achievement. How can strategic leaders influence others to come on the school's strategic journey? What follows are a number of factors which shape the leader's ability to influence others.

The first part of the influence-building process is to consider how people react to the leader, and therefore the first stage is for the leader to look at his or her own leadership style and skills. Strategic leaders need to build trust with their colleagues and staff so others can believe in their motivations and their integrity. Important in this is how others perceive the leader and how effective he or she is at communicating those values and attributes. This credibility has two components. First, the credibility that comes from expertise and the ability to do the job. Second, the credibility that comes from the character and integrity of the individual.

Strongly linked to this idea is the leader's own passion for education and the role he or she can play in enhancing children's learning and life chances. Effective strategic leaders make opportunities to articulate their passion for education and what drives them to create a sense of moral purpose and establish a credibility base grounded on doing what is best for the students and calling on all staff to make a difference in their interactions and role in the school. Moral leadership clearly needs to go beyond the rhetoric. The expression 'see something – do something about it' is a leadership value that needs to permeate the behaviour of all staff. The leader needs to create a moral purpose that translates ideals into action and is the initial catalyst of influence building.

Influencing others by involving them in the process is the starting place, but there are a number of other significant factors, Clearly building a foundation of understanding across the school is based on clear criteria for success but also on effective relationships so that staff are involved in the process. The ABCD model (Figure 6.2) illustrates how this can be done.

Articulate	1	Strategy
Build	2	Images Metaphors Experiences
Create	3	Dialogues – conversations Cognitive/mental map Shared understanding
Define	4	Strategic perspective Outcome orientation Formal plans

Figure 6.2   The ABCD approach (Davies 2006: 93)

The purpose of this is to create a shared language and set of values so that the strategic leader connects to the heart as well as the head. The emotional commitment as well as the logical or rational commitment of staff is vital.

Strategic leaders are strategic talent developers

Talent management is increasingly seen as a critical factor in developing successful organisations and is a strategic priority for businesses. It is just as critical a factor for schools. The growing leadership skill shortage, difficulty in appointing principals (and other senior leaders) and the work–life balance agenda are leading to a shortage of people who are capable of making a difference to organisational performance. A focus on talent management will contribute to other strategic objectives, such as building a high-performance learning environment and adding value to the school. This is different from simple succession planning and filling typical hierarchal leadership roles that exist today because it is a process of providing able and talented people who will create new and different leadership roles in the future.

This is particularly important for strategic leaders as they meet the challenge of developing innovative and imaginative leaders throughout the organisation to meet the needs of school transformation. Individual schools need to develop a talent pool where staff can be presented with a coherent developmental strategy with planned work opportunities in different contexts. This should provide new staff and middle leaders with institutional leadership opportunities, award-bearing qualifications and in-house development to systematically enhance the talent pool within the organisation.

[...]

Strategic leadership is about moving the school on to a new and desirable future, and this can only be achieved by having great people in the organisation. Being a talent manager is the cornerstone of a strategic leader's success.

Strategic leaders balance the strategic and the operational

There is an assumption that strategy is about the long term and it is incompatible with short-term objectives. There are some basic things that an education system should provide for children. It should provide them with definable learning achievements that allow them to function and prosper in society. Where children are not making the progress we expected for them, they need extra support and educational input to help them realise their potential. This, by necessity, requires regular review against benchmarks. We recognise the danger of seeing short-term benchmarks as the outcomes and not indicators of progress. Indeed, if annual tests were seen as diagnostic and generated learning plans for children rather than outcome scores for schools, the problem of testing might be solved overnight. What needs to be done is that the short term should not be seen as separate from the long term, or as in conflict with it, but as part of a holistic framework where short-term assessments are seen as guides on the long-term journey.

This balanced view of the short-term and long-term perspective can be seen in Figure 6.3. It is of little use having a long-term strategic plan if it ignores the short term, as we see in Figure 6.3. The result in the bottom right quadrant will be that short-term crises will prevent the long-term

Operational processes and planning (SDP and target setting)	Effective	*Functionally successful in the short term but not sustainable long term*	*Successful and sustainable in both the short term and long term*
	Ineffective	*Failure inevitable both in the short and long term*	*Short-term crises will prevent longer-term sustainability*
		Ineffective	Effective
		Strategic processes and approaches	

Figure 6.3   Short-term viability and long-term sustainability (based on Davies 2004)

goals ever being achieved. Similarly, merely operating on a short-term perspective, the top left quadrant, will prevent long-term sustainability ever being achieved. What is needed is a balance between the short and long term, as witnessed in the quadrant at the top right.

The challenge for strategic leaders is to use the longer-term vision as a template or framework for operational shorter-term actions. Vision that cannot be translated into action has no impact. Similarly, continuing to manage the now without change and development is not building capacity for the future. We need to balance both the long- and the short-term approach.

Strategic leaders deliver strategic action

[T]he critical importance of the strategic leader [is that] to be effective, he or she has to translate strategy into action. Deciding to do something and actually doing something are very different. A school may have eloquently written plans which do not come to fruition. What are the key things that will make a difference? In terms of implementation, what are the critical factors that will lead to successful implementation?

First is to set clear objectives. The standard leadership maxim 'more from less' is useful here. Schools should focus on the key things that will make a difference and then deliver on them. The volume of the documentation is less important for success than staff understanding and committing to the plan. So a sharp and clear set of objectives that staff can understand and act on is vital. This leads on to the second factor, that of the ability of strategic leaders to align the people, the organisation and the strategy. It is by bringing together these three elements that a strategic leader can translate strategy into action. Very often individuals in organisations can feel that strategy is top down and that they are 'done to' and can end up 'done in'. What is needed is a way of working where the emphasis is 'done with', so an individual and the organisation come together to build the strategy. The third factor is that this can only come into being if strategy is everyone's job and is a learning process. The concept of emergent strategy, where reflection and feedback adjust and change the strategy as the school learns new and better ways of doing things, is a useful way of thinking. Thus a process needs to be established in school for reflection on the effectiveness of strategic actions. This involves assessing what has gone well and less well and what can be learnt for more effective action in the future.

A fourth factor in translating strategy into action is the effectiveness of strategic leadership in delivering strategic change. In doing this strategic leaders need to create the frameworks within which others can act. This involves balancing control and autonomy and developing a risk-taking culture where people are not punished for taking risks, but only for repeating mistakes because they have not learnt from them. In terms of their own leadership skills, strategic leaders need to assess future courses of action and take reasoned decisions based on evidence and data. However, once a decision is made they need to support it wholeheartedly and convincingly and have the courage of their convictions. In moments of uncertainty in strategic change those in the organisation look to the leader, and that leader needs to act decisively in the face of that uncertainty.

Finally, it is worth reminding ourselves that there are always many activities and conversations that leaders can engage in with their colleagues, but deciding which are the critical ones that lead to translating strategy into action is more difficult. Strategic organisations need three things: focus, focus and focus! This means that leaders need to develop both good content questions and good process questions. Working with colleagues, leaders need to define critical areas for strategic development and then take sufficient time to outline the nature and dimensions of the proposed strategic change, so that a complete picture of the critical factors for implementation can be built up. The other side of the coin to 'what we are doing?' is 'how are we going about it?'. Here leaders need to understand the how of implementation. This involves a process of determining the key factors that need to be communicated in order to gain the commitment of colleagues. We suggest that commitment will be more effective if leaders can identify the main elements of the change but also the main implementation points and the possible problems that may arise.

As well as keeping the focus, keeping the implementation process simple is an important contributor to success. This involves both defining and articulating the key stages and significant points of the implementation strategy. Planning the implementation is as important as planning the content of the strategy itself. Clarity of process and establishing definable outcomes along the way are key elements to build into the overall approach.

Strategic leaders define strategic measures of success

How would a strategic leader know their school has been successful in five or seven years' time? Clearly the leader needs to define the strategic measures of success. The leader needs, first, to establish criteria and, second, to find appropriate measures to evaluate whether the criteria have been met. The debate that we 'value what we can measure' rather than 'we measure what we value' is a useful starting point here. It draws into the debate the balance between qualitative and quantitative measures.

Clearly it is important to have hard data such as numbers on roll – without students there is no school. Examination and test results are measures that are used to assess the school; while the results of responses to standardised tests can be reported in a relatively straightforward way they can be made to be more sophisticated by the use of value-added interpretations. While such results can be indicative of underlying ability, they are only 'indicative'; they do not define deep understanding, motivation to learn, or love of the subject area. Other more complex learning, such as social learning, can be witnessed by children's behaviour to each other or towards adults. More complex skills such as problem solving, determination and commitment become more difficult to assess.

A core strategic measure of success could be to create active involvement in sustainable learning for each child. This would start with valuing learning within the school community but, significantly, all children would recognise the need to see learning as an ongoing process throughout their life. [...]

Similarly, with staff, an involvement in active professional reflection and dialogue might have several success criteria such as 'Are staff reflective practitioners?' or 'Do they stay after school and discuss ideas with colleagues and build professional learning communities?'. In terms of organisational learning and development, can the school establish a 'no-blame culture' where individuals try new things and learn from their mistakes? This learning approach can be extended so that collaborative cultures are established within the school and between neighbouring schools where staff share success and failures and learn from each other. Building leadership capacity in schools can be seen when individual teachers take more responsibility for their roles – they take decisions rather than having decisions forced on them.

A good way to think about a success culture is that if you arrived in the school five years in the future, what would the school look like? How would it feel to be part of the culture? What successes would the school be celebrating? These 'rich pictures' are part of envisaging success that encompasses the hard data of results and the soft data of attitudes and behaviour as well as expectations and hopes. A key role of the strategic leader is to give voice to those hopes and aspirations by articulating what success would look like and feel like for the school in five years' time. This is the cornerstone of sustainable leadership (see Davies, 2007) which underpins the long-term development of the school.

Conclusion

This chapter has put forward insights from our research which should assist leaders and potential leaders to reflect on their strategic roles. The challenge facing strategic leaders is twofold. The first challenge is the overwhelming pressure of short-term initiatives. Two decades of major educational reform around the world has caused leaders to respond to multiple innovations, especially in the areas of centralised curriculum, assessment and inspection demands from central government. The 'urgent' agenda imposed on leaders and the increasing accountability demands for managerial responses leave little time for reflection and strategic leadership. The second challenge is that of thinking incrementally and not making 'strategic leaps' to new ways of doing things, which can seriously inhibit transformational educational progress. The first challenge is to find the time to think strategically, the second is to think differently. We hope this chapter will encourage school leaders to do both.

References

Baum, J.R., Locke, E. A. & Kirkpatrick, S.A. (1998), A Longitudinal Study of the Relation of Vision and Vision Communication to Venture Growth in Entrepreneurial Firms, *Journal of Applied Psychology* 83(1): 43–54.

Boal, K.B. & Hooijberg, R. (2001), Strategic Leadership Research: Moving On, *Leadership Quarterly* 11(4): 515–549.

Bolman, L.G. & Deal, T.E. (1991), *Reframing Organisations* (San Francisco: Jossey Bass).

Cheng, Y.C. (2002), Leadership and Strategy, in T. Bush & L. Bell (eds), *The Principles and Practice of Educational Management* (London: PCP).

Davies, B. (2003), Rethinking Strategy and Strategic Leadership in Schools, *Education Management & Administration* 31(3): 295–312.

Davies, B. (2006), *Leading the Strategically Focused School* (London: Sage).

Davies, B. (2007), *Sustainable Leadership* (London: Sage).

Davies, B.J. (2004), *An Investigation into the Development of a Strategically Focused Primary School*. EdD thesis, University of Hull.

Davies, B. & Davies, B.J. (2010), Strategic Leadership, in P. Peterson, E. Barker & B. McGaw (eds), *International Encyclopaedia of Education*, 3rd edition (Amsterdam: Elsevier Science).

Davies, B. & Ellison, L. (2003), *The New Strategic Direction and Development of the School* (London: Routledge).

Davies, B., Davies, B.J. & Ellison, L. (2005), *Success and Sustainability, Developing the Strategically Focused School* (Nottingham: National College for School Leadership).

Eacott, S. (2008), Strategy in Educational Leadership: In Search of Unity, *Journal of Educational Administration* 46(3): 353–375.

Gratton, L. (2000), *Living Strategy: Putting People at the Heart of Corporate Purpose* (London: Financial Times – Prentice Hall).

Hamel, G. & Prahalad, C.K. (1994), *Competing for the Future* (Boston: HBS Press).

Mintzberg, H. (2003), Strategic Thinking as Seeing, in B. Garratt (ed.), *Developing Strategic Thought* (London: McGraw-Hill).

Nanus, B. (1992), *Visionary Leadership* (San Francisco: Jossey-Bass).

Sergiovanni, T.J. (1984), Leadership and Excellence in Schooling, *Educational Leadership* 41(5), 4–13.

Westley, F. & Mintzberg, H. (1989), Visionary Leadership and Strategic Management, *Strategic Management Journal* 10(1): 17–32, June.

[...]

7

The Strategy Lenses

Gerry Johnson, Richard Whittington and Kevan Scholes

There are different academic disciplines underpinning the way strategy is understood. Exploring the subject in terms of different perspectives is helpful because it provides *different insights* on issues relating to strategy and the management of strategy. Think of everyday discussions you have. It is not unusual for people to say: 'But if you look at it this way …'. Taking one view can lead to a partial and perhaps biased understanding. A fuller picture, giving different insights, can be gained from multiple perspectives. In turn these different insights can prompt thinking about different *options or solutions* to strategic problems. There is, therefore, both conceptual and practical value in taking a multi-perspective approach to strategy.

This chapter builds on different perspectives on strategy to develop four *lenses* through which strategy in organisations can be viewed. They are:

- Strategy as design views strategy development as a logical process of analysis and evaluation to establish a clear picture of an organisation's strategic position as a basis for deciding future strategy and planning its implementation. So strategy viewed through the design lens emphasises the use of tools and concepts that encourage such objective analysis for making strategy. It is also the most commonly held view about how strategy is developed and what managing strategy is about.
- Strategy as experience views strategy development as the outcome of people's (not least managers'), taken-for-granted assumptions and ways of doing things. Strategy through the experience lens therefore puts people and their experience centre stage in strategy development.
- Strategy as variety is the view that strategy bubbles up from new ideas arising from the variety of people in and around organisations. The variety lens therefore helps explain why some organisations may be more innovative than others. It also suggests that, if innovation is specially important, managing strategy is about creating the

Source – An edited version of Johnson, G., Whittington, R. and Scholes, K. 'The strategy lenses'.

organisational context to benefit from such variety, foster the emergence of ideas and develop them as they emerge. Whereas the design lens suggests strategy develops in terms of planned direction from the top, the emphasis here is more on bottom-up strategy development. From this point of view it is important to look to the periphery and bottom of the organisation to discover the organisation's future strategy.

- Strategy as discourse is the view that the language is important as a means by which managers communicate and explain and change strategy, but by which they also gain influence and power and establish their legitimacy and identity. The discourse lens suggests it is important to unpick the language managers use to justify their strategy in order to uncover hidden assumptions and political interests: the view that language is a resource.

The rest of this chapter explains the lenses in more detail. In so doing, the discussion suggests how the lenses relate to and shed light on three key dimensions of managing strategy:

- *Rationality*. The extent to which the development of strategy is a rationally managed act. Of course the design lens assumes this is the case, but the other lenses raise questions about it.
- *Innovation and change*. The extent to which the management of strategy is likely to develop innovatory, change-oriented organisations; or conversely, consolidate strategies rooted in past experience, established ways of doing things and existing power structures.
- *Legitimacy*. How strategy and the involvement in the management of strategy provide a basis of power, authority and influence in their organisations.

Strategy as design

The design lens builds on two main premises. The first is that managers are, or should be, rational decision-makers. The second is that they should be taking decisions about how to optimise economic performance of their organisations. The principles of economics and the guidelines provided by the decision sciences support and feed the notion that this is what strategic management is all about. Moreover most managers would probably agree that is what they are there to do.

Rational choice implies that managers can and should be able to weigh the benefits and disbenefits of different strategic options on the basis of evidence that informs them of likely outcomes of decisions they make (see March, 1994: 1–35). This is the way strategic management is often explained in textbooks, by tutors and indeed by managers. Stated more fully, the assumptions typically underpinning a *design* view of strategy are as follows. First, in terms of *how strategic decisions are made*:

- *Systematic analysis*. Although there are many influences on an organisation's performance, careful analysis can identify those most likely to influence the organisation significantly. It may be possible to forecast, predict or build scenarios about future impacts so that managers can think through the conditions in which their organisation is likely to operate.

- *Strategic positioning.* This analysis provides a basis for the matching of organisational strengths and resources with changes in the environment so as to take advantage of opportunities and overcome or circumvent threats.
- *Analytic thinking precedes and governs action.* Strategy-making is often seen as a *linear process.* Decisions about what the strategy should be in terms of its content come first and are managed down through the organisation. Decisions about what the strategy should be are therefore separate from and precede its implementation.
- *Objectives* should be clear and explicit and the basis upon which *options are evaluated.* Given a thorough analysis of the factors internal and external to the organisation to inform management about the strategic position of the organisation, a range of options for future strategic direction are then considered and evaluated in terms of the objectives and that analysis. A strategic decision is then made on the basis of what is considered to be optimal, given all these considerations.

Second, the design lens makes assumptions about the *form and nature of organisations*:

- *Organisations are hierarchies.* It is the responsibility of top management to plan the destiny of the organisation. They make important decisions, and lower levels of management, and eventually the rest of the organisation, carry out these decisions and implement the strategy decided at the top.
- *Organisations are rational systems.* Since the]omplexity organisations face can be understood analytically such that logical conclusions are reached, the associated assumption is that people in the organisation will adopt and accept such logic. The system can be controlled rationally too. *Control systems* (for example, budgets, targets, appraisals) provide the means by which top management can measure whether or not others in the organisation are meeting expected objectives and behaving in line with the strategy.
- *Organisations are mechanisms* by which strategy can be put into effect. They are analogous to engineered systems or, perhaps, machines. So how an organisation is structured and controlled needs to be suited to the strategy. Mechanisms to ensure that strategy is, indeed, being considered rationally and dispassionately are also needed.

Implications for management

Managers often talk as if strategy comes about – or *should* come about – much as the design lens suggests: it is seen as valuable by managers. Arguably there are five main reasons for this:

- *Dealing with complexity and uncertainty.* Strategy as design provides a means of coping with and talking about complex and uncertain issues in a rational, logical and structured way. Indeed there are many *concepts*, *tools* and *techniques* to help managers with this.

- *Management power and legitimacy*. Managers, particularly CEOs, face complex and often challenging situations. The assumptions, tools and techniques of design provide them with ways in which they can feel in control and exercise control in such circumstances.
- Rationality is *deeply rooted* in our way of thinking and in our systems of education. We also live in a world in which science and reasoned solutions to the problems we face seem to surround us and provide many benefits. In this sense the design lens is embedded in our human psyche. So, for example, even when managers admit that strategy is not actually developed in ways the design lens suggests, they often think it should be.
- *Stakeholder expectations*. Important stakeholders such as banks, financial analysts, investors and employees may expect and value such an approach. So it is an important means of gaining their support and confidence.
- *The language of strategy*. In many respects the design lens, especially in its emphasis on analysis and control, is the orthodox approach to strategy development most commonly written about in books, taught at business schools and verbalised by management when they discuss the strategy of their organisations. So it is a useful language to know (see the discourse lens below).

In summary, the design lens is a useful way of viewing the management of strategy on the basis of *analysis and planning*. The associated assumption is that change and innovation can, or at least should be able to, be achieved through such rational and mechanistic approaches. However, the emphasis on analysis and control may well result in conformity rather than innovation. Indeed insights from the experience and ideas lenses that follow help explain why this is so. As Figure 7.1 also shows, since a rational/analytic approach is typically seen as being central to the management of strategy, those who see their role like this may also be seen as, or seek to position themselves as, credible, influential (and therefore legitimate) strategists.

We argue that the design lens is indeed a useful explanation of how strategy is managed but is not sufficient. Other lenses provide insights that are also useful.

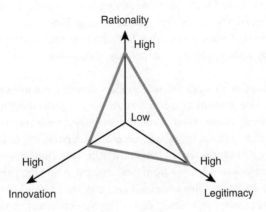

Figure 7.1   Design lens

Strategy as experience

Much of the evidence from research on how strategies actually develop gives a different picture than that seen through the design lens. As early as the 1950s, Nobel prize winner Herbert Simon and management theorist Charles Lindblom (see Lindblom, 1959; Simon, 1960) pointed out that rational decision-making models were unrealistic. It is not possible to obtain the information necessary to achieve the sort of exhaustive analysis required; it is not possible to predict an uncertain future; there are limits in terms of cost and time in undertaking such analysis; organisations and environments are changing continually, so it is not possible for managers to take long-term decisions at a point in time. There are also psychological limitations on managers themselves which mean that they cannot be expected to weigh the consequences of all options or be the objective analysts such rationality would expect – a point which is discussed more fully below. The best that can be expected is what Simon termed 'bounded rationality'; managers do the best they can within the limits of their circumstances, knowledge and experience. The experience lens recognises this boundedness in viewing strategy development as the outcome of people's individual and collective taken-for-granted assumptions and ways of doing things.

Individual experience and bias[1]

Managers make sense of their complex world by drawing on their previous experience. Human beings function in their everyday lives not least because they have the cognitive capability to make sense of problems or issues they encounter. They recognise and make sense of these on the basis of past experience and what they come to believe to be true about the world. More formally, how we interpret issues we face can be explained in terms of the mental (or cognitive) models we build over time to help make sense of our situations. Managers are no exception to this. When they face a problem they make sense of it in terms of their mental models. This has major advantages. They are able to relate such problems to prior events and therefore have comparisons to draw upon. They can interpret one issue in the light of another. Making sense of situations in this way is fast and, most often, efficient. Indeed, if managers did not have such mental models they could not function effectively; they would meet each situation as though they were experiencing it for the first time.

There are, however, downsides. Mental models simplify complexity. It is not possible for managers to operate in terms of 'perfect knowledge'. Understanding the effects of such *simplification processes* is important. Even if managers have a very rich understanding of their environment, they will not bring that complex understanding to bear for all situations and decisions. They will access part of that knowledge (see Dutton et al., 1989, intro). This is called *selective attention*: selecting from total understanding the parts of knowledge that seem most relevant. Managers also use *exemplars* and *prototypes*. For example, commonly competitors become prototypical. Television company executives came to see other television companies – even specific channels – as their competitors. They therefore readily accepted that satellite broadcasting could introduce new competition because it would introduce new television channels. However, they failed to see that the Internet and sites such as YouTube would become an alternative to watching television. There is also the risk that the 'chunk' of information most often used becomes the only information used and that stimuli from the environment are selected to fit these dominant representations of reality. Information that squares with other television channels being the competitors is taken on board, whilst information counter to that is not. Sometimes this distortion can lead to severe errors as managers miss crucial indicators because they are, in effect, scanning the environment for issues and events that are familiar or readily recognisable (Tversky and Kahnemann, 1975).

In summary, there are three important points:

- *Cognitive bias is inevitable*. The idea that managers approach problems and issues of a strategic nature entirely dispassionately and objectively is unrealistic.
- *The future is likely to be made sense of in terms of the past*. Managers typically make sense of new issues in the context of past issues; so when it comes to strategic decisions they are likely to resolve a problem in much the same way as they dealt with a previous one seen as similar. This is one explanation of why strategies tend to develop incrementally from prior strategy.
- Nonetheless, *experience may confer legitimacy and power*. Managers with extensive experience may well be seen as experts or have significant influence in an organisation.

However, managers do not operate purely as individuals; they work and interact with others in organisations, and at this collective level there are also reasons to expect similar tendencies.

Collective experience and organisational culture

How people make sense of situations and issues is not just a matter of individual cognition, but has a collective aspect to it. In this context cultural influences are important: indeed culture was defined by the anthropologist Clifford Geertz as 'socially established structures of meaning' (Geertz, 1973: 12). Central to the concept of culture is the importance of what is 'taken for granted' in terms of assumptions and in terms of activities or practices – 'the way we do things around here'. In everyday life, for example, there are assumptions such as those about the role of the family in bringing up children and about behaviour within the family. These assumptions and associated ways of behaving differ between societies in different parts of the world. In organisational life, an equivalent example might be assumptions about top management, their roles and how they should behave. These also differ, for example between Western firms and Japanese firms. Taken-for-granted aspects of culture also exist at different levels: for example, within a managerial function such as marketing or finance; an organisational unit such as a business; or more widely a professional grouping, such as accountants, an industry sector or even a national culture. The important point here is that these assumptions and taken-for-granted ways of behaving influence strategy in three ways.

First, cultural influences help to explain why managers within a group – an organisation or a department, for example – may see things in similar ways and respond to situations similarly. Second, given this, they help explain why such managers may adhere to familiar strategies and be reluctant to change them. However, third, differences in culture also explain why different groups see things differently; Japanese managers may see things differently from European managers or marketing managers differently from accountants. In turn, and together with the differences in people's personal experience and biases, this helps explain why the management of strategy is often characterised by a good deal of bargaining and negotiation to reconcile such differences.

Implications for management

The experience lens, then, puts people, their experience and the culture in which they work at the centre of strategy development. Figure 7.2 summarises its implications in relation to the three dimensions of strategic management. Rationality, in the sense of the careful weighing of options in a search for optimal solutions, is not the emphasis: rather strategies develop as managers try to relate their experience, individual and collective, to the strategic issues that they face. Managers' experience may, however, be seen by colleagues as relevant and important and therefore bestow a high degree of legitimacy. However, strategic change or innovation is likely to be problematic. It should not be assumed that analysis or reasoned argument necessarily changes deeply embedded assumptions or ways of doing things; readers need only think of their own experience in trying to persuade others to rethink their religious beliefs or, indeed, allegiances to sports teams to realise this.

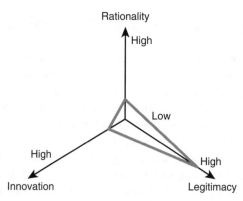

Figure 7.2   Experience lens

In turn this provides insights into two other important phenomena associated with managing strategy:

- *Strategic drift* is a risk. If managers are 'captured' by their own and their colleagues' experience the strategy of the organisation gradually drifts away from the realities of its environment and towards an internally determined view of the world. This can lead to significant performance downturn and, potentially, the demise of the organisation.
- *Bargaining and negotiation* may take place between managers on the basis of different interpretations of events according to their past experience or cultural differences. This is the more likely, since managers' personal reputation and standing are likely to be based partly on such experience. This perspective is reflected in discussions of strategy development as a political process.

Strategy as variety

The extent to which the two lenses described so far help explain innovation is rather limited. The variety lens helps explain innovative strategies, processes and products; and how organisations faced with fast-changing environments and short decision horizons, such as those in high-technology businesses or the fashion industries, cope with the speed of change and innovation required.

The variety lens builds on complexity theory[2] and evolutionary theory.[3] McKinsey consultant Shona Brown and Stanford academic Kathy Eisenhardt (Brown and Eisenhardt, 1998) have shown these are helpful when it comes to explaining the conditions that help generate innovation. The basic tenets of evolutionary theory – variation, selection and retention – provide an understanding of how organisational context is important in relation to the generation of new ideas and how managers may help shape that context. The emphasis of complexity theory on how systems cope with uncertainty in non-linear ways adds to that understanding. Viewed through the variety lens, top-down design and direction of strategy is de-emphasised. Rather, strategies are seen as emerging from ideas that bubble up from the variety in and around organisations.

The importance of variety

New ideas are generated in conditions of variety whereas conditions of uniformity give rise to fewer new ideas. Whether the concern is with species, as in the natural world, people in societies or indeed ideas in organisations,[4] uniformity is not the norm; there exists variety. There is an ever-changing environment, different types of businesses, a variety of groups and individuals, a variety of their experience and ideas, and there are deviations from routine ways of doing things.[5] Evolution helps explain how any living system, including an organisation, evolves through natural selection acting upon such variation.

Variety is likely to be greatest where the environment is changing fastest. For example, in our biological world there has been the rapid development of new strains of viruses given the advances in modern medicine to fight them. There are parallels with regard to organisations. Organisations in industry sectors that are developing and fragmented tend to be more innovative than those in mature and concentrated industries (Acs and Audretsch, 1988) – because of the variety of ideas that exist in such dynamic conditions. Take the example of the microelectronics industry. It is a fast-changing industry. This has spawned many different types of businesses, from hardware manufacturers through to software boutiques and firms engaged in applications of such technology. Within these organisations, in turn, there develop new ideas as people interpret opportunities and potential applications differently.

A good deal of this variety occurs naturally and quite likely outside managers' direct control. Since sensing of its environment takes place throughout an organisation, new ideas quite likely come from low down in an organisation, not just from the top.[6] Such ideas will be more or less well informed, may not be well formulated and, at the individual level at least, they may be very diverse. Complexity theorist Bill McKelvey refers to this as the 'distributed intelligence' of an organisation.[7] Moreover, innovation in large organisations often comes from outside their boundaries, perhaps from smaller businesses (von Hippel, 1988).

Managers may seek to generate such variety and some of the ways they do this are discussed below. Variation may not, however, always be intentional. In the natural world, change and newness come about because of *imperfections* – a mutation of a gene, for example – that may provide the basis for a 'fitter' organism in a changing environment. In organisations, ideas are also copied imperfectly between individuals, groups or organisations. Some of these will give rise to innovations better suited to the changing environment. A research chemist's idea may be taken up by a marketing executive but interpreted differently from the original idea. Managers in one organisation may seek to copy the strategy of another, but will not do things in exactly the same way. Some of these imperfect copies will not be successful; but others may be. A famous example is Post-its, which originated in an 'imperfect' glue being applied to paper, but resulted in a semi-adhesive for which the researcher saw market potential. There may also be surprises and unforeseen circumstances in the environment; for example the unexpected skills or views introduced by new appointees or unintended consequences arising from management initiatives.

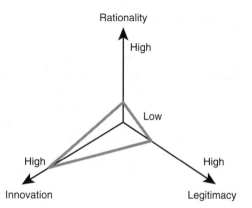

Figure 7.3   Variety lens

Selection and retention

The implication of the design lens is that the selection of a strategy is a matter of deliberate choice to optimise some sort of outcome, for example competitive advantage leading to enhanced profits. The variety lens and evolutionary theory in particular do not deny the deliberate acts of managers. They do suggest, however, that selection is 'blind'[8] in the sense that outcomes cannot be known. Managers may exercise judgement and choice, indeed may use or refer to management tools to do so, but the strategies that develop are also the result of other processes of selection and retention. These include:

- *Experience and culture*. People's experience and the culture of an organisation act as filters of ideas that do not 'fit'. Formal processes of control, planning and evaluation act to regularise what ideas will and will not go forward. The self-interest of powerful managers may block ideas counter to their own. So pressures for conformity may see off potential new ideas.
- *Functional benefit*. An idea may meet the needs of environmental and market forces. However, many of these (from climate changes to competitor responses) can at best be partially known. There may, however, be other functions such as serving the interests of individuals within the organisation, for example in furthering career aspirations.
- *Alignment*. An idea is likely to be more successful if it aligns with other successful ideas, for example because it is what other organisations are doing or it fits the culture and experience of the organisation itself.
- *Attraction*. Some strategic ideas, by their very nature, are more or less attractive than others (Weeks and Galunic, 2003). For example, ideas that are altruistic tend to spread and get adopted most.[9] In line with this, complexity theory emphasises the need for sufficient support or 'positive feedback', and some ideas are more likely to attract this than others. For example, a new product idea in a science-based company persisted despite strong evidence of its lack of commercial viability because it addressed 'green' issues and its potential benefits interested colleagues in other divisions and friends and families of the managers developing it.
- *Retention*. As well as processes of selection, there are processes of retention. 'Retention occurs when selected variations are preserved, duplicated or otherwise reproduced' (Aldrich, 1999), leading to their future repetition. One key factor here is the extent to which ideas become routinised and thus retained. Routinisation varies from formal procedures (for example, job descriptions), accounting and control systems, management information systems, training, organisation structuring, to the formal or informal standardisation of work routines and the eventual embedding of such routines in the culture of the organisation.

Implications for management[10]

A key insight from the variety lens is that managers need to be wary of assuming they can directly control the generation and adoption of new ideas. However, managers can foster new ideas and innovation by *creating the context* and conditions where they are more likely to emerge.

First, they can do this by considering what the appropriate *boundaries* are for the organisation. The more the *boundaries between the organisation and its environment* are reduced, the more innovation is likely to occur. For some high-technology businesses it is difficult to see quite what their boundaries are. They are networks, intimately linked to their wider environment. As that environment changes, so do the ideas in the network. For example, in Formula One motor racing the different teams are intimately linked with the wider motor industry as well as other areas of advanced technology. As a result of this networking new ideas get imitated (but changed) very rapidly. In contrast, where people are insulated from the environment, perhaps by relying on particular ways of doing things, as in a highly rule-based bureaucracy, an organisation will generate less variety of ideas and less innovation.

Second, managers can promote behaviours likely to encourage new ideas in at least five ways:

- *Interaction and cooperation* within organisations encourage variety and the spread of ideas. There is a danger that organisational structures become too established such that people's relationships become too predictable and ordered; rather, ideas tend to be generated more where there are 'weak ties' based on less established relationships (Granovetter, 1973). However, there may be limits to this. Too many 'connections' may lead to an over-complex system (McKelvey, 2004). All this may help explain why so much effort is spent by managers in changing organisational structures in the search for the most appropriate working environment.
- *Questioning and challenge* of 'received wisdom' are important. For example, large organisations often move executives across businesses or divisions with the specific intention of encouraging new ideas and challenging prevailing views.
- *Experimentation* is important. This may take different forms. Some organisations have formal incentive programmes to encourage experimentation. Others have established it as part of their culture. For example, Google gives staff 20 per cent of their time to pursue their own projects. Strategic experiments at an organisational level, such as alliances and joint ventures, are also ways in which organisations may try out possible strategy developments and generate new ideas without over-commitment.
- *Adaptive tension.* Some complexity theorists argue that innovation and creativity emerge when there is sufficient order to make things happen but not when there is such rigidity of control as to prevent such innovation. This is the idea of 'adaptive tension' or 'edge of chaos'.[11] Innovation occurs most readily when the organisation never quite settles down into a steady state or equilibrium and volatility arising from variation is given sufficient rein (see Figure 7.4), though of course not to the extent that the organisation cannot function.
- *Order-generating rules.* Complexity theory also suggests there is no need for elaborate control to create sufficient order for an organisation to work effectively; that ordered patterns of behaviour can come about through just a few 'order-generating rules' or 'simple rules'. In organisations in which innovation is important, managers need to be very clear about the very few overarching requirements that have to be met, but then allow flexibility and latitude in how they are achieved.

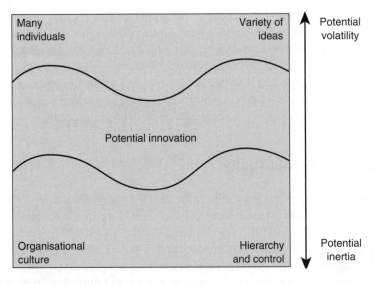

Figure 7.4   Adaptive tension

Finally, top management need to consider their role in developing strategy. They need to be able to discern promising ideas, monitor how they 'function' and 'fit' (see above) as they develop, be sensitive to their outcome and impact, and mould the most promising into coherent strategies. Strategy development by top management is therefore more about '*pattern recognition*' than formal analysis and planning. Managers need to develop the competences to do this rather than being over-reliant on the formal tools and techniques of the design lens.

In addition, since new ideas are unlikely to emerge fully formed – indeed they may be the result of 'imperfect copying' – managers have to learn to tolerate such imperfection and allow for failures if they want innovation.

In summary, the variety lens helps an understanding of where innovative strategies come from. It de-emphasises the directive role of managers and their rationality and therefore poses questions about whether or not top management really have control over strategic direction to the extent the design lens suggests. In this respect and in its emphasis on the dispersed nature of ideas, it also questions the legitimacy of top management as the strategic directors and source of the success (or failure) of organisations. Figure 7.3 summarises this.

Strategy as discourse

In many ways management is about discourse. Managers spend 75 per cent of their time communicating with others (Mintzberg, 1973) in gathering information, persuading others of a course of action or following up decisions. In particular, the management of strategy has a high discursive component. Managers and consultants talk about strategy and strategy is written as formal plans and mission or vision statements, explained in annual reports and in newspaper releases. Efforts to get managerial colleagues, employees and other stakeholders to buy into strategy are also fundamentally discursive; and managers use the language of strategy for their own ends, to gain influence and establish their legitimacy as strategists. The ability to use discursive resources effectively can, then, be an advantage and competence for a manager. Looking at strategy development in terms of strategy as discourse therefore provides insight into how the language of strategy is used by managers to persuade others, to gain influence and power or establish their identity as strategists.[12]

Discourse and rationality

As discussion of the design lens pointed out, rationality is a central component of the orthodox language of strategy. From a management point of view, then, appearing rational is key to making strategy: 'To be rational is to make persuasive sense' (Green, 2004). Strategic management must seem more than just hunch and intuition; it should be more like science and the models like scientific models. As such, managers familiar with such logic can call on it and employ it to justify the 'rightness' of their arguments and views. Indeed typically, even when managers find themselves unable to achieve the goals of strategy – unable, for example, to achieve competitive advantage – they do not deny the logic of the strategy, merely the ability of the organisation to achieve it (Knights, 1992). They may employ this language because they are themselves persuaded of the logic of a strategy, because they believe that by doing so their arguments will carry more weight with others, because it is the typical way in which strategy is communicated or because, by so doing, it positions them as an authority on the subject.

Discourse and influence

The language of strategy has characteristics that make it convincing to others (Barry and Elmes, 1997). Strategy is not only written about in impressive documents – strategic plans or annual reports, for example – but also written about in relation to important phenomena such as markets, competitors and customers. It is often associated with 'heroic' chief executives or successful firms. Strategy discussions take place in important places such as boardrooms or strategy away-days. There is also evidence that the employment of strategy discourse works. Managers consciously employ the vocabulary and concepts of strategy to effect change (see for example, Hardy et al., 2000: 1231; Heracleous and Barrett, 2001), to justify and legitimise strategies that are to be followed (Suddaby and Greenwood, 2005; Sillence and Mueller, 2007), or to ensure conformity to the right ways to manage strategy (Oakes et al., 1998). In other words, managers draw on the concepts of strategy and the apparent 'rightness' of strategy concepts to convince others they should comply.

Discourse, identity and legitimacy

How managers talk about strategy also positions them in relation to others, either by their own deliberate choice or as a result of how they are perceived. Discourse is therefore also related to the identity and legitimacy of managers. The common use of the language of rationality has been highlighted above. At other times or in other circumstances managers may also employ different discourse. For example, in trying to get a strategy implemented at an operational level down the line a manager may draw on previous experience as a 'hands-on worker'. In other circumstances reference to prior experience in turning around an organisation may matter. In other contexts the language of the 'visionary leader' or the innovative entrepreneur may be employed.

Strategy discourse may also be consciously or unconsciously employed by managers – particularly top managers – to provide certain benefits for themselves (Knights and Morgan, 1991). It helps legitimise a manager as a knowledgeable strategist, employing the right concepts, using the right logic, doing the right thing and being at the forefront of management thinking. It also provides the sense of centrality, of 'making a difference' to the most important aspects of organisational survival. Since over time different strategy discourses have been more or less fashionable, some elements of discourse are likely to be more effective than others at different times. In the 1960s and 1970s it was the language of corporate or strategic planning; in the 1980s there was more of an emphasis on organisational culture; and latterly strategy has become discussed and communicated more in terms of capabilities and competences.

Discourse as power

In turn the discourse of strategy is linked to power and control. By understanding the concepts of strategy, or being seen to do so, it is top managers or strategy specialists who are positioned as having the knowledge about how to deal with the really difficult problems the organisation faces. The possession of such knowledge gives them power over others who do not have it. It 'allows managers to imagine themselves as controllers of ... economic life' (Spicer, 2004: 1256).

Thus the discourse of strategy can also operate as social control. Groups may adopt particular ways of thinking, behaving and speaking about strategy. For example, some organisations, especially firms of consultants, have developed their own discourse on strategy. Or there may develop ways of approaching strategic issues that are embedded in particular discourse. For example, the need to cut costs may be indisputable in certain circumstances. However, it can foster a mindset in which cutting becomes the norm such that it is difficult to propose a strategy that would not lead to reduced costs. Similarly, 'offshoring' and 'the world is flat' have become common terms amongst Western businesses, helping to legitimise the transfer of work from highly paid employees in home countries to cheaper labour in Asian countries. Such discourse may become so taken-for-granted, so difficult to question or change that it becomes a powerful influence on behaviour. In this sense discourse is associated with power when it attracts followers and is self-reproducing and self-reinforcing.

Implications for management

In summary, as shown in Figure 7.5, the discourse lens raises the question of the extent to which managers rely on the appearance, rather than the reality, of rational argument.

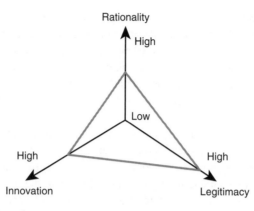

Figure 7.5   Discourse lens

Discourse is used not only to justify strategies, but as ways of seeking power, identity, recognition (and therefore legitimacy). The extent to which such discourse promotes innovation and change will depend on the motivations of the managers and the nature of the language used, though there is evidence that language can play an important role in the management of change.

The fundamental lesson for managers is that the language of strategy they employ matters. The discourse lens highlights this, provides a way of considering how this is so and in practical terms offers concepts and cues by which managers can manage more effectively, for example:

- *Discourse and context*. Different strategy discourses are likely to be more or less effective in different contexts and circumstances. How a strategy is explained and justified to a potential investor may call for a major emphasis on logic and reason under-pinning a financial case. A similarly rational approach may be needed to persuade fellow managers, but perhaps with an additional component related to the benefits in terms of their own interests, future influence and standing. A similar explanation to the workforce of an organisation will have to address the implications for job security, but perhaps also needs to be expressed in ways that reinforce confidence in management. A press release on strategy will likely need to give thought to the main headlines or 'sound bites'. Careful thought needs to go into how strategy is explained and justified to whom.
- *Discourse and the management of strategic change*. Strategy discourse plays an especially important role in the diffusion of innovations, new management practices and the management of change (see, for example, Hardy et al., 2000). In particular, different forms of language may be more or less useful in achieving the adoption and retention of new practices. Language that appeals to emotion and self-interest may help adoption, but a reliance on this may lead to the early rejection of new practices. A more rational approach may mean that it takes longer to achieve adoption but will be less likely to result in early rejection. Language that appeals to or relates to accepted ways of doing things may, however, help ensure retention.

- *Common discourse*. It may be beneficial to seek to develop a common language of strategy in an organisation. This is a common reason for management development programmes in relation to strategy. The argued benefit is that managers can then communicate on the basis of a common set of generally understood concepts, terms and tools of strategy which makes strategy debate more effective. It is also a role management educators provide in the diffusion of strategy concepts and language, of course.

- *A critical perspective for managers*. A critical perspective on the discourse of strategy should prompt managers and students alike to question just how substantial concepts and models to do with strategy really are. Are they really based on sound evidence and theory; do they really make a difference? Or are they a discourse being employed because it seems to be what is expected; because it is 'the language of strategists'; or a way for managers to gain power and influence? In this sense, seeing strategy as discourse can prompt the healthy questioning of concepts, ideas and assumptions that might otherwise be taken for granted.

Conclusion

The core assumptions and the key implications of the four lenses of design, experience, variety and discourse are summarised in Table 7.1. They are not offered here as an exhaustive list. They are an attempt to encapsulate different approaches and insights into the complex concept of strategy. Indeed, the suggestion is that you may usefully extend

Table 7.1   A summary of the strategy lenses

	Strategy as:			
	Design	Experience	Variety	Discourse
Strategy develops through...	A logical process of analysis and evaluation	People's experience, assumptions and taken-for-granted ways of doing things	Ideas bubbling up from the variety of people in and around organisations	Managers seeking influence, power and legitimacy through the language they use
Assumptions about organisations	Mechanistic, hierarchical, rational systems	Cultures based on experience, legitimacy and past success	Complex and potentially diverse organic systems	Arenas of power and influence
Role of top management	Strategic decision-makers	Enactors of their experience	'Coaches', creators of context and pattern-recognisers	Exercising or gaining power and influence over others
Key implications	Undertake careful and thorough analysis of strategic issues	Recognise that people's experience is central and needs to be built upon but also challenged	If innovation is important look for ideas bubbling up from the bottom and periphery of the organisation	Unpick the language used by managers to uncover hidden assumptions and political interests

your exploration of different lenses yourself. It should be apparent in what you have read so far that the lenses presented here actually include several perspectives themselves. For example, the experience lens builds on explanations from cognition, sociology and cultural anthropology and the variety lens builds on both evolutionary theory and complexity theory. So, within these lenses there are finer-grained insights that can be gained and the references should help with that. In addition there are whole books written that provide multiple perspectives on strategy, from the four that Richard Whittington (Whittington 2000) offers to the ten of Henry Mintzberg and his co-authors (Mintzberg et al., 1998).

However, there are two overarching messages that come through consistently. The first is the one with which this chapter began: in considering a topic like strategy, it helps to take more than one perspective. The second is that, in so doing, there is a need to question the conventional wisdom of strategy encapsulated in the design lens. In particular the central tenet of managers at the top planning and directing strategy through machine-like organisations is too limited a view of what strategic management is about.

[...]

Notes

1. For a thorough explanation of the role of psychological processes in strategy, see Hodgkinson and Sparrow (2002).
2. For a fuller discussion of complexity theory in relation to strategy, see Stacey (2000) and Burnes (2005).
3. For a systematic discussion of the implications of evolutionary theory on management, see Aldrich (1999).
4. An excellent discussion of the development of ideas (or what the authors refer to as 'memes') and the relationship of this to the role and nature of organisations can be found in Weeks and Galunic (2003).
5. Feldman and Pentland (2003) show how 'performative' variations from standardised (they call them ostensive) routines may create variation which creates organisational change.
6. See Johnson and Huff (1998). Patrick Regner (2003) also shows how new strategic directions can grow from the periphery of organisations in the face of opposition from the centre.
7. Bill McKelvey (2004), a complexity theorist, argues that the variety within this distributed intelligence is increased because individual managers seek to become better informed about their environment.
8. The concept of blind selection is explained more fully in the chapter by D. Barron on evolutionary theory in the *Oxford Handbook of Strategy* (2003).
9. The role of altruism and other bases of attraction is discussed by Susan Blackmore in *The Meme Machine* (1999).
10. For other implications, see Stacey (2000), Brown and Eisenhardt (1998) and McKelvey (2004).
11. This is the term used by Brown and Eisenhard (1998), amongst others.
12. In the *Handbook of Discourse Analysis* (2001), T.A. Van Dijk writes: 'Critical Discourse Analysis primarily studies the way social power abuse, dominance and inequality are enacted, reproduced and resisted by text and talk in the social and political context' (p. 352).

References

Acs, Z.J. and Audretsch, D.B. (1988) 'Innovation in large and small firms: an empirical analysis', *American Economic Review*, 78: 678–90.

Aldrich, H. (1999) *Organizations Evolving*. Thousand Oaks, CA: Sage.

Barron, D. (2003) 'Evoluationary theory', in D. Faulkner and A. Campbell (eds) *Oxford Handbook of Strategy*. Oxford: Oxford University Press.

Barry, D. and Elmes, M. (1997) 'Strategy retold: toward a narrative view of strategic discourse', *Academy of Management Review*, 22(2): 429–52.

Blackmore, S. (1999) *The Meme Machine*. Oxford: Oxford University Press.

Brown, S.L. and Eisenhardt, K.M. (1998) *Complexity on the Edge*. Harvard: Harvard Business School Press.

Burnes, B. (2005) 'Complexity theories and organizational change', *International Journal of Management Reviews*, 7(2): 73–90.

Dutton, J., Walton, E. and Abrahamson, E. (1989) 'Important dimensions of strategic issues: separating the wheat from the chaff', *Journal of Management Studies*, 26(4): 380–95.

Feldman, M.S. and Pentland, B.T. (2003) 'Reconceptualizing organisational routines as a source of flexibility and change', *Administrative Science Quarterly*, 48: 94–118.

Geertz, C. (1973) *The Interpretation of Culture*. New York: Basic Books.

Granovetter, M.S. (1973) 'The strength of weak ties', *American Journal of Sociology*, 78(6): 1360–80.

Green, S.E. Jr. (2004) 'A rhetorical theory of diffusion', *Academy of Management Review*, 29(4): 653–69.

Hardy, C., Palmer, I. and Phillips, N. (2000) 'Discourse as a strategic resource', *Human Relations*, 53(9): 1227–48.

Heracleous, L. and Barrett, M. (2001) 'Organizational change as discourse: communicative actions and deep structures in the context of information technology implementation', *Academy of Management Journal*, 44(4): 755–78.

Hodgkinson, G.P. and Sparrow, P.R. (2002) *The Competent Organization*. Maidenhead: Open University Press.

Johnson, G. and Huff, A.S. (1998) 'Everyday innovation/everyday strategy', in G. Hamel, G.K. Prahalad, H. Thomas and D. O'Neal (eds) *Strategic Flexibility: Managing in a Turbulent Environment*, pp. 13–27. Chichester: Wiley.

Knights, D. (1992) 'Changing spaces: the disruptive impact of a new epistemological location for the study of management', *Academy of Management Review*, 17(3): 514–36.

Knights, D. and Morgan, G. (1991) 'Corporate strategy, organizations and subjectivity', *Organization Studies*, 12(2): 251–73.

Lindblom, C.E. (1959) 'The science of muddling through', *Public Administration Review*, 19: 79–88.

March, J.G. (1994) *A Primer on Decision Making: How Decisions Happen*. New York: Simon & Schuster.

McKelvey, B. (2004) 'Simple rules for improving corporate IQ: basic lessons from complexity science', in P. Andriani and G. Passiante (eds) *Complexity, Theory and the Management of Networks*. London: Imperial College Press.

Mintzberg, H. (1973) *The Nature of Managerial Work*. New York: Harper & Row.

Mintzberg, H., Ahlstrand, B. and Lampel, J. (1998) *Strategy Safari*. Upper Saddle River, NJ: Prentice Hall.

Oaks, L., Townley, B. and Cooper, D.J. (1998) 'Business planning as pedagogy: language and institutions in a changing institutional field', *Administrative Science Quarterly*, 43(2): 257–92.

Regner, P. (2003) 'Strategy creation in the periphery: inductive versus deductive strategy making', *Journal of Management Studies*, 40(1): 57–82.

Sillence, J. and Mueller, F. (2007) 'Switching strategic perspective: the reframing of accounts of responsibility', *Organization Studies*, 28(2): 175–6.

Simon, H.A. (1960) *The New Science of Management Decision*. Upper Saddle River, NJ: Prentice Hall.

Spicer, A. (2004) 'Book review of *Recreating Strategy*', *Organization Studies*, 25(7): 1256.

Stacey, R.D. (2000) *Strategic Management and Organizational Dynamics: The Challenge of Complexity*, 3rd edn. Harlow: Pearson Education.

Suddaby, R. and Greenwood, R. (2005) 'Rhetorical strategies of legitimacy', *Administrative Science Quarterly*, 50: 35–67.

Tversky, A. and Kahnemenn, D. (1975) 'Judgments under uncertainty: heuristics and biases', *Science*, 185: 1124–31.

Van Dijk, T.A. (2001) 'Critical discourse analysis', in D. Schiffrin and H. Hamilton (eds) *Handbook of Discourse Analysis*. Oxford: Blackwell.

Von Hippel, E. (1988) *The Sources of Innovation*. Oxford: Oxford University Press.

Weeks, J. and Galunic, C. (2003) 'A theory of the cultural evolution of the firm: the intra-organizational ecology of memes', *Organization Studies*, 24(8): 1309–52.

Whittington, R. (2000) *What is Strategy – and Does it Matter?* 2nd edn. London: Thomson Learning.

8

The Practice of Leadership in the Messy World of Organizations

Jean-Louis Denis, Ann Langley and Linda Rouleau

Introduction

Some researchers have proposed taking what is called in social sciences the 'practice turn' (Schatzki et al., 2001) for studying leadership (Alvesson and Sveningsson, 2003a, 2003b; Carroll et al., 2008; Knights and Willmott, 1992) grounded in social theories of practice. A practice perspective focuses on human action and praxis in order to understand how people participate in the production and reproduction of organization and society and in this case of leadership. It is in this sense that Alvesson and Sveningsson (2003a, 2003b) have suggested looking at leadership as the 'extraordinarization' of mundane activities, emphasizing, for example, the importance of listening and chatting as foundational practices of leadership exercised in the daily activities of managers. A practice theory view thus tends to focus on micro-level activities, examining in a very fine-grained manner how they achieve their effects. To date however, there have been relatively few empirical studies that explicitly adopt a practice perspective on leadership, and most of these studies have remained focused on relatively narrowly defined situations.

In this chapter, we revisit data from two case studies of leadership experiences in the context of change in the health care field, attempting to combine a focus on micro-level practices (Carroll et al., 2008) with an understanding of the broader overall processes

Source – An edited version of Denis, J-L., Langley, A. and Rouleau, L. (2010) 'The practice of leadership in the messy world of organizations'.

(Pettigrew, 1992) within which they are embedded. We use this analysis to illustrate the *dynamic, collective, situated* and *dialectical* nature of leadership practices, suggesting a need to encourage an awareness of [these dimensions] among practitioners.

The health care setting that forms the backdrop for this analysis is somewhat extreme in terms of the ambiguity of its authority relationships – it is a particularly 'messy' world in which multiple groups with different values, interests and expertise compete for influence (Mintzberg, 1997). [...] Yet some might claim that almost all large organizations are at least to some extent pluralistic in the sense of incorporating multiple foci of power, and diverse interests, values and expertise (Denis et al., 2005, 2007).

We begin by briefly presenting the two case studies that form the basis of our analysis, and then review how each study illustrates the four dimensions mentioned above. Finally we consider the implications of this analysis for practice.

Two illustrative case studies

The two case studies considered here were originally developed as part of a long-term program of research on organizational change in health care organizations that has given rise to several previous publications (Denis et al., 1996, 2000, 2001, 2006, 2009). [...]

In order to enrich understanding of the key points developed in the body of the chapter, we begin by providing a short narrative vignette for each case followed by illustrative quotations from interviews showing perceptions of the particular practices and approaches of a key leader playing an important role in the case history. We focus more particularly here on two specific individuals who were at the centre of the action: John for Case 1 and Ivor for Case 2 (fictitious names).

Case 1 vignette: change leadership under ambiguity

The first case study focused on the leadership of major change in a hospital character-ized by diffuse authority and power relationships. Several people played leadership roles in this context, but perhaps the most interesting figure in the process was John, a public health physician who at the start of the study did not hold a particularly central position in the organization. However, when the CEO ran into difficulties with a planning proc-ess, he called on John to help out. From this point on, John began to play an increasingly important role, promoting the designation of the hospital as a teaching institution and mobilizing colleagues from the medical staff and the board around his ideas. His approach was very entrepreneurial and hands-on. When he felt something needed doing, he tended to go for it, becoming successively involved in managing financial downsiz-ing, and negotiating with the ministry of health and with the university. He was extremely effective in most of these enterprises, producing impressive substantive results in terms of fiscal equilibrium and the teaching affiliation, but his activities were not always appreciated by people who felt pushed aside or ignored in his unrelenting drive to move things forward. Eventually, he and his main collaborators lost the support of key members of the medical staff who felt that the organization was moving too quickly. John left the hospital and moved on to other things, while the change process he had initiated slowed down.

John as a leader:

'He was a guy who shook up a lot of things.' (Doctor-manager)
'He's a guy who's very dynamic, he assembles people, he's a doer, he can find the glue to stick rubber to plastic.' (MD)
'He was a catalyst, he seeded ideas.' (MD)
'Things were done in a cavalier fashion … people were profoundly upset by the way things were done.' (Manager)
'People need to slow down. You cannot keep on breaking the china all the time.' (Manager)

Case 2 vignette: the process of integration of a new leader

The second case study focused on the process by which a new leader – called here Ivor – integrated into the CEO position in a large and prestigious teaching hospital. Ivor had acquired a reputation for excellent communication skills in his former post as CEO of a smaller hospital and this was one reason why the medical establishment was particularly keen to hire him – they felt that their hospital needed to develop a higher profile. However, they were also hiring someone who had a strong taste for innovation – something that members of this more conservative organization were not quite ready for.

The case shows how difficult it may be for a new leader, even a CEO, to impose his way of thinking on an organization with strong incumbent stakeholders. While his integration was ultimately successful. Ivor found himself forced to adopt many of the perspectives preferred by the powerful medical staff and he went through numerous difficult trial and error negotiations with his administrative team concerning quality management practices. Ivor's 'open-door' style and practices, his skill in communications and his informality in relations with others were popular with physicians. They enabled him to rapidly assimilate the perspectives that the medical staff favoured. He became adept at finding ways to develop initiatives that met their concerns and interests but that also contributed positively to organizational performance. On the other hand, the same practices caused difficulties with the administrative team who sometimes found themselves shut out. Moreover, Ivor gradually came to realize that his 'open-door' policy might undermine other managers and leave him with little recourse when a change of direction was required.

Ivor as a leader:

'A man of imagination, of creativity of projects, of considerable ambition, of unbounded energy.' (Manager)
'He has an open-door policy and receives all sorts of people in his office. But sometimes, it looks like interference.' (Manager)

'I think he is gradually becoming imbued with our culture. Like an angel cake – when you add the syrup, it seeps in.' (MD)

'He took the culture, adopted it and adapted it.' (Manager)

'I've learned some fascinating things. You have power by remaining distant here. If you are too involved from the beginning, you lose your impartiality.' (Ivor)

[…]

Doing leadership

The perspective presented in this chapter emphasizes the importance of looking at the micro-practices through which leadership is constituted. Specifically, drawing on the two cases sketched earlier, we highlight successively the *dynamic, collective, situated* and *dialectical* character of *doing* leadership as a practical activity. Table 8.1 summarizes how these basic dimensions apply to the two representative studies of health care organizational change.

Leadership as *dynamic*

Leadership studies that reduce leadership and its consequences to inter-related sets of variables are clearly very limited in their capacity to grasp the temporally rich experience of what it means to be a leader visible even in the very short vignettes provided earlier. Our research program and the two cases in particular reveal the nature of leadership as a *dynamic* phenomenon – a process that evolves over time in context. Indeed, a longitudinal research perspective seems essential to better understand how context and leadership interact through time and how changes take place. Leadership emerges, shifts, changes and flows around organizations as leaders and others engage in everyday activities, interpret the meaning and consequences of prior actions and engage in further actions.

At the centre of the dynamics of leadership is the recursive relationship between leadership practices and their consequences. One way of looking at these consequences is to consider them in three categories: substantive, symbolic and political (see also Denis et al., 2001). Substantive consequences are those that concern concrete structural change. Symbolic consequences concern the evolution of meaning among relevant stakeholders. Political consequences refer to the evolution in leadership roles themselves. Political consequences such as increased or decreased credibility and changes in formal position are particularly important for determining leaders' future scope for action. The *dynamics* of leadership are strongly related to these political issues in the two cases.

For example, in Case 1, John's ascension to a key leadership role and eventual withdrawal constitute a dynamic process that can only be understood by looking at his activities and their consequences over time. His initial interventions were rather popular. He took over the strategic planning process, succeeded in generating consensus among his medical colleagues (something that the CEO had not achieved), and piloted a report that demonstrated that the hospital was underfinanced. The result of these initiatives was to create a

Table 8.1   Illustrations of four features of the practice of leadership in the two case studies

	John: change leadership	Ivor: becoming a leader
Leadership as Dynamic: *Leadership actions at one time can change the potential for effective leadership later*	John's initial successes led to increased power, but as his actions threatened other interests, they made it impossible to continue.	Ivor's earlier assimilation to the values of the medical staff enabled him to convince them to change later.
Leadership as Collective: *Leadership depends critically on a constellation of co-leaders who play complementary roles*	John built effective alliances with the medical council chairman Chris and Board member Mitch, each playing complementary roles in promoting change.	Ivor had to negotiate his position with respect to the very powerful medical staff and Board as he entered the organization.
Leadership as Situated: *Leadership is manifest in the micro-activities of leaders in interaction with others in specific contexts*	John's leadership was manifest in the way he was able to persuade a team to adopt a contrary orientation to the one they had in mind previously, using energetic and inspiring arguments linked to desirable strategic goals.	Ivor's leadership was manifest in the way he connected warmly and naturally with other people in interactions, acquiring both visibility externally and recognition internally.
Leadership as Dialectic: *Practices that seem to be effective often have a downside. The strengths of leaders can become weaknesses*	In opposing a variety of organization members using practices such as those in the box above, John stepped on a lot of toes. He succeeded in the moment, but created opposition that would later have its day.	Ivor's open and accessible style described in the box above enabled him to gain credibility, but sometimes meant decisions were taken too quickly and he was left without a final recourse in case of problems.

web of support across the organization that encouraged him to pursue these proposals further and gained him a promotion to an administrative position. In pursuing the teaching hospital affiliation, his role widened further. His negotiations with the government led him to propose a retrenchment plan, something that previously had been considered inconceivable. As one board member noted, 'It was a curious thing to see. The Board tipped completely from one side to the other. Suddenly sentences that before made everyone jump – we need a balanced budget – were uttered. Because now we were told that a balanced budget was needed to get the university affiliation'. This constituted the height of John's influence in the organisation, but also a turning point as certain people began to see his contribution in less positive terms. Concerns became more and more evident as certain key members of the medical staff began to see other potentially negative consequences of the university affiliation. As opposition to the proposal grew, John's store of credibility as a leader diminished and it became urgent to move on.

The dynamic processes described here were also inherent to Ivor's integration as a new leader described in Case 2. Ivor successfully succeeded his predecessor but had to go through an integration process that took considerable time (27 months) and was differently achieved throughout the organization. During this time, he used several mechanisms to build his leadership. As illustrated in the vignette, with the medical staff, he found himself obliged to shift his perspective to meet their expectations before being able to convince them to consider moves in new directions. In parallel with these processes, he engaged in a long period of trial and error with the administrative team around the implementation of a quality-improvement project. The extensive support he had acquired from the medical staff early in the process of integration was, however, helpful in protecting him in his struggles with the administrative team. His credibility with physicians made it easier to survive these conflicts and adjustments. A new leader entering in an organization needs to be aware that leadership is a dynamic process in the sense that one action or one form of integration may be a precursor of another. The interactive and dynamic integration process between leader and organization was summed up by one observer as follows: 'Each side compromised in their approach and now we see that there is harmony'.

[...]

Overall, our point here is that leadership is something that evolves and manifests itself over time, interacting with its context. As circumstances change, leaders may easily gain or lose influence. Moreover, leaders may contribute either wittingly or unwittingly to their own leadership gains and losses through their activities and practices at any particular point in time and the consequences these may bring. As Case 1 illustrates, and as we shall develop further in a later point, activities that seem to be effective in achieving substantive impact may sometimes become problematic later. This emphasis on the dynamic nature of leadership strongly recalls Pettigrew's (1992) call for a processual perspective on the emergence, development and evolution of leadership roles.

Leadership as *collective*

Our research program also drew attention to the *collective* nature of leadership. We argue with others (e.g. Gronn, 2002) that there is value, even within more hierarchical organizational forms to considering leadership not simply as an individual attribute but as a coalitional phenomenon both throughout the organization and among leaders at the top. While the 'upper echelons' approach proposed by Hambrick (2007) and others has moved the focus away from CEOs towards their top management teams, more could be done to open up our understanding of how team members interact and coalesce dynamically in the context of practical activity. In the vignettes shown earlier, we emphasized the roles of two key individuals. However, in each case, the activities that are central to their practices would have been impossible if these individuals had not succeeded in aligning themselves with others in leadership positions with whom they then coordinated their actions. Indeed, part of the dynamics of leadership described earlier involves the construction and evolution of what we call 'leadership constellations', following Hodgson et al. (1965). We now briefly illustrate the importance of these constellations to the two cases.

John's leadership activities in Case 1 would have been impossible if he had not constructed strong alliances with a number of people who played co-leadership roles. Central among these was Chris, a physician who had been elected to the hospital's medical council and who had extensive political connections as well as a desire to see the organization develop, and Mitch, a proactive board member rather tired of what he saw as the defeatist tone dominating board meetings. The CEO also contributed to the constellation by maintaining his support despite the somewhat invasive initiatives of John and Chris. Various respondents described the relationships among these protagonists: 'Chris had been looking for some time for a Director of Professional Services he could work with' (John); 'John's arrival was a precipitating factor for Chris. This is the guy we need' (Manager); 'Chris was a good politician ... there was an alchemy between John and Chris ... They had good relations with Mitch on the board which helped move things along' (Manager). The group created a powerful constellation of people who mutually coordinated their actions, playing differentiated but complementary roles (see also Denis et al., 1996, 2001). Without this circle of collaborators, constructed over time, none of the protagonists would have been able to achieve much in an organization where power and influence were widely distributed.

Case 2 also clearly shows the collective nature of leadership. As a new CEO, Ivor had to take into account the configuration of coalitions in place, and in particular the three key poles of influence in this organization: the Board, the Medical Council Executive and the administrative team. Indeed, his task as a new leader involved inserting himself into an existing constellation, and gradually finding a way to inflect its evolution over time. In this case, the prestigious medical staff exercised enormous influence requiring Ivor to develop linkages with them before he could begin to attempt moves in new directions. The process of leader integration seen in this case study contrasts quite strongly with a more traditional perspective on leader integration as 'taking charge' (Gabarro, 1987). Instead, the process can be viewed as one of mutual accommodation and interdependence, in which the capacity to lead collectively emerged gradually over time. As one doctor put it towards the end of the study, 'It is impossible that the medical council executive and the CEO not have the same information on the institution. We have a common front'.

[...]

Overall, building on the original work of Hodgson et al. (1965), we suggest that a constellation of leaders will be more effective if it presents three characteristics: *specialization*, *differentiation* and *complementarity*. Specialization refers to what each member of the constellation brings in term of expertise and legitimacy (e.g. clinical expertise, expertise in managing professionals, in setting up decision-making processes). Differentiation refers to the division of labour among the coalition in order to avoid excessive overlap and possible competition among leaders – a non-negligible risk in contexts where individuals may have forceful personalities and strong ambitions. Complementarity refers to the scope of the resources (expertise, legitimacy, relationships) that a constellation has in regard to the challenges faced by the organization. The idea here is that the more a constellation is aligned with the issues faced by an organization, the more its leaders will be in a position to have an impact.

Leadership as *situated*

Leadership is also contextually *situated* and practically enacted. Such a view implies a need to look simultaneously at the properties of context and at the micro-level detail of leadership practices in situ to understand how they achieve their results, as suggested by Alvesson and Sveningsson (2003a, 2003b) and Carroll et al. (2008). To illustrate this idea, we zoom in on some particular episodes in the two cases, illustrating activities of the two leaders that appeared characteristic of how they actually *did* leadership in the here and now. An optimal source of data for capturing the micro-practices of leadership is the observations of leaders in action. Another source that offers a useful perspective on practice is leaders' own accounts or narratives of their practice (Rouleau, 2009). Although these accounts may be less detailed and comprise elements of impression management, they provide deeper insight into the thinking behind individual leaders' behaviours, and the knowledge driving their practices. This is the source of data we use in our illustrations for Cases 1 and 2.

To illustrate episodes of leadership practice for Case 1, we present two short narratives or verbatim stories from an in-depth interview with John. These are shown in Table 8.2.

Table 8.2 Two micro-narratives of John's leadership practice

Story 1: the big COUP	Story 2: redirecting the fund-raising campaign
People were saying we were underfinanced. So the Finance Director proposed a process for demonstrating this with an accounting firm … And I came right in and said, 'No – we'll take a different route and do a financial analysis in the context of the current situation and for our future strategy'. And we called it the 'Big COUP' because jokingly I said we needed to give a big kick ['coup de pied' in French] and create the *Committee* for the *Organization, Unification* and *Promotion* of the hospital. And so we agreed to that, so it was a very participative strategy that created a wide movement to recognize the financial difficulties of the hospital … It enabled consideration of the implications of our strategy that we hadn't done yet. I profited from this to do that. This wasn't necessarily appreciated by the Finance Director who had his consulting firm lined up and they lost a contract. But the CEO and the Board approved it.	In the summer, the CEO with the foundation decided to undertake a fund-raising drive [for the anaesthesia department]. That isn't easy to sell but it had been accepted by the Board of the hospital and the foundation. They asked me to come and talk to the Board of the Foundation and to tell them about anaesthesia … I went to the meeting, the Board Chair was there, and I started talking about traumatology. I said I thought that anaesthesia was a terrible theme to sell to the community, that the hospital couldn't really identify with that, but with a more strategic choice which was traumatology. In the end, the Board decided to convene a couple of days later and from one thing to the next, they converged around traumatology. And the only person who changed that was me because the anaesthetists were very happy to go ahead with anaesthesia but the rest of the hospital wanted traumatology. So we had a fundraising campaign around that and I was the spokesperson for the hospital.

These stories describe two micro-episodes that have striking similarities despite their very different context. They both reveal John's influence as a leader. In both cases he enters a situation arguing in opposition to plans promoted by people who have apparent organizational authority and legitimacy, and he succeeds in driving things in a completely different direction. His persuasiveness clearly reposes at least in part on the strength of his arguments but also on the excitement and enthusiasm he manages to create around his ideas. In each case, he moves people away from a short-term operational choice that he presents as dull and bureaucratic towards a more strategic and even glamorous decision compatible with the strategic plan he has previously been involved in developing. His ideas are all driven by an articulate and integrated vision that no one else seems to be providing, and moreover, it is one that looks to the future optimistically. In the first story, the symbolic language and wide participation of the 'big COUP' is able to generate enthusiasm across the hospital around the potential for development. In the second story, the idea of encouraging investment in a prestigious traumatology program is clearly far more attractive and strategic than the CEO's original plan to orient the campaign around anaesthesia. John's success in moving people around to his views is also related to his obvious entrepreneurial drive and willingness to place his own energy in the service of these initiatives. He became the coordinator of the 'big COUP' and the spokesperson for the traumatology fundraising drive. Thus the highly concrete and situated nature of leadership practice is evident in these specific incidents. It is through such episodes that leadership is enacted.

At the same time, these micro-level manifestations of leadership do not occur in a vacuum. It is here that the *dynamic* and *collective* dimensions of leadership as processes are important to consider as a backdrop to *situated* practices. For example, in order to fully appreciate John's success in persuading others in the above cases, it is important to understand what had happened before these incidents that might make his message particularly credible. John's success with the prior strategic planning exercise as well as his recent very skilful handing of a local environmental crisis in which the hospital's performance was seen as exemplary were elements that almost certainly made him a person worth listening to. In addition, the strong collaborative relationship he had already developed with Chris ensured that when he spoke, other members of the leadership *collective* were already with him. Thus situated practice is embedded in and indeed partly constructed by these underlying dynamics.

To illustrate Ivor's situated practices in Case 2, we look briefly at an account from a middle manager towards the end of the integration period describing her reactions to the new leader:

> He has created breakfasts with the staff and two of my employees were part of these breakfast talks. So … for them, I think what came out was that he was someone who is accessible. Contrary to the image of a Director General that everyone has – you know a big man who walks around with a briefcase (laughter …) who is just not accessible … He has demystified that image that people had … You know, in meetings, he will say, 'We met with people from the ministry, or we're going to Quebec next week, and we will discuss this and this'. Before we had information, but it was always very general … When Ivor arrived, all of a sudden I realized the Director General exists (laughter) and he sees us, he meets with us.

In this quotation, the very existence of a leader within the organization is literally made manifest by his practices of accessibility. At the same time, accessibility to his own employees also acquires value because of his visibility and prestige in the local scene: 'He has wide visibility outside the hospital in the media and everything … and at some point, people say … that's our Director General'. At this point, it is clear that Ivor has been successfully integrated into a leadership role, he has been appropriated as such by his 'followers', and that the practices described in the two quotations appear to have contributed to that. Once again however, it would be simplistic to consider the effects of these practices in isolation without also examining the *dynamic* process of adjustment that led to this point, or without considering the strong alliance that he had developed with the medical staff (i.e. the *collective* dimension of leadership) that gave him the credibility to appear in public and with employees as a leader.

[…]

In summary, the two leaders studied showed different patterns in their situated practices as revealed in these illustrations. John's entrepreneurial moves succeeded in deviating colleagues from preconceived paths by offering attractive alternatives embedded in an overall strategic vision. Ivor's skilful communication practices brought him appreciation from the people who looked to him for leadership and enabled him to become integrated. In both cases however, the micro-level effects of their situated practices could not be understood without knowledge of the context in which they occurred (i.e. the broader *dynamics* of the process, and the relationships developed with key co-leaders – the *collective* dimension). It is important to realize also that these situated practices embed contradictions. Their effects are not so simple or one-sided as we may have implied in this section. This brings us to the fourth dimension we wish to emphasize in this chapter.

Leadership as *dialectic*

Throughout the research program described here, we encountered contradictions in the exercise of leadership in situations of change. Collinson (2005) drew attention to three dialectic dimensions of leadership practices that he labels control/resistance, consent/dissent and men/women. He suggests, for example, that apparently successful leadership practices inherently generate their own resistance, that consent may be manufactured and hide overt or passive practices of dissent among followers and that gender relations may be embedded in these tensions. He notes that:

> a dialectical approach suggests that studies need to acknowledge the deep-seated asymmetrical power relations of leadership dynamics. It recognizes that leaders exercise considerable control and that their power can also have contradictory outcomes which leaders either do not always understand or of which they are unaware. (p. 1435)

The cases we studied reveal that leadership has dialectic qualities based on the equivocal nature of many leadership actions and practices. Indeed both of the vignettes suggest a cyclical process in which each leader's practices had a 'dark side' that ultimately came to the surface and that we now explore in more depth.

If we consider Case 1, a second look at the two practice narratives in Table 8.2 suggests that John's practices of entrepreneurial leadership were not without risk. For example, in the Grand COUP story, we see that the Finance Director has been largely undermined by John's proposed solutions. In the fund-raising story, there are also losers, starting with the anaesthetists who had expected to be the main beneficiaries of the hospital's campaign. One might also surmise that the CEO who had initially supported the anaesthetists might find the situation somewhat uncomfortable. Through practices like these in which he aggressively promoted his strategic ideas. John created pockets of dissatisfaction and tension surrounding himself even as he achieved immense strides in developing the hospital and in improving its performance in collaboration with Chris, Mitch and others. Ultimately, as one observer put it, 'You cannot keep on breaking the china'. After some time in their positions, John and Chris had created too many enemies and it was time to move on. It is perhaps no accident that the person who replaced Chris as the new President of the Medical Council was the chief anaesthetist.

Ivor's situated practices, as described earlier, also had contradictory effects. While his 'open-door' policy and accessibility were appreciated by the medical staff and employees, they became a bone of contention for his executive team who felt that this practice tended to bypass their authority. Indeed, one manager offers a somewhat different perspective on this practice from that indicated earlier:

> He says I will go and eat with you in the cafeteria, and we are there at the table at lunchtime with the employees of the hospital and the Director General in shirtsleeves who says, 'Let's talk'. Well, people who have never seen that in their lives think that at last they have access to the pipeline. They take anything that is said for a decision. Participation is opened up – everyone wants to participate, but should it be around the Board table or at the proper level and then it goes up through the organization? ... So now he risks having everyone's problems in his office.

Ivor himself also gradually came to see the risks of excessive openness and found himself modulating his approach as illustrated in the following narrative:

> I'm going up the stairs ... and I meet a doctor, a service head, coming down. He says, 'Hi, look, I have a great idea for my service ... we need to do things this and this way'. I say, 'That's very interesting, we should think about it'. Two days later, I have a department head come into my office and say, 'You authorized $300,000 for the complete reorganization of the service'. You have to be very careful in an organization like that to create an environment and structures that allow formal, democratic and open decision making.

[...]

In summary, as shown in this section, the *situated practices* of leaders rarely have unequivocally positive effects. Even apparently successful practices embed within themselves contradictory effects – a dark side – that may and often does come back to haunt leaders.

Indeed, leadership roles are by nature transient, and leaders are subject to unexpected forces for change, including the consequences of their actions, practices, and decisions. They evolve in complex systems of interactions including patterns of power and interests that they cannot fully control. Nor can they perfectly anticipate the context and the outcomes of their decisions. This brings us full circle to the *dynamic* nature of leadership processes. Indeed, we would argue that the dialectic nature of leadership practices is a major force behind the dynamics of leadership (see also Denis et al., 2001). Specifically, John's practices in Case 1 were often substantively effective, but as time went on politically problematic. Ivor learned to adapt his practices over time to avoid their more problematic political effects and use them increasingly to his advantage. [...]

Lessons for leaders

The implications of seeing leadership as *dynamic, collective, situated* and *dialectical* for practitioners are numerous. First, while attributions of leadership are often made in the short term, it is only in the longer term that the full ramifications of leaders' actions and behaviors are revealed. The *dynamic* nature of leadership means that the capacity to influence action may wax and wane as the context changes and as the consequences of prior actions become clearer. Leadership roles and practices must be expected to shift with the demands of the situation.

The image of leadership as a *collective* enterprise further draws attention to the importance of creating a functional group of leaders. Leadership cannot be competently exercised in large, complex and 'messy' organizations without taking into account the multiple, dynamic and more or less fragile coalitions that constitute them. Thus, leadership should not be viewed as an external authority or symbol influencing others from outside. Rather, leaders need to see themselves as embedded in networks that they do not fully control. This perspective also demands more humility from people in leadership positions. Leaders are transient in the sense that challenges and dilemmas change and a given leader may not be the best person to contribute to organizational development in a changing context. Individuals in a position of leadership need to accept the need to leave space for others in an existing constellation – something that can be hard to do in many cases. Moreover, to construct and sustain a supportive leadership constellation, they need to tap into the value systems that reflect key aspects of organizational identity and practices.

In addition, the *situated* nature of leadership practices implies that day-to-day interactions are critically important. It is through these that the work of leading actually gets done. Moreover, it is also through their day-to-day interactions and actions that leaders shape and hone their leadership capacity. The knowledge they gain of the in-depth functioning of their organization through daily interactions is an invaluable resource of learning. At the same time, successful performance in the here and now relies on their cumulated experience as well as the credibility they have generated through prior actions. Thus, John's persuasive interventions in meetings and Ivor's skilful 'listening and chatting' with employees (Alvesson & Sveningsson, 2003a) depend in part for their success on everything that has gone before as well as the collaborators and allies that are brought onto the scene to support them either physically or virtually.

Finally, our observations of the *dialectic* nature of leadership practices suggest that almost any apparently successful leadership intervention or practice could have a potential downside. As Collinson (2005) indicated, power does not come free: leaders need to understand that their activities create waves of substantive, symbolic and political consequences that may not always be fully evident in the passing moment. These will contribute inevitably to constituting subsequent leadership opportunities and challenges in a never ending dynamic process.

References

Alvesson, M., & Sveningsson, S. (2003a) 'Managers Doing Leadership: The Extra-ordinarization of the Mundane', *Human Relations* 56(12): 1435–59.

Alvesson, M., & Sveningsson, S. (2003b) 'The Great Disappearance Act: Difficulties in Doing Leadership', *Leadership Quarterly* 14: 359–81.

Carroll, B., Levy, L., & Richmond, D. (2008) 'Leadership as Practice: Challenging the Competency Paradigm', *Leadership* 4(4): 363–79.

Collinson, D. (2005) 'Dialectics of Leadership', *Human Relations* 58(11): 1419–42.

Denis, J.L., Lamothe, L., & Langley, A. (2001) 'The Dynamics of Collective Leadership and Strategic Change in Pluralistic Organizations', *Academy of Management Journal* 44(4): 809–37.

Denis, J.L., Langley, A., & Cazale, L. (1996) 'Leadership and Strategic Change Under Ambiguity', *Organisations Studies* 17(4): 673–99.

Denis, J.L., Langley, A., & Pineault, M. (2000) 'Becoming a Leader in a Complex Organizations', *Journal of Management Studies* 37(8): 1063–99.

Denis, J.L., Langley, A., & Rouleau, L. (2005) 'Rethinking Leadership in Public Organizations', in E. Ferlie, L. Lynn, & C. Pollitt (eds) *The Oxford Handbook of Public Management*, pp. 446–67. Oxford: Oxford University Press.

Denis, J.L., Langley, A., & Rouleau, L. (2006) 'The Power of Numbers in Strategizing', *Strategic Organization* 4(4): 349–77.

Denis, J.L., Langley, A., & Rouleau L. (2007) 'Strategizing in Pluralistic Contexts: Rethinking Theoretical Frames', *Human Relations* 60: 179–215.

Denis, J.L., Lamothe, L., Langley, A., Breton, M., Gervais, J., Trottier, L.-H., Contandriopoulos. D., & Dubois, C.-A. (2009) 'The Reciprocal Dynamics of Organizing and Sensemaking in the Implementation of Major Public Sector Reforms', *Canadian Public Administration* 52(2): 225–48.

Gabarro, J. (1987) *The Dynamics of Taking Charge.* Boston, MA: Harvard Business School Press.

Gronn, P. (2002) 'Distributed Leadership as a Unit of Analysis', *Leadership Quarterly* 13(4): 423–51.

Hambrick, D.C. (2007) 'Upper Echelons Theory: An Update', *Academy of Management Review* 32(2): 334–43.

Hodgson, R.C., Levinson, D.J., & Zaleznik, A. (1965) *The Executive Role Constellation.* Boston, MA: Harvard Business School Press.

Knights D., & Willmott, H. (1992) 'Conceptualizing Leadership Processes: A Study of Senior Managers in a Financial Services Company', *Journal of Management Studies* 29: 761–82.

Mintzberg, H. (1997) 'Toward Healthier Hospitals', *Health Care Management Review* 22(4): 9–18.

Pettigrew, A.M. (1992) 'On Studying Managerial Elites', *Strategic Management Journal* 1: 163–82.

Rouleau, L. (2009) 'Studying Strategizing Through Narratives of Practice', in D. Golsorkhi, L. Rouleau, D. Seidl, & T. Vaara (eds) *Cambridge Handbook of Strategy as Practice.* Cambridge: Cambridge University Press.

Schatzki, T., Knorr-Cetina, K., & von Savigny, E. (2001) *The Practice Turn in Contemporary Theory.* London: Routledge.

Part 3

Leadership in Context

9

Reframing the Role of Organizations in Policy Implementation: Resources *for* Practice, *in* Practice

James P. Spillane, Louis M. Gomez and Leigh Mesler

Introduction

In this chapter we revisit the local organization and its role in policy implementation.

We begin by examining 'change' and 'organization' – two key constructs in the study of the role of local organizations in policy implementation. Our discussion points to the complexity of the term *change* and, following Karl Weick (1979), argues for thinking about organizations in terms of organizing. Next, we argue for thinking about organizing and implementation in terms of resources that enable and constrain practice as it unfolds in the interactions among two or more people. Resources are constellations of physical, financial, human, and social assets that individuals and organizations use to accomplish their work. We argue for thinking about resources as having both ostensive and performative aspects. We then develop our argument by focusing on four key resources: (a) human capital, (b) social capital, (c) technology, and (d) organizational routines. These resources feature prominently in the literature on organizational change in general and we consider how they might be differentially distributed, accessed and activated through policy. Our list of resources is illustrative rather than exhaustive.

Source – An edited version of Spillane, J. Gomez, M. and Mesler, L. (2009) 'Reframing the role of organizations in policy implementation'.

Change and organization

Discussions of policy implementation would be difficult without the words 'change' and 'organization'. Our goal in this section is to underscore the ambiguity surrounding these constructs.

What change for policy analysis?

Policy is an intentional effort on the part of government agencies to change existing behavior or practice. And, for policy analysts, a key concern is whether practice changes in a direction that is roughly analogous with policy makers' intentions. One analytic distinction we make is between planned change and unplanned change (Poole, 2004). Policy is mostly about planned change.

Schools and local school districts are often portrayed as hostile to change – bastions of constancy. As a result, implementation scholarship often reads as laments for policy failure – that is, the failure of schools and local school systems to change in response to policy makers' 'good' intentions – their planned change.

Still, policy scholars cannot ignore unplanned change To begin with, policy makers are sometimes prompted by unplanned change – a widening achievement gap, teacher shortage, changing demographics in a neighborhood or city, and so on – to make policy. Further, policy makers planned changes frequently butt heads with unplanned change in the organizations it targets. As planned change, policy plays out in organizations where unplanned change is a constant.

Policy makers often appear to work on an outdated model of organizational change where freezing, changing, and refreezing is the standard operating procedure (Lewin. 1951), rather than the model of where change is a constant. As Kanter et al. (1992) put it, planned change is better conceptualized as being about grabbing part of the constant motion in an organization and steering it so that the members of the organization will interpret it as a new way of 'doing business'. In this view, policy is an attempt to harness and nudge the continuous unplanned change in local schools and school systems in a particular direction. Understanding and fomenting planned change necessitates careful attention to unplanned change – you cannot understand one without the other.

In considering change, planned or unplanned, it is important to not forget about constancy: it is a critical ingredient in understanding change in organizations. *Some* things change, and *other* things remain the same. Change and constancy go together, and we need to treat them accordingly.

Planned change never eradicates the past in its attempts to craft the future. Policy makers' grand designs do not play out on blank slates, rather they are layered on and entangled in current ways of doing things. In this way, the past lives even when things change. In those immortal words of Faulkner (1951, p. 92), 'The past is never dead. In fact, it's not even past'.

Policy makers try to orchestrate planned change by manipulating resources. But organizations are not frozen but in constant motion (Kanter et al., 1992). Policy makers do not acknowledge this constant because it is much easier to imagine frozen organizations that will be subjected to policy and then unfrozen. Further, for policy makers to acknowledge unplanned change would amount to recognizing the limits of policy in enabling planned change in a constantly changing world. [...]

What organization for policy implementation?

In education policy implementation, the notion of organization is ambiguous. Much of the literature dwells on the school organization, suggesting that the school is the key local organizational unit in instructional reform (Meyer and Rowan, 1977; Purkey and Smith, 1983). Strong instructional leadership, trust among teachers and among teachers and administrators, and a sense of collective responsibility for students learning can create incentives and opportunities for teachers to implement policy and revise their practice (Bryk and Schneider, 2002). [...]

Schools are situated in [Local Education Agencies (LEAs)] that research suggests are influential in the implementation process (Spillane, 1998; Supovitz, 2007). District administrators' 'constant and active support' for a reform is a necessary condition for local implementation (Berman and McLaughlin, 1978, p. 33). The LEA as a government jurisdiction and its administrative wing – the district office – are important aspects of the local organization when it comes to policymaking and policy implementation. Each subunit with its own responsibilities and jurisdictions often works relatively independently of one another and posing challenges for state and federal policies that attempt to align the guidance about instruction that teachers are given (Spillane, 1998).

Looking within the schoolhouse, what counts as the relevant unit of analysis for examining the role of the organization in implementation is also murky. Most scholars focus on either the attributes of teachers and administrators or on school level attributes which they typically measure by aggregating up the responses of school staff to say something about the organizational conditions in the school. Both approaches have merit but together they miss or gloss over another key organizational dimension – the subgroup or subunit within schools.

At the high school level, subject matter departments can be an important context for teachers' work (Little, 1993; Siskin, 1994). High school teachers differ in their conceptions of the subjects they teach, and these differences have consequences for curricular practices such as teachers' control of content and curriculum coordination and standardization, differences that may mediate the influence of reform on practice (Stodolsky and Grossman, 1995). Even beyond the high school with its departmentalized structure around school subjects, subgroups of staff within a school are likely a critical organizational dimension in any investigation of implementation (Hayton and Spillane, 2008).

To put one final wrinkle on what counts as the organization at the local level, various extra-system agencies and agents are also an important consideration (Hill, 1999; Rowan, 2006). Teachers' participation in professional networks that extend beyond the schoolhouse are often critical to the implementation of reform (Little, 1993; Talbert and McLaughlin, 1994). [F]or-profit and non-profit agencies also thrive right alongside local school systems, offering an expanding array of goods and services to the formal system. Any effort to under-stand change in schools would be remiss without serious attention to these extra-system organizations (Rowan, 2006) which can influence the resources critical for school improve-ment and policy implementation.

What counts as the relevant unit of analysis, then, with respect to the nexus of policy implementation and organizational behavior is not immediately obvious. Investigations that focus on one level – the high school department or grade level, the school building, or district office – while foregrounding that particular level need to be sensitive to other lev-els and how they interact with the level under investigation. We argue for a reframing of how we think about organizations and policy implementation by taking up the challenge posed by Karl Weick (1979) and thinking about organizing (rather than organizations) – 'a consensually validated grammar for reducing equivocality by means of sensible inter-locked behaviors' (p. 3). Weick argues that small units such as double interacts, dyads, and triads are 'sensible as places to understand the major workings of organizations' (p. 236). Such an approach enables us to conduct analysis that cuts across organizational bound-aries (e.g. school – school district or school – external consultant) and that is driven by a consideration of work practice as it unfolds in the interactions among people.

Focusing on resources enables analysis to move back and forth among different levels of the local school system, and the extra system and lends itself to a consideration of orga-nizing rather than organization. Resources are a useful analytical lens because they offer a common frame that can be applied across different levels while simultaneously allowing us to examine how they become instantiated in practice in different ways depending on the level and interactions. Moreover, the focus on resources underscores the inter-dependency among levels of the system and the extra system.

[…]

Policy implementation, practice, and resources

It is important to think about the behavior or more accurately, the interactions, of people in organizations as more than the sum of their parts. Hence, we focus on practice rather than organizational or individual behavior in organizations. In our view, practice is consti-tuted or defined in interactions among people and is not equivalent to the actions of an individual or a set of behaviors.

Organizational members are not free agents; their sense-making and practice is shaped or structured by the organizations in which they work. Though frequently used in sociol-ogy and related fields, the concept of structure has definitional problems. Following Giddens (1979, 1984), we view structure as both the medium and the outcome of practice. Practice is constituted by organizational structure (and indeed broader societal social structure) that provides the rules and resources upon which it is based. At the same time practice is constitutive of organizational structure as it is created, reproduced, and potentially transformed in practice by human agents in interaction (Giddens, 1979). The structural properties that enable practice in organizations exist as they are 'instantiated in activity' or remembered as rules of conduct or 'rights to resources' (Whittington, 1992, p. 696).

We use the term *practice* to refer to patterns of behavior that emerge from people's interactions with each other, as mediated by aspects of the situation over time (Bourdieu, 1981). Hence, practice is not a synonym for best practices or strategies or individual actions, because ignoring the situation disconnects behavior from the 'urgency of practice' (Bourdieu, 1990). Individuals act, but they do so in relation to others – and it is in these interactions that practice takes form in organizations. Although practice unfolds in the present, it is tied to the past as people draw on a logic that is informed by their past interactions (Bourdieu, 1990, p. 86). While actions are obviously important in understanding practice. interactions are paramount. We see school work practice, as fundamentally about interactions among people, interactions that are mediated by aspects of the situation (Spillane and Diamond, 2007). We can think of at least some of these aspects of the situation as resources.

[…]

Organizational resources: ostensive and performative aspects

We conceptualize organizational structure in terms of resources that enable and constrain practice. A focus on resources has at least two advantages. First, it underscores that organizational structure is dynamic and not necessarily fixed or static. Second, it gives us traction on how that structure can simultaneously be both constitutive of and constituted in practice. Resources enable us to bridge two distinctly different perspectives on how organizations mater in practice and thereby for policy implementation.

As noted earlier, we define resources as a constellation of physical, financial, human, and social assets that people, both individually and collectively, used to accomplish organizalional work. For resources to effect an organization's output they must be available *and* they have to be *recognized* and *used* by *organizational* members. […]

Building on Latour's work (1986) we can think about resources as having two aspects – an ostensive aspect and a performative aspect (see also Feldman and Pentland, 2003). The *ostensive aspect* is the abstract, generalized idea of the resource (Feldman and Pentland, 2003). The ostensive aspect serves as a script for the resource, the resource as designed or intended. The performative aspect refers to the resource in use in particular places and at particular times. It is the performative aspect of a resource that allows for agency as the resource is used, in practice, in particular situations at particular times (Feldman and Pentland, 2003).

Hence, to understand how policy implementation is enabled and constrained by the local organizations we must examine the role that resources play in daily practice in these local organizations. The issue is *how* resources are both constitutive of and constituted in practice. By and large, policy (especially from the policy makers' perspective) centers on the ostensive aspect. However, on the ground it is how people make sense of – notice and understand – the resource, distributed by policy, and use it in practice that is important for policy implementation. Thus to get analytic traction we must attend to both the ostensive and performative aspects of resources and, most importantly, the relations between the two.

Resources do not determine practice. Rather, people draw on resources through which they deploy strategies of action to address issues they face (Swidler, 1986). In this way resources from human capital to organizational routines might be conceptualized as, to borrow Swidler's term, a *tool kit* that does not determine action but instead provides resources for action from which people pick and choose to create desired strategies. Focusing on practice in terms of interactions rather than actions, means that individual choices are dependent in part on those with whom they are interacting. Hence, how resources are configured in practice is critical and these configurations may differ when 'objective' resources are similar or even identical.

While resource distribution is important, resource access and activation are also important (Lin, 2002). An organization may be rich in a particular resource, but *access* to that resource is more or less constrained, depending on where one is situated in the organization. A third issue concerns the activation of resources. By activation here we mean the use of a resource for instrumental purposes – in practice – to attain a particular goal or end. Access to a resource does not guarantee its activation. [...]

Human capital

Human resources refer to individual knowledge, skill, and expertise that are part of the stock of resources available to an organization for doing its work. Human capital involves investing in these human resources in order to improve productivity and thus generate higher returns to the organization (Smith, 1937; Becker, 1964). Improving teachers' or administrators' knowledge about teaching or learning enables them (at least in theory) to practice in new ways, and this new practice can, in turn, improve student achievement either directly or indirectly.

In the education policy world, human capital has received considerable attention, especially in efforts to improve teacher quality (Kane et al., 2007). While there is variation in the estimation of teacher quality, the evidence suggests that students whose teachers are near the top of the quality distribution learn significant amounts more than students whose teachers are near the bottom of the distribution (Rowan et al., 2002). A one standard deviation increase in teacher quality is associated with between one- and three-tenths of a standard deviation in student achievement gains (Rivkin et al., 2005).

Perhaps most troubling from a policy perspective is that the best teachers are unevenly distributed across schools. Work in New York state, for example, shows that teachers in urban schools are less qualified (based on their experience, schooling, certification, and certification test pass rates), and that low-achieving and non-White students tend to be taught by the least qualified teachers (Lankford et al., 2002). Further, teacher effects are much greater in low-socioeconomic state (SES) schools than in high-SES schools (Nye et al., 2004). Still, the evidence suggests that there is substantial within-school variation in teacher quality, even in schools that enroll large numbers of students living in poverty (Rivkin et al., 2005).

Even more troubling from the perspective of schools that enroll poor, minority, and underachieving students is that the racial, achievement, and income composition of the student population in the school contributes to teacher mobility and choice of school as much or more than wages do (Boyd et al., 2005). These 'unplanned' changes are difficult for policy makers to manipulate through public policy. Moreover, these trends in teacher movement have major implications for policy designed to improve student achievement and narrow the achievement gap. Specifically, if schools that serve the lowest performing students are indeed the weakest in terms of the human capital of staff, then these same schools are the least likely to successfully implement policy. Moreover, if work conditions are stronger motivators than monetary rewards, the reach of public policy in transforming the imbalance among schools in human capital distribution may be limited.

[…]

From a policy implementation perspective, human capital – the knowledge and skill of teachers and other local staff used in practice – is critical in that it influences relations between policy and practice in at least two ways. First, what teachers and administrators understand about reforming their existing practice depends in part on their existing knowledge (Hill, 1999; Spillane, 2004). [...] Policy usually implies learning and what we learn depends in part on what we already know (Cohen and Barnes, 1993). Hence, if policy makers want to transform students' opportunities to learn in order to improve their achievement, their success will depend in great part on the human capital of local educators.

As local organizations vary in human capital, the ways that local educators make sense of and implement policy will also vary (Spillane, 2004). The implementation challenge is accentuated by the current patterns of human capital distribution, in which schools and school districts that enroll the most disadvantaged students are least well-endowed with human capital. Many of those schools that policy makers are intent on improving lack the human capital necessary to successfully implement the policies that are designed to improve achievement and narrow the achievement gap.

State and federal policy makers can leverage some change in the ostensive aspect of human capital by attempting to increase the supply of high quality teachers and other professionals through improved preparation and professional development programs. The reach of policy, however, is much more limited with respect to the performative aspect of human capital that is crucial for the success of state and federal policies designed to improve classroom instruction in order to improve student achievement and narrow the achievement gap. Unplanned changes, such as the tendency for highly qualified teachers to migrate to better performing schools and school districts, reduce the human capital available in the poorest performing schools and school districts and thereby undermines the planned changes pressed through public policy.

Social capital

Social capital concerns the relations among individuals in a group or organization (Adler and Kwon, 2002; Coleman, 1988). Developing social capital involves investing in social relations by changing the way people relate with each other in order to achieve particular goals and enhance outcomes of practice. These new ways of relating enable people to do things that would not be possible in the absence of these relations. Social capital is a resource for action (Coleman, 1988).

The evidence suggests that social capital influences policy implementation and school reform in general in a number of ways. First, social capital influences the flow of information within an organization and between organizations. Teachers' collective sense-making from and about policy was shaped by their patterns of interaction – who is talking with whom – and the nature of the conversations.

Social capital is also used to refer to social influence or pressure. Frank and Zhao (2004), for example, in a study of the implementation of technology, argue that the effects of social capital (perceived social pressure, help and talk), though moderate, were as important as the effects of teachers' perceived value of the technology and adequacy of the resources. As Frank and Zhao point out, social capital is a critical consideration in implementation because it leverages human capital – expertise and knowledge.

Social capital is also used to refer to the nature of the relations among organizational members, especially norms and habits of trust and obligation among organization members, and with organizations in their environment. Bryk and Schneider (2002) conceptualize social capital as relational trust and argue that it operates as a resource for school improvement in four ways. First, organizational change involves risks for all participants, as teachers, parents, and principals must engage with changes that they are not certain will work. When relational trust in a school community is strong, the sense of uncertainty and vulnerability is moderated as participants confront the demands of school reform. Second, relational trust improves problem solving in the organization because participants trust one another and are less likely to question the motives behind changes. Third, schools with high levels of relational trust benefit from clear understandings about role responsibilities that are regularly reinforced. Fourth, relational trust adds a moral dimension to improvement efforts by pressing school staff to constantly work to advance the best interests of students. Schools that had stronger base levels of relational trust were more likely to improve than schools with weak base levels of trust. Research on school districts also suggests that social capital is an important resource when it comes to policy implementation (Spillane and Thompson, 1998).

The available evidence suggests that an organization's social capital is an important predictor of policy implementation. Schools and school districts that are better endowed with social capital are better equipped to implement policy. Social capital is not equally distributed among local school systems. For example, schools with stable school communities are likely to have higher levels of relational trust, as it is easier for school professionals to develop and maintain social relationships with students and parents who remain in the school community for an extended period of time (Bryk and Schneider, 2002). Here again unplanned change (e.g. teacher and student mobility) is consequential for the local implementation of policy makers' efforts to forge planned change through public policy.
[…]
Social capital can be instrumental in policy implementation in local organizations, but the extent to which it is will depend in part on the organization's human capital. After all, if the knowledge and skill of organizational members is generally weak, social ties among organizational members will have limited influence in enabling policy implementation. Similarly, the extent to which an organization's human capital enables implementation will

depend on access to and activation of the organization's social capital. For example, the likelihood that the human capital of a handful of expert teachers will be accessed and activated in the cause of implementing a policy school-wide is substantially reduced in a school where social ties are weak and/or these relations lack trust.

Social capital can have negative consequences (Adler and Kwon, 2002). Aspects of social capital such as strong ties and trust among school staff that enable policy implementation in one school can in another school bring staff together to build a coalition in opposition to the policy that undermines its implementation.

A key issue concerns whether district, state, and federal policy can reach into schools to influence social capital distribution, access, and activation. Coburn and Russell (2006) suggest that policy can in fact play a role in influencing some dimensions of teachers' social networks, including tie strength, access to expertise, and depth. Their analysis also suggests that some aspects of teachers' social networks are perhaps beyond policy intervention – social networks are an emergent phenomenon. Finally, while building social ties among organizational members might improve access to social capital it does not guarantee that the social capital will be activated or mobilized in practice to support policy implementation.

Organizational routines

Practice in organizations is structured by organizational routines that are incorporated into daily life through planned and unplanned changes (Cyert and March, 1963). School and district staff often encounter and make sense of state and federal policy through their participation in organizational routines. […]

The design and deployment of organizational routines or redesign of existing routines is another means of leveraging change in local practice (Resnick and Spillane, 2006; Spillane et al., 2007). Policy makers attempt to leverage change directly and indirectly using organizational routines. [They] mandate particular routines and specify more or less the various components that need to be included (i.e. the ostensive aspect of the routine). [They] also work indirectly to change organizational routines in schools through supporting the development of extra-system providers (e.g. Comprehensive School Reform models) and either mandating or providing inducements for schools to adopt these models. Each of these models includes a set of routines and a more or less specified process about implementing the routine with varying degrees of support in the form of coaching and monitoring. Both planned and unplanned change are important considerations with respect to organizational routines.

These efforts at planned change through organizational routines, however, face a number of challenges. Hence, policy makers and school reformers can at best provide broad scripts for organizational routines (i.e. the ostensive aspect), leaving a substantial tacit component that is difficult to codify to be worked out in local practice. Even when these scripts are more specified and accompanied with various tools and supports (e.g. coaching, modeling) to sustain their implementation, much remains tacit. Further, efforts to leverage change in organizations through routines must also contend with unplanned change in organizational routines. Organizational routines often undergo continuous change through experiential learning rather than purposeful design decisions of organizational members (Cohen and Bacdayan, 1996).

The implementation of a routine in practice – the performative aspect – depends in part on an organization's human and social capital. For example, consider the Learning Walk, an organizational routine designed to engage school and district leaders in ongoing conversations about classroom instruction and its improvement (Resnick and Spillane, 2006). In organizations that are rich in social capital the Learning Walk will be more readily taken up compared with organizations that have limited social capital. Further, the fidelity of implementation will depend in important part on the human capital of the walkers. Organizational members can go through the motions of an organizational routine – following each of the prescribed steps to the letter, but lacking the human or social capital, failing to realize the underlying intent or purpose of these steps – the spirit of the organizational routine. While policy can specify the ostensive aspects of routines and develop technologies to help with their implementation in local practice, the reach of policy is much more constrained when it comes to the performative aspect of organizational routines.

Technology and tools

The term *technology* is expansive and can encompass many tools. Organizational members do not act directly on the world nor interact directly with one another. Various tools mediate human interactions in organizations (Barley, 1986). Tools, by virtue of their affordances and constraints, structure interactions in a manner that is constitutive of practice. Tools do more than simply enable organizational members to execute their plans of action more or less efficiently and effectively. Tools can foreground some elements in interactions and background other elements or they change the power relations among organizational members (Barley, 1986; Spillane, 2006). Although this added structure limits the ways in which practice can unfold, tools never constrain practice completely – the same tool in different hands can be used in different ways. It is only *in* practice that the researcher is able to comprehend how tools *constitute* practice (Cole, 1996).

[…]

Organizational routines as designed by policy makers and school reformers are often encapsulated within protocols designed to assist in the execution of the routine. The introduction of new technology has the potential to change practice in planned and/or unplanned or unanticipated ways. [It] can alter institutional roles and patterns of interaction among organizational members – practice – that in turn transform the organizational structure (Barley, 1986).

For the better part of two decades, technology has been a hot topic in the conversations about improving education. As the capabilities of readily available technologies have improved, discussions of their potential utility as a resource to teaching and learning have proliferated. With some notable exceptions (e.g. Blumenfeld et al., 2000), the conversations about education and technology have been tightly focused on how particular technologies or suites of technologies can contribute to the solution of rather tightly construed teaching and learning problems. [...]

While noteworthy, this literature gives little insight into how technology and tools are constitutive of and constituted in work practice in organizations. What is not well understood is how technology unfolds in implementation in schools and school districts as it is understood and put to use in practice. By and large, work focused on technology and its impact on education is not framed within larger organizational contexts and work practice. We believe framing of this sort is critically important to characterize the sustained organizational impact of technology beyond a more circumscribed effect of a classroom or school trial. From a resource deployment perspective, technology, when activated in particular settings, may not fit well into practice and the various configurations of other resources such as human capital and organizational routines. A simple organizational routine like 55-minute class periods can fail to accommodate a new tool. Wenglinsky (1998), in a summary report, suggests that when systemic factors like teacher preparation to use technology are taken into account, the use of computers can be shown to be associated with improvements in student performance. We argued that understanding local contexts necessitates attention to work practice in schools and school districts. When practice is richly accounted for and technologies are designed based on an understanding of practice, new technology is more likely to be taken up in local organizations.

Resources in practice in situ: the case of curricular domains

[The interdependencies among different] organizations and subunits within organizations are critical in understanding the distribution, access to, and activation of resources in practice. For example, a decision by a set of schools or subdistrict in an urban school district to build human capital by firing weak teachers and recruiting high quality teachers through various incentive arrangements can contribute to weakening the human capital in other subdistricts or schools within the school district.

Practice is situated in various ways and the situation or context is an important consideration with respect to resource distribution, access, and activation. The available evidence suggests that the distribution, access, and activation of resources such as human capital and social capital may differ depending on the school subject.

These school subject differences in the distribution of and access to resources in part reflect the broader policy environment. State and federal agencies regulate the different school subjects differently, with mathematics and language arts receiving far more attention than other subjects (Rowan, 2006). Differences across school subject areas are also reflected in the organization and activities of extra-system agencies, including textbook and test publishers, professional associations, and the university sector. Some subject-specific professional networks, for example, are much better organized both locally and nationally than others. When it comes to the distribution of, and access to, key resources such as social capital and human capital, these professional networks can be especially relevant.

Still, we know relatively little about how resources are activated in practice and why activation differs across school subjects. Developing a better understanding of how resources are activated in schools will necessitate closer attention to practice – double interacts, dyadic and triadic interactions – the building blocks of organizing.

[…]

Conclusion

Policy and its implementation is especially a matter of local organizations. Any serious consideration of organizations has to be fundamentally about work practice in organizations. Organizational practice is not simply a matter of individual or organizational behavior; rather the practice policy makers' intend to transform takes shape in the interactions among the people who inhabit these organizations as mediated by key aspects of their situation. Acknowledging the emergent property of practice complicates policy makers' task of bringing about planned change in practice in local organizations where change is a constant. At the same time, thinking systematically about the distribution of, access to, and activation of those resources essential for the performance of practice is suggestive of whether and how policy might matter in changing it.

Public policy is perhaps best understood as a tool for distributing resources for particular instrumental ends and thereby a somewhat blunt instrument. Policy influences work practice in schools, district central offices, and other organizations indirectly through the resources it distributes for particular purposes. It is in the activation of these resources that local practice may change.

References

Adler, P. S. & Kwon, S. K. (2002). Social capital: Prospects for a new concept. *Academy of Management Review*, 27, 17–40.

Barley, S. R. (1986). Technology as an occasion for structuring: Evidence from observations of CT scanners and the social order of radiology departments. *Administrative Science Quarterly*, 31, 78–108.

Becker, G. S. (1964). *Human capital: A theoretical and empirical analysis with special reference to education*. New York: National Bureau of Economic Research.

Berman, P., & McLaughlin, M. W. (1978). *Federal programs supporting educational change. Vol. 8: Implementing and sustaining innovations*. Santa Monica, CA: RAND.

Blumenfeld, P., Fishman, B. J., Krajcik, J., Marx, R. W., & Soloway, E. (2000). Creating usable innovations in systemic reform: Scaling up technology-embedded project-based science in urban schools. *Educational Psychologist*, 35, 149–164.

Bourdieu, P. (1981). Men and machines. In K. Knorr-Cetina & A. V. Cicourel (Eds.), *Advances in social theory and methodology* (pp. 304–317). London: Routledge.

Bourdieu, P. (1990). *The logic of practice* (Trans, R. Nice). Stanford, CA: Stanford University Press. (Original work published in 1980)

Boyd, D., Lankford, H., Loeb, S., & Wyckoff, J. (2005) Explaining the short careers of high achieving teachers in schools with low-performing students. *American Economic Review*, 95, 166–171.

Bryk, A. S., & Schneider, B. L. (2002). *Trust in schools: A core resource for improvement*. New York: Russell Sage Foundation.

Coburn, C. E. & Russell, I. (2006). *Exploring the determinants of teachers' social networks*. Paper presented at the Annual Meeting of the American Sociological Association, Montreal, Canada.

Cohen, D. K., & Barnes, C. A. (1993). Pedagogy and policy. In D. K. Cohen, M. W. McLaughlin, & J. E. Talbert (Eds.), *Teaching for understanding: Challenges for policy and practice* (pp. 207–239). San Francisco: Jossey Bass.

Cohen, M. D., & Bacdayan, P. (1996). Organizational routines are stored as procedural memory: Evidence from a laboratory study. In M. Cohen & L. S. Sproull (Eds.), *Organizational learning* (pp. 403–129). Thousand Oaks. CA: Sage.

Cole, M. (1996). *Cultural psychology: A once and future discipline*. Cambridge, MA: Belknap Press of Harvard University Press.

Coleman, J. S. (1988). Social capital in the creation of human capital. *The American Journal of Sociology*, 94, 895–I20.

Cyert, R. M., & March, J. G. (1963). *A behavioral theory of the firm*. Englewood Cliffs, NJ: Prentice-Hall.

Faulkner, W. (1951). *Requiem for a nun*. New York: Random House.

Feldman, M. S., & Pentland, B. T. (2003). Reconceptualizing organizational routines as a source of flexibility and change. *Administrative Science Quarterly*, 48, 94–121.

Frank, K. A., & Zhao, Y. (2004). Subgroups as a meso-level entity in the social organization of schools. In L. Hedges & B. Schneider (Eds.), *The social organization of schooling* (pp. 279–318). New York: Sage.

Giddens, A. (1979). *Central problems in social theory: Action, structure, and contradiction in social analysis*. Basingstoke, UK: Macmillan.

Giddens, A. (1984) *The constitution of society: Outline of the theory of structuration*. Cambridge, UK: Polity.

Hayton, P., & Spillane, J. (2008). Professional community or communities? School subject matter and elementary school teachers' work environments. In J. MacBeath & Y. C. Chen (Eds.), *Leadership for learning: International perspectives* (pp. 59–71). Rotterdam, Netherlands: SENSE Publishers.

Hill, H. C. (1999). *Implementation networks: Nonstate resources for getting policy done*. Unpublished doctoral dissertation, University of Michigan, Ann Arbor.

Kane, T., Rockoff, J. E., & Staiger, D. O. (2007). What does certification tell us about teacher effectiveness? Evidence from New York City [Electronic version]. *Economics of Education Review*, 27, 615–631.

Kanter, R. M., Stein, B. A., & Jick, T. D. (1992). *The challenge of organizational change: How companies experience it and leaders guide it*. New York: The Free Press.

Lankford, H., Loeb, S., & Wyckoff, J. (2002). Teacher sorting and the plight of urban schools: A descriptive analysis. *Educational Evaluation and Policy Analysis*, 24, 37–62.

Latour, B. (1986). The powers of association. In J. Law (Ed.), *Power, action and belief: A new sociology of knowledge* (pp. 264–280). New York: Routledge.

Lewin, K. (1951). *Field theory in social science: Selected theoretical papers*. New York: Harper and Row.

Lin, N. (2002). *Social capital: a theory of social structure and action*. Cambridge: Cambridge University Press.

Little, J. W. (1993). Professional community in comprehensive high schools: The two worlds of academic and vocational teachers. In J. W. Little & M. W. McLaughlin (Eds.), *Teachers' work: Individuals, colleagues, and contexts* (pp. 137–163). New York: Teachers College Press.

Meyer, J. W., Rowan, B. (1977), Institutionalized organizations: Formal structure as myth and ceremony. *American Journal of Sociology*, 83, 340–363.

Nye, B., Konstantopoulos, S., & Hedges, L. V. (2004). How large are teacher effects? *Educational Evaluation and Policy Analysis*, 26, 237–257.

Poole, M. S. (2004). Central issues in the study of change and innovation. In M. S. Poole & A. H. Van de Ven (Eds.), *Handbook of organizational change and innovation* (pp. 3–31). New York: Oxford University Press.

Purkey, S. C., & Smith, M. S. (1983). Effective schools: A review. *The Elementary School Journal*, 83, 426–132.

Resnick, L. B., & Spillane, J. P. (2006). From individual learning to organizational designs for learning. In L. Verschaffel, F. Duchy, M. Boekaerts, & S. Vosniadou (Eds.), *Instructional psychology: past, present and future trends. Sixteen essays in honor of Erik De Corte* (pp. 259–276). Oxford, UK: Pergamon.

Rivkin, S. G., Hanushek, E. A., & Kain, J. F. (2005). Teachers, schools, and academic achievement. *Econometrica*, 73, 417–458.

Rowan, B. (2006). The school improvement industry in the United States: Why educational change is both pervasive and ineffectual. In H. D. Meyer, & B. Rowan (Eds.), *The new institutionalism in education* (pp. 67–86). Albany: State University of New York Press.

Rowan, B., Correnti, R., & Miller, R. J. (2002). What large-scale survey research tells us about teacher effects on student achievement: Insight from the prospects study of elementary schools, *Teacher College Record*, 104, 1525–1567.

Siskin, L. S. (1994). *Realms of knowledge: Academic departments in secondary schools.* London: Falmer.

Smith, A. (1937). *The wealth of nations.* New York: Modern Library. (Original work published 1776)

Spillane, J., Mesler, L. Croegaert, A., & Sherer Zoltners, J. (2007) *Organizational routines and school level efforts to establish tight coupling: Changing policy, changing work practice?* Unpublished manuscript.

Spillane, J. P. (1998). State policy and the non-monolithic nature of the local school district: Organizational and professional considerations. *American Educational Research Journal*, 35, 33–63.

Spillane, J. P. (2004). *Standards deviation: How schools misunderstand education policy.* Cambridge, MA: Harvard University Press.

Spillane, J. P. (2006). *Distributed leadership.* San Francisco: Jossey-Bass.

Spillane, J. P., & Diamond. J. (Eds.) (2007). *Distributed leadership in practice.* New York: Teachers College Press.

Spillane, J. P., & Thompson, C. L. (1998). *Looking at local districts' capacity for ambitious reform* (CPRE Policy Bulletin). Philadelphia: Consortium for Policy Research in Education.

Stodolsky, S. S., & Grossman, P. L. (1995). The impact of subject matter on curricular activity: An analysis of five academic subjects. *American Educational Research Journal*, 32, 227–249.

Supovitz, J. A. (2007). *The case for district-based reform: Leading, building, and sustaining school improvement.* Cambridge, MA: Harvard Education Press.

Swidler, A. (1986). Culture in action: Symbols and strategies. *American Sociological Review*, 51, 273–286.

Talbert, J., & McLaughlin, M. (1994). Teacher professionalism in local school contexts. *American Journal of Education*, 102, 123–153.

Weick, K. (1979). *The social psychology of organizing* (2nd ed.). New York: McGraw-Hill.

Weglinsky, H. (1998). *Does it compute? The relationship between educational technology and student achievement in mathematics.* Princeton, NJ: Educational Testing Service.

Whittington, R. (1992). Putting Giddens into action: Social systems and managerial agency. *Journal of Management Studies*, 29, 693–712.

10

Contextualizing Leader Dynamics: How Public Service Leaders Endeavour to Build Influence

Mike Wallace and Michael Tomlinson

Leaders make things happen...

Experience, research (Bryman, 2004; Hunter et al., 2007) and theory building (Osborne et al., 2002; Van Wart, 2003) suggest that one leadership context is simultaneously like all other leadership contexts, like some other leadership contexts, and like no other leadership context. Depicting context as 'out there' underplays how leadership is 'situated' (Grint, 2005). Leaders proactively 'read the situation', interpreting their context and mediating it through shaping contextual factors that are manipulable, and feeding back the consequences of their actions into this context (Mowday and Sutton, 1993).

... But things make leaders happen too

Increasing attention is now being accorded to the interpenetration of context and leader activity, foregrounding the 'embeddedness' of leaders in general (Collinson and Grint, 2005; Whittington, 1992) and of 'top' leaders of organizations (Storey, 2005) in particular, within their wider political, economic, social and technological milieu.

Source – An edited version of Wallace, M. and Tomlinson, M. (2010) 'Contextualizing leader dynamics: how public service leaders endeavour to build influence'.

The agency of leaders is delimited by stakeholders who lead them, and by stakeholders they lead. Thus public service leaders are embedded as 'piggies-in-the-middle' (Hoyle and Wallace, 2005) of a state-sponsored, multiple stakeholder-governed, multi-organizational, professionally staffed system (Rainey, 2003). Leaders' vision and practice must comply with parameters imposed by their political masters. [...] [Successive English governments] have prioritized public service reform as means for the quasi-marketization and account-ability regimes of the 'New Public Management' (NPM) pursued by governments across the world (Ferlie et al., 1996, 2003; Hood, 1991). Marketization places an expectation on leaders to be 'entrepreneurs' (Du Gay, 2000) but accountability places an expectation on leaders to ensure their service organizations meet externally imposed targets (Barber, 2007).

Additionally, leaders' agency is variably delimited by the led. Sociological studies of the professions have long pointed to an inherent tension between bureaucratic and professional modes of organizing work (Davies, 1983; Farrell and Morris, 2003). Professionalized staff expect a significant measure of autonomy, and use what professional power they possess to protect it (e.g. Abbott, 1988; Kitchener, 2002; Ferlie et al., 2005). [...] Leaders depend on the acquiescence at least and endorsement at best of other stakeholders affected (Wallace and Pocklington, 2002).

This tension has not been resolved by moves to incorporate professionals into manage-ment (Causer and Exworthy, 1999) and now leadership (Hoyle and Wallace, 2009) under the aegis of new managerialism (Deem et al., 2007), the ideology behind the 'control tech-nologies' of NPM. But whatever public service leaders' mix of professional allegiances, they are still subject to top-down political and bottom-up 'citizen-consumer' pressure (Clarke et al., 2007).

Public service organizations, moreover, do not operate alone. Expanding emphasis on 'joined-up' provision of seamless multiple services entails inter-organizational, and even inter-service collaboration (e.g. Crosby and Bryson, 2005; Huxham and Vangen, 2000; Newman, 2005). Power sharing trades the delimitation of leaders' agency within their own organization, due to increased external influence, against enhancement of their agency – beyond their formal 'span of control' – through gaining influence over other organizations in the collectivity. Thus to be reasonably comprehensive, a contextual orientation should take account of things that make leaders happen (Bolman and Deal, 1991), alongside con-textual factors that leaders can readily – or just possibly – manipulate.

Accordingly, we conceive context as a mixture of factors which leaders generate and shape, and those framing leaders' activity. We construe leaders as both context-creating and context-dependent as they proactively negotiate the more structural aspect of their contexts. They draw on the creative and evolutionary use of agency, acknowledging explicitly or subliminally that it is delimited by identified structural parameters, yet remain unaware of others that may be observed to mould their thoughts and deeds.

[...]

Theorizing context and leader dynamics

Underlying the dynamics of leader activity lies the assumption that leaders can make a positive difference. They may pursue different goals through different means, influencing followers to contribute to selecting these goals and working towards them more or less wholeheartedly. Over time, the consequences of pursuing earlier goals accrue to constitute part of the context, facilitating (or inhibiting) the pursuit of subsequent goals. However, their power to choose goals and means is never unlimited. Not only do the intended or unintended consequences of earlier leader activity recursively form part of the structural order framing the range of later choices. There are also wider structural factors constraining choice possibilities or lying beyond their compass. Giddens (1979, 1984) conceives the workings of agency within structural parameters as a process of *structuration* through which social production and reproduction occurs.

Social systems, including public services, are viewed as patterns of social relations constituted through human agents. Their activity is enabled or constrained by structural properties of the systems that define the rules guiding action and resources empowering it. But rules can be broken, resources redistributed. Since social systems are the product of agency, they can be reworked through it. So the relationship of agency to structural properties of social systems is that of a duality. Each variably implicates the other in a dialectical relationship. It may be more or less agentistic or structurally delimited, but never unhindered or predetermined. There is always some potential for change. Thus while public service organization leaders are piggies-in-the-middle of a system subjecting them to political pressure for reform, they retain sufficient power within the dialectic of control to take their own initiatives and mediate this pressure.

[...]

Burgeoning academic interest in understanding the mobilization and mediation of public service reform resonates with structuration. Mediation at service organization level has been a persistent theme in the analysis of public professionals' shifting identity (Gleeson and Knights, 2006; Newman and Nutley, 2003; Wajcman and Martin, 2004).

The goals pursued by the organization leaders in our illustrative research are affected by the changing political economy surrounding public service reform. Various service sectors have undergone significant restructuring, not least in their relationship with state funding and the private sector (Moran, 2003). Such imperatives, coupled with dominant discourses of the knowledge economy, market-driven reform, global competition and technological change, form a backdrop which public service organization leaders must negotiate. Yet the relative autonomy leaders have affords them significant agency to effect change and shape their organizational context. They may choose fully to embrace economic imperatives, downplay the significance of these imperatives for their organization, or emphasize other goals outside the economic domain, thus making creative use of agency. The organizational context is, however, never divorced from a wider political and economic context that structurally bounds such activity.

In sum, leaders' goal–achievement activity variably shapes some aspects of their immediate context and so generates part of the future context for subsequent activity, while variably being shaped by these and wider structural aspects of context. We conceptualize the agency–structure relationship in terms of intrinsic, complementary dimensions of leader activity: (1) the *atemporal* dimension of leader's agency linked to context manipulability and the specificity of contextual factors concerned; (2) the *dynamic* dimension of cumulative and recursive manipulation of context to expand leaders' influence.

The two linked figures depict these dimensions and their relationship. In Figure 10.1 the arrow symbolizes the atemporal agency–structure dimension. Leaders' relative degree of agency ranges from very high (but never absolute), through moderate (where structural factors become more salient but are still open to the operation of leaders' agency), through very low (where structural factors leave only marginal scope for agency) to non-existent (beyond structural limits where agency is ruled out). The degree of leaders' agency reflects the extent of their capability to manipulate different contextual factors (discussed later), which tend to operate at particular analytic levels. Thus relatively high agency is linked with 'readily manipulable' aspects of the micro-level context. Moving along the agency-structure dimension, the more moderate the degree of agency becomes, and the more contextual factors become only 'possibly manipulable' at the meso-level. As agency becomes relatively low due to encroaching structural delimitation, leaders may be aware of 'marginally manipulable' contextual factors at the macro-level. They retain sufficient agency to influence how these factors impact on their organization. Yet they must nevertheless accept the import of such factors and operate within the limits imposed.

Beyond the structural limits of agency, contextual factors that might be considered hypothetically for manipulation lie beyond leaders' awareness: they are not manipulable because they are 'unthinkable'. Our conceptualization allows for the possibility that the mix of

Degree of leaders' agency and its structural delimitation		Extent to which context is manipulable	Level of analysis	Illustrative range of contextual factors
towards very high agency, very low structural delimitation	↑	readily manipulable	micro	• strategic vision • local initiatives • selective response to policy • allocation of resources • management arrangements
moderate agency, moderate structural delimitation	¦	possibly manipulable	meso	• existing professional culture • local context • relations with intermediaries
towards very low agency, very high structural delimitation	¦	marginally manipulable	macro	• globalization and wider economy • policy climate • social change • technological change
non-existent agency, beyond structural limits	↓	not manipulable (because unthinkable)		• (e.g. operation with potentially unlimited resources available)

Figure 10.1   Linkage between leaders' agency and the manipulability of different contextual factors

Cumulative and Recursive Focus of Context–Leader Dynamic

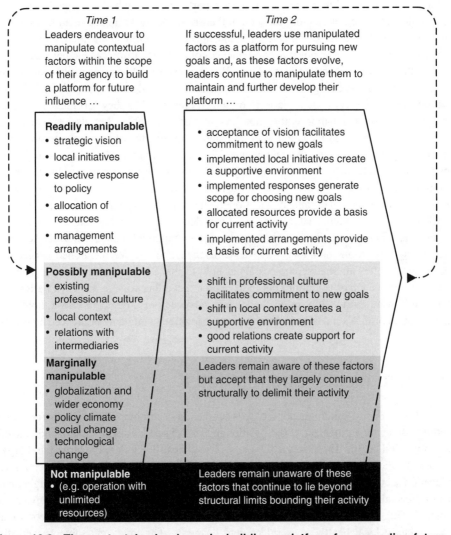

Figure 10.2   The context–leader dynamic: building a platform for expanding future influence

contextual factors which leaders will perceive as highly, possibly or marginally manipulable will vary across micro- to macro- levels, so affecting their *profile* of goals. The illustrative research indicates how there were differences between these profiles among leaders from different public service sectors, reflecting divergence in their sectoral histories.

What may happen over time is brought into the dynamic dimension. In Figure 10.2 time is symbolized as passing from left to right. The first column (Time 1) considers how leaders try to manipulate contextual factors ranging from the readily to possibly manipulable, while being aware of other factors which they perceive as only marginally manipulable. The factors in Figure 10.1 arising from our research exemplify those that may be salient along the agency–structure dimension. Our leaders reported how they had attempted to manipulate particular contextual factors early on in their role. Doing so helped them to create and sustain a receptive context, enhancing their capacity for influencing their colleagues in pursuing future goals. The positive consequences of doing so, from leaders' perspective, are represented by the second column (Time 2). Here each readily to possibly manipulable contextual factor has changed cumulatively as a result of leaders' earlier activity, now constituting part of the contextual platform on which they build as they formulate new goals. The context–leader dynamic is thus not only in part cumulative, but also recursive. Past contextual manipulation feeds into present leader activity, and will continue to do so with the further passage of time. It should be noted that leaders may remain aware of marginally manipulable contextual factors, accepting that at most they may retain a little 'wriggle room' at the micro-level. (Any impact at the macro-level would flow from the aggregate of micro-level responses in organizations throughout this national public service, and beyond.)

Changes in contextual factors may imply leaders' success, enhancing their degree of agency. Yet their manipulative failure could also cumulatively and recursively feed into present activity in an inhibitory way, reducing their agency. We mentioned earlier how leadership implies alternative choices about how to make a positive difference. The outcomes of these choices could turn out to have no effect either way, or a negative effect – as where followers do not 'buy in' to the leaders' advocacy of a strategic vision, holding to their existing professional culture and denying the legitimacy of being influenced by leaders.

Research focus and methods

The data comprise 18 individual interviews conducted in summer 2007 with the incumbent of the most senior formal leadership position in English service sector organizations within education and health. These services were selected because they are the largest and organizationally most complex overall. Within each service we focused on two sectors. The education sectors are public funded secondary schools, and part-public funded higher education, formally more autonomous from government. The health sectors are primary care trusts (PCTs) – created in 2001 as part of central government-driven reform to coordinate and purchase local healthcare services, and hospitals. The interview subjects were five headteachers, five vice-chancellors, four PCT and four hospital chief executives.

[…]

Leaders' accounts of the variable manipulability of contextual factors

Here we portray how the relative degree of agency possessed by our informants from the four public service sectors was reflected in the range of contextual factors they tried to manipulate or perceived to lie outside their jurisdiction. Our account is primarily comparative.

Table 10.1   The pattern of contextual factors mentioned by leaders from different public sectors

	No. leaders mentioning each factor in different public sectors			
Manipulability by leaders of different contextual factors	Secondary schools (5 headteachers)	Universities (5 vice-chancellors)	Primary Care Trusts (4 chief executives)	Hospitals (4 chief executives)
Readily manipulable				
• strategic vision	5	1	0	3
• local initiatives	5	5	4	4
• selective response to policy	5	4	4	4
• allocation of resources	5	5	2	4
• management arrangements	5	4	3	4
Possibly manipulable				
• existing professional culture	3	3	4	4
• local context	4	2	4	3
• relations with intermediaries	5	2	4	4
Marginally manipulable				
• globalization and wider economy	3	3	0	1
• policy climate	4	5	4	4
• social change	5	2	3	2
• technological change	3	1	0	2
Not manipulable – unthinkable	0	0	0	0

Table 10.1 summarizes the proportion of leaders in each sector mentioning the contextual factors in our first three categories. That all referred to readily, possibly and marginally manipulable factors suggests that dealing with variably manipulable aspects of context was a common experience. Yet the most salient factors also differed between sectors, as with strategic vision.

The remaining discussion qualitatively contextualizes these summary figures.

Addressing the readily manipulable

At the high agency end of the atemporal dimension, informants perceived themselves to work within a context which was fluid and readily manipulable, capable of yielding immediate tangible change. The five contextual factors mentioned by most informants across the sectors involved leaders' efforts to orchestrate independent and organizationally initiated changes subject to minimal constraint, which could assist with creating favourable conditions for pursuing educational or healthcare goals:

1. The development of a strategic organizational vision constituting the template for more specific goals, shaping the organizational orientation towards the direction and management of change.
2. The instigation of locally driven, organization-specific changes and refashioning of existing resource and operational structures to facilitate the development of new working arrangements.

3. A selective response to and adaptation of wider policy based on a creative mediation of salient policies to suit leaders' contingent circumstances.
4. The allocation of resources within the organization.
5. The development of organizational management arrangements.

[...]

While there are similarities in leaders' perceptions across sectors, there are also sectoral variations in the degree of manipulability for each factor. They reflect contrasting views about both the salience of and obligation to implement NPM-related reforms. Thus in schools, developing a strategic vision was perceived as an aspect of context where leaders could draw on a very high degree of agency in effecting organization-wide change. Strategic vision was crucial to forming a template which anchored local initiatives and provided a platform for the pursuit of future goals. However, leaders in PCTs possessed only moderately high agency: their scope for visioning and embedding organizational values was constrained by pre-defined and largely state-driven imperatives (see Pollitt, 2007), though they still retained the jurisdiction to introduce initiatives.

Indeed, leaders across all these sectors reportedly enjoyed sufficient autonomy to generate local initiatives and to find creative ways of adapting and appropriating external policy pressures. They perceived this thrust as key to their leadership role, often distinguishing it from the operational tasks of management. University vice-chancellors in particular described their role in agenda setting, shaping local policy frameworks and reshaping existing management arrangements. Such perceptions were premised on the semi-autonomous status of higher education as a part-funded public service, giving vice-chancellors significant jurisdiction to broker change agendas: 'When I came here I thought that ... the university needed to change, and I was of the view that that was also the opinion of the people who appointed me, and in particular the lay members of the university'.

Such convictions were evident in leaders' attempts to mediate government policy according to their professional beliefs and values, indicating that their incorporation into professionalized leadership was far from complete. Many regarded their role as contextualizing external pressures and making them meaningful for other organization members. [...] One [hospital chief executive] had been involved in a merger:

> The two hospitals into one, the work that we've done in changing some of the service, they're all outside government policy. They're in the line of government policy but that's the trick isn't it? How you adapt what you want to see for your organization, describe it in the line of government policy, is the essence of public sector management.

Taking on the possibly manipulable

Here the scope for agency was more moderate, but enough to make the effort of context manipulation worth while. Achieving influence was tougher because contextual factors were at the meso-level, beyond the domain of leaders' authority and so contributing to structural parameters framing their activity. The three contextual factors mentioned were:

1. The existing professional culture to which organization members subscribed.
2. The local context surrounding the organization.
3. Relationships with intermediary organizations.

One [headteacher] perceived that staff allegiance to a change-resistant *professional culture* endemic to state schools was reflected in widespread non-receptivity and even active resistance to change. Yet he saw his task as trying to render this culture more positive through lifting colleagues' morale. He enhanced classroom resources, reduced individual workloads, and invited more staff to participate in decision making.

The headteacher was also proactive in working round constraints imposed by the Local Authority (responsible for supporting schools within its jurisdiction), a key *intermediary organization*. He attempted to by-pass its administrative control wherever possible and to deal directly with central government, which allowed for more institutional autonomy.

The existing professional culture was a factor whose manipulability differed significantly between sectors, depending on how far it impinged on leaders' agency to effect change. Both school and hospital leaders reported negotiating carefully with colleagues over change agendas – particularly middle managers (in the case of hospitals, clinical managers), who were used to working in 'silos' and were more change-resistant, confirming research findings highlighted earlier (e.g. Ferlie et al., 2005) about entrenched professional values and resistance. University and PCT leaders viewed culture as potentially more manipulable. PCT chief executives felt that the novelty of their organizations, created as part of government-driven healthcare reforms, meant that the organizational history was too short to have developed an entrenched professional culture across this new sector.

However, most school leaders perceived a tension between deploying a managerial strategy to effect change and the values and interests associated with long-standing professionalism in their organizations. Similarly, university vice-chancellors perceived the existing professional culture as only partially manipulable because of the long-standing allegiance of academics to their discipline and the continued adherence to collegiality. But they mostly identified with this culture and tried to harness rather than constrain it.

Across all sectors, leaders expressed varying antipathy towards intermediary state agencies which played a significant role in resource allocation, local accountability and local framework setting. In the words of one headteacher:

> The government use Local Authorities as they're a conduit to schools. Because if I was in government I wouldn't want to take the flack if anything goes wrong, and I'd like to have the man in the middle … I sometimes think that Local Authorities are the drag in all this.

Such bodies were viewed as delimiting leaders' agency to embark on service consumer choice and other change agendas, absorbing effort that leaders would prefer to have devoted to other change tasks. Leaders were acutely aware how intermediary body resource allocation policies could facilitate or inhibit the pursuit of their goals.

All chief executives in the PCTs and hospitals implied that their agency was constrained by directives from regulatory intermediary bodies, especially Strategic Health Authorities. PCT leaders perceived a tension between nurturing commitment to the PCTs' health-related goals of providing care speedily to the local population and facilitating these stakeholders' acceptance of change on the one hand, and being constrained by rigid regulatory planning on the other. Their experience reflects the tension within NPM between promoting flexibility alongside top-down mandates, often mediated through intermediary bodies (Farrell and Morris, 2003).

The potential expression of professional power, especially in resisting change agendas that threatened professional interests, was a recurrent theme in leaders' accounts, testifying to [the] enduring strength of 'counterpower' despite the delimiting effects of accountability reforms such as performance management. The need for generating receptive contexts was generally acknowledged, but most forcefully in hospitals where clinical groups and professional managers (consistent with other research previously discussed) played a key mediating role in the generation of change agendas.

Living with the marginally manipulable

Macro-level contextual factors had reshaped service provision through stimulating the government reforms, now forming a structural framework within which organization leaders operated. They could not expect realistically to impact directly on such factors at the macro-level. But these factors were marginally manipulable insofar as leaders could engage with them at the micro-level. Reference was made to four macro-level factors, with frequent acknowledgement of their interrelationship:

1. The shift towards globalization and an increasingly knowledge-based economy, which itself had far-reaching implications for the responses of public service organizations – particularly in the education sectors. Related responses included workforce reform, new skill demands and changing forms of educational credentials and professional development, alongside organizational restructuring and the move towards more flexible and efficient workplaces.
2. Social change including new models of public choice and consumer sovereignty linked to the rise in market plurality.
3. An altered policy climate marked by the spread of quasi-marketization bringing competition into public services. Pressure was increasing on individual organizations to be responsive and accountable to more discerning and active 'consumer-citizens'. Government-driven reforms were designed to raise standards and efficiency and ensure progress through ongoing quality audits and the monitoring of service output.
4. Technological developments including more complex administrative data management arrangements and new virtual learning spaces.

[…]

The responses of leaders from different sectors to the effects of economic change on workforce and in labour market demands contrasted significantly. Leaders in the school and university sectors saw globalized economic change as forming a structural backdrop to their work which was largely impossible to manipulate. Their service provision directly concerned building the capacity of the UK workforce to compete internationally in this new economic environment. Whereas economic imperatives were given strong prominence in the secondary schools sector, social agendas connected to child welfare and personalized learning were also mentioned. They were seen to offer headteachers reasonable scope for mediating the wider policy thrust.

Such external pressure was less salient for their counterparts in PCTs and hospitals. However, the new policy climate was perceived by all hospital leaders as far-reaching. They felt pressured to meet stringent government targets for speed of provision and quality of outcomes, and to comply with related stipulations of the government health department and the various health regulatory bodies. Similarly, several PCT chief executives acknowledged the constraining role of commissioners in slowing their attempts to establish 'world-class' local service provision.

While relatively few leaders from all sectors mentioned technological change as having a major bearing on their activity, they were aware of its impacts on service provision – from on-line learning to more sophisticated health treatments – and used their agency to embrace the new possibilities presented. Living with the marginally manipulable thus had salience for all our leaders. They constituted 'givens' on which some leaders might be able to capitalize at the micro-level.

[…]

Realizing the potential of conceiving context and leadership as interactive

There is more to context than meets the eye of those who regard it as external to leadership. First, the context of leadership was revealed by our conceptualization and data to be partially integral to leader dynamics, consistent with the theoretical thrust to relocate context as both external and internal to the leadership nexus (Collinson, 2005; Grint, 2005). Many aspects of context therefore exist in an evolutionary two-way relationship intrinsic to leader activity while others constitute external structural framing that largely delimits these activities. None of our leaders denied the wider pressures flowing from changes in the global economy, nor did any ignore dominant political pressures for reforming their services. But, crucially, all attempted to work creatively around these structural limits within the parameters of their agency.

Second, the import of contextual factors in our empirical settings was shown to be contingent on both individual organizational characteristics and sectoral history. Comprehending how leaders 'read their situation' (Grint, 2005) entails a sensitivity to those factors that are common to all situations, to some situations (as with the sectoral history), and to no other situation (as with individual organizational features).

Third, common to all sectors were the numerous aspects of context open to manipulation and so to leader activities which are potentially generative: their outcomes may facilitate the cumulative and recursive development of a platform for leaders to expand their influence. Agency implies choice, and today's choices may significantly alter the course of tomorrow's action and contextual factors that evolve as an intended or unintended consequence.

Fourth, by implication, decontextualized theories of leadership are confirmed to be missing something that matters for grasping leader dynamics (and so the more complex nexus of leadership dynamics). An emphasis on engaging with context thus offers greater potential for a nuanced understanding of the contingency of leadership than continuing to pursue universality in the face of accruing evidence of contextual diversity.

Our conceptualization captured in Figures 10.1 and 10.2 offers a heuristic for exploring the complexity and contingency of context through an inclusive, 'both–and' approach. The focus is multi-dimensional, embracing both the variable manipulability of different factors and the dynamic implications of manipulation efforts over time. Our modest ambition here has been to interpret leadership as both context-creating and context-dependent through a limited focus on leader dynamics.

Acknowledgements

The research was supported by the Economic and Social Research Council under grant number RES-000-23-1136. The views expressed in this chapter are those of the authors, and do not represent the view of the ESRC. We are indebted to our informants for enabling us to explore their leader activity in some depth.

References

Abbott, A. (1988) *The System of Professions: An Essay on the Division of Labor*. Chicago, IL: University of Chicago Press.

Barber, M. (2007) *Instruction to Deliver: Tony Blair, Public Services and Achieving Targets*. London: Politicos.

Bolman, L., & Deal, T. (1991) *Reframing Organizations: Artistry, Choice Leadership*. San Francisco, CA: Jossey-Bass.

Bryman, A. (2004) 'Qualitative Research on Leadership: A Critical but Appreciative Review', *The Leadership Quarterly* 15: 729–69.

Causer, G., & Exworthy, M. (1999) 'Professionals as Managers Across the Public Sector', in M. Exworthy & S. Halford (eds) *Professions and the New Managerialism in the Public Sector*, pp. 83–101. Buckingham: Open University Press.

Clarke, J., Newman, J., Smith, N., Vidler, E., & Westmarland, L. (2007) *Creating Citizen-Consumers: Changing Publics and Changing Public Services*. London: Sage.

Collinson, D. (2005) 'Dialectics of Leadership', *Human Relations* 58(11): 1419–42.

Collinson, D., & Grint, K. (2005) 'Editorial: The Leadership Agenda', *Leadership* 1(1): 5–9.

Crosby, B., & Bryson, J. (2005) 'A Leadership Framework for Cross-sector Collaboration', *Public Management Review* 7(2): 177–201.

Davies, C. (1983) 'Professionals in Bureaucracies: The Conflict Thesis Re-visited', in R. Dingwall & P. Lewis (eds), *The Sociology of the Professions*, pp. 177–94. Basingstoke: Macmillan.

Deem, R., Hillyard, S., & Reed, M. (2007) *Knowledge, Higher Education, and the New Managerialism*. Oxford: Oxford University Press.

Du Gay, P. (2000) *In Praise of Bureaucracy*. London: Sage.

Farrell, C., & Morris, J. (2003) 'The Neo-Bureaucratic State: Professionals, Managers and Professional Managers in Schools, General Practices and Social Work', *Organization* 10(1): 129–56.

Ferlie, E., Fitzgerald, L., Wood, M., & Hawkins, C. (2005) 'The Nonspread of Innovations: The Mediating Role of Professionals', *Academy of Management Journal* 48(1): 117–34.

Ferlie, E., Hartley, J., & Martin, S. (2003) 'Changing Public Service Organizations: Current Perspectives and Future Prospects', *British Journal of Management* 14: S1–S14.

Ferlie, E., Pettigrew, A., Ashburner, L., & Fitzgerald, L. (1996) *The New Public Management in Action*. Oxford: Oxford University Press.

Giddens, A. (1979) *Central Problems in Social Theory*. Berkeley, CA: University of California Press.

Giddens, A. (1984) *The Constitution of Society*. Cambridge: Polity Press.

Gleeson, D., & Knights, D. (2006) 'Challenging Dualism: Public Professionalism in "Troubled Times"', *Sociology* 40(2): 277–95.

Grint, K. (2005) 'Problems, Problems, Problems: The Social Construction of Leadership', *Human Relations* 58(11): 1467–94.

Hood, C. (1991) 'A Public Management for all Seasons', *Public Administration* 69 (spring): 3–19.

Hoyle, E., & Wallace, M. (2005) *Educational Leadership: Ambiguity, Professionals and Managerialism*. London: Sage.

Hoyle, E., & Wallace, M. (2009) 'Leadership for Professional Practice', in S. Gewirtz, P. Mahony, I. Hextall & A. Cribb (eds) *Changing Teacher Professionalism*, pp. 204–14. London: Routledge.

Hunter, S., Bedell-Avers, K., & Mumford, M. (2007) 'The Typical Leadership Study: Assumptions, Implications, and Potential Remedies', *Leadership Quarterly* 18: 435–46.

Huxham, C., & Vangen, S. (2000) 'Leadership in the Shaping and Implementation of Collaboration Agendas: How Things Happen in a (Not Quite) Joined up World', *Academy of Management Journal* 43(6): 1159–75.

Kitchener, M. (2002) 'Mobilizing the Logic of Managerialism in Professional Fields: The Case of Academic Health Center Mergers', *Organization Studies* 23(3): 391–420.

Moran, M. (2003) *The British Regulatory State*. Oxford: Oxford University Press.

Mowday, R., & Sutton, R. (1993) 'Organizational Behaviour: Linking Individuals and Groups to Organizational Context', *Annual Review of Psychology* 44: 195–220.

Newman, J. (2005) 'Enter the Transformational Leader: Network Governance and the Micro-politics of Modernization', *Sociology* 39(4): 717–34.

Newman, J., & Nutley, S. (2003) 'Transforming the Probation Service: "What Works", Organizational Change and Professional Identity', *Policy and Politics* 31(4): 547–63.

Osborne, R., Hunt, J., & Jauch, L. (2002) 'Towards a Contextual Theory of Leadership', *The Leadership Quarterly* 13(6): 797–837.

Pollitt, C. (2007) 'New Labour's Re-disorganization: Hyper-modernism and the Costs of Reform – a Cautionary Tale', *Public Management Review* 9(4): 529–43.

Rainey, H. (2003) *Understanding and Managing Pubic Organizations*. San Francisco, CA: Jossey-Bass.

Storey, J. (2005) 'What Next for Strategic-level Leadership Research?', *Leadership* 1(1): 89–104.

Van Wart, M. (2003) 'Public-sector Leadership Theory: An Assessment', *Public Administration Review* 63(2): 214–28.

Wajcman, J., & Martin, B. (2004) 'Markets, Contingency and Preferences: Contemporary Managers'
    Narrative Identities', *Sociological Review* 52(2): 240–62.
Wallace, M., & Pocklington, K. (2002) *Managing Complex Educational Change: Large Scale
    Reorganization of Schools*. London: RoutledgeFalmer.
Whittington, R. (1992) 'Putting Giddens into Action: Social Systems and Managerial Agency',
    Journal of Management Studies 29(6): 693–713.

11

Stories of Compliance and Subversion in a Prescriptive Policy Environment

John MacBeath

The 12 English headteachers, six primary, six secondary, whose interviews are the source of this chapter, had all signed up to The Learning How to Learn Project.[1] [...]

Interviews with the headteachers were structured around their learning agenda at pupil, teacher and organizational levels, setting these within the current policy context. [...]

In examining the [interview] transcripts reference to external authorities was chosen as a focus for specific analysis, identifying ways in which headteachers located themselves and their schools in relation to those authorities – to DfES and Ofsted[2] as main points of external reference. The following discussion is based on close reading and re-reading of these texts, systematic analysis of key recurring ideas, identifying references to external bodies and the way in which these were contextualized within the narrative. The problematization of policy development or the absence of such critique proved to be salient aspects of these narratives.

Policy environment

In all these 12 narratives an embedded theme is the relationship of school practice to the policy environment in which these heads found themselves. Light is thrown on government policy but constructed variously among this group of 12 school leaders. Two markedly differing accounts of policy and how it impacts on practice provide the extremes of a continuum, at one end depicted as a positive force for change and highly influential in supporting and improving practice while the polar opposite view describes a government

Source – An edited version of MacBeath, J. (2008) 'Stories of compliance and subversion in a prescriptive policy environment'.

imposing dysfunctional strategies on schools, deskilling and disempowering teachers' practice. These two polar positions, both from primary school headteachers, serve as a frame for the more nuanced or ambivalent narratives which fall between these two extremes.

Policy environment as supportive

The following is a distillation of one headteacher's perception of the policy environment:

> The policy environment is one that has helped to move schools on, to challenge uninformed or simply sloppy practice. It has given teachers something tangible to go on. The Literacy and Numeracy Strategies[3] provide models that work. 'It's the first time we've been given anything to go on'. 'It was brilliant to be told what to do'. The three/four part lesson with starter, input, work, plenary has been most helpful in lending pace and variety to lessons. Good ideas and innovative techniques for teachers have succeeded in engaging pupils more actively in their own learning. By providing teachers with tools to use, National Strategies have provided support for weaker teachers. They have encouraged a rigorous approach to teaching and learning. They have focused teachers' attention on outcomes and given an emphasis to targets and target setting. Ofsted too has played its part in making a contribution, affirming good practice, spotlighting areas for development and providing key areas for focus in improving quality and standards. (Headteacher secondary school B)

Policy environment as oppressive

The following offers an alternative construction of the policy environment:

> The policy dictat is so tight that to survive and do what is important for staff and children one has to be subversive. The policies are both over prescriptive and condescending, deskilling rather than empowering teachers. Richness and creativity are lost by formulaic prescription. The literacy strategy is so superficial we have to take risks in order to free up teachers to take back ownership of teaching and learning. After teachers have gone through the training and jumped through the hoops we help them 'to go wild', while recognising that for their own career promotion needs, in other places they have to be astute in knowing when to toe the line and play the game for inspection purposes. However, 'if people would get off our backs just a little the learning could just rocket because children and people in the schools were doing what they wanted to do and passionately believed in'. We try to help staff to 'fly', to go the way they want rather than having to feel the burden of having a master outside the school. (Headteacher primary school L)

The contrast between these two depictions of policy may be characterized using Perkins' (2003) notions of 'taming the wild' and 'wilding the tame'. In the first of these narratives the wild is tamed by clear targets, predetermined outcomes and focusing of teachers' attention on templates of good practice. 'Being told what to do', as in the first narrative, provides a sense of comfort and security and affirmation by the authority of Ofsted, reassuring staff that practice falls within the bounds of government mandates. Pace and variety in lessons is injected to engage pupils more actively with the task at hand with the formula of the three/four part lesson as a containment, thwarting diversions and offering support and clear direction for weaker teachers. Taken together these routines are seen as provide the rigour that was previously seen to be missing.

'Wilding the tame' suggests a recognition of domestication and a conscious attempt to loosen the ties that bind teachers to mandated practice. This is explicitly stated in the process of learning to jump through the hoops before 'going wild'. Another metaphor is of shedding the burden so that teachers are able to fly on their own. The term 'empowerment' is used to convey a sense of agency, the rediscovery of richness and creativity in learning and teaching and of reinstatement of professional self-confidence. This is depicted as 'risk' because of its non-compliance with mandated practice, but at the same time recognising the nature of the political 'game' which allows teachers to meet expectations of Ofsted when required. While in the first narrative the locus of change is attributed to external influences, in the second narrative there is explicit reference to leadership (the 'we') in helping teachers to go wild.

The difference between a healthy and an unhealthy organization, argue Senge et al. (2004: 32), lies in members' awareness and ability to acknowledge their 'felt needs to conform' and their ability to challenge their habits of seeing and responding to external pressures. How the policy environment is described is as much a reflection of a school's stage of development, of a particular headteacher's construction at a given time or revealing of a more deep-seated conception of the school policy interface. Nor are these polar positions as crisp and static as these archetypes suggest. As becomes clear through the analysis of these texts, they conceal a deeper struggle for leadership in navigating the path between compliance and subversion.

The implication for leadership is to know what stance is appropriate at a given time and in relation to specific policy movements. Giroux's (1992) counsel is to be alert to the 'omniscient narrator', the authority who speaks on your behalf. There is no grand narrative that can speak for us all, he argues, and therefore professional educators must take responsibility for the knowledge they organize, produce, mediate and translate into practice. If not there is a danger that they come to be seen as simply the technical intervening medium through which knowledge is transmitted to students, erasing themselves in an uncritical reproduction of received wisdom. Rather than internalising the master narratives, Giroux suggests, the task of leadership is to examine how these narratives become constructed, what they mean, how they regulate our social and moral experience, how they presuppose particular views of the world and pre-empt debate as to what is worthy of attention.

Setting the school in context

We are offered a glimpse of how these headteachers view the policy world in their response to the researcher's invitation to set the school in context. How heads choose to describe the salient features of their schools provides a clue to how they validate their own practice in relation to external pressures. On the one hand their accounts may be constructed predominantly with reference to the external validation of success, or with a more inward focus in which there is validation of the school's own criteria of success. For example, in one transcript a secondary headteacher gives an extended account of his school's success referring exclusively to the school's normative standing in performance tables and the validation of practice by the most recent Ofsted report. By contrast, another secondary head working in a similar urban environment chooses to tell the story in terms of the challenges in putting learning and teaching centre stage and creating a professional development culture. In the course of her lengthy introduction to the school neither Ofsted nor GCSE attainment scores are cited. Validation of the school's progress is by reference to students' and teachers' evaluation of important priorities and through her own efforts as a school leader to create the kind of environment for learning which she values.

These two heads, in common with the ten others in this sample, describe their efforts to put learning centre stage, acknowledging the tensions in trying to accommodate a concern for the 'how' of student learning within a drive for raised achievement. All of them refer to the impact of Key Stage Strategies, to changing lesson structures, to external pressure and accountability. Their approaches to assessment of achievement appear to be broadly similar but it is in the degree of embrace of government policies or a critical distancing from them that differences among these 12 schools begin to emerge most saliently.

[…]

Learning journey

The journey is a much used metaphor in relation to learning and progress. It is construed as one undertaken more in expectation than hope. That is, the destination is clearly understood by the pupil as the next 'level' or the next handhold on the climbing frame:

> I want them to be level three by the end of year one, you know, it's checking that sort of progress and getting them to want to improve the journey together. (Headteacher primary school J)

There is a broad consensus that students are increasingly internalising that frame of reference and able to articulate their journey in terms of baselines and targets:

> I think they are able to say, 'this is where I want to be', 'this is where I think I am. There's where I want to be and this is what I need to get there' I think they're clever at doing that too. And I suppose the fact that we put letters and numbers with it merely makes it refined and comprehensible rather than the airy-fairy way I would have of assessing people. (Headteacher primary school J)

The journey towards agreed targets is from one level to the next, a model that now appears to be deeply embedded in teachers' thinking about learning. The extent to which these permeate practice is illustrated by one secondary head:

> I should be able to go into a classroom, I should be able to ask the child what level they're working at and I should be able to ask what level or what they have to do to improve from that level. (Headteacher secondary school B)

There is a kind of religious tenor to a statement by one headteacher, referring to 'picking up children who have lapsed', conveying an image of 'backsliding' or losing the faith.

Targets and levels combine to provide the 'road map' and are made explicit and visible on classroom walls, stamped on front of books and sometimes on each piece of work, or portrayed on posters on the walls. Targets are often reviewed at the start of lessons, reinforced and highlighted at every opportunity. While the intensity and visibility of targets and levels differs among the 12 schools, in all of them it is a preoccupying concern. Targets have, as one primary head says, 'become a topic of endless discussions'. This appears to reflect a fairly wide agreement that pupils need to know the level they are working at and that parents too should be equally informed and take part in the target-setting process.

There is also one dissenting voice among the 12. One primary headteacher argues against this as a form of labelling and as a self-fulfilling prophecy, which she sees as lending itself to a purely instrumental approach to learning:

> I try very hard not to let the children know what their actual level is. I want them to know where they are and what they want to do to improve but I don't want them to get a handle on what level they are because that has lots of baggage with it and they go home to their parents and say, 'I'm a level three' and then, you know, there's the inevitable, the pressure on them that they need to do, you know, they need to be a level four or they want level five so they'll go in the top class of secondary school. (Headteacher primary school J)

While this head tries to dissuade staff from sharing levels with pupils, she is aware that it creates a tension with a policy of openness and transparency and parental partnerships where informed parents are anxious to know their children's stage or level of progress. This headteacher, who has a commitment to assessment for learning as an integral aspect of a Learning How to Learn Project, is aware of the difficulty in recasting parental expectations.

The challenge for leadership is to work with the paradox of a closer collaborative relationship with parents, providing the security of summative assessments while at the same time trying to undo the successful embedding of marks and grades, a commitment to which has over time penetrated deep into the affections of parents.

[...]

Learning and teaching

There is, running through the conversations, a conflation of the language of learning evidenced in the frequent references to 'teachingandlearning' as one single conjoined concept, particularly when referring to strategy as in 'teaching and learning strategies'. The language of teaching appears at times to be confused with that of learning, and references made in the context of a discussion about learning frequently tend to refer more to what the teacher is doing or to teacher intention rather than to student activity or intention. Occasionally this results in an awkward straddling of two distinct and inherently conflicting ideas.

> I think we're aiming to enable every individual student to maximise their potential, to be challenged, to be stimulated, to produce learning outcomes for themselves. (Headteacher secondary school E)

This is exemplary of a statement that appears on the surface to be about learning but in its language of outcomes betrays a more school-centred frame of reference. It may be nothing more than a child-centred view which, it is felt, needs to be dressed up, ill-fittingly, to conform to a dominant political discourse. The following is a further example of a conceptual slide from a child-centred view to a teaching strategy.

> The children are partners in that enterprise [learning] and a whole range of strategies for keeping everybody on task. (Headteacher primary school H)

Equally difficult to reconcile is the student taking responsibility while the teacher is 'in control of the learning'.

> [Students] taking the responsibility for themselves, the way they manage themselves in the school. So we're not now talking about the teacher being in control of the child in the same way but they [teachers] are still in control of the learning. (Headteacher secondary school B)

It may be inferred from these comments that headteachers are struggling with a cognitive resolution between a learning-centred or 'personalized' agenda, on the one hand, and a highly prescriptive set of teaching strategies on the other. There is an implicit, and sometimes explicit, recognition that teaching and learning strategies have to be contextualized within a curriculum and assessment framework, the rationale of which is not derived from individual learning needs but from a body of conventional wisdom as to what knowledge is of most worth, and reinforced by strong coalitions of interest in maintaining subject status. Strategies which attempt to be learner-centred have to work from a set of logistical givens about the structure of the school day, week and year, so that references to 'pace', variety, beginnings of lesson, time on task, all refer to extracting the maximum learning returns from 'lessons', tightly structured in order to cover the ground with maximal efficiency. [...]

Lessons are framed by objectives at the outset and review of objectives achieved at the lesson's end, and the approach is consistent across the school.

> A consistent approach to teaching, all teachers make sure they tell the children the learning objectives for each lesson, all the teachers link to the planning, the planning's linked to assessment. There's a very consistent approach throughout the school, and all staff follow the policy and the ethos of the school. (Headteacher primary school G)

Consistency is a key word that runs through the pages of these transcripts. 'Enlightened policies are uniformly implemented by all teachers', claims one secondary head while another uses the word 'consistency' 24 times in the course of the interview. Its importance is reiterated with regard to Key Stage Three, with regard to independent learning, study skills, homeworking policy, training areas, 'across colleagues', in the use of LSAs (Learning Support Assistants) and with reference to parents.

> We need to achieve that consistency across all those subjects so a parent would know that a level five in English means the same thing in subject-specific terms, a level five in maths or music or whatever. (Headteacher secondary school B)

The prevalence of this theme offers a sharp contrast with the absence of terms such as dialogue, dissent, disagreement, or conflict. Conflict is mentioned only in relation to children, or in one case as a management style that heads off potential conflict. Dissent is not in the lexicon of policy and improvement. 'Dialogue' is mentioned in four interviews, in each case referring to an instrumental use – between teacher and pupil in order to set targets, in communication with parents, 'open dialogue' following classroom observation and 'professional dialogue' as integral to appraisal.

While there is a wide scale adoption of a new government discourse, and a generally high level embrace of National Strategies there is at the same time a critical distancing and accompanying critique. Pace, for example, as dictated by the teacher's agenda is seen as in conflict with the emphasis on thinking, or 'wait' time.

> I don't think we give them enough thinking time either, because of the pace we've been pushed so hard on pace of lessons, that before you know what's happened, you've not given them any thinking time at all. (Headteacher secondary school A)

A much stronger statement comes from a primary head who, having implemented the Strategies, is highly critical of their effects on learning.

> The literacy came in and it was just unbelievable, the formality of the lessons and I found that … well, I just felt that it was obscene, the, way we were expected to teach literacy. In fact, it just made literacy die a death in my opinion. The excitement was out of it. (Headteacher primary school J)

Another critique is of what a head describes as 'the do it by numbers rationale', claiming that it had 'stopped teachers thinking'. Yet another primary head talks of 'the need for a breather to get away from the routine of literacy'. The Literacy and Numeracy Strategies, says another, have encouraged a culture of 'tell me what to do and I'll do it', pushing people too fast, not allowing time to grow or assume ownership.

> [It is] not helpful for teachers' own self-esteem because their teaching styles and their teaching repertoire have been challenged in a way which has not enabled them to feel they have any part in it, they have no ownership of it. (Headteacher primary school L)

Compliance with Government imperatives has entailed 'ducking and weaving' one's way through the 'narrow' demands of curriculum, striving for the enrichment of the 'wider' curriculum and 'widest' possible opportunities for learning. The vocabulary of 'narrow' and 'wide' are deeply embedded in a discourse of achievement which sets in opposition the pressures for attainment of competitive targets and the more person-centred mission of the school. The words 'passion' and 'excitement', which occur within the learning conversation, sit alongside the embrace of the three/four part lesson and a grateful endorsement of Ofsted, resulting in a curiously ambivalent set of implicit theories.

Ofsted 'warrant'

All heads make unprompted references to Ofsted in the course of the interview. [...]

In one secondary school Ofsted was cited 21 times in the course of the interview, testimony to the extent to which the Ofsted approach to evaluating teaching had been internalized by the school. To an English observer or insider this may be seen as commonplace and unsurprising, so deeply is this now embedded in school and national culture. It is only when seen through the eyes of visitors from other countries that the depth of impact of Ofsted in the lives of schools and headteachers becomes conspicuously apparent.

[...]

The headteachers' relationship with Ofsted is one replete with paradox. Its endorsement is highly valued and made public. There is an apparently enthusiastic embrace of much that Ofsted has to offer by way of direction and templates, and inspectors' observations often serve to strengthen the headteacher's hand. There is also a hint of strategic manoeuvring, as described by this secondary head.

> From a head's point of view, you're wanting obviously to get a good relationship with your Ofsted team because it's actually the essential thing. You learn this, that it is a key thing. (Headteacher secondary school D)

He adds by way of self-revelation:

> Talking to this guy he said, 'Well, of course, a school like yours, I'm going to give you a real high-powered team'. And I sat down and I said, 'Oh good' where I was really thinking, 'Oh bugger!' You know, can't I have some thick ones who will just do what I tell them.

There are also frequent allusions to playing the game. Any latitude within the three/four part lesson is set aside for inspection purposes. One primary head talks about the 'tightening up' of the lesson which excludes the normal routine of listening to pupils who come with stories and are eager to relate their experiences. The use of the word 'slippage' is highly significant in signalling the teacher agenda as against a more pupil-centred classroom ethos.

> When Ofsted did come in, the slippage, which they call it, was tightened up because we're all able to do that. It doesn't matter on some occasions. You don't have to teach the minute they [the pupils] come in because sometimes there are desperately important things that they have to tell you. (Headteacher primary school J)

This head adds '[human behaviour] that is not allowed. Not during Ofsted week'. Again, resistance to the idea of being 'hide bound' is conveyed in this contrast between what teachers would normally do and what they would do for an inspection team.

> I don't like having it laid down and to be honest, unless it's Ofsted, you're not that hide-bound by it. There is room to put in a bit of interest if you want to and something else. During Ofsted, probably not. (Headteacher primary school H)

The strength of compliance from headteachers contrasts markedly with the sense of authority and conviction that these heads express in the context of their own schools. To stand up for yourself in an Ofsted context appears to require an extra measure of strength and confidence.

> You have to be very strong. You have to be confident enough to say this is where we are, this is where we know we need to go and we will take that in our time and in our own way to advisors and to Ofsted. (Headteacher secondary school D)

[…]

Leadership and management

While leadership was not explicitly addressed in discussions of culture, nor talked about as a key interview theme, leadership styles and values permeate almost every aspect of the discussion. There is a clear and consistent message that headteachers set the vision and culture of the school and that schools carry the imprint of those personal or professional values. One secondary head reflects this widely held view when he says, 'You wouldn't be a headteacher unless you had a very strong philosophy yourself, unless you had a very strong vision of what a school would be about'. Sometimes the values are alluded to apologetically as having 'a bee in my bonnet', without appeal to evidence or to higher authority.

Most heads make a distinction between what is and isn't negotiable. By virtue of their office, heads have the freedom to decide, or impose, ways of working. Ownership of core principles or practices is explicitly seen by one headteacher as lying with the senior team and not the staff.

> So there's a few core things that come from me and the senior team that they're not for ownership, they are and if you don't submit to that, it's not really a place to work. (Headteacher secondary school A)

At its most extreme it takes the form of what Maccoby (2001) terms 'narcissistic leadership' in which 'self' is conspicuously centre stage in the transcript. The following are a few examples from an interview in which the use of 'I', 'me' and 'myself' was the continuous strand in describing policy development within the school:

This policy has got a lot of me in it. It's largely me.

That wasn't from the staff. That was from myself.

It comes from me, an awful lot of it comes from me.

The policy has got a lot of me in it. It's largely me.

It was quite brutal. It was tough. It was me. (Headteacher secondary school D)

The use of words like 'tough' and 'brutal' are one expression of what is widely referred to as 'strong' leadership. It encapsulates ideas of sticking to your own principles, raising the stakes, creating willing followership. One secondary head describes having to 'force' ideas on to his colleagues, involving 'battles' to get people to accept his plans for the school.

This tough stance tends by most heads to be seen as applying in the early stages of head-ship when the challenge is to get everyone on board and moving in the same direction. The balance of command, consultation and consensus is conceived as one that changes over time as vision and direction are established and key principles become embedded in practice.

On my arrival here it was the case and I think within the first six months we had a new assessment policy. I think that wasn't something that I consulted on. I was fairly dictatorial on that. (Headteacher secondary school C)

'Stepping back' from a more directive mode and adopting a lower profile is seen as pos-sible once the school has moved towards a more collegial non-hieraichical culture, one in which people feel empowered to take initiative for themselves, to both lead and follow their colleagues.

What I'm now trying to do is step back and let different things run. And that does seem to be working. So that's what I see as a learning organization. People take the initiative in a non-hierarchical way, people reflect on what they're doing, they share that practice. (Headteacher secondary school C)

There is, none the less, a sense of tension among heads between their own driving values and a desire for ownership and empowerment on the part of staff. This ambivalence is explicitly conveyed by a secondary head who talks of empowering people to arrive at the right decisions.

… process is the empowering of people and as you empower them they will then be making that decision, having that input within the school, knowing that they're doing it within what we agreed is important for the school. (Headteacher primary school K)

In some cases there is a more honest and forthright acknowledgement of this process as manipulation. The word 'forcing' in the following statement is in uneasy juxtaposition with the implied ownership:

I think teachers have got to feel that they're making decisions but what I suppose I'm forcing them to do is making those decisions. (Headteacher secondary school D)

As in this case, a 'strong' directive leadership style can be dressed up as consultation, and what makes for genuine consultation among equals becomes hard to discern. One secondary head claims that 'The staff write the policies. I don't write the policy, they're not written by me, they're written by them'. The next statement by this head, however, contains an ambiguity which is picked up by the interviewer:

> They [policies] weren't imposed, they were negotiated and people were challenged in their thinking so that they would look to see what it is that we felt were important issues about the school.
>
> Interviewer: Who were 'we' at that point? When you say 'we' …
>
> Head: Well, that would be very much, I think, the management within the school. (Headteacher primary school K)

The 'we' is a contentious area in building a genuine learning community and while trying to include, or 'move', all staff toward a common goal there is recognition of the disparate attitudes, values and motivation that comprise a professional body. Schratz (2001) characterizes a school, or perhaps any organization, as containing missionaries, true believers, lip servers, spectators, underground workers, outright opponents and emigrants, distributing themselves along a spectrum, according to the degree to which they 'buy into' the vision and mission of the school, with varying degrees of enthusiasm.

In schools which do encompass a range of motivations the change strategy, as defined by a number of these heads, is to invest efforts at the fertile end of the attitudinal spectrum (the missionaries and true believers) where you can expect high returns for minimal investment. 'You play to your winners', says one secondary head. The view that 'other people will respond to what they're seeing going on around them' suggests an implicit theory of epidemiological change (Gladwell, 2000; Hargreaves, 2004) in which interesting or 'breakthrough' practice spreads and reaches a tipping point. The strategy includes an encouragement to leave for those who don't fit, or can't adjust to the changing culture, replacing them with carefully selected true believers, in tune with the school's, or perhaps more accurately, the head's, vision.

One head whose school is highly successful in terms of its GCSE results and Ofsted report, ascribes his success to a highly directive style of leadership, aggressive recruiting of quality staff and incentive policies to both attract and retain them.

> I suppose fundamentally I think people make things happen and people are what the school's about and I think I know very quickly when I meet people whether they're people I want here that will make a difference or make it exceptional. (Headteacher secondary school A)

There are references to 'the thinkers', 'the innovators', the change agents', the 'champions' whom heads rely on and 'use' to foster a climate of change. These people may have no formal status, 'without portfolio', but more commonly they occupy a middle leadership role. In secondary schools departmental heads or departments as a whole are seen as spearheading change. The leading edge departments, or 'those at the sharp end' tend to be seen as those which have been involved most centrally in the National Strategies, offering a core of changed practice and modelling which extends outward to other departments.

In contrast to the departmental focus, and in some cases complementary to it, are cross-department groups or working parties devising policies, testing ideas and feeding back to senior leadership. These may take the form of teaching and learning groups, for example, designed to include staff with differing strengths or groups with specific functions, such as professional development, and include members of staff with no formal status – newly qualified teachers, for example. While these accounts contain a hint of a welcome for diversity and challenge to the everyday practice, the latitude for dissent or radical reappraisal of mainstream orthodoxy remains a more open question.

Conclusion

The clearest message to emerge from these 12 extended interviews is the success of government policies in leaving a depth of imprint on school practice and shaping the discourse which accompanies it. The success of National Strategies is vouchsafed by the compliance of headteachers, for the most part willingly, and by the imprimatur of Ofsted inspection. There is, at the same time, an accompanying critique of the formulaic nature of aspects of the Strategies. There is dissatisfaction with assessment measures such as SATS and a more general depiction of Ofsted inspection as an occasion for strategic conformity. Yet, from an ethnographic perspective, the lack of challenge offered to external authorities is striking and hard to reconcile with the authority and conviction of these heads as powerfully influential within their own schools.

There is a strong sense of a new orthodoxy running through these accounts. It reveals itself in an almost uniform view of learning, bearing the hallmark of brain-based theories of learning styles and multiple intelligences which, while widely endorsed, is contained uncomfortably with highly structured lesson units in which 'delivery' is a predominant metaphor. At the same time there is an almost complete absence of critical reflection on the embrace and advocacy of learning styles (see, for example, Coffield et al., 2004; White, 2004), while the all-consuming nature of targets and levels conveys a ruthlessly cumulative image of learning in which any deviation or distraction from the journey to curricular goals is to be eschewed.

All heads agree on the importance of a culture of learning and use every opportunity to reinforce the message. Peer observation, often across subject boundaries, is the mechanism by which the dialogue around learning is fostered, yet the conversations tend to betray a more teaching focused perspective. Use of the Ofsted model focuses observation on what the teacher is doing and the normative scale to evaluate teaching tends to close down rather than open up a more critical discourse.

The apotheosis of a learning culture is portrayed as a consensual one. Intellectual bonding appears to follow on the heels of social bonding and one has a sense of the individual being buried under the weight of the policy and beneath the pressure for a uniformity of practice. A sense of agency on the part of teachers is hard to detect and even the strong sense of agency among the heads appears to be contingent on policy direction. The apparent lack of room for dissent risks locking schools into what Argyris and Schön (1978) call single loop learning – a continuous loop of defined objectives, planning, implementation and evaluation. The 'double loop', apparent in glimpses in these narratives, is one which provides space to stand back outside of that process, inviting critique, dissent and even subversion of orthodoxy. 'Organizations require a minimal degree of consensus but not so much as to stifle the discussion that is the lifeblood of innovation' write Evans and Genady (1999: 368), arguing that the constant challenge of contrasting ideas is what sustains and renews organizations.

Schools that play safe, driven by external mandates, set tight parameters around what can be said and what can be heard. Such schools are antithetical to the notion of a learning organization which, by definition, is always challenging its own premises and ways of being. For Evans and Genady organizational effectiveness is inherently paradoxical. It is dynamically balanced between control and flexibility, internal and external focus, by the tensions between means and ends. There is freedom to break rules because the culture is resilient enough to learn from it. Their (1999: 369) aphorism 'organize one way and manage another' implies that the greater the external pressure and the tighter the hierarchical constraints the greater the need for flexibility, diversification and agency.

The paradox of agency is that in a context of a top-down cascade of government initiatives, reaffirmation of teachers' experience is paramount. It is the prime source of knowledge on which a learning organization both rests and moves forward (Senge, 1990, Senge et al., 2004; Boreham and Morgan, 2004). However great the constraints of organizational structures, resource provision and political imperatives, individual agency means that teachers are not only in control of their own practice but able to exert their influence on the very structures which contain them. In Giddens' (1984: 5) terminology it may be described as a dynamic co-construction of change, driven internally by 'a continuing theoretical understanding of the ground of their activity'. Beane and Apple (1999: 7) offer three critical conditions for democratic schools:

- The open flow of ideas, regardless of their popularity, that enables people to be as fully informed as possible.
- Faith in the individual and collective capacity of people to create possibilities for resolving problems.
- The use of critical reflection and analysis to evaluate ideas, problems, and policies.

The 12 schools of this study may be described in Ofsted terminology as 'well led'. The vision and enthusiasm of these senior leaders shines through the transcripts. The words 'passion' and 'excitement' reoccur and there is a prevailing sense of these schools being driven by uncompromising principles. There are elements of heroic and narcissistic leadership, sometimes juxtaposed with an espousal of distributed leadership and a continuing struggle to resolve the tensions between individual and shared leadership, policy dictat and ownership, but needing to be resolved within the school as a unit of improvement in a competitive environment. In a Danish context where schools were beginning to feel the brunt of political pressure, Moos et al. (2000) warn that school leaders can easily find themselves blindsided unless they are able to bring a more critical 'reading' to the larger policy context of their leadership activities. In a similar vein, Frost (2000) describes the process of 'getting colleagues on board' as one which may fall prey to the rhetoric of collaboration 'as a euphemism for strategic manipulation' (2000: 17).

The individual efforts of these heads to improve their schools has to be seen in a context of 'challenging circumstances' which apply not simply to the problematic social context in which they are set but to policy directions which exceed national boundaries. The overriding concern of raising standards and meeting targets is owed in large part to the continuous flow of data from OECD and other sources of international comparison. This is allied to a global trend for self-management at local level and tougher government intervention at national level, combined with higher stakes accountability and external evaluation. These trends, driven primarily by an economic rather than an educational logic, leave headteachers to work out their own salvation within the bounds of their own schools, in a continuous quest to find a marriage of convenience between dutiful compliance and intellectual subversion.

Notes

1. A four-year research project, 2001–5, funded by the Economic and Social Research Council.
2. The then Department for Education and Skills, and the Office for Standards in Education, the government agency which inspects and evaluates schools and colleges in England.
3. The Literacy and Numeracy Strategies – government programmes designed to raise achievement in English and Maths, which prescribed detailed content and lesson plans.

References

Argyris, C., and Schön, D. (1978) *Organizational Learning: A Theory of Action Perspective.* Reading, MA: Addison Wesley.

Beane, J.A. and Apple, M.W. (1999) 'The Case for Democratic Schools', in M.W. Apple and J.A. Beane (eds) *Democratic Schools: Lessons from the Chalk Face.* Buckingham: Open University Press.

Boreham, N. and Morgan, C. (2004) 'A Sociocultural Analysis of Organisational Learning', *Oxford Review of Education* 30: 307–25.

Coffield, F., Moseley, D., Hall, E. and Ecclestone, K. (2004) *Should We be using Learning Styles? What Research has to Say to Practice.* London: Learning Skills Research Centre.

Evans, P. and Genady, M. (1999) 'A Diversity-based Perspective for Strategic Human Resource Management', *Research in Personnel and Human Resource Management, Supplement* 4: 368.

Frost, D. (2000) 'Teacher-led School Improvement: Agency and Strategy', *Management in Education* 14(4): 21–4 and (5): 17–20.

Giddens, A. (1984) *The Constitution of Society: Outline of the Theory of Structuration.* Berkeley, CA: University of California Press.

Giroux, H. (1992) *Border Crossings.* London: Routledge.

Gladwell, M. (2000) *The Tipping Point.* New York: Little, Brown and Company.

Hargreaves, A. (2004) 'Sustainable Leadership, Sustainable Reform'. Paper delivered at the First World Summit on Educational Leadership, November, Boston.

Maccoby, M. (2001) 'The Incredible Pros, the Inevitable Cons', in *What Makes a Leader?* Boston, MA: Harvard Business School Press.

Moos, L., Møller, J. and Johansson, O. (2000) 'A Scandinavian Perspective on the Culture of Educational Leadership'. Paper presented at AERA in New Orleans, April.

Perkins, D. (2003) 'Taming the Wild and Wilding the Tame'. Invited lecture to the Faculty of Education, University of Cambridge, June.

Schratz, M. (2001) Conference presentation, Leadership for Learning, Cambridge, June 28.

Senge, P. (1990) *The Fifth Discipline: The Art and Practices of the Learning Organisation*, New York: Doubleday.

Senge, P., Scharmer, O.C., Jaworski, J. and Flowers, B.S. (2004) *Presence: Human Purpose and the Field of the Future.* Cambridge, MA: The Society for Organizational Learning.

White, J. (2004) 'Unpick Woolly Thinking', *Times Educational Supplement*, 12 November.

12

Evaluation, Accountability, and Performance Measurement in National Education Systems: Trends, Methods, and Issues

Katherine E. Ryan and Irwin Feller

Introduction

Across nations, policy initiatives and proposals relating to the governance, missions, revenue sources, and performance standards of both K-12[1] and higher education systems are suffused with the precepts and language of accountability and performance measurement. Influenced by a cluster of propositions about knowledge economies loosely packaged together under the term *globalization*, these trends include increased emphasis on education at all levels as a critical determinant of national economic competitiveness; intensified demands on educational institutions, as with many other public sector entities, that they document their accountability to larger publics for the quantity and quality of the services they provide; increasing formal requirements that this performance be documented by standardized assessment means; and an increasing reliance on market forces, such as competition among providers and fee-based provision of services to determine the size and apportionment of educational services.

[…]

In this chapter, we […] examine how these trends affect the evaluation of national education systems. Our approach is both multilevel, encompassing both K-12 and higher education, and comparative, involving vignettes from many countries. We sketch the multiple, complex, and variegated denotations and connotations of the concepts of accountability and performance measurement, singly and interactively, as they engender changes in

Source – An edited version of Ryan, K. and Feller, I. (2009) 'Evaluation, accountability, and performance measurement in national education systems'.

the educational evaluation arena, subjecting these concepts to the same type of analytical scrutiny that their use imposes on organizations, policies, and programs.

These analytical brushes produce a pointillist landscape that highlights the complex, diverse, and, at times, contradictory policy and program implications of implementing initiatives directed at fostering accountability and performance measurement in national education systems. This highlighting also makes more visible the importance of context, both within and across national borders, in designing and conducting policy- and program-specific evaluations. This perspective also leads to the identification of several looming and latent challenges for evaluators of educational programs that extend beyond standard methodological strictures or debates about evaluation's various modes, methods, or functions. As analyzed next, *performance assessment* and *measurement* are not synonymous terms and activities with *program evaluation*, considered in the specific sense as a means for determining the worth, value, or impact of an intervention (Mark et al., 2000).

The concept of globalization with its sub-themes, as sketched previously, also presents an immediate problem for program evaluation as it creates the surface appearance of common problems that are thus susceptible to common solutions. National education systems differ in many ways, however. These differences include constitutional and legislative provisions for public sector regulation and financing of education across levels of support of education; the relative importance of public and private institutions, especially in higher education; external and internal governance; size; historic and current levels of absolute and relative performance; and so forth. These contextual differences confound, or so we argue, attempts to generalize the applicability of the precepts subsumed under globalization or the findings from evaluations of seemingly kindred policy interventions from one setting to another.

The chapter begins with a general overview of international trends toward new, more formal requirements for accountability and performance measurement. These trends are manifestly visible among Organisation for Economic Co-operation and Development (OECD) countries, but also are evident across several Latin American and Asian countries (Altbach and Balan, 2007; Cozzens and Turpin, 2000; Organisation for Economic Co-operation and Development, 2005). This overview emphasizes dominant 'global' requirements on public sector organizations to demonstrate accountability and document performance (Power, 1997) and examines precepts termed the *new public management* (NPM) that guide how public sector activities are to be managed, monitored, and measured. Later parts of the chapter examine how these trends and programs play out in the context of 'local' national systems of education, citing specific national and international events to illustrate particular analytical themes. [...]

The landscape of accountability and performance measurement

Accountability is a political and legal concept. It denotes the responsibility of an organization or individual (i.e. an agent) to perform within the specified boundaries set by some higher political authority (i.e. a principal) and to report to and justify one's actions to this authority. Accountability is a basic tenet of democratic political systems. As noted by Smith and Lipsky (1993), 'Democratic governance requires that government adequately hold accountable all agencies that implement public policy, whether they are government bureaus, businesses, or nonprofit contractors' (p. 13).

As Behn (2001) has highlighted, however, accountability has different meanings depending on the context in which it is used. It can mean proper use of appropriated funds; appropriate behavior by an agency in terms of prescribed rules, regulations, or prevailing norms of equity and fairness; production of the goods and services, or outcomes, expected of it; as well as various combinations of these items. For the most part, our concern is with accountability as defined and measured in terms of performance.

Performance measurement, by way of contrast, is an amalgam of organizational and economic concepts that relate to the means and measures by which an organization demonstrates that its activities have produced the outputs, outcomes, and impacts for which it was established and provided resources. More broadly, performance measurement is a compound product of the objectives for which an organization was established, the criteria used to measure attainment of these objectives, and the measures used to operationalize the criteria.

Logically separate, accountability and performance measurement have become intertwined concepts. Accountability increasingly has come to include explicit requirements for documented (improved) performance; performance measurement is the increasingly preferred or mandated means by which agencies are expected to provide evidence to authorities and stakeholders that they are fulfilling their required or expected performance objectives.

This intertwining takes on true force when decision makers use evidence of an organization's past or current performance to make decisions that affect its future. These decisions can relate to the organization's continued existence, size, scope, mission, resources, structure, leadership, personnel, and more (Cronbach et al., 1980).

What makes accountability and performance measurement fertile and important subjects of interest is that they are closely linked to other principal components of the NPM paradigm. Generally associated with a portfolio of government reforms in New Zealand beginning in the late 1980s (Nagel, 1997), the paradigm has diffused widely across other countries. As noted by the OECD in 1995, 'A new paradigm for public management has emerged, aimed at fostering a performance-oriented culture in a less centralized public sector' (Organisation for Economic Co-operation and Development, 1995, p. 8). Among the paradigm's central features are: decentralized decision making and control of resources 'so that authority corresponds with accountability'; 'operational specification of goals through substantial investment in performance measurement'; and 'accountability for performance through reliance on competition (among both public and private service providers), explicit contracts, and material incentives' (Nagel, 1997, p. 350). Decentralization is designed to increase the flexibility and adaptability of organizations closer to end users than national or state ministries to customize programs that meet the needs of diverse audiences and to more quickly, effectively, and efficiently respond to new or changing needs or opportunities. Competition among public sector providers – and especially between public and private sector providers – is seen as compelling the former to meet customer needs lest those customers vote with their feet, reducing political support or otherwise causing organizational revenues to fall. Competition also serves as a means of establishing real-world benchmarks that can be used to identify differential performance and thus prod average and below-average performers to attain the performance levels of best practice performers.

National education systems

General trends

National systems of K-12 and higher education have not escaped scrutiny or coverage from these trends. Initiatives relating to accountability, performance measurement, and the new public management permeate proposals for reforming K-12 and higher education in many countries. These proposals originate both from political and economic sectors external to the organizations that compose a nation's K-12 and higher education systems, as well as from within these organizations or systems, where they serve as internal management tools, often associated with quality improvement initiatives.

International competitiveness

In the context of a knowledge economy worldview, a national goal of being (or becoming) the home of globally competitive research universities moves from being a solipsistic parlor game played by academics in their ivory towers to strategic assets that are to be developed and deployed as part of larger national policies. Likewise, for K-12 education, performance of elementary school students on international standardized achievement tests moves from being a reputational symbol of limited policy interest to a closely watched indicator of a nation's current and prospective international economic competitiveness (Miller et al., 2007). A related consequence of this internationally shared perspective, as Gardner (2004) has noted, is that, although distinctions clearly remain, 'there is surprising convergence in what is considered a pre-collegiate education in Tokyo or Tel Aviv, in Budapest or Boston' (p. 238).

Databases and data mining

Another development abetting the spread of performance measurement systems is that of large-scale, readily accessible databases tied to new analytical and data-mining techniques that make it possible to construct comparative performance measures for academic units (e.g. departments, colleges, and research centers) and universities. International policy units such as the OECD, International Education Association (IEA), and National Center for Educational Statistics (NCES) have targeted policy initiatives supporting the organization and development of these databases. For example, cross-national K-12 comparisons on international assessments such as the *Programme for International Student Assessment* (PISA) are directly connected to the proposition that educational quality is critical for educational development within a global economy (Kellaghan and Greaney, 2001; Stronach, 1999). National assessment systems likewise have been implemented worldwide – for example, in Chile, Argentina, and Uruguay in Latin America (Bienveniste, 2002) and in Uganda and Zambia in Africa (Kellaghan and Greaney, 2003). In the United States, the

No Child Left Behind[2] legislation (NCLB, 2002) created a new institutional environment in which students, teachers, schools, and districts are held accountable through auditable performance standards and assessments.

Similar developments in data collection, especially relating to publication and citation counts, patents, licenses, and number of spin-off firms, have become increasingly popular means – both for good and bad – for evaluating department and institutional outputs, impact, or productivity (Feller, 2002). Bibliometric-based or reputational rankings, such as the Times Higher Education Supplement rankings of the world's top 200 universities, have become influential measures by which academic administrators and national and regional policymakers evaluate the performance of colleges and departments, even in the face of considerable criticism by specialists in the field (Goldstein and Spiegelhalter, 1996; van Leeuwen, 2004; Weingart, 2005).

Yet another influence is the ability of individuals or organizations, but especially the media, to call attention to what they deem to be the underperformance of educational institutions. Notable examples of the press playing this role have surfaced in various countries. In Brazil, for example, a local newspaper spurred attention to the performance of Sao Paulo University by calling attention to the number of scholars with zero publications (Pereira et al., 1996). In the United States and Canada, the respective rankings produced by *U.S. News and World Report* and *Maclean's* command enough attention from various publics that university administrators at times either laud their standings, especially upward moves, or feel obligated to account, usually on methodological grounds, for downward moves.

Educational accountability

Accountability, notes Burke (2005), 'raises several deceptively simple but devilishly difficult questions,' such as '*Who* is accountable to *whom*, for *what* purposes, for *whose* benefit, by *which* means, and with *what* consequences' (p. 2). Answers to each of these questions can differ across levels of education and countries. In the following section, we outline some of these differences.

K-12 educational accountability

The rationale for educational accountability includes improving both educational quality and educational equity (Bienveniste, 2002; Linn, 2000). Although the conceptualization and implementation of educational accountability differs to some extent across nations, the trend has been for the locus of responsibility for performance to shift from the government to schools (decentralization). It is the latter that are now accountable for both educational program quality *and* improving educational achievement. Further, through legislation or other forms of regulation, the state prescribes the means and provisions of holding schools accountable. Included with varying degrees of formal authority and informal influence are national, regional, and local governmental units, as well as parents, students, teachers, schools, and other educational units.

In some cases, the role of parents, communities, and the public (i.e. ordinary citizens interested in or affected by concerns and representing multiple viewpoints) at the local level has changed substantially with this rearrangement. The function and character of educational evaluation also shifts with the introduction of the accountability relationship between the state and schools. Although educational evaluation has often played a part in external control of education, introducing managerial and supervisory accountability affects the evaluator's role and practices.

The 'what' facet of accountability also has undergone change. In K-12, educational actors are increasingly held accountable for ensuring that students have the essential skills and knowledge to ensure that their respective countries can remain competitive in the global economy. The consequences of accountability also vary. In the market-based approach of the United States, students are allowed to change schools if their school does not meet performance standards. There is in some sense 'competition' among schools because parents as consumers can register dissatisfaction by moving to a different school with more desirable services signaled by higher test scores. In contrast, in England, when a school is determined to be failing based on a site visit inspection, the school is required to implement a school improvement plan, which is subsequently monitored by additional governmental site visits. Kenya has historically used a more indirect approach. Teachers and schools are held accountable by publicizing how students in particular schools performed on public examinations (Kellaghan and Greaney, 2003). It is assumed that by introducing this form of competition, called *incentive information*, teachers will be motivated to improve instruction.

The institutional structures – including management, government, administration, professions, policymakers, and discourses enabling the machinery of educational accountability requirements – also vary across nations. Two generic approaches to implementing accountability dominate, albeit with considerable local variation: (a) outcomes-based educational accountability, and (b) school self-evaluation. The educational evaluator's role and relationship to this machinery can differ in important ways.

Outcomes-based educational accountability

Outcomes-based educational accountability involves some mandated form of systematic assessment of student achievement based on educational standards (e.g. content). Other indicators may be incorporated (e.g. teacher quality, school completion rates) for making judgments about whether educational standards are being met. Performance on these standardized assessments and indicators is a proxy that essentially defines educational quality. Within this institutional arrangement, the educational evaluator's role is designated as a 'measurement technician' assisting with the assessment, analysis, and interpretation of reporting requirements (Benjamin, 2008).

High-stakes outcomes-based educational accountability provisions, reflecting decentralization and NPM, employ market- and incentive-based strategies as the key means for improving student achievement. The US federal educational accountability system exemplifies high-stakes educational accountability in a decentralized, market-based environment. With NCLB, a historically unparalleled degree of federal government regulatory involvement was introduced into the workings of schools (Manna, 2007). Reflecting the complexities of decentralization, schools, instead of districts or the state (central authority), are now held accountable for achieving specific educational standards (performance standards). At the same time, schools have autonomy and responsibility for improving student learning in order to meet performance standards measured with outcomes-based assessments.

'High stakes' (sanctions) are introduced when graduated school-level sanctions are implemented when schools repeatedly fail to make annual yearly progress (AYP) toward meeting those standards. These sanctions range from school choice (students can legally enroll in another school) to school closing. Within this set of institutional arrangements based on notions of competition and markets, schools unable to compete successfully are removed from the 'school market' when they are closed. Further, in the United States, some states (e.g. Tennessee) have implemented reward and/or sanction-oriented compensation systems, where teacher salary increases are tied to improved achievement.

Latin American countries such as Argentina and Chile also have implemented top-down, high-stakes educational accountability systems that are substantively linked to deregulation and market competition environments (Bienveniste, 2002). In Chile, rewards include honoraria to professional staff for schools identified as effective based on educational indicators (e.g. standardized test scores), signaling teacher responsibility for student achievement. Similarly, high-performing schools in Argentina have received additional monies or in-kind awards (Bienveniste, 2002). At the same time, there are differences in the extent to which countries provide additional resources to schools that are not effective. For example, Chile provides low-performing schools with supplementary resources, whereas the United States does not.

Introducing the notions of markets and competition designates parents and students as consumers in high-stakes outcomes-based educational accountability. This rearrangement is expected to provide significant options (e.g. school choice) when their neighborhood schools are not adequate (Biesta, 2004; Ryan, 2007). As part of the market-oriented milieu, parents and students exercise consumer choice to change schools instead of advocating for local school improvement. Although the consumer role is intended to empower parents and students by offering school choice when their home schools are not adequate, opportunities for parents, other citizens, and communities to improve local schools then become more limited. Changing schools is the solution, instead of marshalling resources (e.g. local, state) to improve local schools.

The weakening of accountability linkages between families and schools has led to concerns about whether the interests of educational actors (e.g. teachers), schools, and families were included in the development and implementation of high-stakes educational accountability systems (Linn, 2008; McDonnell, 2008). An additional issue that has received heightened attention in the United States relates to whether NCLB accountability actually improves equity and achievement or provides sufficient information to help schools (e.g. Fuller et al., 2007). These questions, in turn, have led to renewed interest in policy alternatives based on 'low-stakes' outcomes-based educational accountability systems and school self-evaluations (Linn, 2008; McDonnell, 2008; Ryan, 2005).

Low-stakes outcomes-based educational accountability provides descriptive information about student achievement levels and school performance. The underlying notion here is that information will motivate teachers, principals, communities, and other stakeholders to improve school performance, either individually or collectively (McDonnell, 2008). For example, Uruguay has implemented a large-scale standardized assessment program where results are used to describe student achievement. Developed with community collaboration, the public receives descriptive information about *national* student performance similar to the United States 'Nation's Report Card', based on the *National Assessment of Educational Progress*. In Uruguay, reflecting the 'low-stakes notion,' school-level information is reported only within the educational community and is not made available to the public.

Using test results for descriptive accountability (a low-stakes technique) is receiving substantial attention in the United States as an alternative to high-stakes outcomes-based accountability (Linn, 2008). Although low-stakes approaches have several attractive features (e.g. including collaboration with parent, community, and public interests), moving from a high-stakes outcomes-based model may be difficult to accomplish in a market and deregulation milieu. However, school self-evaluation (SSE), another approach, is being implemented with some success in other regions and countries (e.g. England) that are committed to deregulation and market-based competition.

SSE

SSE or school-based evaluation is aimed at improving teaching and learning with some forms oriented toward external accountability requirements (e.g. MacBeath, 1999; Nevo, 1995; Ryan, 2005). SSE involves examining and monitoring the extent to which schools' goals are met by educational staff members or interested parents (Ritchie, 2007). Numerous protocols have been developed and implemented, particularly in Europe and Hong Kong (see MacBeath et al., 2000, for a study comparing school self-evaluation across 18 countries; Pang, 2003). Many countries (e.g. England, Iceland, The Netherlands) mandate SSE involving some kind of inspection by a national or regional educational authority (Nevo, 1995). In England, for example, school visitations have involved an accountability dimension since 2000 (Ritchie, 2007). Schools are visited (inspected) for several days by a team of examiners from the Office for Standards in Education (1999). The SSE form, completed by the school prior to the visit, serves as the visit agenda.

SSE with an external accountability component integrates features from school effectiveness and school improvement theories. School effectiveness theory focuses on student outcomes and identifies characteristics that contribute to successful schools, whereas school improvement approaches are aimed at improving student learning by improving teaching and learning. In England, the goal of the inspection is to make a judgment about school quality with particular emphasis on leadership and capacity for school improvement. In addition to on-site observations, various forms of evidence are examined by inspectors in making judgments about schools, including performance data and teacher, parent, and student feedback. Examiners can judge a school as failing, recommending plans for improvement (Ritchie, 2007). The inspection report is an accountability provision that (a) goes beyond test scores to include a broader perspective about school performance, and (b) makes recommendations about how to increase capacity to improve (McDonnell, 2008; Ritchie, 2007).

[...]

Incorporating a school improvement component directly by providing feedback to schools about what to do and how to do it complements school report cards or league table information about school performance. Moreover, within this model, educational actors, parents, students, and community interests are served when, as part of the process, they provide feedback and advocate for local school improvement.

Within these kinds of institutional arrangements and value commitments, including improvement and effectiveness, the educational evaluator role expands substantially to 'capacity builder' (Benjamin, 2008). The educational evaluator can serve the public good as an educational evaluation consultant helping educational institutions to increase their capacity to improve, as a meta-evaluator, and in other ways.

Higher education accountability

Accountability, in the case of national higher education systems, is viewed here in terms of two different but overlapping variables: (a) governance and administrative structures, and (b) sources of funding.

The tripartite governance and administrative structure framework formulated by Clark (1983) and widely used in comparative studies of higher education systems provides a baseline for describing recent developments. In this framework, national governance systems are described as being organized about one of three core models or ideal types: (a) bureaucratic control, as exercised by state ministries (e.g. France, Germany, Italy); (b) oligarchic, or collegial, control, as exercised by professionals operating on the basis of shared values and traditions (e.g. United Kingdom); and (c) market control, as expressed via competition for resources and standing (e.g. United States) (Dill, 1992).

The models reflect the relative degrees of control exercised respectively by governmental authorities and college and university personnel over decisions relating to higher education's core production processes. These decisions include both macrolevel ones (e.g. criteria for admitting students, curricula content, graduation criteria, selection of university administrative officers and faculty, revenue structures) and microlevel policies and actions (e.g. purchasing arrangements and per diem travel expenses). The finance variable relates to the share of the revenues provided to a nation's higher education institutions by, respectively, the public sector, including both national and subnational governments, and the private sector, including tuition, endowments, nongovernmental contributors, and others. National systems vary considerably here.

A connection between a government's contribution to, and control over, university revenues and its ability to require financial and performance accountability is to be expected. National systems in which the government supplies almost all or the larger share of university revenues can be expected to control more aspects of a university's behavior than those in which the share is smaller.

A more complex setting, however, arises in national higher education systems character-ized by a mix of public and private institutions. Here, one observes differential degrees of control exercised by political authorities over different facets of public and private univer-sity operations, with these differences in turn affecting the competitive position of one set relative to the other. Thus, public universities may find one or more legislative constraints on tuition rates, salary structures, intellectual property policies, and the like, at the same time that they compete in national- or state-level markets for students, faculty, and external resources with less regulated private universities.

Holding aside this complexity and diversity, the general trend in accountability arrangements for higher education is a shift away from direct, detailed control of inputs historically characteristic of the bureaucratic model toward what has been termed *gov-ernance* by *instruments*. As described by Dill (2003), 'The new policy strategy can be seen as a "stepping back" by governments from detailed centralized control through encouraging higher education institutions to be more autonomous, self-regulating and market oriented in their operations, albeit within an overall framework of government priorities' (p. 4).

An underlying driver of these changes is the workings of what Behn (2001) has termed the *accountability dilemma*, which arises because 'the accountability rules for finance and fairness can hinder performance. Indeed, the rules may actually thwart per-formance' (p. 10). Adding to the acuteness of this dilemma is another international trend – namely, that public sector funding has failed to keep up with the rising costs of higher education (Institute for Higher Education Policy, 2007). Thus, several governments are seeking to improve the overall research and educational performance of their higher educa-tion systems at the same time that competing pressures on the size and apportionment of government budgets constrain the share of these budgets that they are willing or able to devote to building globally competitive universities.

The widely pursued way out of this situation has been the adoption of policies that explicitly or implicitly constitute moves to a market model. Universities have been freed from the micromanagement controls formerly exercised by government ministries, but are expected to generate a larger percentage of their operating budgets. In effect, a new social compact has been entered into between government and higher education in which institu-tions continue to receive the larger – if relatively smaller – share of their revenues from government, but are expected to generate relatively larger portions of their revenues in the form of fees (tuition) or from partnerships with the private sector (Krull, 2004). A further part of the bargain is that universities gain increased discretion about how to allocate these resources in exchange for more explicit and quantifiable commitments to attain agreed-on education, research, and third-mission objectives.

For example, Japan's national universities, although funded primarily by the govern-ment, have been converted into independent administrative agencies, thus gaining more autonomy and flexibility (Kahaner, 2007). They are permitted – indeed encouraged – to seek funding from industry. Germany has a process of differentiating the missions of its universities; with a view toward establishing a select number of globally competitive research universities, it has opened up a competition for supplemental funds that would permit establishment of graduate schools, excellence clusters, and strategic institutions.

In Canada, in 2005, the province of Ontario committed itself to major investments in postsecondary education, but required in turn that universities commit themselves to multi-year performance agreements centered mainly around targets related to student enrollments, access, retention, and instructional quality.

The impact of new commitments to accountability and performance measurement on governance structures do not, however, lead only in one direction. As described next, in nations currently characterized by collegial control or market models, such as the UK and the United States, increasing linkages of accountability and performance measurement have provided a rationale for increased governmental control over the educational or research performance of institutions of higher education. Within the UK, for example, the changed situation with respect to government funding of academic research has been described as shifting the locus of decision making from a group of academics acting as a quasi-ministry for higher education to the prime minister and his cabinet, each taking a closer interest in higher education. This interest, however, is not dictated by a full understanding of the issues involved in running universities. Rather, as argued by Shattock (2007), it is shaped by externally driven reforms needed to modernize all public services, such as top-down performance management, market incentives, and related new public management.

[...]

Educational accountability contradictions

In both the K-12 and higher education sectors, educational accountability is presented as a policy strategy designed to improve educational quality. Decentralization and market competition, in turn, are tactics adopted to implement this strategy. Tensions, at times outright contradictions, however, can and do exist between strategy and tactics. With K-12 and higher education sectors, the state is maintaining authority while transferring responsibility over educational processes and outcomes (Bienveniste, 2002).

Within the K-12 sector, there are significant tensions in shifting the relationships among the state, schools, teachers, and other stakeholders. Paradoxically, the market-based consumer role diminishes the power and recourse of local communities, citizens, and groups to address specific local school issues such as the need for adequate financial resources. There is no direct accountability between schools and their public constituencies (i.e. communities, parents, and students; Biesta, 2004). By contrast, educational entities such as schools and districts (or other subunits) are accountable to the state for making progress toward performance standards, but not necessarily to parents, citizens, or the community.

Tensions also exist within higher education about the effects of thrusts toward increased accountability and performance measurement on governance and financing arrangements between governments and institutions. A notable example here is the United States, where the US Department of Education's efforts to expand its regulatory authorities in order to foster a robust culture of measurement, accountability, and transparency have been opposed by many universities, especially private universities, as an unwarranted and dysfunctional intrusion on their historic autonomy.

Educational performance measurement

Performance measurement presents analytical complexities and contradictory perspectives, both in general and with specific reference to education. Performance measurement is obviously not a new concept in education; students have long had their performance evaluated by exam scores, decisions on faculty promotion tenure traditionally have involved some consideration of publication counts and survey responses about teaching effectiveness, and institutional eligibility for specific government programs with federal or state regulations have long been based on quantitative evidence of performance (or compliance).

What is new is that more aspects of the performance of K-12 and higher education institutions are being subjected to performance measurement requirements. Educational performance measurement is endorsed and promoted based on the assumption that (a) this kind of numerical information represents progress toward objectives, and (b) increases in the indices can be interpreted as reliable and valid indicators of higher quality education. However, Wholey's (1994) theory involving performance measurement identifies important precursors that are essential for quality performance measurement. A program's definition must be elaborated, and the program logic must be adequately developed before indicators can be selected (Wholey, 1994).

Current educational performance measurement practices are not always well aligned with Wholey's performance measurement theory. In education, the indicators are emphasized as opposed to the complex educational constructs that the indicators represent – an important deviation from 'best practice recommendations' (Wholey, 1994). This problem is closely related to construct validity issues – namely, whether the measures chosen to assess performance of the several sectors of a nation's educational system accurately capture the values, outcomes, or impact sought by the larger system (Kane, 2006). Sizeable literatures exist about the strengths and weaknesses and the uses and misuses of each of the several measures – student test scores, bibliometrics, patent statistics – that currently form the portfolio of techniques used to assess the performance of the K-12 and higher education sectors, and of individual organizations within these sectors. […]

Performance measurement contradictions

By reducing complexity about educational performance to simple quantitative terms, [performance measurement] pose[s] at least three broad sets of issues for evelution. The first is the setting of the criteria by which performance is to be gauged. As noted earlier, to establish performance criteria requires (or implies) agreement about the purposes of education. The risk here is that technique and data preempt educational objectives: selection of measures may implicitly determine educational values or priorities, rather than the reverse. Relatedly, use of specific measures because of their availability, manipulability, or correlation with proxies for ultimate outcomes may mask or mislead consideration of fundamental educational objectives and associated societal values.

As the stakes associated with the use of these measures increases, so too must the attention paid to these construct validity critiques. The reasons here extend beyond methodological niceties about reliability and validity, although these obviously are important. The further consideration is a growing recognition of 'situations where more measurement of quality may lead to everything else but better quality' (Dahler-Larsen, 2007, p. 19; see also McPherson and Schapiro, 2007; Perrin, 1998). Gaming the measures, or opportunistic behavior, has quickly (and predictably) accompanied the introduction of several performance measurement systems. For example, [...] [in] K-12 education, unintended negative consequences such as 'teaching to the test' have been documented globally (e.g. United States, The Netherlands; de Wolfe and Janssens, 2007).

The third issue is why – at least to date – with few exceptions, the linkages between performance measurement systems and budgets appear to remain relatively loose and limited, even in those countries or states that have adopted such systems. The international and national surveys cited previously indicate that despite the considerable attention they have received, and even when formal requirements exist for their use, the rewards and penalties attached to mandated performance measurement systems appear to be implemented infrequently and then typically only in modest ways. This pattern suggests that the opposing forces represented, on the one hand, by adherents of the NPM and, on the other hand, by those speaking on behalf of the autonomy of educational institutions, especially for higher education, have arrived at a 'low level' equilibrium involving the introduction of relatively modest reporting requirements with relatively modest prizes and penalties associated with meeting/not meeting performance goals.

Conclusion

This cross-country scan highlights the extent to which the consequences of implementing accountability and performance measurement requirements can mean different things in different national contexts, as well as between K-12 and higher education systems within nations. Some of these outcomes can be positive and in accord with desired end results; at other times or in other places, introduction of these requirements may fail to produce their intended outcomes or, indeed, produce undesirable – if at times predictably dysfunctional – outcomes. This statement means more than 'one size doesn't fit all'; it means that the wrong styles may be chosen.

[...]

Notes

1. Note that the authors of this chapter use the term K-12 to refer to stages of education preceding higher education, i.e. early years/nursery, primary, secondary and further education.
2. No Child Left Behind – US government legislation measures requiring schools to boost the educational achievement of all students.

References

Altbach, P., & Balan, J. (Eds.). (2007). *World class worldwide*. Baltimore: Johns Hopkins University Press.

Behn, R. (2001). *Rethinking democratic accountability*. Washington, DC: Brookings Institution.

Benjamin, L. M. (2008). Evaluator's role in accountability relationships: Measurement technician, capacity builder, or risk manager. *Evaluation, 14*(3), 323–343.

Bienveniste, L. (2002). The political structuration of assessment: Negotiating state power and legitimacy. *Comparative Education Review, 46*(1), 89–118.

Biesta, G. J. (2004). Education, accountability, and the ethical demand: Can the democratic potential of accountability be regained? *Educational Theory, 54*(3), 233–250.

Burke, J. (Ed.). (2005). *Achieving accountability in higher education*. San Francisco, CA: Jossey-Bass.

Clark, B. (1983). *The higher education system: Academic organization in cross-national perspective*. Berkeley: University of California Press.

Cozzens, S., & Turpin, T. (2000). Processes and mechanisms for evaluating and monitoring research outcomes from higher education: International comparisons. *Research Evaluation, 8*, 3–4.

Cronbach, L., Ambron, S., Dornbusch, S., Hess, R., Hornik, R., Phillips, D., et al. (1980). *Toward a reform of program evaluation: Aims, methods, and institutional arrangements*. San Francisco, CA: Jossey-Bass.

Dahler-Larsen, P. (2007). Constitutive effects of performance indicator systems. In S. Kushner & N. Norris (Eds.), *Dilemmas of engagement: Evaluation and the new public management* (pp. 17–35). Amsterdam: Elsevier.

de Wolfe, I. F., & Janssens, F. J. G. (2007). Effects and side effects of inspections and accountability in education: An overview of empirical studies. *Oxford Review of Education, 33*(3), 379–396.

Dill, D. (1992). Administration: Academic. In B. Clark & G. Neave (Eds.), *The encyclopedia of higher education* (Vol. 2, pp. 1318–1329). Oxford, UK: Pergamon Press.

Dill, D. (2003, March). *The regulation of academic quality: An assessment of university assessment systems with emphasis on the United States*. Symposium on University Evaluation for the Future: International Trends in Higher Education Reform, Tokyo, Japan.

Feller, I. (2002). Performance measurement redux. *American Journal of Evaluation, 23*, 435–452.

Fuller, B., Wright, J., Gesicki, K., & Kang, E. (2007). Gauging growth: How to judge No Child Left Behind. *Educational Researcher, 36*(5), 268–278.

Gardner, H. (2004). How science changes: Considerations of history, science, and values. In M. Suarez-Orozco & D. M. Qin-Hillard (Eds.), *Globalization: Culture and education in the new millennium* (pp. 235–258). Berkeley: University of California Press.

Goldstein, H., & Spiegelhalter, D. (1996). League tables and their limitations: Statistical issues in comparisons of institutional performance. *Journal of the Royal Statistical Society*, Series A, *159*, 385–443.

Institute for Higher Education Policy. (2007). *The global state of higher education and of the rise of private finance*. Washington, DC: Author.

Kahaner, D. (2007). Japanese technology policy: Evolution and current initiatives. In C. Wessner (Ed.), *Innovation policies for the 21st century* (pp. 121–128). Washington, DC: National Academies Press.

Kane, M. (2006). Validation. In R. L. Brennan (Ed.), *Educational measurement* (4th ed.). New York: American Council on Education and Praeger.

Kellaghan, T., & Greaney, V. (2001). The globalization of assessment in the 20th century. *Assessment in Education, 8*(1), 87–102.

Kellaghan, T., & Greaney, V. (2003, December). *Monitoring performance: Assessments and examinations in Africa*. Paper presented at the annual meeting of the Association for the Development of Education in Africa, Grand Baie, Mauritius.

Krull, W. (2004). Towards a research policy for the new Europe: Changes and challenges for public and private funders. *Minerva*, *42*, 29–39.

Linn, R. L. (2000). Assessments and accountability. *Educational Researcher*, *29*(2), 4–14.

Linn, R. L. (2008). Educational accountability systems. In K. E. Ryan & L. A. Shepard (Eds.), *The future of test-based accountability* (pp. 3–24). Mahwah, NJ: Lawrence Erlbaum Associates.

MacBeath, J. (1999). *Schools must speak for themselves: The case for school self-evaluation*. London: Routledge Falmer.

MacBeath, J., Jacobsen, L., Meuret, L., & Schratz, M. (2000). *Self-evaluation in European schools. A story of change*. London: Routledge.

Manna, P. (2007). *School's in*. Washington, DC: Georgetown University Press.

Mark, M. M., Henry, G. T., & Julnes, G. (2000). *Evaluation: An integrated framework for understanding, guiding and improving public and non-profit policies and programs*. San Francisco, CA: Jossey-Bass.

McDonnell, L. A. (2008). The politics of educational accountability: Can the clock be turned back? In K. E. Ryan & L. A. Shepard (Eds.), *The future of test-based accountability* (pp. 23–46). Mahwah, NJ: Lawrence Erlbaum Associates.

McPherson, M., & Schapiro, M. (2007). Moral reasoning and higher education policy. *The Chronicle of Higher Education*, *54*(2), B10ff.

Miller, D., Sen, A., & Malley, L. (2007). *Comparative indicators of education in the United States and other G-8 countries: 2006* (NCES Publication No. 2007–006). Washington, DC: U.S. Government Printing Office.

Nagel, J. (1997). Editor's introduction. *Journal of Policy Analysis and Management*, *16*, 349–356.

Nevo, D. (1995). *School-based evaluation: A dialogue for school improvement*. Kidlington, Oxford: Pergamon.

No Child Left Behind Act of 2001. (2002). Pub. L. No. 107th Cong., 110 Cong. Rec. 1425. 115 Stat.

Office for Standards in Education. (1999). *Inspecting schools: The framework*. London: Author.

Organisation for Economic Co-operation and Development. (1995). *Governance in transition: Public management reforms in OECD countries*. Paris: Author.

Organisation for Economic Co-operation and Development. (2005). *Modernising government*. Paris: Author.

Organisation for Economic Co-operation and Development. (2006). *Education at a glance 2006*. Paris: Author.

Pang, S.-K.N. (2003). Initiating organizational change through school self-evaluation. *International Journal of Knowledge, Culture and Change Management*, *3*, 245–256.

Pereira, J., Pires, M., Duarte, P., Paes, A., & Okana, V. (1996). Introducing a method of research evaluation into a university: Medical research at the University of Sao Paulo, Brazil. *Research Evaluation*, *6*, 37–42.

Perrin, B. (1998). Effective use and misuse of performance evaluation. *American Journal of Evaluation*, 19, 367–379.

Power, M. (1997). *The audit society*. New York: Oxford University Press.

Ritchie, R. (2007). School self-evaluation. In S. Kushner (Ed.), *Dilemmas of engagement: Evaluation development under new public management and the new politics* (pp. 85–102). Chevy Chase, MD: Elsevier.

Ryan, K. E. (2005). Making educational accountability more democratic. *American Journal of Evaluation*, *26*(4), 443–460.

Ryan, K. E. (2007). Changing contexts and changing relationships. In S. Kushner (Ed.), *Dilemmas of engagement: Evaluation development under new public management and the new politics* (pp. 103–316). Chevy Chase, MD: Elsevier.

Shattock, M. (2007). From private to public governance of British higher education: The state, the market and competing perceptions of the national interest, 1980–2006. In *The crisis of the publics: Proceedings of a symposium organized by the Center for Studies in Higher Education* (pp. 187–200). Berkeley: University of California.

Smith, S., & Lipsky, M. (1993). *Nonprofits for hire.* Cambridge, MA: Harvard University Press.

Stronach, I. (1999). Shouting theatre in a crowded fire: Educational effectiveness as cultural performance. *Evaluation, 5*(2), 173–193.

van Leeuwen, T. (2004). Descriptive versus evaluative bibliometrics. In H. Moed, W. Glanzel, & U. Schmoch (Eds.), *Handbook of quantitative science and technology research* (pp. 373–388). Dordrecht, The Netherlands: Kluwer Academic Publishers.

Weingart, P. (2005). Impact of bibliometrics upon the science system: Inadvertent consequences? *Scientometrics, 62*(1), 117–131.

Wholey, J. S. (1994). Assessing the feasibility and likely usefulness of evaluation. In J. Wholey, H. Hatry, & K. Newcomer (Eds.), *Handbook of practical program evaluation* (pp. 15–39). San Francisco, CA: Jossey-Bass.

13

'Blended Leadership': Employee Perspectives on Effective Leadership in the UK Further Education Sector

David Collinson and Margaret Collinson

Introduction

This [chapter] examines the findings from a research project on effective leader–led relations in the UK Further Education (FE) sector. Informed by critical approaches to leadership studies, the project was concerned to explore the complex relationships between leaders and led and to locate these dynamics within their sector-specific conditions and consequences. While the FE sector is distinctive in many ways, it also has a number of overlaps and collaborations with UK Higher Education (HE). Accordingly, having outlined our main findings, we then consider some of the wider implications of our analysis for researching leader–led relations in the HE sector.

This project recognized that leader–led dynamics occur within particular shifting local, regional, national and global contexts and have complex intended and unintended effects. Context is especially important for understanding FE leadership dynamics. 'FE' covers a diverse range of post-compulsory educational provision for people over 16, taught primarily in general and tertiary FE colleges (similar to community colleges in the USA), sixth-form colleges and specialist colleges. FE colleges (FECs) offer a wide range of courses, from basic literacy and numeracy to academic and vocational qualifications for all post-school adults.

Source – An edited version of Collinson, D. and Collinson, M. (2009) '"Blended leadership": employee perspectives on effective leadership in the UK Further Education sector'.

The 361 FE colleges in England have a total income of over £6bn, employ over 23,000 staff and educate approximately 3 million people each year (Association of Colleges, 2008). […]. As teaching organizations, FECs are closely monitored and operate within a complex and turbulent funding and policy environment. […]. FECs are also subject to regular inspections by Ofsted, the Quality Assurance Agency (QAA), the Adult Learning Inspectorate (ALI) and various financial auditors. Hence, while HE institutions (HEIs) award their own degrees and validate their teaching and research activities through external examining and peer review, FECs are more tightly regulated through numerous external awarding and inspection bodies.

[…]

Our [chapter] begins by briefly reviewing two primary discourses in the leadership effectiveness literature: the heroic and the post-heroic. It then outlines our research findings which reveal that FE employees often value leadership practices that combine elements of both discourses. Drawing on other research that provides support for the view that paradoxical blends of apparently irreconcilable opposites might form the basis for effective leadership, the [chapter] considers the implications of this analysis for the study of HE. It concludes by highlighting the potential value of more dialectical approaches to the study of leadership, which acknowledge paradox, ambiguity and multiplicity.

Leadership 'effectiveness': a contested terrain

In recent years, 'effective leadership' has come to be seen as vital for improving organizational performance, particularly in the UK public sector. This view has informed the launch of various government-funded bodies within education specifically designed to improve leadership […]

Within the leadership literature, 'effectiveness' remains a contested terrain. Informed mainly by functionalist assumptions and focusing on leaders' behaviours and competencies, heroic discourses have been highly influential. For example, effective leaders are typically deemed to provide a clear sense of direction, be strategic, inspirational, charismatic and self-confident, communicate a vision, and foster trust, belonging and commitment (Bryman, 2007). While influential studies document a variety of possible leadership styles and their variation according to context (Goleman, 2000), current debates focus on whether effective leaders are best seen as: creative risk takers, charismatic domineering battlers, ruthless pursuers of performance, dedicated servant leaders or quiet stoics (Wheeler et al., 2007).

However, heroic perspectives have been criticized for romanticizing leaders (Meindl et al., 1985) and adhering to exaggerated views about what individual leaders do and what they can achieve. For Meindl and colleagues, leaders' contribution to a collective enterprise is inevitably somewhat constrained, closely tied to external factors outside a leader's control such as those affecting whole industries. Similarly, Mintzberg (2006) criticizes the obsession with heroic leaders, and argues in favour of rethinking organizations as communities of cooperation where leadership roles are shared by various people according to their capabilities.

Such critiques have informed the development of post-heroic discourses, less tied to 'top-down', hierarchical models and more concerned with enhancing communities through dispersed and networked interactions. Post-heroic writers view effective leadership in more relational ways, as 'distributed' (Gronn, 2002), 'shared' (Pearce and Conger, 2003), and 'collaborative' (Jameson, 2007). Others examine the effectiveness of 'co-leadership' and executive role sharing where complementary partnerships are deemed to enhance decision making (Alvarez and Svejenova, 2005). Within education, where there is considerable interest in the ways that leadership can be distributed (e.g. Spillane, 2006), these ideas would seem particularly pertinent given that teachers act as pedagogical leaders in the classroom.

This post-heroic discourse has also informed a growing interest in 'followership' (Howell and Shamir, 2005). Particularly in the context of flatter hierarchies and greater team working, 'exemplary' followers are seen as essential for successful organizations (Riggio et al., 2008). Challenging traditional views of followers as passive and homogenous, recent writers have emphasized followers' agency (Shamir, 2007), knowledgeability (Collinson, 2005), differences (Kellerman, 2008) and their potential for constructive dissent (Chaleff, 2003; Collinson, 2006, 2008). Hence, while studies of the solo 'heroic leader' have tended to predominate in leadership studies, there has been growing interest in more collective, distributed and 'post-heroic' approaches. These respective discourses that view effective leadership as either an individual or a collective phenomenon are typically competing and in tension with one another. Against this background, we now consider our research findings which explore the perspectives of FE employees on effective leadership.

Exploring effective leader–led relations

Research on leadership effectiveness raises questions about causality. If an organization is performing 'well' or 'poorly', can we attribute this directly to the practices of the current leader? As Meindl et al. (1985) suggested, the effectiveness of individual leaders is difficult to specify because organizations are collective, interdependent enterprises. Rather than presuppose an overly mechanistic causal link between variables (as is sometimes the case in leadership studies) this project was designed to explore respondents' own definitions of effectiveness and attributions of causation.

While our qualitative methodology explored leaders' accounts, it also sought to drill down into organizations to examine subordinates' views about what constitutes effective leadership. Employees would seem particularly well placed to comment on leadership effectiveness since they directly experience the impact of leaders' decision making. Indeed our research in various private and public sector UK organizations over the past 25 years has found that those in subordinate positions are often acutely aware of and sensitive to the signals and symbols that leaders convey, both consciously and unwittingly (e.g. Collinson, 2003). Interviews with those who are required to implement college policies also enable the verbal accounts and claims of leaders to be subjected to a certain degree of verification and scrutiny.

[…]

Kouzes and Posner's (2007) large-scale study found four key qualities that followers value in their leaders: being honest, forward looking, competent and inspiring. Of these, honesty was 'the single most important ingredient in the leader-constituent relationship' (p. 32). The more qualitative research findings presented in this [chapter] tend to concur with Kouzes and Posner's findings. Yet, FE respondents also articulated more nuanced and complex perspectives based on their own experience of leadership practices.

Our research project examined how leadership is enacted, distributed and experienced at various hierarchical levels within FECs. Rather than treat leadership as the mysterious, charismatic properties of individual 'heroes', the project explored the dynamic and asymmetrical nature of relationships between those in senior and in more junior positions. It focused on in-depth research in seven English FE colleges over a 2.5 year period. Between 2004 and 2006, 140 research interviews were conducted within these general FE colleges, which included two sixth forms. While we explored leader–led relations in seven main colleges, we also researched in another four specialist sub-divisions of these colleges. All the colleges had HE students enrolled and some had separate 'university centres'. The case study organizations were selected to provide a diverse range of organizations in terms of size, performance, location and local community features. Although each FEC was treated as a separate 'case', for the purposes of this [chapter], findings are presented in terms of general patterns.

Respondents were interviewed at different hierarchical levels, beginning with Principals and Heads then moving down into the organization. Given the possible sensitivities involved, all interviewees and institutions were assured of confidentiality and anonymity. Semi-structured research interviews covered the same questions and typically lasted approximately one hour. The same standard list of 12 interview questions was used, but as much space as possible was left open, enabling respondents to raise additional themes. In addition to conducting the research interviews and examining documentary material, information was gleaned in feedback sessions with case study colleges and in presentations at sector-specific workshops and conferences.

Across all seven colleges interviewees consistently viewed leadership as a vital ingredient and as one of, if not the most important aspect of college governance. Respondents' views about the vital importance of leadership were remarkably consistent. By contrast with Gemmill and Oakley's (1992) thesis that leadership is simply a way of placating followers' 'childlike' insecurities, our respondents emphasized the vital strategic, financial, organizational and motivational importance of effective leadership.

In relation to the question, 'What in your view constitutes effective leadership in this sector?' many respondents expressed a preference for open, engaged and collaborative practices. When describing their own approach, those in senior and middle leadership positions typically highlighted their preference for consultation and participation. However, while respondents preferred a consultative leadership style, they also valued leaders who were clear and decisive. They articulated a consistent preference for what we term 'blended leadership', a view that emphasizes the inter-relatedness of leadership behaviours often assumed to be incompatible dichotomies. Respondents frequently interpreted apparent dichotomies in heroic and post-heroic perspectives as mutually compatible and equally necessary for leadership effectiveness. To illustrate these themes, we now examine three inter-related dualities that consistently emerged in employees' views on effective leadership, namely respondents' preference for both delegation and direction, both proximity and distance and both internal and external engagement.

Both delegation and direction

Across all seven colleges, interviewees stated that they wanted to be consulted and listened to, but they also valued clear and consistent direction from those in leadership positions. To most respondents, distributed leadership meant 'top-down' delegation rather than any alternative notion of 'bottom-up' engagement. Interviewees generally viewed this kind of distributed leadership very positively, as a means of enhancing team-working and employee commitment, but they also wanted leaders to provide direction, vision and clear expectations.

For example, a course manager in one large FEC argued that the Principal's 'firm' leadership style was particularly valued:

> Here we like a firm leadership approach. We like to know what has to be done and needs to be done. We like straight talking and the Principal is a very straight talker. Without strong management and leadership we would not know what we are doing. Honesty is the key thing. We like rigorous leadership. People like to know where they are. I give my staff a list of all their duties. Once they know what their roles and responsibilities are, they feel comfortable doing their job. So, clarifying what is expected of staff and creating the structures and conditions that allow them to perform their duties is absolutely essential.

As this respondent illustrates, clearly defined job tasks, reporting structures and decision-making processes were widely valued as a key to effective leadership. For those in less senior positions, ambiguity and uncertainty about responsibilities or direction (which respondents often associated with excessive delegation) could foster a lack of accountability, leading to unfair practices and mistrust. Indeed a number of respondents criticized leaders (mainly from past experience) who failed to clarify decisions and whose selection practices appeared to be unfair.

Employees at one particular college highlighted the current Principal's leadership style which combined delegation with decisive decision making. This college is one of the largest of its kind in post-16 UK education, attracting over 23,000 student enrolments per year and employing over 1000 staff. When the new Principal was appointed (four years earlier), the College was losing £2.25 million each year, and student retention and achievement rates were well below the national average. The College is now financially stable, student retention is high and results compare favourably with colleges around the country. In explaining this turnaround, the Principal pointed to the new culture of delegation:

> This is a very large FE college. In fact, we've got faculties here that are bigger than some colleges so delegation is essential. It provides tremendous benefits. I'm not running all over the place. I trust people to do their job. Of course there are negatives. People at times step beyond their responsibility and sometimes they make mistakes, but it's important to support them when they do. We've got to help them to learn. In a college you've got to have people who can take chances. That's the sort of person we want to nurture here. The key principle is that if you produce an initiative you get the credit. The worst situation, and the one I definitely do not want, is where the Principal gets all the credit for everything that's done in the college. I stay well away from that. If they get the credit then they will stay motivated.

College employees at various levels confirmed that, in contrast with the previous incumbent, the new Principal provided a sense of direction: 'The Principal gives direction by making decisions. He'll say, "This is where we're going. Now, how are we going to get there?"' (Lecturer). It was generally believed that the College turnaround was in large part due to the Principal's policy of combining delegation with direction and decisiveness, as a lecturer explained:

> The Principal has built a reputation for delegation. He's well known for it. But there is a side to him that is also very firm. That's important too. If he says something is going to happen, it does happen. Somebody now is making decisions. Some decisions he has had to make are not very nice, but at least he made them. He grasped the nettle.

Another lecturer confirmed the positive impact of the Principal's blended leadership style:

> He has created a delegating culture and this has given an immediate sense of stability across the college. His finger is on the pulse and he's well connected. He also has a strong moral conscience and is very approachable. He's always happy to go out for lunch but he does not have favourites. This is exactly what you need to be a good Principal.

Interviewees confirmed that by combining delegation with direction, the Principal had facilitated a strong sense of community and a confident and motivated workforce.

Across all seven colleges employees expressed a preference for leadership that blends delegation and distribution with direction and decisive decision making. Underpinning this preference was another apparent dichotomy in relations between leaders and led, namely that between distance and proximity.

Both proximity and distance

In order to satisfy external assessors and to provide the clarity, consistency and fairness that employees value, structures and practices have to be relatively formal and impersonal. This in turn requires a degree of distance between leaders and led. However, our research revealed that the dominant workplace culture in all the FECs we researched was largely informal. In this context a detached and impersonal leadership approach could be ineffective and even counter-productive. Several respondents suggested that leaders who are perceived to be remote are unlikely to generate employee respect and trust.

Many interviewees stated that leaders need to be 'approachable' and able to communicate at all levels of the institution. They highlighted the need to 'value people' as a key aspect of effective leadership and as an essential precondition for enhancing employee morale and a sense of community. One repeatedly mentioned example of how leaders could demonstrate approachability was through their willingness to be personally involved with specific tasks and available to help at critical moments, as one junior manager explained:

When there is a particularly difficult problem we are struggling with, it is important to know that people in leadership positions are willing to step in to help if we think it is necessary. Leaders need to be approachable and willing to help.

Several respondents stressed that one way leaders could 'value people' was by being available to assist staff with difficult issues. These views highlighted an unusual notion of leadership, one that is very operational and 'hands on'.

Principals also recognized their 'approachability' and its importance, as one stated:

To be liked is not important for this job but staff have got to feel they can approach you. You've got to be approachable. It really worries me when people are hiding information and not communicating with us. I say, 'Come on, why did you not say that?' I get really disappointed when people feel they can't say what they think is important.

Seeking to ensure his approachability, this Principal informed all colleagues that anyone could ask to see him at any time, and that they could bypass middle managers. He also organized regular meetings with all 65 managers in the college and held annual year-end meetings (in groups of ten) with all staff in the College, as he explained, 'this gives employees a chance of face-to-face discussions with me on any issue concerning the college'.

Many of the FE employees we interviewed expect those in senior positions to be visible, close to operational matters and willing to be involved in everyday college processes. The need for leaders to 'get their hands dirty' was very frequently mentioned as a prerequisite for establishing mutual trust and respect. This was especially the case with regard to the leadership qualities that women respondents considered very important. Stressing the importance of 'leading by example', women at various levels consistently stated that they would never ask anybody to do anything they would not do themselves, as one female middle manager stated: 'I would never ask my staff to do anything I would not do myself. There is no difference between me and the cleaner. I am prepared to do anything because I believe in the College and what we have to offer'. Women respondents considered it particularly important that those in senior positions are willing to undertake any task which they request of others. [...]

The degree of distance and proximity between leaders and led is currently an important topic in leadership studies (e.g. Weibler, 2004). Much of the literature suggests that leaders need to retain a distance from followers (e.g. Antonakis and Atwater, 2002) and that this distance can take many different forms (e.g. psychological, social, hierarchical, physical and/or interaction frequency). Clearly, maintaining a degree of distance might assist leaders to focus on long-term strategic issues, retain confidential information and facilitate meritocratic decision making.

Yet, our findings indicate that, in a sector where informality is particularly valued, leaders who are deemed to be effective seek to maintain a balance in their dealings with staff between being distant enough (to see the bigger picture and provide direction) and close enough (to be approachable and assist with particular problems). Employees expect leaders to be flexible and able to shift between (degrees of) distance and proximity according to changing circumstances, demands and pressures. As Goffee and Jones (2006: 135) contend, effective leaders skilfully manage a forever shifting and paradoxical balance between distance and closeness.

The repeated preference for leader approachability is an important feature of the informal culture in FE. Yet, while this expectation of approachability can facilitate internal collaboration, it can also create tensions and dilemmas because FE leaders are also required to be externally oriented, both in representing their organizations within the local community and in ensuring that colleges are accountable to various external funding and inspection bodies. These dual responsibilities of community representation and college accountability can reinforce senior leaders' concern to prioritize external matters, leaving internal issues to more junior colleagues. As the next section elaborates, retaining a balance between internal and external engagement can be extremely challenging.

Both internal and external engagement

FECs engage with multiple external stakeholders at a local and regional level (e.g. regional development agencies, training standards, sector skills councils, community organizations, local employers, local community leaders, etc.) as well as with numerous national-level funding, auditing and inspection bodies. Consequently, leaders are required to be externally accountable to multiple stakeholders. For FECs, community engagement is increasingly vital, as one Principal emphasized:

> In my first two years here, my role was very internal. I never set foot outside. But it is more and more external, trying to locate the college as a big player in the local community. This is now really important.

Most respondents agreed that effective FE leaders need to develop an external presence. However, many also emphasized that this external engagement should not be at the cost of internal college matters. A number of interviewees were concerned that, in focusing on external issues, leaders could become too distant from equally important internal concerns.

For example, during his first year in post, one particular Principal invested a considerable amount of time trying to raise the profile of the College in the local and regional community. Prior to his appointment, the College had been struggling for several years and improving its external reputation was seen as a key part of the new Principal's remit. However, when a financial crisis developed within the College, the Principal was forced to redirect his energies and dedicate more attention to internal matters. In doing so he found it difficult to connect with staff, as he explained:

> At Principal level, when you spend so much time out in the community, trying to raise the profile of the College you can lose touch with internal issues. I realized that, even when I was in the College, I was thinking about external issues. This must have shown on my face as my secretary told me that, when I toured the College, I needed to relax and smile more. She explained that as I had been focused on external matters, the employees did not really know me, and although I was more visible now, when staff saw me I always had a really serious face and this led to anxiety within the College. I didn't realize such a small thing could affect staff so much! Just that little statement from my secretary has led me to really make an effort to engage with staff throughout the College in a more approachable way.

Trying to redress a previous imbalance (too internally focused), the present Principal had created the opposite imbalance (too externally focused).

Interviews with employees at this College confirmed that in his first 18 months in post, the Principal had been widely perceived to be rather detached. They also acknowledged that his subsequent efforts to connect with staff had produced positive results, as a lecturer confirmed:

> We didn't have many dealings with the Principal at first, he was always out and about, but recently he has been much more visible in college. I used to think he was quite detached and severe but I think a lot of people are beginning to see another side to him. At a recent staff meeting he had some very supportive things to say about the College and he even cracked a few jokes. Although things are still difficult with the funding cuts, I know it made people feel he was more in touch with us all.

This case illustrates that when leaders become overly 'outward looking', they risk being seen by employees as remote and aloof. When employees believe that senior people are too externally focused, they can also begin to suspect that their leaders are mainly concerned with their own visibility and career.

Accordingly, retaining a balance between internal and external engagement was identified by many respondents as a key aspect of effective FE leadership. Such a balance is especially important given the high cultural value attributed by respondents in FE colleges to leader approachability. Yet, achieving and maintaining this kind of balance can be extremely challenging for those in senior positions, particularly because of the numerous external funding and inspection processes to which colleges are now subject.

[...]

Senior respondents were frustrated by the perpetual changes they perceived in government education policies, as another Principal explained:

> There are a lot of pressures from outside, a multitude of targets and at times, conflicting targets. There are real pressures to achieve phenomenal targets. Nobody objects to being accountable but this constant changing of the goalposts is very difficult. Funding regimes in FE are highly complex. If Government would just get off our backs for five minutes!

At the outset of this research project, we had assumed that FE leaders were empowered to lead their colleges. Yet, our research found that those in leadership positions frequently felt significantly constrained, and were widely perceived to be under intense, multiple pressures. We were struck by how often college leaders talked as if they were followers, required to adhere closely to government policy, rather than as leaders designing and implementing a strategic vision for their college.

Tight financial targets can also conflict with the traditional inclusive role of colleges as the providers of community-based learning opportunities. Our research suggests that, while formalized processes are designed to raise standards by increasing accountability and transparency, an excessive audit culture can have unintended and counter-productive effects that may erode the potential for effective leadership, reproducing a recurrent tension between (internal) approachability and (external) accountability.

[...]

Our research suggests that FE employees expect those in leadership positions to be approachable yet also able to balance the external, multiple responsibilities of community representation and college accountability. It was important for respondents that, in their pursuit of external strategic positioning, leaders did not neglect important internal concerns. These findings suggest that a key challenge for FE leadership is to interact effectively with multiple communities in ways that retain a (perceived) balance between these diverse responsibilities.

Conclusion

This [chapter] has highlighted FE employees' preference for subtle and flexible practices that we have termed 'blended leadership': a way of understanding and enacting leadership in which apparently separate and incompatible dichotomies are reevaluated as inter-related and mutually necessary. While heroic and post-heroic discourses on leadership are often seen as competing, our research suggests that many employees view them as complementary and mutually implicated in effective leadership. They preferred leadership practices that combine a paradoxical blend of seemingly irreconcilable qualities. Although employees across all seven colleges valued distributed and shared leadership, they also expressed a preference for aspects of more directive and 'firm' leadership, valuing leaders who were detached enough to appreciate the big picture, but also close enough to be approachable and 'down to earth'.

These findings suggest that FE leaders who are able to balance strategic priorities and competing responsibilities are most likely to be seen as enacting effective leadership and our study identified examples of such versatile practices in specific FECs. This is not, however, to suggest that blended leadership is invariably enacted in all FECs or that it constitutes 'a one best way' to lead. An important feature of such practices is their versatility. They are likely to take different forms and to shift according to specific circumstances and interpretations. Equally, we recognize that maintaining this kind of flexible approach is especially challenging in FE, particularly because of the multiple, shifting and sometimes contradictory (auditing) pressures under which colleges operate.

[…]

Research by Bolden et al. (2008, 2009) in UK HEIs recorded similar employee responses in relation to preferred leadership approach. They found that while acknowledging that leadership was generally distributed, HE respondents also valued 'strong and inspiring leadership within the university'. Similarly, VCs talked about 'the constant juggling act' of balancing central direction with devolving responsibility. These findings suggest that if HE leaders are overly directive they may damage employee morale but if they are not directive enough they may be unable to ensure fair, lawful and consistent practices across the institution. Hence, the identification of salient tensions, contradictions and paradoxes as well as strategies for their resolution may be a relatively productive focus for researchers studying leadership in HEIs (the growing literature on 'ambidexterity', which has considered universities, is also relevant here; e.g. Ambos et al., 2008).

A number of US studies suggest that this focus on paradoxical dichotomies and blended practices may also have a wider generalizability. For example, Collins (2001) found that organizations which had moved from 'good to great' over a 20-year period were run by 'level 5' leaders who were, paradoxically, modest yet wilful, humble yet fearless, resolute yet stoic. Cameron et al. (2006) argue that effective leaders tend to be 'simultaneously paradoxical', integrating factors usually seen as competing, contradictory and even incompatible. They encourage leaders to rethink apparent opposites by replacing 'either/or' with 'both/and' thinking. Kaplan and Kaiser (2003) argue that effective leaders are those who have the versatility to move freely between apparently opposing leadership practices. Highlighting the need for leaders to be both 'forceful' and 'enabling' and both 'strategic' and 'operational', they found that employees consistently regarded versatile managers as the most effective leaders in their organizations.

These arguments are also compatible with recent conceptual developments in leadership studies. A number of writers have criticized the rather simplistic dualistic assumptions found in much of the leadership literature (e.g. transformational/transactional, task/people orientation). Problematizing binaries such as organic/mechanistic and participative/autocratic, Fairhurst (2001) argues that the primary dualism in leadership studies is that between individual and collective forms of analysis. Bowring (2004) asserts that the binary opposition between leaders and followers is typically reinforced by a gender dualism in which men are privileged while women are marginalized. These arguments are supported by Gronn's (2008) proposal for researchers to replace distributed leadership with a focus on 'hybridity'. Acknowledging that both individual and collective dimensions will invariably co-exist in leadership configurations, Gronn's notion of hybridity is very compatible with the blended leadership dynamics described here.

In sum, this growing conceptual interest in dialectical studies of leadership has led to alternative approaches being proposed that seek to address the dynamic tensions and interplay between seemingly opposing binaries. Drawing on our empirical research in FE, this article has sought to contribute to this growing interest in dialectical analysis by highlighting the potential value of exploring employee perspectives on effective leadership and blended leadership practices that can incorporate apparently irreconcilable opposites through a focus on paradox, multiplicity, ambiguity and inter-connectedness.

[...]

References

Alvarez, J. L., & Svejenova, S. (2005) *Sharing Executive Power*. Cambridge: Cambridge University Press.

Ambos, T. C., Makela, K., Birkinshaw, J., & D'este, P. (2008) 'When Does University Research Get Commercialized? Creating Ambidexterity in Research Institutions', *Journal of Management Studies* 45(8): 1424–47.

Antonakis, J., & Atwater, L. (2002) 'Leader Distance: A Review and a Proposed Theory', *The Leadership Quarterly* 13(6): 673–704.

Association of Colleges (2008) www.aoc.co.uk

Bolden, R., Petrov, G., & Gosling, J. (2008) 'Tensions in Higher Education Leadership: Towards a Multi-level Model of Leadership Practice', *Higher Education Quarterly* 62(4): 358–76.

Bolden, R., Petrov, G., & Gosling, J. (2009) 'Distributed Leadership in Higher Education: Rhetoric and Reality', *Educational Management, Administration and Leadership* 37(2): 257–77.

Bowring, M. A. (2004) 'Resistance is Not Futile: Liberating Captain Janeway From the Masculine–Feminine Dualism of Leadership', *Gender, Work and Organization* 11(4): 381–405.

Bryman, A. (2007) *Effective Leadership in Higher Education*. London: Leadership Foundation for Higher Education.

Cameron, K. S., Quinn, R. E., Degraff, J., & Thakor, A. V. (2006) *Competing Values Framework: Creating Value in Organizations*. Cheltenham: Edward Elgar.

Chaleff, I. (2003) *The Courageous Follower*. San Francisco, CA: Berrett-Koehler.

Collins, J. (2001) *Good to Great*. London: Random House.

Collinson, D. (2003) 'Identities and Insecurities: Selves at Work', *Organization* 10(3): 527–47.

Collinson, D. (2005) 'Dialectics of Leadership', *Human Relations* 58(11): 1419–42.

Collinson, D. (2006) 'Rethinking Followership: A Post-structuralist Analysis of Follower Identities', *The Leadership Quarterly* 17(2): 172–89.

Collinson, D. (2008) 'Conformist, Resistant and Disguised Selves: A Post-structuralist Approach to Identity and Workplace Followership', in R. Riggio, I. Chaleff, & J. Lipmen-Blumen (eds) *The Art of Followership*, pp. 309–24. San Francisco, CA: Jossey-Bass.

Fairhurst, G. (2001) 'Dualisms in Leadership Research', in F. Jablin & L. Putnam (eds) *The New Handbook of Organizational Communication*, pp. 379–439. Thousand Oaks, CA: Sage.

Gemmill, G., & Oakley, J. (1992) 'Leadership: An Alienating Social Myth', *Human Relations* 45(2): 113–29.

Goffee, R., & Jones, G. (2006) *Why Should Anyone Be Led by You?* Boston, MA: Harvard Business School.

Goleman, D. (2000) 'Leadership That Gets Results', *Harvard Business Review* March/April: 78–90.

Gronn, P. (2002) 'Distributed Leadership as a Unit of Analysis', *The Leadership Quarterly* 13(4): 423–52.

Gronn, P. (2008) 'Hybrid Leadership', in K. Leithwood, B. Macall, & T. Strauss (eds) *Distributed Leadership According to the Evidence*, pp. 17–40. New York: Routledge.

Howell, J., & Shamir, B. (2005) 'The Role of Followers in the Charismatic Leadership Process: Relationships and Their Consequences', *Academy of Management Review* 30(1): 96–112.

Jameson, J. (2007) *Investigating Collaborative Leadership in Learning and Skills*. Lancaster: Centre for Excellence in Leadership.

Kaplan, R., & Kaiser, R. (2003) 'Rethinking a Classic Distinction in Leadership: Implications for the Assessment and Development of Executives', *Consulting Psychology Journal: Research and Practice* 55(1): 15–26.

Kellerman, B. (2008) *Followership*. Boston, MA: Harvard Business School.

Kouzes J. M., & Posner, B. Z. (2007) *The Leadership Challenge*. San Francisco, MA: John Wiley.

Meindl, J., Ehrlich, S. B., & Dukerich, J. M. (1985) 'The Romance of Leadership', *Administrative Science Quarterly* 30(1): 78–102.

Mintzberg, H. (2006) 'The Leadership Debate with Henry Mintzberg: Community-ship is the Answer', *The Financial Times*. Available at: www.FT.com

Pearce, C. L., & Conger, J. A. (eds) (2003) *Shared Leadership*. Thousand Oaks, CA: Sage.

Riggio, R., Chaleff, I., & Lipmen-Blumen, J. (eds) (2008) *The Art of Followership*. San Francisco, CA: Jossey-Bass.

Shamir, B. (2007) 'Introduction: From Passive Recipients to Active Co-Producers: Followers' Roles in the Leadership Process', in B. Shamir, R. Pillai, M. C. Bligh, & M. Uhi-Bien (eds) *Follower-centered Perspectives on Leadership*, pp. ix–xxxix. Greenwich, CT: IAP.

Spillane, J. P. (2006) *Distributed Leadership*. San Francisco, CA: John Wiley.

Weibler, J. (2004) 'Leading at a Distance', in J. MacGregor Burns, G. R. Goethals, & G. J. Sorenson (eds) *Encyclopaedia of Leadership*, pp. 874–80. London: Sage.

Wheeler, S., McFarland, W., & Kleiner, A. (2007) 'A Blueprint for Strategic Leadership', *Strategy and Business* 49 (winter).

[…]

14

Leadership for Diversity and Inclusion

Jacky Lumby

Introduction

Each of the words of the title of this chapter has multiple and contested meanings. The words 'diversity' and 'inclusion' are also commonly used in practitioner discourse and in policy documents at organisational, local and national levels. How the terms are understood is as contested and varied as is leadership. This chapter begins by considering the multiple ways in which these key elements are conceived. It explores how diversity has been researched and therefore how relevant knowledge has been generated. Finally, it considers how leaders can act to lead for and with diversity and to be inclusive, and what preparation or support might aid them.

There is a very large and wide range of literature focused on issues of diversity and inclusion related to both staff and learners. The chapter has not space to address in detail the specific issues that may arise in relation to individuals or groups of staff or learners with particular needs. Rather it sets out the overarching ideas, relevant research and actions which leaders might consider to achieve a strategic orientation to leading for diversity and inclusion.

Definitions and understandings

How we understand who leaders are and what activity constitutes leadership is an important foundation for the chapter. Identifying leaders is contextually sensitive. While theories of distributed leadership have found a following in many anglophone areas of the world, in other countries a more hierarchical approach is the norm, with 'leader' understood as the

---

Source – An edited version of Lumby, J. (2010) 'Leadership for diversity and inclusion'.

person who formally has a role invested with authority. For the purposes of this chapter, an inclusive but also partial approach is taken. Leaders are assumed to be all those in educational organisations who deliberately create and transmit the organisation's values and use influence to ensure that values inform practice. Such action is arguably the most fundamental act of leadership (Begley, 2003). The latter may involve more than this, but the question of values is particularly pertinent to diversity issues, and so is selected here as the heart of leadership.

Diversity is a term which is used ubiquitously and variously. It is sometimes used as synonymous with ethnicity or race. Sometimes it is used to indicate the presence of individuals with the range of characteristics embedded in equality legislation such as ethnicity, gender, disability and age; sometimes it is used to acknowledge the very wide range of characteristics which differentiate human beings, including both visible and non-visible attributes of the physical person and their background, preferences and beliefs (You-Ta et al., 2004). How diversity is conceived has an impact on how leaders construct action in response. Diversity is defined here as the range of human characteristics which result in socially-constructed advantage and disadvantage (DiTomaso and Hooijberg, 1996); that is, it is not, for example, being black or fe/male or having a disability which is critical. What matters is how others react to the characteristic and by their reaction create unjustified advantage or disadvantage. Reynolds and Trehan (2003: 167) put it succinctly: 'differences that matter and those that do not, depending on whether they reinforce inequality'.

Inclusion is the final concept central to the chapter. It can be related to multiple strategies to achieve particular outcomes for staff and learners, including equal opportunities, affirmative action, multiculturalism, and capabilities approaches. The differing terminologies and desired outcomes relate to varied understandings of fairness and social inclusion. Rather than adopt a single definition, the chapter explores the different goals related to alternative understandings of what inclusion might mean.

Researching diversity

Addressing issues related to diversity can draw on many disciplines, including, for example, social psychology, cultural anthropology and socio-biology. It can also consider neuro-epistemological theories about the degree of agency leaders may have to adjust the fundamental thinking processes which underpin attitudes to diversity and inclusion. The relevant literature can focus on single characteristics, as does feminist literature and critical race theory or, increasingly, can adopt intersectionality approaches which insist on understanding the effect of each individual's multiple characteristics in synergy.

With every area of inquiry, there is a relationship between knowledge production, theory and practice. In relation to diversity, McCall (2005) suggests three different approaches. The first is anti-categorical complexity, that is, rejection of the notion that it is possible to meaningfully research human beings using categories. Litvin (1997) argues this strongly. She believes that categorising people, for example into ethnic groups, inappropriately adopts a biological taxonomy approach. 'The categories constructed through the discourse of workforce diversity as natural and obvious are hard pressed to accommodate the complexity of real people' (1997: 202). Even the most apparently incontrovertible category, that of gender, is challenged by queer theory which attacks essentialist notions of gender and insists gender is a variable and constructed performance that is related to other characteristics (Sloop, 2007). McCall's second approach is inter-categorical complexity, using historic categories of disadvantage as an organising framework. Many individuals and groups assert that it is extremely important to consider groups, such as black people or girls/ women or those who have a particular disability, as groups, because that is how they are often seen by others and stereotyped as a result. Membership of the group is therefore one root of the disadvantage they experience. The final approach, intra-categorical complexity, explores the nature of the making of categories and boundaries and their effects on research, knowledge and practice. Why we create groups and the effect of the group on how we see people is therefore another area of knowledge production.

The links to policy and action are evident. If leaders resist categorising people into groups, then their response to diversity and inclusion is likely to stress the need to consider each individual as a unique being. By contrast, leaders of schools in inner cities might believe it is crucial to focus on equality and inclusion for a particular ethnic group, for example African Caribbean youths in England. In South Africa, school, college or university leaders might believe it necessary to focus on addressing the effect on students of intersections of characteristics, such as ethnicity, language, gender and religion (Lumby and Heystek, 2008). In each case different conceptions of diversity call on different kinds of research/literature which in turn lead to different goals and orientations to practice.

Identifying goals

For diversity

Leading *for* diversity, that is, achieving a representative profile of staff or students, is still a widely adopted goal internationally (Bush et al., 2006; Hartle and Thomas, 2003). It is seen to offer measurable progress and by accepting people into areas from which they have previously been excluded, potentially to redress the prior imbalance of power. There are, however, issues with such a goal. First, while it is widely adopted in relation to staff, it is far from universal in relation to learners. Schools may engineer their intake in various ways, and having a profile of learners which reflects, for example, the ethnicity or socio-economic background or prior attainment of the local or national population is not always the intention. For many staff and parents a 'good' school is one which has an intake skewed towards learners with a more advantaged background and higher prior attainment. By contrast, throughout the world many schools take professional pride in meeting the needs of all the children who live locally, who may have no option but to attend their local school. There is no question of engineering intake. For other schools, fee payment or selection processes may aim at an unrepresentative learner body. Elite universities in the UK experience pressure from central government to ensure a range of socio economic backgrounds in their intake. Representation is therefore a goal which is much more widely adopted in relation to staff. The result is potentially a dissonance between a staff body which is currently, or in aspiration, representative of the local and/or national population and a learner body which is not, or vice versa. Such disparity may constitute a hidden message which undermines any intended communication of commitment to diversity and inclusion (Lumby and Heystek, 2008).

The second issue is deciding of what population staff or learners are to be representative and which characteristics are most pertinent. A gender balance often appears more likely to be seen as relevant and achievable than, for example, a staff profile which is representative of the number of people nationally who are minority ethnic or have a disability, particularly if the local population is perceived as 'not diverse' (Lumby et al., 2005). Whether representation is in relation to the local or the national population becomes a key choice.

A third issue is controversy about what representation in itself achieves. If staff or learners are recruited who are perceived as different to the majority or a usually unstated norm, but the culture and practice of leadership, or teaching and learning remain static, representation may be achieved at the cost of assimilation, where the dominant group of people may consciously or unconsciously impose on all their own parameters for values, thinking and practice (Lumby with Coleman, 2007). The progress indicated by increasing representation is seen therefore as apparent only and as 'entryism' (Davies, 1990: 16), that is, merely injecting under-represented people without attention to an inclusive culture (Grogan, 1999). [...] Others argue that representation is an important goal, despite the issues it raises, and that a first step to greater equality is for those previously excluded to at least have the chance to progress to formal leadership roles and to influence practice and outcomes.

How far the goal of representation is achieved is hard to assess. The data on the degree of representation amongst educational leaders is difficult to come by, even in Organisation for Economic Co-operation and Development (OECD) countries such as Australia, Canada and the UK (Cruikshank, 2004; Sobehart, 2008). Increasingly the goal is seen as representation plus; that representation may both be preceded by and support further the consideration of how culture and practice can be inclusive of all those currently in the school, college or university community and of potential future members (Milliken and Martins, 1996).

Leading with diversity

The term 'inclusion' is used as ubiquitously as diversity and often with as undefined a meaning. In relation to learners, in the UK the Office for Standards in Education's definition describes inclusion as equal opportunities for all, and goes on to identify particular groups requiring attention to ensure they have equal chances, such as children in care, or those of a particular ethnic background. By contrast, another kind of definition focuses on how the individual experiences the organisation, rather than the supplier's intention to offer equality:

> When individual and group differences are regarded as valued resources, as in an inclusive environment, differences no longer need to be suppressed. Those who cannot fit into the old mono-cultural model no longer need waste their energy trying to be what they are not, and those who can successfully suppress or hide their differences no longer need waste their energy doing so. (Miller and Katz, 2002: 17)

It is essentially all experiencing a sense of belonging which characterises inclusion for Miller and Katz.

[...]

Those leading for diversity and inclusion therefore face an important initial task in agreeing with others how diversity is conceived and what the goal(s) might be. Is the target particularly 'differences that matter' (Reynolds and Trehan, 2003: 167)? Are the groups with characteristics enshrined in equality legislation to be the focus? Is progress to be assessed by increasing the representation of those employed at all levels or, for learners, a more representative profile of those studying particular subjects, achieving accredited outcomes and progressing to further education or training? The gulf between the achievement of some learner groups and others might demand specific attention to redress imbalance in outcomes. For example, Shields (2008) reports the huge discrepancies of funding for white and black students in Chicago, USA and in South Africa:

> In the Chicago area, for example, the highest per pupil expenditure of $17,291 is to be found in Highland Park and Deerfield, districts with a 90% White population and only 8% low income students, while in Chicago itself, with 85% low income students and 87% Black and Hispanic, the per pupil expenditure is $8,482 ... Similarly, in South Africa, Dunn (1998) reported that 'for every dollar spent on a black student, seven were spent on each white' (p. 2). (Shields, 2008: 5)

Leaders of schools in such inequitable contexts will indeed feel the pressure to address particularly 'differences that matter' (Shields, 2008). By contrast, in schools or colleges where there are multiple sources of disadvantage which intersect to heighten or lessen disadvantage, leaders might feel that to support all individuals, staff and learners, to be enabled to live a life they value, both in the present and the future, is the appropriate goal. In such a case, progress is more likely to be assessed by the satisfaction people feel with their experience, and particularly with the quality of their relationships and the support to achieve what they may, as much as the accredited outcomes they achieve. This is not to condone complacency about attainment outcomes, but to emphasise that how learners experience the process of education and training may matter as much as the final outcome (Lumby and Morrison, 2009).

Development of leaders for future diverse and inclusive schools, colleges and universities

There are very many guidance documents emerging from public sector bodies, interest groups, national reviews and local working groups. These offer a range of possible actions to increase equality, representation, family-friendliness, physical access and other goals. They focus outwards on action. This chapter goes on to consider such outward-orientated action, but first looks inwards. There is much evidence that inequality is embedded not only in structures but most profoundly in the attitudes of individuals, including educational leaders (Bush et al., 2006; Cushman, 2005; Decuir and Dixson, 2004; Rusch, 2004).

The majority of leaders would assert a commitment to equality, however they understand the term, in relation to both learners and staff. Yet there is historical and universal evidence of sexism, racism and other forms of discrimination (Gillborn, 2005; Walker 2005). Such behaviour is often not a conscious choice, but an arguably instinctive (Sapolsky, 2002) or socially embedded reaction (Simons and Pelled, 1999). An encounter with another who is perceived as different to oneself evokes uncertainty, which in its turn leads to anxiety. Cognitive processes habitually deal with such anxiety by avoidance or by a quick fix adoption of stereotyping, which allows categorisation of an individual and shapes the response to take account of what is 'known' about the stereotyped group. Stone and Colella (1996: 358) define stereotypes as 'largely false "overgeneralized" beliefs about members of a category that are typically negative'. Once a stereotyping process has been initiated, the leader's capacity to react to the person as an individual becomes limited:

> Cognitively anxiety leads to biases in how we process information. The more anxious we are, the more likely we will focus on the behaviours we expect to see, such as those based on our stereotypes, and the more likely we are to confirm these expectations and not recognize behaviour which is inconsistent with our expectations. (Gudykunst, 1995: 14)

There is no panacea for replacing such responses amongst oneself, other staff and learners with a more accurate and mindful interaction with the individual as a unique person, rather than as a member of a group. Lakomski (2001) and Allix and Gronn (2005) both argue that what needs to change [are] neurological patterns which may have been established by repetition over a lifetime. As a consequence, learned responses are 'highly resistant to eradication, or forgetting … implicit learning gives rise to a phenomenal sense of intuition in that subjects respond the way they do because it simply "feels right", or natural' (Allix and Gronn, 2005: 187). Token 'sheep dip' training days will do little to shift deeply embedded attitudes, which are often unconscious and in contradiction to consciously held beliefs. A much more persistent range of strategies is needed to embed ongoing pressure to shift thinking.

One might hope that the presence of those perceived as 'other' might offer help in challenging such thinking patterns, but there are obstacles. Those who are disadvantaged by a particular characteristic or characteristics may adopt strategies to disguise their 'otherness' rather than foreground their distinctive nature. Gurin and Nagda (2006), writing in a US context, identify ways students (and potentially staff) may deal with minority status. They may de-categorise, emphasising that they are not to be seen as a member of a disadvantaged group, such as black or a woman, but as an individual. Such de-categorisation aims to encourage the in-group to see the individual as such, and not as a member of an out-group. Re-categorisation draws the out-group into the in-group, in order to create one single group. If those who are disadvantaged adopt such strategies in order to blend with the majority or those who are dominant, they are not likely to offer the kind of information and support which helps understand difference. Rather, the latter is minimised as far as possible. The stigmatised characteristic is subject to misdirection, as a magician will attempt to divert attention away from what he or she does not want the audience to see

(Goffman, 1986). The result may be to encourage blindness to difference and its significance. Colour blindness is one result. White staff do not focus on their whiteness as a significant characteristic. They also may not see the ethnicity of others as relevant (Cochrane-Smith, 1995; Mabokela and Madsen, 2003). The assertion that an individual 'does not notice colour' in others is widespread (Walker, 2005). In this way those who view themselves as the norm collude with those who are perceived as different, to maintain that difference does not matter. Leaders may need consistently to insist that people are different, that difference matters in a range of ways, and that some differences matter more than others in the advantage or disadvantage they accrue.

Key actions to achieve a diverse leadership

In order to lead in a diverse society and to foreground differences among learners and staff in a way that is positive, leaders may need intercultural competence skills, and to reconsider the purpose of leadership if the transformation of society is a goal (Stier, 2006). [...] Iles and Kaur Hayers (1997: 105) describe cultural fluency involving three dimensions: 'cognitive complexity, emotional energy and psychological maturity'. Their work draws on research concerning transnational corporations, but increasingly the intercultural competence needed in such contexts is equally relevant to the diverse communities served by many schools, colleges and universities. The kind of inner strength and moral energy depicted as necessary is a long way from the leader development which hinges on short-term training or guidance documents. The latter have a place, but are only likely to be effective if they are founded on a bedrock of the kind of 'mindfulness' described by Gudykunst (1995: 16). Rather than actions which focus outward on other staff or learners, the leader's first task may be to look inward and over time to continue to challenge one's own stance.

The stance of other staff and the purpose and structures of the organisations may also require attention. As outlined earlier in the chapter there are, of course, very many possible goals and actions.

Key areas of action for leading for diversity and inclusion

There are many prescriptions of how to achieve 'equality', deriving from national governments, from advisory bodies, and from research. Synthesising the content, some key questions emerge. The first is the location of responsibility. In some cases, the principal/headteacher may take personal responsibility, believing the area is foundational, and therefore rightly a part of the principal's brief. More often, the organisation may embed a diversity role as part of a member of the senior leadership team's portfolio. In larger organisations, such as colleges or universities, there may be a diversity manager, often situated within a human resource department, or a diversity champion/multicultural co-ordinator within the teaching and learning staff structure. If the role is low status, that is, perceived by the majority as not central to the success of the organisation, then wherever responsibility is placed, diversity will remain a minor issue. In a study of colleges in the UK, a diversity manager placed high in the organisation hierarchy nevertheless felt, 'You're a lone voice in an ocean … a bolt-on to the business of the college' (Lumby et al., 2007). The locus of responsibility alone will not achieve diversity issues being perceived as high priority, but it could contribute to achieving such an aim. Responsibility for diversity issues placed with a junior role with little time or resource will give a clear message about its unimportance. Placing it higher will not necessarily give the contrary message unless linked to a degree of resource indicative of its importance. […]

Appointing/allocating someone to address diversity issues is of itself unlikely to bring about much change. Other signals will be deciphered to interpret the meaning of such action. Similarly, many organisations collect diversity data of various kinds. Collection in itself may achieve little. The attention paid to the kind of data and the use made of it signals whether the activity is ritual compliance with legislative requirements, or a matter of genuine concern to those who hold status in the school or college. Data monitoring as a displacement activity for real change is a common strategy (Deem and Morley, 2006). Commitment to a direction for change cannot be faked, or at least not for long. Both staff and learners will read the runes to decipher attitudes to diversity and the necessity for change or otherwise.

Assuming that there is a real intention to move towards greater equality, and that how this is understood has been discussed and agreed by staff and learners, there are many sources of ideas for action. Norte (1999) suggests a five-point framework for developing school practice for inclusion; that policy and practice be considered in relation to:

1. Content: the subject matter of focus (including vision, curriculum and support/counselling services for learners).
2. Process: how people engage the subject matter (planning, use of data, consultation engagement with all staff, student and local communities).
3. Structure: how time, space and people are organised and configured (encouragement of interaction between individuals and between school or community groups).
4. Staffing: the roles to which personnel are assigned (recruitment and selection, promotion, development opportunities and support, employment conditions and personal security).
5. Infrastructure: the physical setting (safety, accessibility and a positive environment and facilities for all).

If leaders reviewed each of these aspects of the school, college or university to consider their support of diversity and inclusion, substantial change is likely to be indicated. For example, if staff are unrepresentative of the local or school community, changing the situation may demand determination and creativity. Existing staff may be resistant, arguing against what they erroneously perceive as unfair positive discrimination (Lumby et al., 2005). A long-term and detailed strategy might emerge to address attitudes and practice if each of the five points were considered in all aspects.

Aguirre and Martinez (2007) present two options for responding to diversity which they term co-option and transformational strategies. There is evidence that much leadership for and with diversity in many parts of the world is co-option; that is, it treats diversity as a relatively minor issue which can be tacked on to other more central policies and acted upon periodically (Dass and Parker, 1999). Transformation approaches which place diversity as central are less frequent.

The practice gulf

While many, perhaps most, educational leaders recognise that there may be issues of inequality in their organisation related to particular individuals or groups of learners or staff, progress in addressing them is inhibited by the gulf between intention, enactment and experience. Evans (2003: 419) distinguishes 'policy espoused', 'policy enacted' and the impact on individuals' and groups' lives as 'policy experienced'. Official policy documents, policy espoused, generally commit to increasing equality of opportunity or social justice. The enactment of such policy is weak in many schools, colleges and universities. There is lack of action, peripheral tokenistic action or action primarily driven by compliance with legislation, which results in systems that do not impact deeply on people's attitudes and daily practice. The locus of both the existence of significant inequality and the responsibility for addressing it is often placed elsewhere. A kind of double-think is in existence, where leaders acknowledge that, for example, racism exists everywhere, but also that it is not particularly pertinent among their own staff or in their own practice. Numerous studies in different parts of the world suggest otherwise; that inequality is deeply and universally embedded and persistent, and that many staff and leaders consider diversity issues either irrelevant or low priority, or are actively hostile to them (Phendla, 2008; Rusch, 2004; Sinclair, 2000; Walker and Walker, 1998). There is a widespread overestimation of the impact of action. Research in the UK (Bush et al., 2006; Fazil et al., 2002), in South Africa (Lumby and Heystek, 2008; Phendla, 2008), in the USA (Lugg, 2003), in Canada and Australia (Gaskell and Taylor, 2003) and in Korea (Brooker and Ha, 2005), among many other countries, reveals persisting unjustified disadvantage and consequent underperformance resulting from attitudes to ethnicity, gender, sexual orientation, disability and socio-economic class, among other characteristics. There are, of course, exceptions where individuals and organisations have fully embraced the necessity to engage with issues of diversity in a positive and determined fashion (Lumby et al., 2005). One case study college provides evidence of such leadership in action, where the principal focused on and, evidence suggests, achieved:

- a focus on diversity issues as fundamental to organisational development
- a senior management team representative of the local community gender and ethnic profile
- responsibility for diversity and inclusion both embedded in the whole senior team and in specific roles
- a detailed and well-resourced equality action plan

- frequent and rigorous scrutiny and response to diversity data analysis
- ongoing and frequent development activities for all staff both in relation to generic leadership (in which diversity is foundational) and particular diversity issues
- participation in organisational, local and national networks supporting individuals and groups working towards greater equality (Lumby, 2009).

Staff of varied levels in the case study perceived diversity as integrated within every aspect of their own and organisational practice. However, the research cited in this section suggests that the majority of those leading and those preparing leaders who might identify with such practice are likely to be over-optimistic. The main thrust of this chapter has been to outline not only what might be done to address issues related to diversity, but also to stress what a long way remains to go.

References

Aguirre, A. Jr and Martinez, R.O. (2007) 'Diversity leadership in higher education', *ASHE Higher Education Report*, 32(3), San Francisco, CA: Jossey-Bass.

Allix, P. and Gronn, P. (2005) '"Leadership" as knowledge', *Educational Management, Leadership and Administration*, 33(2): 181–96.

Begley, P. (2003) 'In pursuit of authentic school leadership practices', in P. Begley and O. Johansson (eds), *The Ethical Dimensions of School Leadership*. London: Kluwer Academic.

Brooker, L. and Ha, S.J. (2005) 'The cooking teacher: investigating gender stereotypes in a Korean kindergarten', *Early Years*, 25(1): 17–30.

Bush, T., Glover, D. and Sood, K. (2006) 'Black and minority ethnic leaders in England: a portrait', *School Leadership and Management*, 26(3): 289–305.

Cochrane-Smith, M. (1995) 'Color blindness and basket making are not the answers: confronting the dilemmas of race, culture, and language diversity in teacher education', *American Educational Research Journal*, 32(3): 493–522.

Cruikshank, K. (2004) 'Towards diversity in teacher education: teacher preparation of immigrant teachers', *International Journal of Teacher Education*, 27(2): 125–38.

Cushman, P. (2005) 'It's just not a real bloke's job: male teachers in the primary school', *Asia-Pacific Journal of Teacher Education*, 33(3): 321–38.

Dass, P. and Parker, B. (1999) 'Strategies for managing human resource diversity: from resistance to learning', *Academy of Management Executive*, 13(2): 68–80.

Davies, L. (1990) *Equity and Efficiency? School Management in an International Context*. London: Falmer Press.

Decuir, J. and Dixson, A. (2004) '"So when it comes out, they aren't that surprised that it is there": using critical race theory as a tool of analysis of race and racism in education', *Educational Researcher*, 33(5): 26–31.

Deem, R. and Morley, L. (2006) 'Diversity in the academy? Staff perceptions of equality policies in six contemporary higher education institutions', *Policy Futures in Education*, 4(2): 185–202.

DiTomaso, N. and Hooijberg, R. (1996) 'Diversity and the demands of leadership', *The Leadership Quarterly*, 7(2): 163–87.

Evans, K. (2003) 'Uncertain frontiers: taking forward Edmund King's world perspectives on post-compulsory education', *Comparative Education*, 39(4): 415–22.

Fazil, Q., Bywaters, P., Ali, Z., Wallace, L. and Singh, G. (2002) 'Disadvantage and discrimination compounded: the experience of Pakistani and Bangladeshi parents of disabled children in the UK', *Disability and Society*, 17(3): 237–54.

Gaskell, J. and Taylor, S. (2003) 'The women's movement in Canadian and Australian education: from liberation and sexism to boys and social justice', *Gender and Education*, 15(2): 151–68.

Gillborn, D. (2005) 'Education policy as an act of white supremacy: whiteness, critical race theory and education reform', *Journal of Education Policy*, 20(4): 485–505.

Goffman, E. (1986) *Stigma: Notes on the Management of Spoiled Identity*. New York: Simon & Schuster.

Grogan, M. (1999) 'Equity/equality issues of gender, race and class', *Educational Administration Quarterly*, 35(4): 518–36.

Gudykunst, W. (1995) 'Anxiety/uncertainty management (AUM) theory', in R. Wiseman (ed.), *International Communication Theory* Vol. XIX. London: Sage.

Gurin, P. and Nagda, B.R.A. (2006) 'Getting to the what, how and why of diversity on campus', *Educational Researcher*, 35(1): 20-4.

Hartle, F. and Thomas, K. (2003) *Growing Tomorrow's School Leaders – The Challenge*. Nottingham: NCSL.

Iles, P. and Kaur Hayers, P. (1997) 'Managing diversity in transnational project teams: a tentative model and case study', *Journal of Managerial Psychology*, 1(2): 95–117.

Lakomski, G. (2001) 'Organizational change, leadership and learning: culture as cognitive process', *The International Journal of Educational Management*, 15(2): 68–77.

Litvin, D.R. (1997) 'The discourse of diversity: from biology to management', *Discourse and Organization*, 4(2): 187–209.

Lugg, C.A. (2003) 'Sissies, faggots, lezzies, and dykes: gender, sexual orientation, and a new politics of education?', *Educational Administration Quarterly*, 39(1): 95–134.

Lumby, J. (2009) 'Leaders' orientations to diversity: two cases from education', *Leadership*, 5(4): 423–46.

Lumby, J. and Heystek, J. (2008) 'Race, identity and leadership in South African and English schools', paper presented to the Biennial Conference of the Commonwealth Council for Educational Administration and Management, 'Think Globally, Act Locally: A Challenge to Education Leaders', 8–12 September, Durban, South Africa.

Lumby, J. and Morrison, M. (2009) 'Youth perspectives: schooling, capabilities frameworks and human rights', *International Journal of Inclusive Education*. First article: 1–15. http://dx.doi.org/10.1080/13603110801995920 (accessed 5 May 2009).

Lumby, J., Bhopal, K., Dyke, M., Maringe, F. and Morrison, M. (2007) *Integrating Diversity in Leadership in Further Education*. London: Centre for Excellence in Leadership.

Lumby, J., Harris, A., Morrison, M., Muijs, D., Sood, K., Glover, D. and Wilson, M. with Briggs, A.R.J. and Middlewood, D. (2005) *Leadership, Development and Diversity in the Learning and Skills Sector*. London: LSDA.

Lumby, J. with Coleman, M. (2007) *Leadership and Diversity: Challenging Theory and Practice in Education*. London: Sage.

Mabokela, R.O. and Madsen, J. (2003) '"Color-blind" leadership and intergroup conflict', *Journal of School Leadership*, 13(2): 130–58.

McCall, M. (2005) 'The complexity of intersectionality', *Signs: Journal of Women in Culture and Society*, 33(3): 1771–96.

Miller, F.A. and Katz, J.H. (2002) *The Inclusion Breakthrough: Unleashing the Real Power of Diversity*. San Francisco, CA: Berrett-Koehler.

Milliken, F.J. and Martins, L.L. (1996) 'Searching for common threads: understanding the multiple effects of diversity in organizational groups', *Academy of Management Review*, 21(2): 1–32. http://search.epnet.com/dierct.asp? an=9605060217 &db=buh (accessed 6 May 2004).

Norte, E. (1999) '"Structures beneath the skin": how school leaders use their power and authority to create institutional opportunities for developing positive interethnic communities', *Journal of Negro Education*, 68(4): 466–85.

Phendla, T. (2008) 'The paradox of Luselo-Lufhanga metaphors: African women defining leadership for social justice', *International Studies in Educational Leadership*, 36(1): 22–40.

Reynolds, M. and Trehan, K. (2003) 'Learning from difference?', *Management Learning*, 34(2): 163–80.

Rusch, E. (2004) 'Gender and race in leadership preparation: a constrained discourse', *Educational Administration Quarterly*, 40(1): 16–48.

Sapolsky, R. (2002) 'Cheaters and chumps', *Natural History*, 111(5): 1–7. http://weblinks2.epnet. com/citation. asp? (accessed 23 May 2006).

Shields, C. (2008) 'Levelling the playing field in racialized contexts: leaders speaking out about difficult issues', paper presented to the Biennial Conference of the Commonwealth Council for Educational Administration and Management, 'Think Globally Act Locally: A Challenge to Education Leaders', 8–12 September, Durban, South Africa.

Simons, T. and Pelled, L.H. (1999) 'Understanding executive diversity: more than meets the eye', *Human Resource Planning*, 22(2): 49–51.

Sinclair, A. (2000) 'Women within diversity: risks and possibilities', *Women in Management Review*, 15(5/6): 237–45.

Sloop, J. (2007) 'In queer time and place and race: intersectionality comes of age', *Quarterly Journal of Speech*, 91(3): 312–26.

Sobehart, H. (ed.) (2008) *Women Leading Education Across the Continents: Sharing the Spirit, Fanning the Flame*. Lantham, MD and Toronto: Rowman and Littlefield.

Stier, J. (2006) 'Internationalisation, intercultural communication and intercultural competence', *Journal of Intercultural Communication*, 11: 1–12. http://www.immi.se/intercultural/ (accessed 14 July 2006).

Stone, D. and Colella, A. (1996) 'A model of factors affecting the treatment of disabled individuals in organizations', *Academy of Management Review*, 12(2): 352–401.

Walker, M. (2005) 'Race is nowhere and race is everywhere', *British Journal of the Sociology of Education*, 26(1): 41–55.

Walker, A. and Walker, J. (1998) 'Challenging the boundaries of sameness: leadership through valuing difference', *Journal of Educational Administration*, 36(1): 8–28.

You-Ta, C., Church, R. and Zikic, J. (2004) 'Organizational culture, group diversity and intra-group conflict', *Team Performance Management*, 10(1): 26–34.

Part 4

Partnerships and Collaboration

15

Reconfiguring Urban Leadership: Taking a Perspective on Community

Kathryn A. Riley

Introduction

This chapter is an exploration of the nature, challenges and opportunities of urban leadership. It maps the nature of school communities in challenging urban contexts, using this exploration to reconfigure the leadership challenges and the ways in which leadership is conceptualised. The starting point for this exploration is context and community.

The children and young people of our cities can experience life at its extremes: an ex-pupil, caught up in the local gang-land drugs culture, is shot and killed; a child is killed by a drunken motorist. However, the daily reality is often far more mundane than this and, for many, includes friendship and support in contexts which are rich and diverse. Nonetheless, despite the abundance of social capital in our cities, many young people have limited access to the opportunities of our cities and are disenfranchised from the cultural inheritance which is rightly theirs. Urban schools can help create pathways for young people into the opportunities of our cities. School leaders' role is to set the climate of expectations which enables this to happen.

Leadership is commonly defined as a role-based function linked to a specific job or institution and to the activities associated with that role (Riley and Louis 2000), or as the actions of heroic individuals who take a lead at extreme moments. While both of these definitions remain, in an increasingly complex, global and diverse world the notion of a

Source – An edited version of Riley, K.A. (2009) 'Reconfiguring urban leadership: taking a perspective on community'.

leader acting in isolation (heroically or otherwise), or having a clearly defined role to be exercised within set and agreed boundaries, is increasingly redundant. There are layers of leadership:

- of, and with, the school community;
- of, and with, the local community; and
- of, and with, the broader locality.

This raises questions about what is meant by community and by community leadership, and about the interface between schools and communities. What is the school's sphere of influence? In what ways should the learning environment change to take account of the experiences of young people in our cities? What does leading for and with community mean? The needs and wants of a community are rarely static, or uniform: Whose views count, why, how and when? Many schools serve very diverse communities: How do schools connect to dispersed communities? How can they create community within school?

Over recent years, the demands on school leaders have grown exponentially. Yet the consequences of taking on a more community-orientated role challenge the scope and practice of leadership. School leaders who are working to connect to communities may discover uncomfortable truths – criminal activities or extremism. What do they do in response to this?

The political context in which urban school leaders struggle to find the answers to these questions is in itself a challenging one. While many features of urban education are connected to broader educational, social and economic issues which extend beyond the immediate urban context (Riley 1998; Whitty et al. 1998; Lupton 2005), to a considerable degree, politicians on both sides of the Atlantic have focused on the negative aspects of urban schooling. The policy discourse, particularly in the USA, has tended to centre on the perpetual crisis of urban education: teacher shortages; cutbacks in services. For some, the term *urban* has become synonymous with 'poverty, non-white violence, narcotics, bad neighbourhoods, an absence of family values, crumbling housing and failing schools' (Kincheloe 2004: 2). In the UK, there have been concerns about how to close the gap in achievement between the youngsters in the most deprived areas and those in the more affluent areas (Bell 2003). The community and the political context set the framework for this discussion about urban leadership.

The chapter is organised into three parts. Part I maps the key features of the urban context, highlighting the nature and intensity of the challenges. Part II goes deeper into the community-related challenges that urban school leaders face. Part III brings these elements together, suggesting that school leaders' ability to take stock of the community context, and to develop self-knowledge about how leadership is experienced, is part of the scaffolding which they need to put in place before they can reconfigure their leadership. Part III also outlines some of the steps that urban school leaders can take to build trust, create a new relationship with communities, and secure an ethical foundation which will enable them to realign their leadership. It concludes by offering a values-driven, community-based model of leadership – a model that sets out some of the key ingredients but does not prescribe how leadership is exercised.

I. The urban context

Cities across the globe attract large and diverse populations and witness societal struggles about the distribution of resources. At their extremes, they are places of:

- *contrast and disparity*: between those living in opulence and those struggling with poverty;
- *opportunity and restriction*: between those who have access to employment and rich cultural experiences and those who do not; and
- *location and dislocation*: between those who have a sense of belonging, and those who live on the margins of society.

These extremes raise issues about how societies educate the children of the most deprived, in close proximity to the most advantaged (Riley and Emery 2007).

Our cities are diverse, with pockets of stability and areas that change fast. Impoverished downtown areas become gentrified in relatively short periods of time: new populations move in and out, influenced by global events and the movement of refugee populations. One urban reality is this ever altering, shifting, varying nature of our communities who form a veritable kaleidoscope of constantly changing groups of people, with their day-to-day realities, hopes and dreams (Riley forthcoming).

Although there are many distinctive differences between our city schools, there are probably a number of defining characteristics of the educational landscape. Writing about the US context, Kincheloe identifies such common features as high population density, areas of profound economic disparity and higher levels of ethnic, racial, religious and linguistic diversity (Kincheloe 2004). The school population of US urban schools is increasingly black and Hispanic and the American urban education landscape is likely to include schools that are typically larger than elsewhere (which means that students can be overlooked and may find it difficult to develop a sense of identity); school districts that face a concentration of problems; and school boards which 'experience factionalized infighting ... over resources and influence' (Kincheloe 2004: 6).

Despite the growing focus in the UK on urban schools, there are problems of definition (Keys et al. 2003). Characteristics include a 'myriad of complex and socially related problems' (Harris 2002) involving social and economic deprivation, for example, ill health, financial pressures, family stress, poor housing (Smith and Noble 1995; Barber 1996). Within-school factors include management, resourcing and interactions with the local community (Cutler 1998; Learmonth and Lowers 1998; DfEE 1999; Englefield 2001; Hopkins 2001).

Nevertheless, the cultural and community diversity of many of our city schools is often a source of great strength. Schools reap the benefits of the multiplicity in our societies: the creativity, the energy and the resilience and exuberance of the children; the rich cultural understanding and experiences. However, cultural and community diversity also has many other implications for schools. There are issues concerning the ability of newly arrived immigrant groups to engage with society; the concentration of socially disadvantaged children, and the demands these create on resources; how to work with an 'underclass' with very low expectations, high levels of disaffection from society and a dismissive attitude towards learning; as well as poverty and mental health problems, for both pupils and their families, which serve to increase the complexity and nature of the challenges. It is this amalgam of complexity, profound need, diversity and speed of change that generates significant challenges for urban school leaders.

II. The challenges and opportunities of urban leadership

Empirical work undertaken for the research and development project *Leadership on the Front-line* indicates that there are two interconnected community-related challenges that school leaders have to contend with. These relate to their ability to:

- make sense of the big picture in our cites – the changes and complexity; and
- understand more about local communities and about children's lives and experiences.

Challenge I: make sense of the big picture

Capturing the distinctive community context of individual schools can be a complex task. While some city schools are located in the centre of the communities they serve, this is not always the case. Some recruit children from a wide geographical area, others are physically located in communities which do not send their children to the school. Even when a school is positioned in the centre of its catchment area, it may serve a range of disparate communities (Riley 2008b). Deciding who the communities are and what is meant by the term community can be a difficult task.

As part of the project *Leadership on the Front-line* we asked participating headteachers and school principals to carry out their own local community audit based on three core questions:

- How do I 'read' my community?
- What's changing?
- What's my role within it?

Leadership on the Front-line

Bringing city leaders together to learn together

Leadership on the Front-line is an ongoing research and development project which brings together headteachers and school principals across the UK and Eire (Belfast, Birmingham, Cardiff, Dublin, London, Londonderry, Liverpool, Manchester and Salford) to develop greater understanding about the context and challenges of urban leadership. To date, the project has brought together over 70 headteachers of schools

---

in challenging urban contexts. The schools are cross-phase (nursery, primary, secondary and special), and reflect the range of types of schools in urban contexts: denominational, integrated, county, girls and boys. The central conceptualization of *Leadership on the Front-line* starts with an external focus on the community. How school leaders interpret and respond to that context, and to the leadership challenges on a day-to-day basis is, in its turn, shaped by underpinning values and beliefs (Riley et al., 2006). The project has focused on:

- The *purposes* of leadership (issues to do with values and beliefs);
- The *practices* (on a day-to-day basis);
- The *challenges* (including how to mediate between different views and beliefs from within the community); and
- The pressures (the personal implications of working in such a challenging role).

In 2007, two further groups of headteachers and lead educators from Salford and Waltham Forest in London joined the project. Each group has its own set of distinctive community challenges. In Salford, there are issues about the poverty, ill-health and low aspirations in a predominantly white working-class community which is now becoming more multiracial. In Waltham Forest, the issues are about community cohesion in a multiracial area which is changing fast and which, in the context of perceived terrorist threats, has been in the public eye. This phase of the project will provide fresh perspectives on urban leadership by supporting collaborations of school leaders and offering a localised focus on the challenges and opportunities. The aim is to review the nature of urban leadership within the broader context of schooling provided by the 'Every Child Matters' Agenda.

Using a tool designed for the project, they mapped their school community on four axes:

- *population* (stable or mobile, e.g. with refugees and immigrants);
- *community profile* (single or multiple communities);
- *levels of engagement* (engaged with education or disengaged); and
- *community identity* (integrated with a strong community identity, or fragmented with disparate communities).

Once participants had undertaken the mapping exercise, they were left with a 'shape' that related to their own community context – an exercise which generated considerable discussion and helped create a shared language to discuss the complexities of context. Based on the mapping exercise, we were able to distinguish four types of urban schools, those that serve:

- an inner-city single, relatively homogenous community;
- multiple and diverse communities within a locality;
- an estate community; and
- multiple and diverse communities over an extended area (Riley forthcoming).

[In] a multiple and diverse community in Liverpool, the headteacher depicted the school as serving a highly mobile and multiple population drawn from a range of communities:

It's a very dysfunctional community, really I think. It's coming to the bottom of a very deep hole of deprivation, problems with drugs, arms, related crime. A lot of disaffected youth in gangs, children between 10 and 16 or 17 maybe. Causing a lot of problems for the people living here. ... I've been a headteacher here for nine years. It was a very stable area ... but I've seen it go down and down, possibly due to the housing policy here where housing is being used to decant people who are having difficulties but the effect has been to move people out of this area who were very stable. Into that mix, I think, comes a lot of people just recently, asylum seeking families, who are having quite a lot of difficulty here.

It's quite a racist area, but there is a lot of short-term housing here. So currently in the school, I think, it's 19% of the children are from asylum seeking families. The mobility rate here is 41% – it's very high. ... There are 17 different languages amongst that group, but what we're finding is that people are coming in and going out, some of them because economically, they are moving around the area. That tends to be Czech Roma families, but there are other families who really are finding it very difficult to come to terms with the aggression. (Riley et al. 2004: 8)

Challenge II: know more about local communities and children's lives and experiences

The word community has many meanings and is used widely because it conveys the sense of individuals working together with shared beliefs and goals. The intrinsic value of community membership has become a cliché: something warm and cuddly that we all want to be a part of. It is a truism today that schools should relate to their community. No one seriously suggests that schools should merely do their best to process the children who come through the school gates every morning, while ignoring whatever goes on outside those gates (Riley and Stoll 2005). Truisms have the advantage of being true, but very often, as in this case, they also have the disadvantage of being rather imprecise generalisations. A review of the literature on schools and communities suggests that there are five main reasons why schools decide to become more engaged with their local communities: to improve student achievement; to make schools more accountable, and to increase democratic involvement; to build social capital within communities, by encouraging schools to collaborate to promote community well-being (for example, healthier or safer communities); to develop the role of schools as moral agents, promoting social justice and responsibility for youth; and to promote schools' self-interest through the development of good public relations (Riley and Louis 2000).

A key element of the investigative work in *Leadership on the Front-line* has been an exploration of the lives and experiences of the young people. Working with nearly 500 children aged 3–17 in 49 of the schools in the project, we asked two broad questions: *What is it like living round here? What is it like being in this school?* Our interviews enabled us to understand more about the intricacies of young people's lives: the disjuncture between school and community; issues to do with safety, space and territory, culture and belief; and issues about territory.

We asked pupils to draw pictures that illustrated their experience of life within the wider community. These images are vivid and looking at young people's lives in new ways has enabled school leaders involved in the project to understand the totality of children's lives and the complexities of community.

These challenges shape the ways in which urban school leaders both experience and exercise their leadership. For the leaders of our city schools, the emotional octane can be intense: highs and lows, as well as the deep satisfaction of seeing the children and young people in their schools succeed. From *Leadership on the Front-line* we have learned much about the pressures and intensity of being a school leader, as well as the personal costs. But, equally, we have also discovered much about the other side of the coin: the exuberance and enthusiasm of our urban children, and the ways in which schools can transform their lives. School leaders have told us how enriching and rewarding the job is: 'The best there is!'

In our first booklet on *Leadership on the Front-line*, we argued that the headteachers and principals of our city schools have much to teach school leaders elsewhere (Riley et al. 2004). There are issues concerned with being at the cutting edge of changes that will shape our society for decades ahead. What the leaders of our city schools need to know and be able to do on a daily basis is what many colleagues in less pressing contexts will need to know and be able do in future years. There are issues concerned with social justice. There are issues concerned with creativity and energy. But the research also revealed that urban school leaders often find themselves caught between what they experience as competing realities – the physical, the social and political; the emotional; and the spiritual or ethical – and that a process of reappraisal and reflection is needed before they can reconfigure their leadership (Riley et al. 2007).

III. Next steps: reconfiguring urban leadership

Underpinning this process of learning and reflection is the need for urban school leaders to understand their own responses to the leadership challenges. Self-knowledge will enable them to understand the *part* they play in leadership – within their school and their locality – and to understand their strengths, as well as their limitations. It will also enable them to centre themselves and develop a sense of wholeness which acknowledges the challenges *and* the joys of leadership (the children and young people: their liveliness and exuberance; and the staff and parents: what they can contribute). And it will enable them to reconcile what, on the face of it, may seem to be the irreconcilable, and strike a balance between the unremitting demands of the job and a sense of personal well-being. It is this balance and focus that will contribute to rich educational gains for students, staff and communities and enable school leaders not only to survive the job, but also to grow and thrive in it.

Nevertheless, the contextual challenges described earlier in the [chapter] inevitably create dilemmas for school leaders:

- If they are to make sense of the big picture, school leaders will need to step back and carry out a thorough audit of the community context. It is also vital that they develop a more strategic and less reactive response to critical social policy issues which have a major impact on the lives of children and young people, such as domestic abuse. This is something which school leaders recognise but often find hard to put into practice.

- Understanding more about local communities and about children's lives and experiences is a precursor to *building trust*. Yet school leaders who work to build trust can feel isolated, particularly if, as suggested, they discover uncomfortable truths about what is happening in their local community and have to balance the needs of families and communities with the demands of other agencies, such as social services, or the police.

In this final section of the [chapter], I outline some of the steps that school leaders can take to build trust, to create a new relationship with communities and to secure an ethical foundation which will enable them to realign their leadership role.

Step I: foster trusting relationships between schools and communities

School leaders have a critical role to play in building trust and mutual understanding between schools and communities. Trust is nurtured through relationships, through information and through knowledge. And although fostering trusting relationships between schools and communities is linked to teaching and learning and to attainment, school leaders acknowledge that it often comes at the bottom of their priority list. The 'Trust' loop looks something like this:

- Schools gather *information* about their local community: the history, geography, key socioeconomic factors.
- That information is then turned into *knowledge* and *understanding*: that is an appreciation of the challenges, riches and complexities of daily life.
- Knowledge and understanding becomes the bedrock for building *mutuality* – a shared affinity and allegiance between schools and communities regarding the education needs of young people.

It is through this mutuality, this signing up to common goals, that schools and communities build that final key ingredient – *trust*. Trust is the 'super glue' that binds these elements together and connects the school's internal community with its outside communities. Trust does not appear out of the ether. It may emerge from respect for a profession (medical), or a calling (a priest or Imam), or a role (tenants' leader), but even then it is dependent on the relationships which people have with those individuals. In our complex and fast-changing world, trust can not be assumed. It has to be created. And it has to be earned (Riley and Stoll, 2005).

This notion of trust is not new (Louis and Kruse 1995; Louis 2007) and the evidence is that educational reforms are doomed to fail, unless trusting relationships are present: among teachers, school leaders, parents and students (Byrk and Scheider 2002). Trust is the basis of real and deep-rooted changes in schools. Trust enables schools to draw on the untapped resources of communities, what have been described as their 'invisible assets', the social capital which includes the networks and relationships which connect communities

(Hargreaves 2003). This notion of trust is strongly an underpinning element of the new leadership relationship.

Step II: create a new relationship with communities

While many school leaders recognise the importance of developing a leadership role which takes them beyond the classroom and the school gate, and which connects to communities, they struggle to identify what this role is, or how to reconcile it with their existing role and the daily demands of the job. Acknowledging these dilemmas, and taking steps towards resolving them, is all part of the process of reflection needed to reconfigure leadership in response to the community (Riley and Louis 2000).

How schools and communities work together is unique to each context and based on intensively personal relationships, which need to be developed. School leaders have a key role to play in valuing children's knowledge and skills. Valuing the richnesses of children's lives in this way is not new but it helps counteract intolerance and ignorance in a national climate which can be hostile to refugees, or to other faiths. The small day-to-day practices within a school – enabling young people to teach their classmates how to say good morning in Amharic; an Islamic prayer; a poem in Jamaican patois – reinforce respect and acknowledge differences (Riley and Stoll 2005).

However, knowing pupils' communities is not just a matter of learning about newcomers, ethnic minorities and non-Christian faiths. It also involves understanding more about longer-standing families in the community – the white working class – who have always been the main source of pupils in our urban schools. There has often been a tension – frequently a very creative tension – between the attitudes and values of teachers who are largely middle class (by profession if not by origin) and their working-class students. It is also important to recognise that these groups are as they always have been. They are evolving too, responding to newcomers and to the many other changes in society.

Step III: secure an ethical foundation

The approach outlined in this [chapter] is based on a series of step changes that are incremental but solidly embedded in core values and beliefs. There is a growing literature on the value and ethics of leadership which is particularly relevant to urban contexts (Burns 1978; Sergiovanni 2000; West-Burnham 2002; Begley and Johansson 2003).

The reconfiguration of urban leadership presented is focused on building mutuality and trust between schools and communities. In the light of the 'Every Child Matters' Agenda of whole system reform of children's services, this implies a willingness to look outwards from schools towards the external community context, and at the range of organisations and agencies that are working with children and young people. The model is shown in Figure 15.1.

It is a collaborative model which has a strong ethical and moral foundation, linked to social justice and to broader concerns about environmental sustainability. It is also a very locality

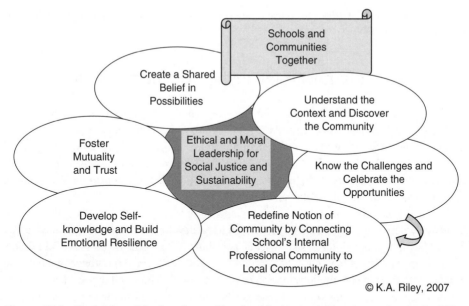

© K.A. Riley, 2007

Figure 15.1   Model for ethical and moral leadership for social justice and sustainability

based model, deriving from the community context, and is dependent for its success on building on, and connecting to, local networks. The specific elements of the model include:

- understanding the local context and discovering the community;
- knowing the challenges and celebrating the opportunities;
- redefining the notion of community by connecting [a] school's internal, professional community to the local community/ies;
- developing self-knowledge and building emotional resilience;
- fostering mutuality and trust; and
- creating a shared belief in possibilities (Riley et al. 2007).

The model implies a process of reaching out to communities. It reinforces the importance of building connections between schools and communities. It also implies that reaching out to help the community is about learning from, and making better use of, existing resources in the community. The goal is to create shared beliefs about what can be achieved for, and by, the young people of our cities.

References

Barber, M. 1996. Creating a framework for success in urban areas. In *Raising educational standards in the inner cities*, eds. M. Barber and R. Dann, 6–23. London: Cassell.

Bell, D. 2003. Access and achievement in urban education: Ten years on. Speech to the Fabian Society.

Begley, P.T., and O. Johansson (eds) 2003. *The ethical dimensions of school leadership*. Dordrecht: Kluwer Academic.

Burns, M.J. 1978. *Leadership*. New York: Harper & Row.

Byrk, A.S., and B. Scheider. 2002. *Trust in school: A core resource for school reform*. New York: Russell Sage Foundation.

Cutler, V. 1998. Highbury Grove – from deconstruction to reconstruction. In *No quick fixes: Perspectives on schools in difficulty*, eds. L. Stoll and K. Myers, 86–95. London: Falmer Press.

DfEE. 1999. *Excellence in cities*. London: Department for Education and Employment.

Englefield, S. 2001. *Leading to success: Judging success in primary schools in challenging contexts*. Nottingham: National College for School Leadership.

Hargreaves, D. 2003. Leading for transformation within the London Challenge. Annual Lecture of the London Leadership Centre, Institute of Education, May.

Harris, A. 2002. Effective leadership in schools facing challenging contexts. S*chool Leadership and Management* 22, no. 1: 15–26.

Hopkins, D. 2001. *Meeting the challenge: An improvement guide for schools facing challenging circumstances*. London: DfEE.

Keys, W., C. Sharp, K. Greene, and H. Grayson. 2003. *Successful leadership of schools in urban and challenging contexts*. Nottingham: National College for School Leadership.

Kincheloe, J.L. 2004. Why a book on urban education? In *Nineteen urban questions: Teaching in the city*, eds. S.R. Steinberg and J.L. Kincheloe, 1–28. New York: Peter Lang Publishing.

Learmonth, J., and K. Lowers. 1998. A trouble shooter calls. In *No quick fixes: Perspectives on schools in difficulty*, eds. L. Stoll and K. Myers, 133–44. London: Falmer Press.

Louis K.S. 2007. Trust and improvement in schools. *Journal of Educational Change* 8, no. 1: 1–24.

Louis, K.S., and S.S. Kruse. 1995. *Professionalism and community: Perspectives on reforming urban schools*. Thousand Oaks, CA: Corwin Press.

Lupton, R. 2005. Social justice and school improvement: Improving the quality of schooling in the poorest neighbourhoods. *British Educational Research Journal* 31, no. 5: 589–604.

Riley, K.A. 1998. *Whose school is it anyway*? London: Falmer Press.

Riley, K.A. 2008a. Improving city schools: Who and what makes the difference? In *New directions for educational change: International perspectives*, ed. C. Sugrue. London: Routledge.

Riley, K.A. 2008b. Leadership and urban education. In *International encyclopaedia of education*. 3rd ed., eds. B. McGaw, E. Baker and P.P. Peterson. Oxford: Elsevier.

Riley, K.A., with K. Edge, J. Jordan, and J. Reed. 2007. *Thriving and surviving as an urban leader: Reflective and analytical tools for leaders of our city schools*. London: Esmée Fairbairn Foundation and London Centre for Leadership in Learning, Institute of Education.

Riley, K.A., and H. Emery. 2007. Reconfiguring urban school leadership: Some lessons from London. In *The global challenges of the city*, eds. T. Brighouse and L. Fullich, 169–96. London: Bedford Way Papers.

Riley, K.A., C. Campbell, C. Currie, K. Edge, J. Jordan, C. Flynn, Z. Lysaght, and J. Reed. 2006. *Leadership on the front-line: Bringing leaders together to learn together*. Working Document. London: London Centre for Leadership in Learning, Institute of Education.

Riley, K.A., T. Hesketh, S. Rafferty, J. Young, P. Taylor-Moore, Y. Beecham, and S. Morris. 2004. *Urban pioneers – leading the way ahead: First lessons from the project leadership on the front-line*. London: Institute of Education, Issues in Practice Series.

Riley, K.A., and K.S.L. Louis, 2000. *Leadership for change and school reform: International perspectives on leadership*. London: Falmer Press.

Riley, K.A., and L. Stoll. 2005. *Leading communities: Purposes, paradoxes and possibilities*. Professorial Lecture, Institute of Education, London.

Sergiovanni, T.J. 2000. Changing change: Towards a design science and art. *Journal of Education Change* 1, no. 1: 57–75.

Smith, T., and M. Noble. 1995. *Education divides: Poverty and schooling in the 1990s*. London: CPAG.

West-Burnham, J. 2002. Invited Lecture, New Heads Conference, National College for School Leadership, Nottingham.

Whitty, G., S. Power, and D. Halpin. 1998. *Devolution and choice in education: The school, the state and the market*. Buckingham: Open University Press.

16

Networks as Power Bases for School Improvement

Tessa A. Moore and Michael P. Kelly

Introduction

Networked Learning Communities (NLC 2003) was launched in 2002 by the DfES in partnership with the National College for School Leadership (NCSL) and with the Innovations Unit (a public services intermediary). To qualify for funding, groups of schools across England were encouraged to form networks of any size (but a minimum number of eight schools), with a commitment to promoting learning at pupil level and at adult level within and beyond the network. Following the success of this initiative, the Primary Strategy Learning Networks (PSLN) initiative was launched in 2005. This was a reform that involved a third of all primary schools in England in the first year. The expectation was that the vast majority of primary schools would be involved in the initiative by 2008. The idea was based on a government commitment to a particular model of collaboration based on groups of 5–8 primary schools working together (DfES 2004) with the purpose of raising standards in literacy and numeracy. The overall aim of the research reported here was to explore these two centrally directed models of collaborative working for raising standards in primary schools nationally. More specifically, the research focused on the idea of networks as organic organisations and their ability to function successfully in a context of imposed bureaucratic structures and external agendas for change.

A key theme that arose in the findings was the criticality of power relationships and how power tensions impacted on the organic nature of networking. This notion was

Source – An edited version of Moore, T. and Kelly, M. (2009) 'Networks as power bases for school improvement'.

influenced by a number of theoretical ideas offered in earlier works and, in particular, Etzioni's (1961) study of power in organisations. Consequently, this [chapter] presents a theoretical model of power relationships developed to interpret this aspect of the empirical findings.

A further key theme that was explored in this research was the tension between organic and bureaucratic organisations for promoting innovation. Thus, the notion of networks as *fluid* organisations and their ability to function successfully within a rigid and prescribed organisational structure was of major interest. This idea was influenced by the earlier work of Burns and Stalker (1961) on different types of organisations. This [chapter] further develops the idea of positive power partnerships to suggest an 'ideal' model for productive networking relationships that acknowledges and supports networks as organic organisations.

Research design

The research had two phases. Phase 1 was a study of a Networked Learning Community (NLC) in the West Midlands. The NLC chosen for phase 1 had existed as a network for two years prior to formalising as a Networked Learning Community and receiving central funding from the NCSL. Phase 1 of the research took place in autumn 2004 after two years of the network's involvement in the NLC initiative. Phase 2 was a study of two London-based Primary Strategy Learning Networks and took place over the course [of] a school year from autumn 2005. The research focused on the first year in the life of these two PSLNs.

The research in both phases was qualitative and data were gathered through semi-structured interviews with participating headteachers in the three networks chosen for this study. Interview questions were designed to determine the perceived benefits and disadvantages of involvement in each of the initiatives.

Definitions

Aspects of power

The term *power* is used in a generic way in this chapter to describe many different forms of control. The term *authority* is used within the networks studied to describe a 'top down' and 'bestowed' power at government, network and school level. The term *influence* is used to describe an informal and social control existing between individuals and groups within and beyond the networks studied. And the term *legitimacy*, drawing on Connolly and James (2006), is used to describe a professional credibility and accepted authority on educational practices. Definitions of authority, influence and legitimacy in this research are explained more fully as follows.

Authority

In the earlier literature, a number of different sources of power that are found within organisations are acknowledged (French and Raven 1960; Etzioni 1961). Each of the sources described by these authors suggests a downward control from superior to subordinate. Authority is regarded in the literature as *formal power*, often conferred legally with the expectation of compliance (Hartley 2007). Etzioni (1961) defines this type of downward control as *normative, remunerative* or *coercive*. *Normative* power is control through persuasion and manipulation (Etzioni 1961). *Remunerative* or reward power is the control over rewards (Etzioni 1961) or 'the ability to give other people what they want, and hence ask them to do things for you in exchange' (French and Raven 1960: 1). *Coercive* power is control over sanctions (Etzioni 1961) or 'when a reward or expertise is withheld' (French and Raven 1960: 1). The principal goal of coercion is always compliance. The research explored these three different types of authority and their prevalence in the networks studied. The research also explored the influence of individuals and groups within the networks and the impact on the networks of the resulting power relationships.

Influence

Theories of micropolitics in organisations acknowledge influence as a significant force. Hoyle (1982) warns against marginalising the major part it plays in power structures and Woods et al. (2006) argue the importance of recognising the 'differences in power and influence between schools that need to be understood and managed' (p. 58) within collaborative groups. The notion of influence was expressed by participants in the networks both positively and negatively. Etzioni (1961) had previously labelled influence as 'social control' (p. 256) and more recent authors, for example Dowding (1996), concur. Power was wielded at all levels through the influence of individuals and groups. In more recent literature, Gunter (2004) suggests that influence is less formal than authority and that it implies manipulation. West (1999) agrees and notes that while formal authority is often 'linked to initiation or development', informal influence is often used by others below the hierarchy 'to inhibit or frustrate' (p. 193). These two definitions imply that influence is a negative force. However, influence can also be a positive force. The influence that participants had within and between groups in the networks in this research – whether positive or negative – affected the 'bottom up' response made to the 'top down' authority. The research further explored the empowerment of individuals, groups and the networks themselves in terms of legitimacy.

Legitimacy

There are two accepted dictionary definitions of legitimacy (Butterfield 2002) – the first being that of 'authorised or in accordance with the law' (p. 432) and the second being that of 'based on correct or acceptable principles of reasoning' (p. 432). In interpreting Connolly and James's (2006) work, legitimacy seems to be an interrelation between the two – thus defined in terms of a professional credibility and an accepted authority on educational practices. However, legitimacy is earned rather than bestowed. The key elements of professional dialogue, empowerment and decision-making offered through networking

(Lieberman and McLaughlin 1992; Stoll et al. 2006), ensure that teachers' knowledge and opinions are valued within the network and allow them to develop professional confidence beyond the network. Thus, the credibility of the group is generated through sharing knowledge and opinions, which, in turn, gives strength to the corporate voice of the network. The status of the network then develops in terms of personal or positional power and ensures its legitimacy (Veugelers and Zijlstra 2005) in the educational and political arena. Legitimacy was developed through the empowerment of individuals and groups within the networks, and through the perceived status of networks and network participants with peers and other educational stakeholders. Rutherford and Jackson (2008) also note legitimacy as a factor in their research on secondary collegiates, where membership 'immediately added to a school's reputation and standing in the City' (p. 7).

Bureaucratic and organic organisations

The notion of bureaucratic and organic organisations is explored in depth by Burns and Stalker (1961) in industrial settings. These authors present a model of two contrasting types of management along a continuum, with a mechanistic bureaucratic type of organisation at one end and an adaptive, organic type at the other. The definition of a mechanistic management system, according to Burns and Stalker (1961), encourages a hierarchic structure of authority, control and communication. This style is seen as appropriate in stable conditions. On the other hand, organic management systems are described by the authors as more appropriate to changing conditions and are seen to flourish in more dynamic, fast-moving conditions (Burns and Stalker 1961).

Because of the complexities of networks (of schools), as organisations of organisations (the schools themselves), it is realistic to assume that they will exist in a climate of ongoing change, turbulence and uncertainties. Changes within the member organisations, along with external pressures, will impact on the structure of a collaborative group or network. Additionally, as time progresses, inevitable changes will take place to the overall purpose of the collaborative group. This [chapter] explores structures of networking that acknowledge change as the norm, along with systems of management that support and encourage change, thus ensuring a more beneficial model than one which assumes total power in terms of authority or control.

The findings

The data revealed a number of requirements and benefits of networks, along with inhibitors and disadvantages. Many of these aspects had previously been observed by others and reported in the literature (e.g. Lieberman and McLaughlin 1992; Huxman and Vangen 2000; Stoll et al. 2006) and they were also evident in both phases of this research. By far the most common response from headteachers on the benefits of networking was the support and insight that working with other colleagues offered. The 'significant claims that networks make on teachers' time and energy' (Lieberman and McLaughlin 1992: 673) was acknowledged when respondents were asked what the worst thing had been about the PSLN initiative. The most common negative responses were centred on time, energy and effort in terms of commitment and other priorities:

> One of the disadvantages is trying to organise things for it [the network], particularly when you're very busy or when people let you down.

The frustration of staff turnover was also expressed by participants, 'where key players had missed out' and headteachers 'were not sure how they would catch up'. An interesting finding to note was that the balance in the number of advantages and disadvantages identified by the participants in the NLC network altered significantly from positive to negative after becoming part of the NLC initiative. What was unclear, however, was whether or not this was as a direct result of an imposed bureaucratic structure or a natural occurrence in the life cycle of the NLC, as this network was already four years old at the time of the research. This needed further investigation. Therefore, the main disadvantages cited in terms of imposed arrangements such as workload, agendas, timescales, bureaucracy, accountability and an imposed model of networking became areas of focus in phase 2 of the research.

The data gathered from phase 2 revealed that the disadvantages of an imposed model existed to some extent. However, participants in phase 2 of the research did not feel as strongly about this as those participants interviewed in phase 1. Although there was general acknowledgement of 'top down' impositions, there seemed to be an acceptance of this from most headteachers:

> Actually [imposed timescales], that's been an advantage. I'm quite glad that it's been a year and that we might see an end to it.

> It's [the imposed agenda] given us the opportunity to look quite closely at something that was one of our [school] concerns.

Interestingly, the bureaucratic structures and the additional workload in terms of meetings, minutes and reports were instigated to a large extent by the networks themselves. The imposed nature of a central government introduced and a local authority directed initiative was viewed, on the whole, as at an appropriate and an acceptable level, with the majority of headteacher participants in the PSLN stating that they would involve their schools in a similar initiative again.

Many of the requirements, benefits and disadvantages of networking that were expressed as either positive or negative features in both phases of the research were often counter-argued with an opposing viewpoint by other headteacher participants in both networking initiatives. The original findings of the research acknowledged that negative features are inevitable, for networks exist as complex organisations of already existing complex organisations (the schools themselves) which, in turn, are composed of complex groups and individuals. What is critical is ensuring that there is a healthy balance between negative and positive features in order to sustain the success of the network. However, network balance was not the only dynamic in the research found to affect the network's success. Additionally, both power and involvement played significant roles in affecting the functionality of the network.

Power and involvement

During the first phase of the research into a Networked Learning Community (NLC), the concept of power was expressed by NLC respondents in both positive and negative terms. In the early days of the life of the network, it was expressed as empowerment. However, power was also seen as a negative element early on and was expressed by participants as the influence of others on the dynamics of the group. Later on, as the network developed in terms of structure and status, power was viewed positively by these same headteachers in terms of legitimacy. This was also noted in the PSLNs and, as one headteacher participant in phase 2 of the research stated:

> What we had taken as our research had become a focus of the local authority as well [and] it really helped us to be in with the running.

The negative aspect of power was apparent at later stages in both networking initiatives and expressed in terms of influence of others on the network's agenda. Some decisive characters at various levels within the NLC network were also perceived as exercising a strong, negative influence and altering the dynamics of the group, thus affecting how it functioned:

> We have some very dominant characters ... who would want to direct a certain aspect of learning in a certain way.

This idea of group dynamics as critical in determining the success and effectiveness of a network is acknowledged in the literature (Stoll et al. 2006). Group dynamics were certainly seen as a positive aspect of networking in phase 2 of the research. PSLN headteacher participants also perceived a positive team culture and strong working relationships as beneficial to the network in the follow-up interviews one year into the research. The positive influence that other network participants had within groups in the PSLN initiative was considered by the headteachers to be empowering and a real force for change:

> I think the dynamics of the group, the management and organisation of the group, has supported its success at the end of the day.

The fact that group dynamics did not arise as a positive aspect of networking with NLC participants in phase 1 of the research was an interesting feature. On reflection, there may be one of several reasons for group dynamics not being mentioned in positive terms in phase 1. First, headteachers in the West Midlands study had been working together for nearly four years, had built up strong working relationships and were very familiar with each other's work patterns to the extent that this aspect was now probably imperceptible within the NLC and, therefore, not mentioned by participants. Or, second, the phase 2 headteachers had more experience in working in a variety of collaborative arrangements and were more adept at drawing out the positive aspects of working groups to the benefit of the network. Or, third, the finding was unique to these networks and is one of the limitations of this research in that small samples can produce evidence in research that is not always generalisable. In order to determine the validity of this finding, it would need exploring over a wider range of networking initiatives.

Shared power

The arising theme of power that was shared with other headteachers was expressed negatively by interviewees as 'too many chiefs' in the NLC network and with 'an awful long time [spent] getting nowhere actually' in the two PSLN networks attempting to action plan and make decisions together. Headteacher participants certainly enjoyed sharing the support of colleagues, but sharing the power for ultimate decision-making was another issue. It could be argued that the nature of schools as traditionally hierarchical structures and the headteacher as the leader tends to conflict with the style of leadership promoted in networks, thus the 'more hierarchical the management structure, the more the liberation of leadership capacity is likely to be stifled' (Hopkins and Jackson 2002: 11). Certainly, to have scenarios where groups of five to eight school hierarchical structures were being merged into one network was a cause of tension for those headteacher participants at the top of the hierarchical structure in their own school. A negative aspect noted was the notion of control through the hierarchical structures developing in the networks and the effect that had on group dynamics. This was expressed as a loss of power.

Loss of power

Loss of leadership power or autonomy arose as an issue fairly early on in the Primary Strategy Learning Networks initiative with school leaders struggling with the notion of delegating responsibility and accountability to others in the group. This issue was noted in the literature where:

> Establishing patterns of distributed leadership is a subtle dance of power and authority. Sharing leadership within schools and across the network can cause confusion, resentment and protection of position and power, especially if the expectations for the differentiation of roles are not clearly specified. (Earl and Katz 2005: 71)

One respondent in the first set of PSLN interviews felt quite strongly about the loss of her leadership power in terms of quality control:

> If you work in a group in your own school, you tend to get it done your way because you're in a senior management position. You don't want things to be presented in

such a way that seems a waste of time for all those people who are listening. The quality of the [network] launch was not as it should have been and if I'd have been doing all of it, it wouldn't have been like that.

Although much had been expressed at the action planning stage with regard to developing leadership potential and distributing leadership down to other network participants, headteachers within the networks were struggling with the notion of releasing the power and control and one interviewee expressed it as a moral obligation to ensure best value:

We've got to do this. We've got to account for that money to make sure we're using it properly.

NLC participants also felt they were losing power because of a 'top down' approach and 'a model which they [NCSL] seemed to expect networks to conform to', thus implying too much central control of the initiative. It is interesting to note that, although there was this growing central accountability agenda observed in the NLC initiative, the issue of accountability in the PSLN initiative was mainly self-perpetuated by the networks themselves and not instigated centrally as a form of external control, substantiating Weber's (1921) observation that if an organisation does not have any bureaucratic restraints, it attempts to create them!

Types of authority and involvement

To summarise, the types of authority and involvement found in the networks studied can be linked to Etzioni's (1961) typology. Etzioni's (1961) types of remunerative and normative powers were the main types of authority or 'downward control' apparent in these networks. With regard to remunerative power, the offer of central government funding with attached conditions in the PSLN initiative ensured that participants 'bought in' to a specific nationally driven school standards agenda. However, a coercive style was also noted later in the NLC initiative, where the threat of withdrawal of central funding was used to ensure attendance at central functions and completion of set documentation by NCSL. With regard to normative power, the use of external and internal accountability ensured compliance with prescribed plans in both networking initiatives. Loss of authority or 'downward control' was expressed negatively by respondents in this research. And one participant compared it to having to 'jump through hoops', implying an imposed agenda. There was reluctance to bestow power down to subject leaders, classroom teachers and other staff within PSLN networks. There was also reluctance noted in the research to share power across the leadership team in the NLC network. It is interesting at this point to refer to the work of Ribbins (2003) on the life cycle or career phases of leaders and to question whether or not successful network leadership may be, in part, influenced by the stages at which those who share the leadership of the network find themselves. It could be argued that the point at which a headteacher's confidence allows his or her 'leadership to become followership, as the occasion demands' (MacBeath 2005: 364) is the optimum phase for network involvement.

Power partnerships

The relationship between 'top-down' authority and 'bottom-up' responses within organisations is critical. The related responses to Etzioni's (1961) three types of authority were calculative, moral or alienative depending on the type of 'top-down' power displayed in his research. Involvement in the networks studied was found to display features of all three types of responses – that of a calculative 'what's in it for me/us' culture; and that of a moral culture pertaining to a commitment to 'the common good' (Foley and Grace 2001) of the network or an obligation to the initiative itself. Etzioni (1961) labels the relationships between power and involvement as 'compliance relationships' (p. 12). However, non-compliance was also apparent in the complexity of relationships studied in this research and an alienative response to some types of authority was observed in the networks studied in terms of negativity and disengagement.

A new concept arose from this research and draws on the researcher's own interpretation of Etzioni's (1961) model of *power, involvement and other correlates*. Etzioni's (1961) remunerative type of authority was redefined in this research as *remunerative/supportive*, acknowledging the need for support from the authority base within a network partnership. Etzioni's (1961) normative type of authority was redefined in this research as *normative/restrictive* to acknowledge a power base that inhibits the organic nature of networking. And Etzioni's (1961) coercive type of authority was redefined in this research as *coercive/punitive* to acknowledge the negative impact of withdrawal of (financial) support in order to impose a 'top-down' agenda on the network which also inhibits the organic nature of networking. These three main types of power partnerships found in the networks studied are defined below as Type A, Type B and Type C. The related outcomes of these power partnerships as observed in this research are further described below in terms of network impact and school improvement.

- *Type A* – A *remunerative/supportive* type of 'top-down' authority in networks offers professional guidance in the form of a flexible model; ongoing funding for time to network; externally delivered support programmes; clear guidance on structures and systems; and a clear plan of action. This encourages a *calculative (type 1)/moral (type 1) involvement*. It is calculative in terms of a creating a 'what's in it for us' culture where participants respond for the 'common good' of the network and make use of their 'corporate voice' for influence in the wider educational field. It is moral in terms of a shared sets of goals; displaying reciprocity between the participating schools; with elements of sharing in a multifaceted way; and professional support from external agents and from the network itself. The resulting outcomes are *productive* in terms of the empowerment of network participants; with evidence of growing professional confidence; and improved leadership capacity at classroom, school and network level. This then leads to innovative practices within the network and legitimacy outside the network. The longer-term impact may be evidenced through improved quality in teaching and learning which ultimately raises standards.

Type A was observed in the small-scale study of a Networked Learning Community when headteacher participants were beginning to form an NLC and were advised and supported by the National College for School Leadership.

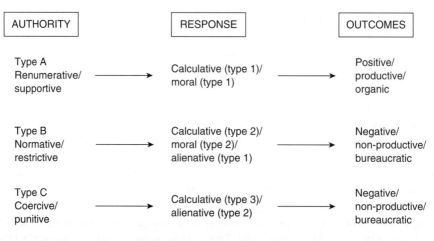

Figure 16.1   Power partnerships and related outcomes

- *Type B* – A *normative/restrictive* type of 'top-down' authority in networks displays external control in the form of a prescribed model; with strict adherence to externally agreed goals; and strong external accountability. The relating response demonstrates a *calculative (type 2)/moral (type 2)/alienative involvement*. It is calculative in the form of a 'what's in it for me' culture and uses persuasion or manipulation for personal or school gain. It is moral only in terms of showing an obligation to the common prescribed agenda and compliance with external/internal accountability. It is alienative in terms of various responses mainly displayed as negative group dynamics and lack of engagement. The resulting outcomes are *non-productive* and demonstrate a lack of reciprocity; limited ownership of the network vision and goals; and unwieldy bureaucracy. This leads to eventual network stagnation and limited outcomes in terms of any sustained impact on standards.

Type B was observed in the main study of the Primary Strategy Learning Networks when headteacher participants were beginning to form as PSLNs and were being controlled by the restraints of the bidding process for central funding.

- *Type C* – A *coercive/punitive* type of 'top-down' authority in networks displays control through threat of withdrawal of funding in reaction to non-compliance. The relative response is *calculative (type 3)/alienative (type 2)*. It is calculative in terms of the necessary compliance of participants in order to ensure ongoing funding. It is alienative in terms of participant withdrawal from networking activities. The resulting outcome is *non-productive* in terms of a loss of commitment and a lack of ownership by network participants.

Type C was observed at the later stages in the small-scale study of a Networked Learning Community when headteacher participants felt under pressure to agree to certain actions due to [the] threat of funding withdrawal.

These three types of power partnerships and their related outcomes as noted in this research are displayed in Figure 16.1. The term 'response' as used in Figure 16.1 acknowledges both compliance and non-compliance within power relationships.

Productive partnerships

What is apparent from the diagram in Figure 16.1 is that positive networking relationships that emanate from Type A – a remunerative/supportive 'top-down' authority – encourage a calculative/moral 'bottom-up' response and complement the organic nature of networking, thus ensuring positive network outcomes. Power partnerships that are overly restrictive or coercive create unwieldy and bureaucratic structures that inhibit the organic nature of networking and produce negative outcomes. This concept forms the basis of an 'ideal' model for productive networking partnerships. West (1999) suggests that explanations of the use of power and influence 'to precipitate, resolve or even to avoid conflict are useful conceptual tools' (p. 189). Therefore, this suggested 'ideal' model is offered for consideration in Figure 16.2. The arrows in Figure 16.2 indicate the flow of the relationship between the government and networks, the networks and the schools, and the schools and the government.

As a further explanation of what Figure 16.2 might look like in practical terms as a model for networking:

- The government relationship with the network would be remunerative and supportive in nature, offering long-term funding and ongoing support in terms of the external structures noted earlier in this [chapter].
- The response from networks would be calculative, but focusing on the common good for all schools in the network rather than personal or individual school gain.

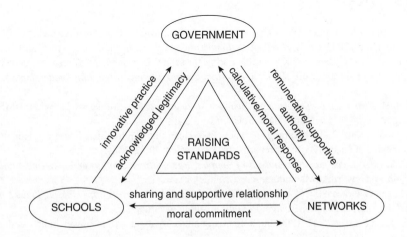

Figure 16.2   An ideal model for productive networking relationships

- The relationship from the networks to the schools would be displayed through the benefits noted earlier in this [chapter] in terms of sharing and support.
- The school's response would be to prioritise its commitment to the network and other participating schools.
- The government's response to the schools, in terms of trust and confidence, would offer legitimacy in educational and political terms.
- Trust and confidence would encourage practitioners to develop innovative practices to ultimately impact on pupil learning.

Conclusion

Power dynamics and power partnerships have a critical impact on the success of networking. They manifest themselves as authority (control *over* the network), micropolitics (influence *within* the network), and legitimacy (validity *beyond* the network). Positive aspects of these three types of power create synergy in networks and provide a real force for change. In contrast, negative aspects of power, such as overly bureaucratic structures, insidious micropolitics or one 'dominant voice', can stifle networking initiatives and limit their potential as power bases for school improvement. This [chapter] argues that positive relationships between key stakeholders need to be nurtured. A model of three-way support and commitment between schools, networks and the government is presented in this research to achieve the government's goal of raising pupil achievement and standards. Acknowledging the organic nature of networks and encouraging ideal types of power partnerships in any centrally promoted model of networking will release the potential of collaborative working arrangements between schools for producing a world-class education system for our children.

References

Burns, T., and G.M. Stalker. 1961. *The management of innovation*. London: Tavistock.
Butterfield, J. (ed.) 2002. *Collins English dictionary plus good writing guide*. Glasgow: HarperCollins.
Connolly, M., and C. James. 2006. Collaboration for school improvement: A resource dependency and institutional framework. *Educational Management Administration and Leadership* 34, no. 1: 69–87.
DfES. 2004. *Primary national strategy: Primary Strategy Learning Networks*. Norwich: HMSO.
Dowding, K. 1996. *Power*. Buckingham: Open University Press.
Earl, L., and S. Katz. 2005. Learning from networked learning communities: Phase 2 – Key features and inevitable tensions. Paper prepared for Aporia Consulting, May.
Etzioni, A. 1961. *A comparative analysis of complex organisations: On power, involvement and their correlates*. New York: Macmillan.
Foley, J., and G. Grace. 2001. *The Birmingham Catholic School Partnership: Holding to the common good in a market competitive age*. London: Institute of Education.
French, J., and Raven, B.H. 1960. http://changingminds.org/explanations/power/french_and_raven. htm (accessed 13 June 2007).

Gunter, H. 2004. Leading edge thinking. Paper presented on the EdD Leaders and Leadership in Education Programme Module 4, University of Birmingham.

Hartley, D. 2007. Leadership studies and theory: An introduction. Paper presented on the EdD Leaders and Leadership in Education Programme, University of Birmingham.

Hopkins, D., and D. Jackson. 2002. *Networked learning communities: Capacity building, networking and leadership learning.* Nottingham: NCSL.

Hoyle, E. 1982. Micropolitics of educational organisations. *Educational Management and Administration* 10, no. 1: 87–98.

Huxman, C., and S. Vangen. 2000. Ambiguity, complexity and dynamics in the membership of collaboration. *Human Relations* 53, no. 6: 771–806.

Lieberman, A., and M. McLaughlin. 1992. Networks for educational change: powerful and problematic. *Phi Delta Cappan* 73, no. 9: 673–7.

MacBeath, J. 2005. Leadership as distributed: A matter of practice. *School, Leadership and Management* 25, no. 4: 349–66.

Networked Learning Communities (NLC). 2003. *Principles.* Nottingham: National College for School Leadership.

Ribbins, P. 2003. Biography and the study of school leader careers: Towards a humanistic approach. In *Leadership in education,* eds. M. Brundrett, N. Burton and R. Smith. London: Sage Publications.

Rutherford, D., and L. Jackson. 2008. Collegiates as a model for collaboration: A new strategy for school improvement. *Management in Education* 22, no. 3: 28–34.

Stoll, L., R. Bolam, A. McMahon, M. Wallace, and S. Thomas. 2006. Professional learning communities: A review of the literature. *Journal of Educational Change* 7, no. 4: 221–58.

Veugelers, W., and H. Zijlstra. 2005. Keeping school networks fluid: Networks in dialogue with education. In *Network learning for educational change,* eds. W. Veugelers and M.O Hair. Milton Keynes: Open University.

Weber, M. 1921. Quoted in Guenther, R., and C. Wittich, eds. 1968. *Economy and society.* New York: Bedminster Press.

West, M. 1999. Micropolitics, leadership and all that … The need to increase the micropolitical awareness and skills of school leaders. *School Leadership and Management* 19, no. 2: 189–95.

Woods, P.A., R. Levačić, J. Evans, F. Castle, R. Glatter, and D. Cooper. 2006. *Diversity and collaboration? Diversity pathfinders evaluation – final report.* London: Institute of Education, University of London.

17

Inter-professional Work and Expertise: New Roles at the Boundaries of Schools

Anne Edwards, Ingrid Lunt and Eleni Stamou

The prevention agenda

The 1990s witnessed a refocusing of work on disadvantage and marginalisation which was signalled by the development of the concept of social exclusion, described by Room as 'the process of becoming detached from the organizations and communities of which the society is composed and from the rights and responsibilities that they embody' (Room, 1995, p. 243). One result was that engagement with society became a personal responsibility that needed to be actively performed (Levitas, 1998), and on which social cohesion depended. At the same time, existing reasons for remedying disadvantage, for example, concerns with equity and with the disruption that alienated youngsters can cause, were augmented by a recognition that there were soon to be too few skilled workers to support an ageing population. Consequently, in policy circles the idea of a child 'at risk' not being able to contribute to society began to replace the notion of disadvantage. From an Organisation for Economic Cooperation and Development perspective, children who were 'at risk' were failing in school and unlikely to enter work (OECD, 1998). The shift from disadvantage to 'at risk' was regarded as helpful because it was future-oriented and allowed governments to consider how social exclusion might be prevented (France and Utting, 2005). It also brought education quite firmly into the frame as part of the prevention system.

The OECD orientation to the future also meshed with research on children's resilience, which has centred on developing individual strengths to prevent a vulnerability to adversity

Source – An edited version of Edwards, A., Lunt, I. and Stamou, E. (2010) 'Inter-professional work and expertise: new roles at the boundaries of schools'.

(Bynner, 2001; Luthar, 2003). The argument is that resilience is a capacity for adaptation to appropriate developmental pathways despite disruptions such as family crises; and the best predictors of resilience are relationships with 'caring prosocial adults' and 'good intellectual functioning' (Masten and Coatsworth, 1998). The advantage of this interpretation of resilience for policy makers is that interventions can be put in place in the early stages of vulnerability which build protective factors around children in order to disrupt those emerging trajectories that are likely to lead to school failure and unemployment. However, this focus on mainly strengthening coping individuals is not without its critics (Colley and Hodkinson, 2001; Edwards, 2007).

Of course, vulnerability is complex and may not be evident unless one looks across all aspects of a child's life: parenting, schooling, health and so on. Equally, building resilience calls for as much consistency as possible in professional responses to children as they move between different settings. Consequently, it was immediately apparent that the services which work with children needed to find ways of enabling collaboration between practitioners (OECD, 1998; Home Office, 2000; Department for Education and Skills [DfES], 2003).

In England the ideas of 'at risk' and resilience have led to policies for *preventing the social exclusion* of children and young people by offering protective factors such as consistent after-school care or mentoring in personalised programmes of support to enable the individual performance of social inclusion.

The study we present examined English secondary schools between June 2007 and September 2008. The finding to be explored here is the emergence of a new space of action at the boundaries of schools which was being opened up by the new role of school-based welfare managers, or equivalents, who worked with other professionals to support children at risk of social exclusion.

These new spaces substantiated Hartley's (2007) suggestion that new work orders of collaboration, marked by notions of 'inter' and 'co', are producing new 'affinity' or 'solution' spaces which do not fit easily with the pedagogic patterns of curriculum delivery and social order in schools. [...]

In this [chapter] we shall locate the secondary school study within broad themes arising in a longer programme of work on inter-professional work for the prevention of social exclusion and on the nature of expertise. We shall examine the emergence of new boundary spaces as sites of collaboration; how schools are responding to the prevention agenda; and the implications of the demands being made on workers in these new spaces for notions of expert professional practice and workforce development.

Themes arising from the study of inter-professional work

Work at the boundaries

The secondary school study was shaped by cultural-historical activity theory (CHAT) (Cole, 1996; Daniels et al., 2007). [...]

In a recently completed Teaching and Learning Research Programme study of learning in and for inter-professional work (LIW) (Edwards et al., 2009), we identified boundary work as an important aspect of inter-professional activity. In LIW this work included the discursive construction of boundaries around newly formed multi-professional teams and struggles at the boundary of a secondary school. The school's attempts to strengthen its boundary, to resist demands that it should work more collaboratively with other services, were met by increasing efforts to destabilise it by representatives of other services who were eager to include the school in an emerging local network of support for children. We were clearly not observing benign 'boundary zones' (Konkola, 2001) which have been described as neutral places where different priorities are respected.

Building on Churchman's view (Ulrich, 1988) that boundaries are social constructions which define who is included and excluded from interactions and what knowledge is considered relevant in those interactions, it reveals them as sites of practice and power-play. Churchman's analysis, for example, can encourage people to push out the boundaries to include more people within them, with all the threats to exclusive expertise, meaning-making and identity that this move might bring.

Midgley [1992] has analysed how differences in values can give rise to differences in where boundaries are drawn and the marginalisation of the less dominant group. [...]

In the LIW study we also observed the personal contradictions (Vasilyuk, 1991) experienced by practitioners as they worked at the boundaries of their own work practices with other professionals. New possibilities for action were opened up for them, but to pursue them they had to 'rule-bend' in their own organisations. We also observed other practitioners 'balancing at the boundaries', looking out at what they saw they might do and perhaps should do if they were to work with their espoused intention of promoting children's well-being, yet being aware that to follow that intention would remove them from the self-sustaining security of the practices of their workplaces. Boundaries, as work sites, simultaneously offer new possibilities and can be unsettling and dangerous places for individual practitioners.

When constituted as local inter-agency partnerships, boundaries are also often sites where government policies can be implemented unmediated by the established practices of local bureaucracies (Skelcher et al., 2005; Edwards et al., 2006). As Hartley (2007) observed, activities in boundary spaces, where collaborative inter-professional responses to the individual needs of clients can occur, are necessary features of the new networked form of governance that makes possible the personalisation that characterises the approach to prevention we have outlined.

Responsive practices in distributed systems

In an attempt to conceptualise the nature of inter-professional collaboration outside established practices of statutory bureaucracies, we have developed the idea of 'distributed expertise' (Edwards et al., 2009). Echoing Bruner's (1996) notion of the 'extended intelligence' of research laboratories and Hutchins (1995) on socially distributed cognition, distributed expertise is seen as spread across local systems, and includes both specialist knowledge and the material resources that sustain knowledge in action.

Our conceptualisation is built, in part, on Engeström and Middleton's (1996) account of expertise as the discursive construction of tasks and solutions. They suggest that expertise is reconstructed in an ongoing dynamic which acknowledges historic values as well as new problems to be worked on, and is not an individual capacity, but is integrated into the dynamics of work systems. [...]

Distributed expertise therefore reflects Nowotny's (2003) analysis that 'Experts must now extend their knowledge ... to building links and trying to integrate what they know with what others want to or should know and do' (p. 155) and Lundvall's (1996) concern with 'know who' as an important aspect of knowledge at work. Emphasising the relational aspects of expertise for inter-professional work, we argue (Edwards et al., 2009), that distributed expertise calls for the capacity to work with others to both expand understandings of the complexity of a child's trajectory, and to respond to that complexity in ways that recognise the priorities of others.

We have labelled this capacity 'relational agency' (Edwards, 2005) and outline it in brief as a capacity for working with others to strengthen purposeful responses to complex problems. [...]

We suggest that it can be learnt and, because it involves working alongside others towards mutually agreed outcomes, is particularly relevant to the work of practitioners who may feel at risk when acting responsively and alone without the protection of established procedures. It is, we think, an additional layer of expertise required by practitioners who negotiate collaboration with other workers who are not members of their work teams; and of particular relevance to practitioners who may find themselves vulnerable when making the moment-by-moment decisions essential to responsive work in isolation.

Workforce implications

[...] Workforce remodelling is presented as central to the English government's personalisation agenda, by creating a 'multi-skilled team to provide effective learning opportunities for children' (from the National Remodelling Team website, cited in Yarker, 2005). Teaching assistants (TAs) were often initially employed to take over mundane tasks for teachers (Bach et al., 2006) and increasingly have become part of teaching teams working alongside qualified teachers, becoming 'ever more significant contributors to pupils' learning' (Cajkler et al., 2007, p. 72).

Describing the deployment of non-teaching staff encouraged by remodelling as 'premised on private sector approaches to achieving a flexible, endlessly trainable workforce', Gunter (2007, p. 6), like Yarker, sees these developments as facilitating the delivery of unmediated curricula rather than promoting the kind of responsive work we have suggested is central to supporting vulnerable children.

However, in a recent examination of an initiative aimed at developing the voluntary and community sector workforce to help parents whose children were at risk of learning delay (Evangelou et al., [2008]), we found practitioners who were working responsively in complex settings with little training. These practitioners were reconfiguring their settings-based or home-visiting practices so that they could model for parents what they could do to help their young children to learn. [...]

The new practices were complex, involving constant professional judgements. Practitioners were required to assess: parents' readiness to engage as educators of their young children; their current understandings of what they might do; the practical possibilities of their carrying forward the ideas that were being passed on to them; and the most appropriate material resources and ideas to use with them. They attended short training events of one day to a week in length, were given access to resources and, in the best situations, found themselves working alongside other practitioners who might support their learning. They learnt quickly. There were few examples of simplistic curriculum delivery; instead we found almost consistent examples of sensitive, responsive work. However, there was considerable frustration among staff arising from their position as flexible and endlessly trainable. They demonstrated what we described as a 'thirst for knowledge'. They knew that they did not know enough to work in the most beneficial ways with parents.

Gunter argues that remodelling is 'located within a very complex struggle over ideas and territory: the amount and deployment of resources; and the culture and practice of professionality' (2007, p. 5). We would agree and suggest that the new site of action where new roles, responsibilities and practices are being shaped offers a timely opportunity to examine new forms of 'professionality' (Nixon et al., 1997) as they are negotiated.

The study

The intention of the 16-month project to be discussed here was to examine secondary schools and teachers in them as they responded to policy demands that they extend their attention to including children in curricula, in order to become part of developing systems of practitioners who were working to disrupt children's trajectories of exclusion.

[…] The study was in three phases. In the first, we selected eight secondary schools in the south Midlands on the basis of Office for Standards in Education (Ofsted) reports which signalled strong engagement with their communities and success with inclusion; discussions with senior educational psychologists; and the need to ensure a mix of differently demanding catchment areas.

We selected the final five on the basis of the range of catchments and their eagerness to engage with the study, seeing it as a way of increasing staff awareness of the shifting inclusion agenda.

In the second phase, the five schools were visited over seven months. We reflected back quickly to the participants in each school their everyday understandings of their work and the contradictions we believed they revealed. Their responses to our analyses of the contradictions allowed us to check our findings and gather additional data about the dynamics at work in the school.

Because the five schools were all located within the same region it was necessary, in phase three, to test the findings with respondents from schools elsewhere in England. We drew on our personal networks to elicit responses from senior teachers in [six regions] through either telephone interviews based on forced choice questions or written responses to the telephone interviews ($n = 46$). […]

The findings

The findings will be discussed in relation to the three themes outlined earlier.

Work at the boundaries

The most striking finding in the five schools was that a new space of action was taking shape immediately outside schools where staff, who were employed by schools, were opening up new pathways of communication and collaboration with practitioners in other agencies. The actual boundaries of the schools as they met the new spaces also varied in strength, with two of the five schools operating with more fluid and open boundaries than the others.

Although there were differences between the schools in who participated in these new spaces, there was one constant: each of the schools had created a new TA-level post variously labelled as 'welfare manager', 'pastoral manager', 'student support worker' or 'achievement support worker'. These practitioners worked both in the schools and in the new space and had usually been employed as either TA or office staff by the schools before being appointed to the new role.

We represented this new space of action to schools as sets of concentric circles (as in Figure 17.1) and mapped who inhabited which areas and their networks. This representation and the amendments that occurred during the feedback sessions revealed the centrality of these new roles, which we will label welfare managers, and indicated that preventative work dealing with vulnerability was occurring in the new space.

The people most frequently included as actors in the space were welfare managers, community police and children and family workers, mental health specialists and practitioners working with children in public care. In some cases education welfare officers were mentioned, along with SENCOs and representatives of within-school inclusion projects. Heads of year or school, the people we had expected to have been primarily involved in the pastoral work of the schools, were rarely included and form tutors were never identified as actors there. Parents were positioned as clients rather than partners, signalling a different relationship with the school from that managed by form tutors, who all described informal relationships where parents were regarded as partners in the support of their children.

The work that occurred in the new space, primarily building new professional networks to support children, was seen as 'plugging a gap' and was in almost every case being driven by the welfare managers. Welfare managers were described as 'completely there for the children' as they were untrammelled by the rigid practices of schools where actions were given shape by the timetable and the curriculum.

Teasing out where the boundaries of this new space were drawn revealed that the schools welcomed its emergence, as responsive preventative practices were incommensurate with the established achievement-oriented practices of the schools. For example, although form tutors were frustrated about the reduction in their pastoral work, they were enmeshed in within-school communication systems based on onward referral of their concerns about children and were not included in those to be found in the new space.

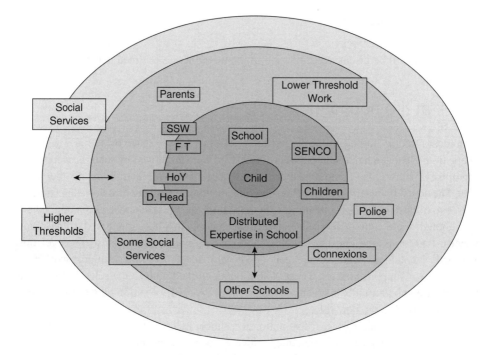

Figure 17.1   The new space of action for preventative work around schools

Analysis of how tools were used in this space centred on the common assessment frame-work (CAF). Welfare managers had usually received training in the CAF. […] Here a welfare manager explained how she used CAF and other information-gathering tools:

> The reason for me [using the CAF] is to ensure that the family and those children are not being neglected … Not going to slip through the net. We could then have all the information before [pupil] came here, so everyone was fully aware of that transition … was going to be quite hard for him … and will obviously follow it through with other meetings.

This use contrasted somewhat with how teachers in the same school talked about the CAF, where it was seen more as a 'what tool', 'just another piece of bureaucracy'.

The division of labour associated with the CAF also indicated the marginalisation of parents in this new space. The 'dividing out of the two roles learning and behaviour', as one senior teacher approvingly described it, seemed to be establishing different sets of relationships with parents. All parents were seen as potential partners in support of their children's learning when working with teachers, while the same parents were less likely to be regarded as partners when the problem was their children's well-being when working with welfare managers. One senior teacher explained that her vehement opposition to the CAF was because the form, and the questions it required, 'patronised' parents.

In the new space parents were discussed as clients, although their voices were 'fed into meetings'. Here a welfare manager described CAF meetings which included parents:

> I think it is also good for the parent because if they feel that they are struggling they know that there are people there to support them and all these people are there to help them.

While this is a sympathetic account of support for needy parents, it is also consigning them to 'profane' status (Midgley et al., 1998) and asserting the superior knowledge of the practitioners in the new space.

Welfare managers were using resources in creative ways to support children's personal trajectories and were negotiating support with other professionals and weaving in what they saw as the intentions of parents. In all these regards, they appeared to be meeting the criteria for negotiated professionality suggested by Nixon et al. (1997). At the same time, the work of teachers appeared to be largely contained within school boundaries in sets of social practices increasingly geared towards pupil achievement.

Distributed systems of expertise

There were two distinct systems of distributed expertise evident in the study: the new space and the schools. Alterations in teachers' pay scales were interpreted by the schools as giving priority to achievement-related work over what had been seen as pastoral responsibilities. We found heads of year or heads of school were now focusing on achievement rather than pastoral work. One senior teacher described the reasons for this refocusing in terms that were echoed in other schools:

> And the government said that we could only give points to people for teaching and learning responsibilities. So they became TLRs, teaching and learning responsibilities and that was it. We had to look at our staffing and say do we really want to get rid of our heads of year? The answer was no; but we had to give them some teaching and learning responsibility ... the heads of year were very upset, they felt that they were having a lot of their job taken away from them.

As the division of labour between heads of year or heads of school and welfare managers changed, so did that of the form tutors. Respondents said that form tutors were less involved in supporting the well-being of children than they had been a few years ago. The form tutors we interviewed all indicated a sense of loss at the delegation of support for pupil well-being to the welfare managers and at making target setting with parents the focus of their links with homes. The phrase 'taken out of my hands' when describing how they worked with vulnerable children resonated across the schools, while senior teachers worried about tutors now being 'left out of the loop'.

The within-school systems that we investigated were in a state of quite dramatic transition and abounded with evidence of the kinds of personal contradictions that are faced by people as they either move between different sets of practices or when practices change around them (Vasilyuk, 1991). Role boundaries were being negotiated and this form tutor was not alone in saying, 'it's difficult to know where your role begins and their [welfare managers'] role ends'. Difficulties over role distinctions seemed to arise from what we have already described as incommensurate systems of practices. There were, in particular, differences in communication rules, with the more informal and responsive communication used by the welfare managers running alongside more formalised systems.

The schools were aware of these transitions, as these senior teachers from different schools explained:

> They [welfare managers] started a year ago and it was a new role, we hadn't had it before so it's kind of continually being invented. I think that's a source of frustration for them because sometimes the boundaries aren't as clear as they would like them to be. And that's an ongoing conversation.

> … we have been aware of the fact that systems don't necessarily marry together – and we're aware of trying so that people are not duplicating things or anything is falling through the net.

These changes were stimulating the development of within-school systems of distributed expertise which tried to bring the work together. One head of school described how the pastoral aspects of the school were now covered in a managed system of roles and responsibilities:

> I have two deputy heads of upper school and I also have three pastoral managers who are non-teaching staff. So it is really a case of leading a team to get to the end objectives … the pastoral managers are very good at filtering out what I need to know.

In the other schools the metaphor of network was pervasive, with complex within-school systems of multi-agency meetings, projects and initiatives revealed to us by senior staff. Projects were made available to pupils on the basis of their referrals in the within-school system and the experiences were based in the schools, to give extra support to pupils. These within-school systems were described by senior teachers as systems of distributed expertise, in this case nested within broader systems:

> I think it's first and foremost an awareness and a sort of constant reference to the fact that you're not working in isolation, you have your role within the school and the school has its role within a network of other agencies … that's really important because I think if you feel that you're doing it all yourself or there isn't any way or any place that you can turn for guidance or assistance or advice even, it's just too much to think about, you just can't sort of suddenly put somebody's life right. So I think it's just that awareness that you have to work as part of a network … So it's that idea that it's a kind of reciprocal arrangement, it's not school you know, it's all kinds of people who are all working together and that's the way it has to be.

However, the external liaison work which linked the within-school systems with those who operated in the new space of action was increasingly falling on the welfare managers. One explained her developing network and 'know-who':

> I've got the sort of rapport with social services that I can ring them up for advice … now I would automatically ring them … can you give me some advice. And if it is not you who should I go to?

[…] The most highly rated statement about what school-based practitioners have to learn in order to deal with the prevention of social exclusion was: 'working flexibly with other services to support a child involves developing new insights into the priorities and practices of other services'. However, as this brief overview of systems in and outside the school suggests, working with the multiple motives of other practitioners and the professional learning involved was located with welfare managers.

Workforce implications

The practices carried out by the welfare managers included many of the features to be expected of being a professional. They were propelled forward by long-term, value-laden goals related to children's well-being which gave shape to their actions and their negotiations (Pickering, 1995; Engeström, 2005); they negotiated these actions with children and other professionals (Nixon et al., 1997); they made judgements about how to work with children (Glisson and Hemmelgarn, 1998); and they carved out new object-oriented practices rather than complying to standard sets of expectations (Edwards et al., 2009). However, they lacked a solid knowledge base of the kind that has traditionally marked being a professional (Wilensky, 1964). The following gives a flavour of the ad hoc-ery of the training received:

> Something I'm going to in a couple of weeks is the [name of project] which is a group of people who used to self-harm so they can be telling welfare officers this is how you should be dealing with it … that's quite good because we have got self-harmers here … because you don't know until you are told. You think you are doing the right thing, but you know, you don't know until you are told.

Their capacity to carry out their work depended almost entirely on their knowledge of local networks. Their expertise was context-dependent and they were consequently keen to learn as much as possible about the resources that were distributed locally. Describing the range of short courses she had attended with practitioners from other agencies, another welfare manager explained:

> I think it is good to keep in with these people. And also it keeps me involved with who these people are and who I can turn to for support, because I think we need it as well.

Their work appeared to have an ephemeral base. Repeatedly their role was justified by senior school staff by their constant availability as a result of not being timetabled; for example, being 'available for students, staff and parents to contact'. Their work was described as 'mushrooming', yet it was difficult to discern what attributes were expected of them apart from being 'very good with children', 'bringing other qualities [other than teaching]', and being 'good at filtering out' problems or 'fact-finding'. Of course, being low paid helped. One senior teacher explained their appointment on the grounds that she could 'not afford five non-teaching heads of year'.

They were also inhabiting and shaping the affinity or solution spaces identified by Hartley (2007). Hartley argued that these spaces which intersect existing organisational structures are necessary if public service provision is to cope with personalisation, or in our terms, following and supporting children's trajectories. [...] The involvement of schools in preventative work was resulting in considerable responsibility being placed on individual practitioners with a relatively thin knowledge base.

When the development of expertise is described in terms of building local networks through attending courses, we may be fast approaching a point where creating networked support is what counts. We would suggest that this is not enough. Relational agency, which we would argue is a prerequisite for inter-professional work, demands more. It is premised on: (a) informed interpretations of, for example, a child's trajectory as an object of activity; and (b) the capacity to make those interpretations explicit. Some element of the exclusive knowledge is therefore important. Relational agency requires that practitioners are not only able to recognise and draw on the expertise that is distributed across local systems, but also to contribute to it.

Concluding points

The study set out to examine how schools were adapting to demands that they augmented their attention to including children in curricula, by becoming part of local systems engaged in preventing the broader social exclusion of their pupils. [...] We did observe that workforce remodelling had combined with a reconfiguration of teachers' pay scales to encourage a separation of the academic and pastoral aspects of the work of schools. These changes in the conditions of practice coincided with the new prevention-focused demands on the pastoral work of schools. The outcome was that welfare managers were not only relieving teachers of the more mundane elements of pastoral activities, such as checking pupil absences, but were also undertaking the responsive practices demanded by preventative work with vulnerable children, both within schools and in the new spaces of inter-professional action that were emerging around schools. [...]

Separation of curriculum from pastoral placed the welfare managers in positions of relative uncertainty when compared with teachers. They were required to follow children's trajectories, negotiate interpretations and responses and, as major players in the new space of action, weave these responses together. The welfare managers were constantly negotiating with young people and with those who might support them. They were, therefore, more likely than teachers to exhibit the professionality described by Nixon and his colleagues (1997). Yet their knowledge base was weak and heavily situated in networks of relationships.

Welfare managers are 'plugging a gap' and developing a relatively limited form of expertise based on know-who as their distinctive contribution to the support of children. We earlier described relational agency as an additional layer of expertise; by that we meant that the know-who aspects of relational agency cannot replace a knowledge base for the complex form of professionality in which welfare managers engaged.

Like the workers in the 2008 Evangelou et al. study, welfare managers were being positioned as flexible and endlessly trainable; like the workers in that study they were also engaging in complex decision making; but, unlike them, they were doing so outside the safety of established structures. While we welcome a renewed focus on pupil well-being, we do have concerns about the long-term well-being of the staff to whom this responsibility has been delegated.

[…]

References

Bach, S., Kessler, I. & Heron, P. (2006) Changing job boundaries and workforce reform: the case of teaching assistants, *Industrial Relations Journal*, 37(1), 2–21.

Bruner, J. S. (1996) *The culture of education* (Cambridge, MA, Harvard University Press).

Bynner, J. (2001) Childhood risks and protective factors in social exclusion, *Children and Society*, 15(5), 285–301.

Cajkler, W., Tennant, G., Tiknaz, Y., et al. (2007) *A systematic literature review on the perceptions of ways in which teaching assistants work to support pupils' social and academic engagement in secondary classrooms* (London, EPPI Centre).

Cole, M. (1996) *Cultural psychology: a once and future discipline* (Cambridge, MA, Harvard University Press).

Colley, H. & Hodkinson, P. (2001) Problems with bridging the gap: the reversal of structure and agency in addressing social exclusion, *Critical Social Policy*, 21(3), 335–359.

Daniels, H., Cole, M. & Wertsch, J. V. (Eds) (2007) *The Cambridge companion to Vygotsky* (Cambridge, Cambridge University Press).

Department for Education and Skills (DfES) (2003) *Every child matters* (London, DfES).

Edwards, A. (2005) Relational agency: learning to be a resourceful practitioner, *International Journal of Educational Research*, 43(3), 168–182.

Edwards, A. (2007) Working collaboratively to build resilience: a CHAT approach, *Social Policy and Society*, 6(2), 255–265.

Edwards, A., Barnes, M., Plewis, I. & Morris, K. (2006) *Working to prevent the social exclusion of children and young people: final lessons from the National Evaluation of the Children's Fund*. RR734 (London, Department for Education and Skills).

Edwards, A., Daniels, H., Gallagher, T., Leadbetter, J. & Warmington, P. (2009) *Improving interprofessional collaborations: learning to do multi-agency work* (London, Routledge).

Engeström, Y. (2005) Knotworking to create collaborative intentionality capital in fluid organizational fields, in M. M. Beyerlein, S. T. Beyerlein & F. A. Kennedy (Eds) *Collaborative capital: creating intangible value* (Amsterdam, Elsevier).

Engeström, Y. & Middleton, D. (Eds) (1996) *Cognition and communication at work* (Cambridge, Cambridge University Press).

Evangelou, M., Sylva, K., Edwards, A. & Smith, T. (2008) *Supporting parents in promoting early learning*. RR039 (London, Department for Children, Schools and Families).

France, A. & Utting, D. (2005) The paradigm of 'risk and protection-focused prevention' and its impact on services for children and families, *Children and Society*, 19(2), 77–90.

Glisson, C. & Hemmelgarn, A. (1998) The effects of organizational climate and interorganizational coordination on the quality and outcomes of children's service systems, *Child Abuse and Neglect*, 22(5), 401–421.

Gunter, H. (2007) Remodelling the school workforce in England: a study in tyranny, *Journal for Critical Education Policy Studies*, 5(1), 1–11.

Hartley, D. (2007) Education policy and the 'inter'-regnum, *Journal of Education Policy*, 22(6), 695–708.

Home Office (2000) *Report of Policy Action Team 12: young people* (London, Home Office).

Hutchins, E. (1995) *Cognition in the wild* (Cambridge, MA, MIT Press).

Konkola, R. (2001) Developmental process of internship at polytechnic and boundary-zone activity as a new model for activity [in Finnish], cited in T. Tuomi-Gröhn, Y. Engeström & M. Young (Eds) (2003) *Between school and work: new perspectives on transfer and boundary crossing* (Oxford, Pergamon).

Levitas, R. (1998) *The inclusive society: social exclusion and New Labour* (London, Macmillan).

Lundvall, B.–A. (1996) The social dimension of the learning economy. Druid working paper, 96–1. Available online at: http://papers.ssrn.com/sol3/papers.cfm?abstract_id=66537 (accessed 24 August 2008).

Luthar, S. S. (Ed.) (2003) *Resilience and vulnerability* (Cambridge, Cambridge University Press).

Masten, A. & Coatsworth, J. D. (1998) The development of competence in favorable and unfavorable environments: lessons from research on successful children, *American Psychologist*, 53, 205–220.

Midgley, G. (1992) The sacred and profane in critical systems thinking, *Systems Practice*, 5(1), 5–16.

Midgley, G., Munlo, I. & Brown, M. (1998) The theory and practice of boundary critique: developing housing services for older people, *Journal of the Operational Research Society*, 49(5), 467–478.

Nixon, J., Martin, J., McKeown, P. & Ranson, S. (1997) Towards a learning profession: changing codes of occupational practice within the new management of education, *British Journal of Sociology of Education*, 18(1), 5–28.

Nowotny, H. (2003) Dilemma of expertise, *Science and Public Policy*, 30(3), 151–156.

Organisation for Economic Cooperation and Development (OECD) (1998) *Co-ordinating services for children and youth at risk: a world view* (Paris, OECD).

Pickering, A. (1995) *The mangle of practice: time, agency and science* (Chicago, IL, University of Chicago Press).

Room, G. (1995) Poverty and social exclusion: the new European agenda for policy and research, in G. Room (Ed.) *Beyond the threshold: the measurement and analysis of social exclusion* (Bristol, Policy Press).

Skelcher, C., Mathur, N. & Smith, M. (2005) The public governance of collaborative spaces: discourse, design and democracy, *Public Administration*, 83(3), 573–596.

Ulrich, W. (1988) C. West Churchman – 75 years, *Systems Practice and Action Research*, 1(4), 341–350.

Vasilyuk, F. (1991) *The psychology of experiencing: the resolution of life's critical situations* (Hemel Hempstead, Harvester).

Wilensky, H. (1964) The professionalization of everyone? *American Journal of Sociology*, 70(2), 137–158.

Yarker, P. (2005) On not being a teacher: the professional and personal costs of workforce remodeling, *Forum*, 47(2–3), 169–174.

18

Approaches to System Leadership: Lessons Learned and Policy Pointers

Beatriz Pont and David Hopkins

Introduction

System leadership is a new and emerging practice that embraces a variety of respon-sibilities that are developing either locally or within discrete national networks or programmes. When taken together they have the potential to contribute to system transformation.

The chapter first summarises what the research and the specialists are saying about system leadership, then continues by examining the actual practices in five different coun-tries. It then analyses the perceived benefits and the potential challenges, and ends with a summary of the key issues and recommendations of the implications of this system leader-ship role for policy makers and stakeholders.

System leadership: a new role for school leaders?

[...]

The concept of system leadership has recently caught the educational imagination. Take for example this quotation from a leading educational commentator whose work has a global reach:

Source – An edited version of Pont, B. and Hopkins, D. (2008) 'Approaches to system leadership: lessons learned and policy pointers'.

... a new kind of leadership is necessary to break through the status quo. Systematic forces, sometimes called inertia, have the upper hand in preventing system shifts. Therefore, it will take powerful, proactive forces to change the existing system (to change context). This can be done directly and indirectly through systems thinking in action. These new theoreticians are leaders who work intensely in their own schools, or national agencies, and at the same time connect with and participate in the bigger picture. (Fullan, 2004)

This quotation contains three implicit assumptions. The first is that if we are ever to achieve sustainable education change, it must be led by those close to the school; the second is that this must have a systemic focus; and the third is that 'system leadership' is an emerging practice. As a concept it has a rich theoretical and research context. The conceptual concerns of system theory for relationships, structures and interdependenies (Katz and Kahn, 1976; Senge, 1990; Campbell et al., 1994) underpin the contemporary work of system leaders in practice. The key insight here has been well summarised by Kofman and Senge (1993: 27) when they state that the '... defining characteristic of a system is that it cannot be understood as a function of its isolated components ... the system doesn't depend on what each part is doing but on how each part is interacting with the rest'.

[...]

[Adaptive leadership] underpins Fullan's (2005) exposition of the role he believes school leaders will need to play as 'system thinkers in action' if sustainable large-scale reform is to be achieved. This, Fullan argues, will necessarily involve adaptive challenges that 'require the deep participation of the people with the problem; [and] that is why it is more complex and why it requires more sophisticated leadership' (p. 53). For Fullan, examples of this new work include: leading and facilitating a revolution in pedagogy (p. 57); understanding and changing the culture of a school for the better (p. 57); relating to the broader community, in particular with parents; and integrating and co-ordinating the work of social service agencies into the school as a hub (p. 61). This will demand '... above all ... powerful strategies that enable people to question and alter certain values and beliefs as they create new forms of learning within and between schools, and across levels of the system' (p. 60).

These demands are further illuminated in theory by Peter Senge (1990), who argues that for organisations to excel, they have to become 'learning organisations', which he defines as 'organisations where people continually expand their capacity to create the results they truly desire, where new and expansive patterns of thinking are nurtured, where collective aspiration is set free, and where people are continually learning to see the whole together' (p. 3).

To Senge, the key to becoming a learning organisation is for leaders to tap into people's commitment and capacity to learn at all levels, to clarify broader systemic interdependencies and how to make them more effective (p. 4).

[...]

The concept of system leadership flows from the general literature on systems theory and thinking and is a theory of action that embraces a range of disciplines in order to exert its power (see for example Elmore 2004, Leithwood et al. 2006). [However] system leadership

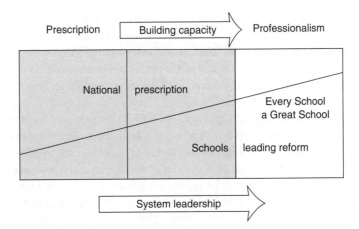

Figure 18.1   Towards system-wide sustainable reform

will only exert any influence to the extent that it focuses on teaching and learning (i.e. is instructional), shares its authority with others (i.e. is distributed), and so on.

[…]

Hopkins claim[s] that:

> There is a growing recognition that schools need to lead the next phase of reform. […] We need a transition from an era of Prescription to an era of Professionalism – in which the balance between national prescription and schools leading reform will change. (Hopkins, 2007, p. 44)

However, achieving this shift is not straightforward. As Fullan (2003, p. 7) has said, it takes capacity to build capacity, and if there is insufficient capacity to begin with it is folly to announce that a move to 'professionalism' provides the basis of a new approach. The key question is 'how do we get there?', because we cannot simply move from one era to the other without self-consciously building professional capacity throughout the system. This progression is illustrated in Figure 18.1. […]

This not an argument against top-down change. Neither top-down nor bottom-up change work by themselves, they have to be in balance – in creative tension. The balance between the two at any one time will of course depend on context.

The right-hand segment is relatively unknown territory. It implies horizontal and lateral ways of working with assumptions and governance arrangements. The main difficulty in imagining this landscape is that the thinking of most people is constrained by their experiences within the power structure and norms of the left-hand segment of the diagram.

One [does not] always have to start from the left-hand side of the diagram and move in some sort of uniform way to the right. Some systems may well start from the middle and move into the right-hand segment, as could be the case in Finland. Others may initially believe that they are in the right-hand segment. […] If this diagram has any value it is as a heuristic.

The OECD report has termed this 'leadership beyond the school borders' and proposes this as one of the key roles for improved school outcomes. These wider engagements focus leadership beyond the people in the school leaders' own buildings to the welfare of all young people in the area and to the improvement of the profession and its work as a whole, but in ways that also access learning and support from others to provide reciprocal benefits for leaders' own communities. [...]

This concept of moving beyond the school borders is also proposed by Hargreaves and Fink (2006), who explain that the key challenge to school improvement today is for school administrators to become leaders who develop and raise high level achievement by working with, learning from and influencing the behaviour of others within and beyond their schools. Educational leaders of the future will be system leaders as well as school leaders. [...]

In summary, linking schools together can contribute to improving capacity of the education system with common purposes and improvement goals. At the heart of this role is the fact that schools and their leaders are not alone, and that working together they can reach higher levels of practice. [...] It can also be something that is coming as a top-down initiative to help improve performance of schools, develop capacity quickly and help rationalise resources.

How are school leaders collaborating and becoming system leaders in practice?

Throughout OECD countries, there is a great deal of school leadership co-operation and collaboration going on. Approaches to co-operation range from informal networking to new management structures, such as the Portuguese or the Dutch approaches. In Hungary 'micro-regional partnerships' have been sponsored for economic and professional rationalisation. In Norway, some schools merge to form an administrative unit governed by one principal. In the Netherlands, the increase in scale following merged schools has led to educational innovations [having] considerable effect on the duties of school leaders. In fact, in all countries participating in the OECD *Improving School Leadership* activity, there are some arrangements for co-operation between schools.

Table 18.1 lists different types of approaches and some of the reasons for co-operation across OECD countries. There are school communities, school pools, networks, possibilities for sharing expertise by principals, actual merging of schools and shared management across schools. We are not able to gauge the extent of their success in most countries but most of these have explicit objectives which concentrate on sharing and rationalising resources, improving coherence of educational provision, supporting well-being and improving educational opportunities and outcomes.

Instead, to explore the practice, we have chosen to focus on a set of innovative practices that we think can provide good examples of systemic approaches to school leadership. These are particular innovative approaches adopted or developed in England, Finland, Belgium, Austria and Victoria (Australia) which are showing emerging evidence of positive results.

Comparing these approaches shows that different countries and different political, social and economic contexts may respond differently to similar challenges and pressures; alternatively, the system approach may be a response arising from different sets of needs. Each

Table 18.1   Co-operation arrangements across OECD countries

Belgium	School communities created as voluntary collaborative partnerships between schools. They aim to have common staffing, ICT and welfare resources management.
Denmark	Co-operation in post-compulsory education promoted by the creation of administrative groups set up locally or regionally to optimise the joint resources of several self-governing institutions.
Finland	2003 legislative reform enhanced school co-operation aiming to ensure integrity of students' study paths.
France	'School basins' implemented to ensure collaborative partnerships between schools to work together in student orientation, educational coherence between different types of schools, common management of shared material and human resources.
Hungary	'Micro-regional partnerships' based on economic and professional rationalisation have resulted in the spreading of common school maintenance in almost all Hungarian micro regions. This network-type co-operation enables professional and organisational learning, leading to new forms of education governance and efficient innovation.
Korea	Small schools cooperate to overcome problems of size in teacher exchange, curriculum organising, joint development activities, and integrated use of facilities.
Netherlands	In primary education, 'upper management' takes management function responsibility for several schools. About 80% of primary school boards have an upper school management bureau for central management, policy staff and support staff.
New Zealand	School clusters based around geographical communities and communities of interest.
Norway	Tendency to merge several schools to form an administrative unit governed by a school principal. Three-level municipalities require networks between schools.
Portugal	Schools commonly grouped together with a collective management structure; executive, pedagogical and administrative councils are responsible for their areas.
Scotland	Important political promotion of collaboration. 'Heads together' is a nationwide online community for sharing leadership experience.
Sweden	Municipal directors of education steer principals. Most are members of director of education steering groups where strategy, development and results are discussed.
UK (England)	[D]ifferent approaches to co-operation stimulated by the government – federations of schools, national leaders of education, school improvement partners …

Source: Pont et al., 2008

individual case has its specificities, as we describe in the following paragraphs, but there are also common patterns and features.

The English practices of system leadership are some of the most developed in this field, and have been publicly developed and supported in recent years. The Specialist Schools and Academies Trust (SSAT) is an independent organisation that promotes school networks of different types. Its network approach to school improvement applies clearly defined tools for principals and its many programmes follow the philosophy 'by schools, for schools'. There are also special training courses to develop the capacity of leaders to become skilled in system leadership. Individuals can work as 'change agents' by acting as mentor leaders in networks or becoming school improvement partners. Also, in England, a group of National Leaders of Education has been created to take on a system leader role and their schools become national support schools (Matthews, 2008).

[...]

In Finland, the OECD team was able to find two approaches which seemed to be systemic. [Firstly] from the way in which Finnish education responsibilities are distributed and shared across the system, one could say that there is system leadership of an organic nature. In order to define [the national curriculum], there is a wide scope of consultation and co-operation from the national down to the school level. Once the curriculum is finalised at all levels, there is a high degree of consensus built around the professional body of teachers, principals and policy makers at local, regional and national level. Teachers are of extremely high quality and have a high degree of professionalism, teamed with a high degree of decentralisation and a national consensus on the value of learning. The whole system cooperates for school improvement. This shows in its excellent PISA results, which are not only consistently the best among all the countries studied but also highly equitable, so that any student is assured high quality education no matter what neighbourhood he or she lives in.

In addition, due to declining school enrolments, declining resources in education, and an increasing workload for principals, municipalities are developing ways to transform school leadership to benefit the broader community. [...] [For example] five school principals were working as district principals, with a third of their time devoted to the district and the rest to their individual schools. This meant also that the leadership was redistributed within the schools.

In Flemish Belgium, the development of communities of schools has tested the benefits and effectiveness of collaboration. The Flemish education department gave these school communities specific competences and additional resources by way of staff points. These competences are establishing agreements in the organisation of education provision, pupil orientation, the establishment of a common staffing policy, establishing teaching labour markets, or ICT co-ordination. They can eventually name a co-ordinating director to ensure that these communities operate smoothly.

This innovative approach has had some positive results (at least at secondary level, where it has been going for longer): at present, communities of schools cover more than 95% of secondary schools in Flanders, with an average of 6 to 12 schools belonging to a community. The immediate effects of the innovation were to establish internal markets which regulated competition for students between schools and increased opportunities for collective action on allocation of staffing and other resources, and for student guidance systems and curriculum. Yet, while these are important features, it must be acknowledged that the scope for collective decision-making was at the margins and did not affect the principals' autonomy.

An extremely interesting aspect of this approach is that it was possible to see how co-operation could be more or less successful, as each community of schools was left to themselves to develop their own strategies. Some schools did not make any changes while at the other extreme a school community has appointed a principal as a full-time co-ordinating director of the community. [...]

The Austrian and Australian innovations concentrate on leadership development, but both also have a systemic dimension to them that merit their inclusion with the rest of the approaches analysed in this report.

In Victoria, Australia, a state-wide approach to leadership preparation and development was developed as part of a broader strategy targeting school improvement. The reform consisted of initiatives aimed at improving practice, enhancing performance and reducing achievement gaps. Leadership development was an essential part of this strategy. There is multi-layered system-wide leadership, which provides a common vision of leadership, promoting a common shared vision of high, evidence-based expectations and collective responsibility. The conceptual framework for this vision of transformational leadership follows a specific model (Sergiovanni) which provides clear domains and descriptions of responsibilities for leadership. Nineteen different training programmes for different stages of leadership underpin this programme.

The Victorian vision of effective schools and culture of leadership development is leading to system leadership capacity with a common view. Through participation in these programmes and the creation of strong networks of common practices, school leaders are contributing to the improvement of Victorian schools as a whole; one of the courses is specifically on developing high-performing system leaders. This results in strategic alignment, and the common language and culture of school improvement are permeating all levels of school leadership. The approach engages the workforce, provides clear expectations and emphasises peer learning.

Austria's approach to support leadership reform is built around the Austrian Leadership Academy, which was launched in 2004 to equip leaders with a new, more proactive and entrepreneurial vision of leadership that would focus on improving school outcomes. [...] The Leadership Academy participants meet twice a year for two years and gain a combination of principles of learning, structure and curriculum, focused on developing leadership skills. They form partnerships, coaching teams, regional and virtual networks. At the outset, participants were school leaders, but as the Academy developed, it was clear that to develop capacity and system change it was also necessary to involve those working in leadership and management at regional and national departments of education. At present, around 20% of the total potential participants have graduated from the Academy, and there are plans to continue until around half of principals, or enough critical mass, has been reached.

The Academy has already begun to achieve a degree of culture and systems change, with a high degree of voluntary participation, engagement and enthusiasm and appears to have positive effects on individual development and improved practice over the long run. It is introducing system change by acting on the agents who are to introduce this change. However, to reach its full potential and to be sustainable it would need to have formal, structured support from the Ministry and be more embedded within the broader initiatives for reform.

These country innovations provide a range of examples of leadership for systemic school improvement. The countries have worked or are working to strengthen leadership practice, through either development or creating co-operation networks that promote going beyond leaders' own schools. These practices have some common features: they are all focusing on preparing and developing leadership for system-wide school improvement through capacity building, sharing of resources and working together.

Benefits of system leadership

Most of these innovations have had some success because they had clearly defined objectives, and strategies to reach them. Yet the results are still tentative, mostly because these practices were just starting when the OECD teams visited the countries. Still we can say that they are slowly producing desired results. They are changing the perception and the practice of school leadership to focus on broader system outcomes, in different ways. [...]

Developing leadership capacity

Strengthening leadership capacity implies creating opportunities for school leaders to work with each other, to share ideas, and to learn through the development of networks and by collaborating in their day-to-day practice. In the English example of a federation of schools, an underperforming school working with a neighbouring school develops its own capacity because the school team has the opportunity to train, to follow more successful patterns of school improvement and to learn. Both schools benefit: even a successful school can learn things from a struggling one. In Finland as well, the leaders who were working one third of their time with the municipality were also developing and strengthening their capacities as system leaders. The broader benefit was that they were all working together for the improvement of the municipality as a whole.

In Victoria and Austria, the leadership training programmes are directly influencing the development of leadership capacity [on] a larger scale. They are aiming at changing the perception and the practice of leadership to focus much more on school outcomes, and to develop clearly defined sets of leadership skills that seem to be missing in the system.

Rationalising resources

Much of the school and school leadership co-operation across countries shows that there is a need to rationalise management processes, sharing appropriate tasks, which may involve financial and resource management. It can allow principals to concentrate on their key pedagogical leadership tasks. Rationalisation can also increase efficiency when budgets are limited. In Finland, for example, budget reductions were one of the reasons for sharing work between the municipality and individual schools. Similarly, in Belgium, part of the rationale behind the creation of communities of schools was rationalisation of resources.

Sharing resources and infrastructures can also broaden the supply of courses or services. The case of special needs provision in England was an example. In local authorities, special needs students were benefiting from the provision of different schools, working together to respond to this specific group.

Increased co-operation

Working together has developed greater interdependence among leadership teams in Belgium, Finland and England. This also happened in Austria and Victoria, through participation in training. A principal in Belgium, comparing how schools used to compete against each other while now they are collaborating, described it as a small revolution. In Finland, this greater degree of co-operation was enhancing a shared culture of trust, co-operation and responsibility in the pursuit of increased effectiveness.

But the Flemish example shows that some communities of schools have not evolved, and pushing co-operation on to agents who are not willing to take on this task may not work. In England, we were told that the federations or networks that worked were based on successful matching up of the partners. This may be crucial.

Distributed leadership

Most of the practices which have called for system leaders have also resulted in greater distribution of leadership within the schools. Principals need to have time to work on their system leader roles and thus need to delegate some of the school management and other tasks more.

In Flanders, some communities of schools added to school leaders' workload and there are calls for middle management to be further developed to take on some of these tasks. In Finland, where the principals are working at the municipality, leadership within larger schools has been redistributed with other staff members. This releases the principal from other responsibilities and develops increased leadership experience and capacity within the schools. In England, the leaders developed strong leadership teams that were able to take on the school roles necessary when the principals were away.

Improving school outcomes

Many of the processes seen in the countries visited were intended to improve the education and outcomes for students. Such success is hard to measure, but it seemed that most of the examples seen were on the way to achieving it to some degree. In broad terms we [found]:

- Improving and rationalising supply of courses or joining forces to provide a broader curriculum and better education for students can improve school outcomes for some.
- Greater integration of services is a way of reaching students and their families better.
- System leadership can lead to better and more consistent pupil orientation and support.

In England, there is significant evidence to show that where a successful school has partnered a school in difficulties, there has been actual improvement in grades of students in both schools within a relatively short (18-month) period of time.

Sustainability

All these examples of approaches to reach systemic improvement are also contributing to sustainability of leadership and of schools. This is happening through developing capacity within and between schools, through the creation of co-operation networks, and through development of institutions that contribute to spread leadership across schools. In Finland, the commitment to co-operation has become so institutionalised that it is now part of the organisational culture of schools. Sustainability depends on building capacity within individual schools. This can also help to strengthen leadership succession [in] the long run.

The challenges to practice

If the concept of system leadership is to be widely implemented, there are considerable challenges to be overcome. We begin with sustainability, as this is inevitably the most critical.

Sustainability

Sustainability is not only a benefit of system leadership, it is also a challenge. Most of the case studies need support [for] these innovations if they are to be sustainable. In Belgium, the OECD team highlighted the need to develop a new collective and distinctive vision through training and development of leaders. In Austria, the question was raised as to whether the Austrian Leadership Academy will continue and whether its training will have effects long-lasting enough to attain systemic change. In Victoria, Australia, this is also a challenge. In England, although there have been a number of short-term successes in improving student learning as a result of system leadership, it is still not clear whether they are sustainable in the medium and long term. In Finland as well, while the systemic reform had produced some positive results and is improving leadership capacity and rationalising practices, unless support is maintained the long-term impact is uncertain.

When looking across these instances of system leadership from the perspective of sustainability, five conditions necessary for effective sustainability stand out:

- *Internal capacity* within the school to sustain high levels of student learning.
- *Between-school capability,* the 'glue' that is necessary for schools to work together effectively.
- *Mediating organisations* that work flexibly with schools to help build internal capacity and the competences necessary for effective collaboration.
- *Critical mass* so that system leadership becomes a movement rather than the practice of a small number of elite leaders.
- *Cultural consensus* across the system that gives school leaders the space, legitimacy and encouragement to engage in collaborative activities.

It is clear that these conditions are not all in place in any of the case studies, but they are all seen in some. It is also apparent that those cases that contain more of these conditions are the more successful in implementing system leadership. These conditions for sustainability therefore act as a useful checklist for the strategic implementation and institutionalisation of system leadership in national and local systems.

School leadership co-operation in an environment of choice and competition

Co-operation among school leaders working in school systems which have been based on competition and school choice may not be easy. [There is] a dilemma of democracy in Flanders, where the education system is strongly committed to competition as a means to increase effectiveness and school quality. At the same time, the communities of schools are aiming to make schools work together, so the nature of the collaboration–competition balance seems unclear.

[…] Although system leadership in England is now a recognisable movement, it is not yet a mainstream practice. Although it is strongly advocated by the national government, it is still not widely accepted by local politicians, local education officers or governors of schools – who worry that collaboration may lead to a dilution of excellent practice in their leading schools.

Policy makers may have to reflect on how system leaders can work beyond their schools to get systems improvement in an environment of competition and choice. It may be a matter of finding spaces for co-operation and sharing of resources where all benefit and competition is not hampered. […] The challenge for policy makers is thus to develop sound and consistent policy with an appropriate, and probably changing, balance between choice/school competition and collaboration. […]

Recognising and supporting system leaders

While taking on this broader role may be beneficial for the education system as a whole, it may not be easy for school leaders with their busy schedules to take on the additional role. The national background reports prepared for this study show that in some countries, individual school leaders are already working long hours; an additional role could be too much. While distributed leadership can support this role, in times of challenges or difficulties, the focus on the individual school will always prevail. In addition, some ask about the accountability of system leaders: who are they accountable to and how? What are the measures of their practice?

[…]

Identifying and recruiting system leaders

It is clear from the case studies that there is currently a lack of clarity about how system leaders can best be identified and the key skills that should be required. There is also a need to differentiate potential candidates in terms of prior experience and current capacity. […]

While appeals to altruism may prove a successful means of attracting high quality leaders, such goodwill cannot be relied upon and it can be exhausted. More formalised incentives can contribute to encouraging and effectively recruiting these system leaders.

These include professional acclaim and recognition of the role they are taking, financial reward, and highlighting the positive challenge and enrichment of a change in the pattern of work.

Professional development of system leaders

Generating a pool of high quality system leaders requires appropriate professional development. System leaders need to focus on the promotion of student learning, the schools' contexts and capacity building, problem-based learning, and a repertoire of practices rather than a single style.

Across the case study countries, approaches to developing system leaders could be categorised:

- *Formal qualifications*: England and Victoria. Benefits of recognition and high level of quality assurance. Concerns that a qualification may not meet needs. May be too detached from the context. May put off existing and aspirant heads who have a heavy workload.
- *Tailored learning*: informal range of learning opportunities that can be personalised to individual need, reflect the experience and aspiration of the leader, focus on contexts and around significant problems and combine theory and practice.
- *Through practice*: Finland and Belgium have shaped system leaders by promoting their practice. Might need to be supported with more formalised training approaches that provide the required skills for successful leadership. [Could] have a negative impact by reproducing leadership styles that might no longer be suitable.

How to move system leadership to scale

In reflecting on the case studies, there appear to be three issues that would become increasingly significant were the model of system leadership be moved to a larger scale. These are:

- *Brokerage*: there needs to be a focus on how the crucial partnership between schools should be brokered. This inevitably needs to be based upon a good knowledge of the context, including the true capacity of each school and the specific challenges facing them.
- *Resourcing*: there are a number of potential costs to consider, such as payment to system leaders to undertake more work and pressure, the financial position of collaborating schools, a short-term improvement fund to achieve urgent changes. The amount and necessity for these recourses is highly contextual.

- *Support*: there is also a concern about the provision of ongoing personal and professional support. This is a critical factor for success and needs to be designed into effective policy. It can require the specification of responsibilities, provision of professional development to school boards and local education officers to better support system leaders, and identification and dissemination of best practice.

Food for thought

School leadership co-operation and collaboration have different traditions and developments across countries. There seem to be clear objectives: capacity building across the system, rationalisation and cost savings, improvements in leadership practice due to a more efficient distribution of tasks, and more coherent supply of educational services for those in the community.

Developing systemic approaches to school leadership needs public support. Objectives and expected benefits need to be clear, and incentives are needed. When schools and school leaders realise the benefits they can reap from co-operation, principals will make time to engage. [...]

As we have seen, there are clear benefits to these approaches, which are contributing to leadership capacity building, to rationalisation of resources, to improved co-operation, to a greater distribution of leadership within schools and to improving school outcomes.

Yet, there are challenges to be overcome if this approach is to be made sustainable. These have been seen as: the difficulty of marrying co-operation and competition (policy choices need to be made); the need to recognise and support distributed leadership within the school; the need to identify, recruit, develop and reward system leaders; and the need to find the right institutional support for the practice.

[...] There is a tension between those system leaders who operate in national programmes that have incentivised activity through organisation, funding and professional development, such as seen in England and Victoria; and those system leaders whose roles are locally developed and contextually responsive, such as in Belgium and Finland. In such activity, professionals not only deploy their experience and skill to lead improvements, they also define the terms on which such activity is undertaken and sustained.

There are of course variations to this bottom-up/top-down dialectic, as has been seen in the five case studies. If, however, a shared criterion is to develop effective system leadership in a growing number of schools, then the following suggestion for more short-term action – *incentivise rather than legislate* – may prove instructive.

The argument is that this leadership needs to come more from principals themselves and from agencies committed to working with them. It is clear that the more bureaucratic the response the less likely it will be to work. A more lateral approach may be to create mediating organisations, such as the NCSL and SSAT in England and the Leadership Academy in Austria, to promote system leadership and collaborative activity. Another approach is to foster local education authorities and municipalities to develop and spread practice, as the Finnish have done. The intention that must be maintained is that instead of creating a new bureaucracy, the brief for these mediating organisations is increasingly focused on facilitating relationships between schools to maximise the potential of purposeful collaboration.

[…]

References

Campbell D., T. Coldicott and K. Kinsella (1994) *Systemic Work with Organisations: A New Model for Managers and Change Agents*, Karnac Books, London.

Elmore, R. (2004) *School Reform from the Inside Out: Policy, Practice, and Performance*, Harvard Educational Press, Cambridge, MA.

Fullan, M. (2003) *The Moral Imperative of School Leadership*, Corwin Press, London.

Fullan, M. (2004) *Systems Thinkers in Action: Moving beyond the Standards Plateau*, Department for Education and Skills Innovation Unit/National College for School Leadership, London/ Nottingham.

Fullan, M. (2005) *Leadership and Sustainability: System Thinkers in Action*, Sage, London.

Hargreaves, A. and D. Fink (2006) *Sustainable Leadership*, Jossey-Bass, San Francisco, CA.

Hopkins, D. (2007) *Every School a Great School*, Open University Press, Buckingham.

Katz, D. and R.L. Kahn (1976) *The Social Psychology of Organizations*, Wiley, New York.

Kofman, F. and P.M. Senge (1993) 'Communities of Commitment: The Heart of Learning Organizations', in Chawla, S. and J. Renesch (eds) *Learning Organizations: Developing Cultures for Tomorrow's Workplace*, Productivity Press, Oregon.

Leithwood, K., C. Day, P. Sammons, A. Harris and D. Hopkins (2006) *Seven Strong Claims about Successful School Leadership*, National College for School Leadership, Nottingham.

Matthews, P. (2008) *Attributes of the First National Leaders of Education in England: What do they bring to the role?*, National College for School Leadership, Nottingham.

Pont, B., D. Nusche and H. Moorman (2008) *Improving School Leadership, Volume 1: Policy and Practice*, OECD, Paris.

Senge, P. (1990) *The Fifth Discipline*, Doubleday, New York.

Part 5

Looking to the Future

19

Leadership, Participation and Power in the School System

Richard Hatcher

The standards agenda is beginning to crumble and in its place is emerging a process of school transformation based on collaboration and networking. This principle is at the very heart of system redesign. (Harris, 2008: 58)

Distributed leadership is undoubtedly the leadership idea of the moment. (Harris, 2008: 13)

Distributed leadership within schools and networks among schools are two central themes in the field of school leadership in England and internationally (OECD, 2003). I am going to argue, drawing on and extending two earlier articles (Hatcher, 2005, 2008), that how the dominant academic and policy paradigm within the field addresses the question of power in and over the school system – managerial power and state power – marks it out as a profoundly depoliticised and idealised ideology, the educational equivalent of Business School management orthodoxy. I will situate leadership and management in the school system in two contexts – private and public sector management, and the capitalist state – and draw on two theoretical perspectives: labour process theory and state governance theory. My starting point is a recognition of the functions of schooling under capitalism.

As has long been recognised, in a capitalist society State education performs a key role in terms of reproducing the labour power essential to meet capital's needs, and transmitting the values and beliefs capable of sustaining a social structure based on inequalities of power and wealth and driven by principles of market exchange ... The relationship between the State and teachers is necessarily one of control in which the State seeks to ensure that teachers function within what might be considered as acceptable parameters. (Stevenson and Carter, 2009: 311–12)

Source – This chapter was commissioned especially for this volume.

In England, state power over and in the school system was exercised by the Labour government of 1997–2010 in the form of a centrally prescribed reform programme, commonly referred to as the 'standards agenda', in two ways. First, externally, by the regulatory framework provided by the National Curriculum, targets, tests, exams and inspections which locks teachers and head teachers into government agendas. The 'standards agenda' generated a logic of action (Ball and Maroy, 2009), backed up by the coercive power of Ofsted[1], which tends 'to determine the horizons of what can be thought and said, and position teachers through a system of constraints and incentives in such a way that the activities that seem to be safest and most productive to follow are those that conform to the dominant agenda' (Jones et al. 2008: 130).

Second, internally, state power was relayed through the managerial authority of head teachers in schools and the role of 'system leaders' in networks. Of course, many school leaders were critical of what they saw as the negative elements of government policies and attempted to mitigate their effects (see Hatcher, 2005). Wright's earlier riposte (2003: 142) – 'heads know that their schools have to succeed in a target-based culture and in the end this will drive what is allowed and what is proscribed' – has been borne out subsequently by Robinson's research:

> The heads in my study were being pragmatic, reluctantly compliant, occasionally resistant or genuine believers with moral purpose, and often a combination of these, and believed they were working to improve children's lives. Their actions however, for whatever motive, have the consequences of implementing much of government policy. (Robinson, 2010: 194)

Distributed leadership

In schools in England, head teachers exercise power over teachers in both their educational and employee capacities (in contrast to many other European countries). The two are linked by performance management, involving power over teachers' appointment and dismissal, workload and promotion. A defining feature of the distributed leadership literature is that it ignores the dual role of the teacher as employee as well as educator and the conflictual potential in both roles. Conflict can occur over workload, conditions and salary issues as well as over educational policy issues, and the two are often intertwined. Yet there is seldom acknowledgement in school leadership literature that school is a contested terrain where dissidents might have legitimate different values and aims. So, for example, Fullan (2005: 100) recognises only 'regressive resistance' to change. There is no recognition, for instance, of the extent of bullying of staff by head teachers, even though teachers, lecturers and employees in education are the largest group of callers to the UK National Workplace Bullying Advice Line (n.d.; see also Association of Teachers and Lecturers, 2010).

However, much of the school management literature typically separates and isolates distributed leadership from this context of state and managerial power. For example, there is no mention of the neoliberal education policy context in Leithwood et al.'s (2009) book on distributed leadership. Harris chooses to discuss distributed leadership in isolation from 'issues of power, authority, legitimacy and micro-politics' (2008: 14), but it is impossible to separate action at school level from the causal structural power of the state over head teachers.

The term distributed leadership is not used in mainstream management literature but it is in fact the manifestation in the school context of management strategies of participation in the private sector.

> It is argued that the future workplace and the 'enlightened organization' must consist of a culture and practice of participation as a vital characteristic of its portfolio of practices. There are various imperatives contributing to the development of partici-pation. It is seen as an essential ingredient of the way organisations may harness employee creativity and commitment for the cause of economic success. Increasingly, management texts and gurus suggest that successful organizations are those that 'involve', 'empower' and 'listen'. (Lucio, 2010: 105)

I want to pursue how 'participatory bureaucracy' (Boxall and Purcell, 2010: 39) in main-stream management discourse is translated into the discourse of distributed leadership in schools, mystifying its three principal managerial functions.

First, cultural integration. Wilkinson et al. (2010: 7) regard employee involvement in companies as a strategy to address 'management's dominant concerns about employee motivation and commitment to organizational objectives'. In schools, distributed lead-ership is intended to engender teachers' commitment to the head teacher's 'vision' so they expend discretionary as well as prescribed effort: 'gaining the buy-in of the work-force', as the PricewaterhouseCoopers/DCSF report puts it (PwC, 2007: 40; see also Hartley, 2004).

Second, cognitive integration.

> Changes in work contexts and content mean that employers are compelled to seek a more intensive utilization of labour power, which I have described elsewhere as a *qualitative intensification of labour*. This includes the moves towards accessing workers' tacit knowledge and skills. (Thompson, 2010: 10)

Schools are complex organisations (Leithwood et al., 2009: 5). Knowledge is dispersed and needs to be shared, for two reasons. First, head teachers are subject to bounded ration-ality and to manage they need detailed knowledge of organisational performance (Marsden, 2007). Second, in order to drive organisational improvement, professional knowledge and practice need to be disembedded from individual teachers' tacit craft knowledge and made available to the whole organisation.

Third, task delegation. According to Harris (2008: 11), 'The teacher leadership literature challenges the notion that distributed leadership is simply delegation by another name'. Of course, it is true that teachers voluntarily undertake informal leadership roles, but the responsibilities and tasks are undertaken on the basis of the licensed autonomy granted, and revocable, by the head. This is why leadership is always, in Gronn's (2009) term, 'hybrid'. The language of the PwC/DCSF report is quite clear: it speaks of 'the delegated task' (PwC, 2007: 92) and refers to a survey of 'the views of ... heads regarding the tasks they would like to delegate' (p. 110).

> Within the schools context, distributing leadership is a potential means of ameliorating some of the workload issues which are currently being faced by school leaders, by making the role more attractive and the size of the job more deliverable. (PwC, 2007: viii)

This can be, as Fitzgerald and Gunter (2008: 334) suggest, 'simply a modernized way to seduce teachers to take on additional tasks and responsibilities without the commensurate increase in their salary or time allowance. This point is rarely debated in the leadership literature'.

Hierarchical power and distributed leadership

There is a utopian strand within mainstream management literature that claims that hierarchical management is being replaced by horizontal forms of coordination.

> Managers are the dinosaurs of our modern organizational ecology. The Age of Management is finally coming to a close ... Autocracy, hierarchy, bureaucracy and management are gradually being replaced by democracy, heterarchy, collaboration and self-managing teams. (Cloke and Goldsmith, 2002, quoted in Wilkinson et al., 2010: 13)

This view is now widespread within the school leadership literature. For Higham et al. (2009: 129), policy changes appear 'to be leading us inexorably towards a transformational moment, where the dominant forms of top-down control can be replaced by more lateral forms of accountability and support'. According to Harris, 'Distributed leadership will have a major role to play as the hierarchical structures fall away, so too, will hierarchical forms of leadership' (Harris, 2009: 254; see also Hargreaves, 2008). It leads to the claim that distributed leadership represents schools operating 'democratically': the distribution of leadership equals the transfer of power. In reality, participatory approaches, while undoubtedly providing a much more congenial school regime than authoritarian forms of managerialism, remain subject to a head-teacher-dominated hierarchy of power.

In the mainstream management field, one feature of employee involvement (EI) is that it tends to be confined to the operational level (in contrast to the rights-based industrial democracy movement of the 1970s).

> These EI initiatives have focused on direct participation by small groups of employees in workplace level information sharing and decision making rather than on employee input into higher level decision-making. (Wilkinson et al., 2010: 8)

In the school context, 'what is to be "distributed" remains very much within the strategic parameters and targets set by government. It is the tactics, not the strategy, which are available for distribution. Hierarchical forms of accountability remain' (Hartley, 2007: 211). This division of labour corresponds to a large extent to the division between the senior leadership team and the rest of the staff (see Hatcher, 2005). This hierarchy of power is demonstrated by the examples of good practice which proponents of 'democratic' leadership practice themselves give. For instance, Harris (2008: 80) refers to the John Cabot Academy which has an extended leadership team with five mini schools, each run by an assistant principal directly responsible to the principal.

Power and networks

I turn now from power over and in schools to power over and in school networks. The notion of network encompasses a spectrum of forms of collaboration from formal governance structures – federations of schools – through structured partnerships such as Networked Learning Communities and 14–19 partnerships, to more informal collaborations. The rationale is that system-wide improvement comes from schools collaborating to innovate through the transfer and development of knowledge and practice (Chapman et al., 2010; West, 2010): what David Hargreaves (2010) describes as the self-improving school system:

- Schools take ownership of problems and reject the notion that the school itself can do little or nothing because it is somebody else's responsibility to provide a solution.
- Solutions are seen to be available from within the school system, provided schools work together to diagnose the problems and devise solutions in their mutual interests. (2010: 8)

I will pursue a similar line of argument to that regarding distributed leadership. The concept of network seems to hold out the promise of innovation generated from the bottom up by horizontal collaborative relationships among teachers, but it is overdetermined by vertical relations of power driven by government agendas. While the institutional status of networks is different from that of schools, they are subject to the same two forms of state control: indirectly, through the overarching regulatory framework within which they operate, and directly, through the role of 'system leaders'.

Networks are of course not unique to education. On the contrary, the network paradigm is a key theme in state governance theory. Jessop (2002) notes the rise of 'heterarchy' – horizontal self-organisation among mutually interdependent actors as a form of governance. He explains this development as the result of a recognition of the limits both of state command action and of market competition.

> It implies that important new problems have emerged that cannot be managed or resolved readily, if at all, through top-down state planning or market-mediated anarchy. This has promoted a shift in the institutional centre of gravity (or institutional attractor) around which policy-makers choose among possible modes of coordination. (Jessop, 2002: 229)

In other words, heterarchy is a form of state management and control:

> the state's increasing interest in heterarchy's potential for enhancing its capacity to secure political objectives by sharing power with forces beyond it and/or delegating responsibilities for specific objectives to partnerships (or other heterarchic arrangements). (p. 237)

The network paradigm doesn't replace either state direction or the market, it provides the state with one management tool among others. In the context of public administration, Klijn and Skelcher deploy the concept of governance networks. 'Governance networks are associated with new systems for public policy deliberation, decision and implementation' (Klijn and Skelcher, 2007: 587–8).

The problem for government is to ensure that school networks are aligned with the government's education agenda. Thompson explains how the state can direct networks 'at a distance'.

> This idea of a 'shadow of hierarchy' relies upon the ability of a hierarchical authority to affect lower level interactions without coordinating these directly or unilaterally (a kind of 'action at a (vertical) distance' ...). It builds upon a distinction between a *hierarchical authority structure* (something difficult to avoid in matters of governance) and *hierarchical direction* operating to override decision preferences of other actors ... Clearly, where there are networks of self-organization and self-government existing in the shadow of the state, we have a case of a hierarchical authority structure but one where the state does not necessarily directly intervene to coordinate decisions and the activity of the networks in any detail. Rather, it establishes the rules under which those networks operate. (Thompson, 2003: 179)

School networks operate within a regulatory framework which establishes the dominant logic of action which governs the network, as a number of research studies demonstrate. Andy Hargreaves, in a review of networks among schools, says: 'although networks have some success in securing short-term test gains, the political culture of targets and testing undermines longer-term or more innovative efforts' (Hargreaves, 2009: 19). A case in point is the Specialist Schools and Academies Trust RATL (Raising Achievement/Transforming Learning) project. Hargreaves notes:

> the limitations imposed by continuing standardization and data-driven surveillance in the surrounding policy environment ... as a result, lateral network activity focuses disproportionately on short-term improvements in delivering existing learning rather than long-term transformations towards creating different and better teaching and learning. (Hargreaves, 2009: 20)

As well as the regulatory framework imposed by the standards agenda, government also has the power to control networks through funding. Moore and Kelly (2009) give two examples, the Primary Schools Learning Network (PSLN) and the National Learning Communities (NLC) network. The latter also demonstrates the role of the National College for School Leadership (now the National College for Leadership of Schools and Children's Services) in relaying and administering government policy.

the offer of central government funding with attached conditions in the PSLN initiative ensured that participants 'bought in' to a specific nationally driven school standards agenda. However, a coercive style was also noted later in the NLC initiative, where the threat of withdrawal of central funding was used to ensure attendance at central functions and completion of set documentation by NCSL. With regard to normative power, the use of external and internal accountability ensured compliance with prescribed plans in both networking initiatives. Loss of authority or 'downward control' was expressed negatively by respondents in this research. And one participant compared it to having to 'jump through hoops', implying an imposed agenda. (Moore and Kelly, 2009: 398–9)

Higham et al. (2009: 141) speak of 'schools joining consortia or loose co-federations primarily because this is where they feel the government will place funding or access to future initiatives and programmes'.

System leaders within networks

'Action at a distance' may need to be supplemented by more direct management of networks to ensure they are aligned with government objectives. This requires new agents – system leaders: a key theme of policy discourse. There is a range of system leadership roles (Higham et al., 2009, Chapter 2). Some system leaders have institutional structural power, as in federations of schools under an executive head. In most cases, these are 'performance federations' of high- and low-performing schools based on a donor–recipient model of school improvement. But most networks do not involve new structural forms of governance. Although there are claims that system leadership can be distributed and is available to any teacher (e.g. Hargreaves, 2010: 11), it generally refers to head teachers. Moore and Kelly (2009: 399), for example, found that 'There was reluctance to bestow power down to subject leaders, classroom teachers and other staff within PSLN networks'. What is being created here is a new professional identity, a new top-level management cadre in the school system.

The principal task of networks is the creation and dissemination across schools of knowledge and practice for system-wide improvement. That cannot be entrusted to teachers in self-organised peer-to-peer networks because only certain forms of knowledge and practice conform to government objectives. The role of system leaders is to manage that selection and implementation process. There are parallels here with distributed leadership in schools.

> The first step in system leadership … is to orient the efforts of all those working in the system towards a core set of goals … Having established a set of overall objectives for the system in which they are operating, system leaders then seek where it is possible to build the autonomy of those working in the system. (O'Leary and Craig, 2007: 13–14)

Autonomy is licensed and subordinate to goals established externally by government and assumed to be consensual (Avis, 2009). Higham et al. (2009: 22), writing as leading advocates of system leadership, state that 'the majority of identified system leaders fall into the nationally developed groupings – the impetus and agency behind the roles are located at a national level often within the Department of Children, Schools and Families (DCSF) – including the national strategies, or the NCSL'. They consider whether system leadership is 'just a cynical government ploy to exert increasing control over the system' or whether there is 'a good deal of agency on the part of the system leader' (p. 133). As with head teachers, system leaders may choose not to simply relay government policy, but Higham et al. acknowledge that this results in 'significant contradictions within, and tensions between, government-led system leadership and those increasing demands for giving school leaders more agency to take the lead' (p. 30). They continue:

> within these opportunities, we may already be witnessing limitations of government-led activity. For, while new leadership roles emerge, the government's tendency to check and control does not seem to diminish significantly. This tendency is related to focus on effectiveness and value for money. But it also seems to portray a government that is still yet to develop sufficient trust in the profession. (Higham et al., 2009: 141)

Power and networks in a marketised system

Neoliberal education policy has taken different forms in different countries, depending on the specific combination of centralised regulation and decentralised quasi-market (Hargreaves, 2009; Lubienski, 2009). England under the Labour government of 1997–2010 exemplified the top-down prescriptive reform model. In May 2010, the Labour government was replaced by the Conservative–Liberal Democrat Coalition government, signalling a radical shift to a less prescriptive, more marketised model. The new secretary of state for education, Michael Gove, announced: 'At the heart of this government's vision for education is a determination to give school leaders more power and control; not just to drive improvement in their own schools, but to drive improvement across our whole education system' (Gove, 2010). At the centre of the Coalition government's programme were two policies: for all schools to become Academies, directly funded by government and independent of local government education authorities; and for parents, charitable organisations and other bodies to be able to set up their own Academies as state-funded 'free schools'. The policies were modelled on charter schools in the USA and free schools in Sweden and, like them, offer opportunities for private organisations to run schools, including on for-profit management contracts (Hatcher, 2010). Most Swedish free schools (75 per cent) are in chains run by private for-profit companies, and many charter schools are in chains run by Education Management Organisations on a for-profit basis.

David Hargreaves welcomed the Coalition government policy as providing a hospitable context for a self-improving school system:

> the Coalition government's plans are evidently intended to change the shape of this system … It would usher in a new era in which the school system becomes the major agent of its own improvement and does so at a rate and to a depth that has hitherto been no more than an aspiration. (Hargreaves, 2010: 4)

But there are two powerful constraints on the autonomy of head teachers: one imposed by government regulation, the other resulting from the school market, itself constructed by government.

The Coalition government, like its predecessor, was under pressure to demonstrate that its policies succeeded in raising standards of attainment in schools, for both economic and electoral reasons. Employers had been strongly critical of the Labour government's education policy for not producing the future workforce with the skills and dispositions they required (CBI, 2010); and the Coalition government's electoral credibility depended on being able to demonstrate that their school policies were more successful than Labour's. But a review of the international research evidence from existing marketised systems of more autonomous schools – including from the Coalition's models, the US charter and Swedish free schools – does not support the claim that they are more effective. They are not more innovative: 'government intervention, rather than market forces, has often led to pedagogical and curricular innovation' (Lubienski, 2009: 45). Nor, in consequence, are they more effective at raising standards: 'it is far from clear that quasi-market forces such as increased autonomy, competition and choice have led to improved outcomes' (Lubienski, 2009: 27). Confirmation comes from specific research studies of charter schools (e.g. CREDO, 2009) and Swedish free schools (e.g. Bohlmark and Lindahl, 2008).

If these experiences of marketised systems are repeated in England, it poses the question of what the Coalition government will do to ensure that standards rise and failure is dealt with. There are two sorts of solution available. One is to become more prescriptive about curriculum, pedagogy and attainment targets. This is the strategy Labour adopted and the Coalition government rejected (with some exceptions such as the teaching of reading). The other strategy is to intervene in the market and remove inefficient providers. In the USA, charter schools are run by providers on statutorily defined performance contracts, awarded, usually by state or district authorities, for a limited time, normally 3–5 years, and terminated if targets are not met (see Hill et al., 2009). Both solutions entail subordinating the autonomy of schools to coercive intervention and a logic of action no less compelling than that which they experienced under Labour.

The second constraint on the autonomy of head teachers arises from the marketisation of networks. Networks of collaboration between schools remained vital for the Coalition government's project of system-wide school improvement. Michael Gove rejected the idea that 'greater autonomy for schools will work against the collaborative model of school improvement that has grown up over the past fifteen or so years' (Gove, 2010). But evidence from the USA and Sweden, and from Academies in England, is that the introduction of private providers into state school systems, whether on a non-profit or for-profit basis, results in the emergence and spread of a particular form of network – branded chains of schools – which impose new forms of control over their constituent schools.

Autonomy at school level is subordinated to the strategic policy making of the controlling organisation, as Hill (2010) found in the case of chains of schools under the Labour government:

> The introduction of trusts and academies and, to an extent, federations, is effectively inventing a new form of school governance. A clearer distinction is being made

between strategic direction and oversight and more operational accountability, with the former being exercised at chain level and the latter at school level. (p. 23)

As Hill also noted, chains tend to impose a standardised model of pedagogy, curriculum and organisation, constraining innovation, a finding confirmed by Lubienski (2009) in an international review of the research evidence, including US charter and Swedish free schools. This is particularly likely in the case of for-profit chains, for reasons of economies of scale.

The growth of branded chains of schools tends to generate competition rather than collaboration. In Sweden, 'The general motivation to cooperate and exchange information on educational issues has decreased between schools since they started to regard each other as competitors with whom one does not happily share successful working methods' (Wiborg, 2010: 16). In England, Hill found that in some areas schools that were part of chains were choosing not to work with other local schools.

The conviction that the particular teaching and learning model they have developed is right could inhibit their openness to learn from the experience of others, particularly since some chains are beginning to claim intellectual property rights for their teaching and learning model. (2010: 32; see also Evans and Stone-Johnson, 2010)

This privatisation of professional knowledge is exacerbated in the case of for-profit school management companies, where it becomes a commodity to be kept locked in the company's schools to give them competitive commercial advantage, or perhaps to be sold to others for profit.

In short, the evidence indicates that the promise of a self-improving school system where innovation is generated and shared among networks of freely collaborating semi-autonomous schools is distorted both by pressure from government for measurable improvement in performance and by the competition between balkanised and quasi-privatised networks of schools created by a more marketised system. In that context, distributed leadership can be as functional for more marketised schools as for more centrally regulated ones. It is, for example, integral to the management philosophy of Edison Learning, one of the largest chains of for-profit Education Management Organisations in the USA (Rutherford, 2006).

The question of democracy

In the dominant school leadership paradigm, the internal democratic deficit within schools and networks is paralleled by the exclusion of any significant role for external popular participation and elected local government in decision making in the local school system. When Harris (2008: 157) asserts that 'The transformational agenda is to be owned by schools and led by schools', she means head teachers: neither school governors nor local authorities appear in her book. Similarly, Hopkins insists that 'the move towards networking should be developed and groups of secondary schools, in particular, should be encouraged to form collaborative arrangements outside local control' (2007: 172). David Hargreaves envisages the role of local authorities under the Coalition government as brokering school networks and then supporting and monitoring their self-improvement, but makes no mention of their democratic representative function (2010: 14). Hill notes the view that the emergence of new forms of network school governance exacerbates the democratic deficit:

> Critics argue that this development, which the establishment of chains is entrenching, undermines the local democratic accountability of schools. They say that any concerns on how a school conducts itself (unless its performance significantly deteriorates) are now outside of the remit of the local authority and that local elected representatives are excluded from any oversight of a schooling system, which is an issue of major concern to local people. (Hill, 2010: 33)

This leadership paradigm articulates and promotes a conception of head teachers as a technocratic managerial elite leading schools and networks of schools unfettered by local democracy at school and local authority levels. It has found its political vehicle in a government which shares its lack of enthusiasm for democratic participation in decision making in the school system, whether by teachers or the wider public, as exemplified by the exclusion of Academies and free schools from local authorities. Thus, at school and network levels, the same contradiction arises between 'authority' and 'influence', between the benefits of participation claimed for distributed leadership and networks and the structural constraints imposed on it by hierarchical management circumscribed and driven by state power. It is a classic instance of what Knights and Willmott (2007) see as a defining contradiction of capitalism:

> as a *mode of production,* capitalism is distinguished by the progressive intensification of the underlying contradiction between the 'socialization' tendency of the forces of production and the persistence of private-property based relations of production. (p. 1372)

In the case of school as a workplace, the contradiction is between the forces of production – specifically, the progressive potential of collective participation by teachers in strategic decision making – and the relations of production – state power over schooling driven by the imperative of ensuring that it reproduces the conditions of capitalist society, and in particular the labour power potential of children and young people as the future workforce. The increasing socialisation of the work process in schools is expressed in different terms in Michael Fullan's (2010) concept of 'collective, collaborative capacity' as the key to system-wide school reform. What needs to be added to Fullan's formulation is that collective, collaborative capacity has to include collective participation in decision making. The same contradiction serves largely to exclude local popular participation in school policy making. While it is not possible to overcome this structural contradiction in the education system, it is possible to ameliorate it. In Hatcher (2005), I offered some examples of radical alternatives, both from other countries and from the early history of the comprehensive school in England (see Chessum, 2011). The challenge for the critical research and policy agendas is not only to continue to critique the technocratic-elite school leadership paradigm and the current policy context in which it flourishes, but also to explore and develop credible alternatives to them.

Note

1. Ofsted is the Office for Standards in Education, the government agency which inspects schools and colleges in England.

References

Association of Teachers and Lecturers (2010) *The Bully*. Available at: www.new2teaching.org.uk/tzone/health_and_safety/Bullying/thebully.asp

Avis, J. (2009) Further education in England: the new localism, systems theory and governance. *Journal of Education Policy* 24(5): 633–48.

Ball, S.J. and Maroy, C. (2009) Schools' logics of action as mediation and compromise between internal dynamics and external constraints and pressures. *Compare* 39(10): 99–112.

Bohlmark, A. and Lindahl, M. (2008) *Does School Privatisation Improve Educational Achievement? Evidence from Sweden's Voucher Reform*, IZA Discussion Paper No. 3691. Bonn, Germany: Institute for the Study of Labor.

Boxall, P. and Purcell, J. (2010) An HRM perspective on employee participation. In A. Wilkinson, P.J. Gollan, M. Marchington and D. Lewin (eds) *The Oxford Handbook of Participation in Organizations*. Oxford: Oxford University Press.

Confederation of British Industry (CBI) (2010) *Fulfilling Potential: The Business Role in Education*. London: CBI.

Chapman, C., Lindsay, G., Muijs, D., Harris, A., Arweck, E. and Goodall, A. (2010) Governance, leadership and management in federations of schools. *School Effectiveness and School Improvement* 21(1): 53–75.

Chessum, L. (2011) *Radical Education in a Cold Climate: What Can We Learn From Countesthorpe College?* London: Continuum.

Center for Research on Education Outcomes (CREDO) (2009) *Multiple Choice: Charter School Performance in 16 States*. Palo Alto, CA: Stanford University.

Evans, M.P. and Stone-Johnson, C. (2010) Internal leadership challenges of network participation, *International Journal of Leadership in Education* 13(2): 203–20.

Fitzgerald, T. and Gunter, H.M. (2008) Contesting the orthodoxy of teacher leadership, *International Journal of Leadership in Education* 11(4): 331–40.

Fullan, M. (2005) *Leadership and Sustainability*. Thousand Oaks, CA: Corwin Press.

Fullan, M. (2010) *All Systems Go: The Change Imperative for Whole System Reform*. London: Sage.

Gove, M. (2010) Speech at National College for Leadership of Schools and Children's Services' Annual Leadership Conference, Birmingham, 17 June.

Gronn, P. (2009) Hybrid leadership. In K. Leithwood, B. Mascall and T. Strauss (eds) *Distributed Leadership According to the Evidence*. Abingdon: Routledge.

Hargreaves, A. (2009) Labouring to lead. In C. Chapman and H.M. Gunter (eds) *Radical Reforms*. London: Routledge.

Hargreaves, D.H. (2008) *Leading System Redesign – 1*. London: Specialist Schools and Academies Trust.

Hargreaves, D.H. (2010) *Creating a Self-improving School System*. Nottingham: National College.

Harris, A. (2008) *Distributed School Leadership*. London: Routledge.

Harris, A. (2009) Distributed leadership and knowledge creation. In K. Leithwood, B. Mascall and T. Strauss (eds) *Distributed Leadership According to the Evidence*. Abingdon: Routledge.

Hartley, D. (2004) Management, leadership and the emotional order of the school. *Journal of Education Policy* 19(5): 583–94.

Hartley, D. (2007) The emergence of distributed leadership in education: why now? *British Journal of Educational Studies* 55(2): 202–14.

Hatcher, R. (2005) The distribution of leadership and power in schools. *British Journal of Sociology of Education* 26(2): 253–67.

Hatcher, R. (2008) System leadership, networks and the question of power. *Management in Education* 22(2): 24–30.

Hatcher, R. (2010) Marketisation, privatisation, autonomy and democracy. Paper presented at 'Education after the Election' BERA Social Justice SIG Seminar, Birmingham City University, 10 June. Available at: www.skolo.org/spip.php?article1234&lang=en (accessed 1 September 2010).

Higham, R., Hopkins, D. and Matthews, P. (2009) *System Leadership in Practice*. Maidenhead: Open University.

Hill, P., Campbell, C., Menefee-Libey, D., Dusseault, B., DeArmand, M. and Gross, B. (2009) *Portfolio School Districts for Big Cities: An Interim Report.* Seattle, WA: Centre on Reinventing Public Education, University of Washington.

Hill, R. (2010) *Chain Reactions: A Thinkpiece on the Development of Chains of Schools in the English School System*. Nottingham: National College.

Hopkins, D. (2007) *Every School a Great School*. Maidenhead: Open University Press.

Jessop, B. (2002) *The Future of the Capitalist State*. Cambridge: Polity Press.

Jones, K., Cunchillo, C., Hatcher, R., Hirtt, N., Innes, R., Joshua, S. and Klausenitzer, J. (2008) *Schooling in Western Europe: The New Order and its Adversaries*. Basingstoke: Palgrave Macmillan.

Klijn, E-H. and Skelcher, C. (2007) Democracy and governance networks: compatible or not? *Public Administration* 85(3): 587–608.

Knights, D. and Willmott, H. (2007) Socialization, Yes. Skill upgrading, Probably. Robust theory of the capitalist labour process, No. *Organization Studies* 28(9): 1369–78.

Leithwood, K., Mascall, B. and Strauss, T. (2009) New perspectives on an old idea: a short history of the old idea. In K. Leithwood, B. Mascall and T. Strauss (eds) *Distributed Leadership According to the Evidence*. Abingdon: Routledge.

Lubienski, C. (2009) Do quasi-markets foster innovation in education? A comparative perspective. Education Working Paper No. 25. Paris: OECD.

Lucio, M.M. (2010) Labour process and Marxist perspectives on employee participation. In A. Wilkinson, P.J. Gollan, M. Marchington and D. Lewin (eds) *The Oxford Handbook of Participation in Organizations*. Oxford: Oxford University Press.

Marsden, D. (2007) Individual employee voice: renegotiation and performance management in public services. *International Journal of Human Resource Management* 18(7): 1263–78.

Moore, T. and Kelly, M.P. (2009) Networks as power bases for school improvement. *School Leadership and Management* 29(4): 391–404.

National Workplace Bullying Advice Line (n.d.) *Information for Teachers and Lecturers Experiencing Workplace Bullying*. Available at: www.bullyonline.org/workbully/teachers.htm

OECD (2003) *Networks of Innovation: Towards New Models for Managing Schools and Systems. Schooling for Tomorrow*. Paris: OECD.

O'Leary, D. and Craig, J. (2007) *System Leadership: Lessons from the Literature*. London: Demos.

PricewaterhouseCoopers (PwC) (2007) *Independent Study into School Leadership*. London: DCSF.

Robinson, S. (2010) Primary headteachers: new leadership roles inside and outside the classroom. PhD thesis, Birmingham City University.

Rutherford, C. (2006) Teacher leadership and organizational structure: the implications of restructured leadership in an Edison school. *Journal of Educational Change* 7(1–2): 59–76.

Stevenson, H. and Carter, B. (2009) Teachers and the state: forming and re-forming 'partnership'. *Journal of Educational Administration and History* 41(4): 311–26.

Thompson, G.F. (2003) *Between Hierarchies and Markets*. Oxford: Oxford University Press.

Thompson, P. (2010) The capitalist labour process: concepts and connections. *Capital & Class* 34(1): 7–14.

West, M. (2010) School to school cooperation as a strategy for improving student outcomes in challenging contexts. *School Effectiveness and School Improvement* 21(1): 93–112.

Wiborg, S. (2010) *Swedish Free Schools: Do They Work?* The Centre for Learning and Life Chances in Knowledge Economies and Societies. Available at: www.llakes.org

Wilkinson, A., Gollan, P.J., Marchington, M. and Lewin, D. (2010) Conceptualizing employee participation in organizations. In A. Wilkinson, P.J. Gollan, M. Marchington and D. Lewin (eds) *The Oxford Handbook of Participation in Organizations*. Oxford: Oxford University Press.

Wright, N. (2003) Principled 'bastard' leadership? *Educational Management and Administration* 31(2): 139–43.

20

The Fourth Way

Andy Hargreaves and Dennis Shirley

Editors' note: Earlier in the book from which this extract is taken, the authors describe three phases of largely unsuccessful educational reform efforts over recent decades, which they term the First, Second and Third Way of Educational Change. A summary of these is shown in the Appendix. In this chapter, Hargreaves and Shirley put the case for a new vision of educational change – the Fourth Way.

The Fourth Way is a way of inspiration and innovation, of responsibility and sustainability. The Fourth Way does not drive reform relentlessly through teachers, use them as final delivery points for government policies, or vacuum up their motivations into a vortex of change defined by short-term political agendas and the special interests with which they are aligned. Rather, it brings together government policy, professional involvement, and public engagement around an inspiring social and educational vision of prosperity, opportunity, and creativity in a world of greater inclusiveness, security, and humanity.

The Fourth Way pushes beyond standardization, data-driven decision making, and target-obsessed distractions to forge an equal and interactive partnership among the people, the profession, and their government. It enables educational leaders to 'let go' of the details of change, steering broadly whenever they can and intervening directly only when they must – to restore safety, avoid harm, and remove incompetence and corruption from the system.

The Fourth Way involves a trade-off for educators. It releases teachers from the tightened grip of government control. It also reduces their autonomy from parents, communities, and the public. Parents become more involved in the daily lives of their children's education, community members become more visible and vocal in schools, and the public gets engaged in determining the purposes of education together rather than simply consuming the services that are delivered to them.

Source – This is a brief extract from Hargreaves, A. and Shirley, D. (2009) 'The fourth way'.

In Linda Darling-Hammond's (2008) terms, the Fourth Way brings about change through democracy and professionalism rather than through bureaucracy and the market. It transfers trust and confidence back from the discredited free market of competition among schools and reinvests them in the expertise of highly trained and actively trusted professionals. At the same time, it reduces political bureaucracy while energizing public democracy. This means a fundamental shift in teachers' professionalism that restores greater autonomy from government and introduces more openness to and engagement with parents and communities. The Fourth Way, therefore, means significant change for everyone – governments, parents, and teacher unions alike (see Figure 20.1).

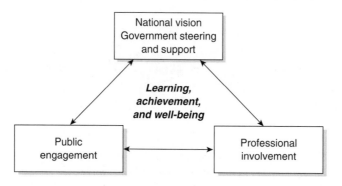

Figure 20.1   The fourth way

This chapter [outlines] the new theory-of-action of the Fourth Way – a Way more suited than previous Ways to building prosperous and competitive knowledge societies, to removing injustice and inequity, to restoring professional expertise and integrity, and to establishing greater cohesion and inclusion in our communities and societies than any of its predecessors. It consists of:

- six pillars of purpose and partnership that support change;
- three principles of professionalism that drive change;
- four catalysts of coherence that sustain change and hold it together.

Six pillars of purpose and partnership

Any theory of action of sustainable change must rest on the original meaning of the Latin verb *sustinere*, to sustain. To sustain means not merely to *maintain* or *endure*, but also to *hold up* or to *bear the weight of* something. What will ultimately bear the weight of sustainable educational change is not an overarching set of bureaucratic policies and interventions that shift from one government to the next, that subject educators to repetitive change syndrome and that undermine the basic trust and confidence that support their relationships with students. Data can enhance and inform these relationships but cannot replace the value of teachers working closely and effectively with students and colleagues, students learning from and supporting each other, and all of them engaging with parents and communities around purposes they develop and deliberate on together.

Research on happiness, including our own, backs this up. The three things that most make people happy are purposes, power, and relationships. Teachers feel positive emotions when their *purposes* are clear, focused, and achievable, and when those purposes belong to them. They become unhappy when purposes are vague, scattered, unrealistic, constantly changing, or are imposed by someone else. Second, teachers, like other people, feel happy when they experience being *empowered*, in control of their work lives and not at the beck and call of others. Last, happiness comes from developing and achieving purposes in positive *relationships* with colleagues and others, whereas unhappiness springs from a professional life that provides no time to develop or sustain any relationships at all. Inspiring purposes developed and achieved with others are the foundation of successful and sustainable educational change.

In the Fourth Way, there are *six pillars of purpose and partnership*. These are:

- an inspiring and inclusive vision;
- strong public engagement;
- achievement through investment;
- corporate educational responsibility;
- students as partners in change;
- mindful learning and teaching.

[…]

Three principles of professionalism

Teachers are the ultimate arbiters of educational change. The classroom door is the open portal to innovation or the raised drawbridge that holds innovation at bay. No plan for sustainable educational change can ignore or bypass the teacher. School leaders can stand on their heads, dish out awards, or wave pom-poms in the air, but none of it matters unless all teachers are engaged in the changes that have to be achieved.

It's time to insist on more than compliance with or 'fidelity' to bureaucratic mandates. It's time to bring teachers back in. The Third Way promoted professional learning communities, but these degenerated into contrived collegiality when the purposes of discussion were confined to increasing achievement scores fixed in advance by policymakers and civil servants in central offices. The Third Way's sponsorship of school networks also increased lateral professional energy, but this was often restricted to fleeting interactions about simple strategies that would give school test scores a quick lift. The Third Way reinvigorated and restored pride among the teaching profession. The Fourth Way pushes this professionalism much farther. Three principles are at the heart of it:

- high-quality teachers;
- positive and powerful professional associations;
- lively learning communities.

[…]

Four catalysts of coherence

The hardest part of educational change is not how to start it, but how to make it last and spread. Pilot projects almost always show early promise, but most attempts to scale them up produce pale imitations of the original. There will always be a few exceptional schools, but we need many more of them. Permissive, voluntary networks work mainly with volunteers and enthusiasts and rarely reach the rest. And leaders of quick turnarounds seldom stay around to see them through.

The challenge of coherence is not to clone or align everything so it looks the same in all schools. If we are all on the same page, nobody is reading the entire book! The challenge, rather, is how to bring diverse people together to work skillfully and effectively for a common cause that lifts them up and has them moving in the same direction with an impact on learning, achievement, and results. The Fourth Way has four catalysts that create this coherence:

- sustainable leadership;
- integrating networks;
- responsibility before accountability;
- differentiation and diversity.

[…]

Conclusion

The Fourth Way is neither about letting a thousand flowers bloom nor about micromanaging everything in detail. It neither exalts the market and its charter school prodigies nor extols the virtues of an all-providing state.

It is not a way to retain autocratic control over narrowly defined goals and targets. The Fourth Way, rather, is a democratic and professional path to improvement that builds from the bottom, steers from the top, and provides support and pressure from the sides. Through high-quality teachers committed to and capable of creating deep and broad teaching and learning, it builds powerful, responsible, and lively professional communities in an increasingly self-regulating but not self-absorbed or self-seeking profession. Here, teachers define and pursue high standards and shared targets, and improve by learning continuously through networks, from evidence, and from each other.

In the Fourth Way, a resilient social democracy builds an inspiring and inclusive vision through courageous national and state or provincial leadership that draws teachers to the profession and grants them public status within it. It involves parents and the public as highly engaged partners, along with businesses that show corporate educational responsibility. In the Fourth Way, a lot is expected of educators, but the burden of narrowing achievement gaps and achieving social justice does not rest on their shoulders alone. It is shared with a strongly supported health service, housing system, and social service sector.

In all this, students in the Fourth Way are not merely targets of change. They are vigorous and active partners with a leading voice in their own development. This partnership is neither paternalistic nor indulgent but calls for educators who demand high standards, do not accept weak excuses or shabby work, and provide the consistent pressure and strong support to raise students to the highest levels of achievement.

The Fourth Way achieves coherence by:

- developing sustainable leadership that is knowledgeable about learning
- placing responsibility before accountability (with accountability serving as a conscience through sampling)
- initiating and supporting but not overregulating professional networks of improvement
- conducting an assault on the excesses of tested standardization that deny diversity and destroy creativity and – most of all –
- developing an inspiring and inclusive educational and social vision that connects the future to the past and leaves teachers collectively responsible for pedagogical decisions and a good amount of curriculum development within it.

The Fourth Way promotes educational change through deepened and demanding learning, professional quality and engagement, and invigorated community development and public democracy. The Fourth Way shares important commonalities with the Third (as well as legacies from the Ways before that), but it is a significant shift from, and even disruption of, Third Way orthodoxy. These shifts and disruptions are represented in Table 20.1.

We are at a turning point in history. The Old Ways can no longer serve us, and some of them have even actively betrayed us. We are in an increasingly interconnected world, financially, politically, and culturally. Unrestrained markets have held us hostage to caprice and greed. Standardization has undermined our capacity to understand and deal with diversity. We will need more innovation and creativity in the 21st century, not less. We will need more connection to and interdependence with our neighbors, at home and abroad, rather than an arrogant insistence on operating alone. It is time to reshape the world and to reinvent ourselves within it. This is the call of the Fourth Way.

We offer no silver bullets and make no promises. There are many tensions in the Fourth Way that will require sound judgment, not simple solutions. The Fourth Way places new demands on teachers *and* students, on top-ranking policymakers *and* bottom-up community organizers. Lateral pressures *and* supports will bring discomfort to some and energize and inspire others. We will need to attend to and integrate both short-term *and* long-term considerations, and sacrifice neither to the other. We must find ways to help our school neighbors in ways that also energize and empower ourselves. At a crucial turning point in global history, we have to make daring and disruptive changes, not incremental adjustments – but without abandoning everything we have valued and achieved in the past. And moment by moment, one issue at time, we have to learn how to steer clearly from the top while knowing how and when to 'let go.'

In the Fourth Way, there will be standards, including public, human, business, and ethical ones, but there will no longer be educational standardization. There will also be targets, and these will be even bolder because dedicated professionals will identify them together. There will be hard work and persistence, but not pointless drudgery. There will be greater support for the education profession, but not unconditionally. Accountability will be our conscience, not our Grand Inquisitor. And our children will be the deposits of learning, generosity, and humanity through which we invest in the future.

The purpose of the Fourth Way is to create the schools that will undergird and catalyze our best values to regenerate and improve society. The time is surely nigh for this. New generations are taking over. The age of unregulated markets and wanton greed is disappearing behind us. People are starting to look within and beyond themselves once more. Now is the time to join them.

Table 20.1   Third Way New Orthodoxy to Fourth Way Solutions

		Third Way New Orthodoxy	Fourth Way Solutions
		from ⟶	*to*
Pillars of Purpose and Partnership	Change	Detailed deliverology	Steering and development
	Control	Bureaucratic, market-related, and professional	Democratic and professional
	Trust	Public confidence	Active trust
	Goals	Competitive, measurable standards	Inspiring, innovative, and inclusive mission
	Public	Parent choice and community service delivery	Public engagement and community development
	Partnership	Entrepreneurial and expedient	Transparent and responsible
	Learning	Customized learning	Mindful learning and teaching
	Students	Targets of teaching and service delivery	Engagement and voice
Principles of Professionalism	Teacher quality	Reward- and performance-driven	Mission- and conditions-driven
	Teacher associations	Bought-off distracters, who consent to change	Agents of change
	Professional community	Data-driven	Evidence-informed
Catalysts of Coherence	Quality assurance	Accountability first	Responsibility first
	Accountability	By census	By sample
	Targets	Arbitrary and imposed	Ambitious and shared
	Leadership	Individually developed	Systemic and sustainable
	Lateral relations	Dispersed networks	Networks plus area-based collaboration
	Diversity and social justice	Narrowed achievement gaps and data-driven interventions	Demanding and responsive teaching

We must be clear where we stand as we face one of the most critical turning points of all time. We must stand aside from the slippery and distracting paths of easy opportunism that merely enhance government 'deliverology'. We must take the more vertiginous route that scales the heights of professional excellence and public democracy. For it is this truly challenging path that will lead us to the peaks of excellence and integrity in student learning and its resulting high levels of achievement.

[...]

Reference

Darling-Hammond, L. (2008) Teaching and the change wars. In Hargreaves, A. and Fullan, M. (eds) *Change Wars*. Bloomington, IN: Solution Tree.

Appendix   From the First Way to the Third Way of Educational Change

	The First Way	The Interregnum	The Second Way	The Third Way
Control	Professionalism	Professionalism and bureaucracy	Bureaucracy and markets	Bureaucracy, markets, and professionalism
Purpose	Innovation and inspiration	Quest for coherence	Markets and standardization	Performance and partnership
Trust	Passive trust	Growing suspicion	Active mistrust	Public confidence
Community engagement	Mainly absent	Parent communication	Parent choice	Delivery of services to communities
Curriculum	Inconsistent innovation	Broad standards and outcomes	Detailed and prescribed standardization	Varying prescription with increased coaching and support
Teaching and learning	Eclectic and uneven	Prescriptively driven by standards and testing	Direct instruction to standards and test requirements	Autocratically data driven yet customized
Professionalism	Autonomous	Increasingly collaborative	Deprofessionalized	Reprofessionalized
Professional learning communities	Discretionary	Some collaborative cultures	Contrived collegiality	Data driven and professionally effervescent
Assessment and accountability	Local and sampled	Portfolio and performance-based	High-stakes targets and testing by census	Escalating targets self-surveillance, and testing-by-census
Lateral relations	Voluntary	Consultative	Competitive	Networked

Index

ABCD model of strategic influence, 90
ability model of emotional intelligence, 53–5
accountability, 94, 146, 175
  in education, 1, 5, 47–8, 173–83
  and performance measurement, 174–6
  as a politico-legal concept, 174–5
  see also self-accountability
achievement-oriented leadership, 78
action competences, 27, 31
adaptive leadership, 68–70, 254
adaptive tension, 106–7
adaptive work, 14, 67–70, 72
Adult Learning Inspectorate (ALI), 190
affective leadership, 52, 61–2
agency of leaders, 126, 146–7, 150–6
  atemporal dimension of, 148, 151
  delimitation of, 146, 148, 153–4
  paradox of, 171
Aguirre, A., 209
alignment of strategies, 73, 105, 259
Allen, K.E., 67
Allix, P., 206
allocation of resources, 50, 148–9, 151–4, 258
Alvesson, M., 115, 121
antecedent-focused regulation, 59
Apple, Michael, 32
approachability, 194–7
Argentina, 179
Argyris, C., 170
Ashforth, B.E., 59
Australia, 256, 258–60, 265
Austria, 256, 258–60
Austrian Leadership Academy, 259, 262
authentic leadership, 44, 50, 56, 58–80, 76–7
authority, 2, 6, 16, 126, 175, 229
  and accountability, 177, 183
  definition of, 228
  legitimacy of, 97, 122, 239
  loss of, 275

authority cont.
  in networks, 228–30, 234–7, 279
  sources of, 22
  structures of, 4, 67, 230, 274
  types of, 234
autonomy
  and educators, 34, 268, 271, 277
  and leadership, 11, 22, 87, 92, 146–7, 152
  loss of, 233
  of schools and colleges, 1, 179, 182–3, 185,
    275, 277
Avolio, B., 58, 73–4, 78

Badarraco, J., 18
Ball, S., 1
Bass, B., 58, 76
Baum, J.R., 89
Beane, James A., 32
Begley, Paul T., 3, 38–50
Behn, R., 175, 182
Belgium, 256, 258, 260–1, 265
Bennett, Nigel, 1–7
Bernstein, Basil, 27
bildung see action competencies
Binney, G., 18
Blair, Tony, 14
blended leadership, 5, 192, 194, 198–9
Boal, K.B., 88
Bolden, R., 198
Bolman, L., 88
Boon, M., 72
boundaries
  organisational, 2, 16, 20, 106, 134
  within schools, 6, 241–2, 245, 247–9
bounded rationality, 100, 271
Bowring, M.A., 199
Branson, C., 45
Brown, Shona, 103
Bruner, J.S., 242

Bryk, A.S., 138
bureaucratic organisations, 228, 230–1
Burke, J., 177
Burns, T., 228, 230

Calas, M.B., 19
Cameron, K.S., 199
Canada, 183
capitalism, 269, 279
Carroll, B., 121
Carter, B., 269
change, 97
    in behaviour, 79–80
    envisioning of, 79
    management of, 3–4, 93, 110
    organisational, 132, 138
    see also evolutionary change, 78
charisma of purpose, 72
charismatic leadership, 76–7
Cheng, Y.C., 88
Chicago, 205
Chile, 179
Churchman, C. West, 242
citizenship, 27–8, 31, 40
Clark, B., 181
Cloke, K., 272
Coburn, C.E., 139
coercive power, 229, 235–6, 270
cognitive bias, 101
cognitive capabilities, 100
Cole, M., 140, 241
Colella, A., 206
collaborated distribution, 30
collaborative leadership, 62, 67, 70, 192
collaborative partnerships, 1, 6, 257
collaborative practices, 61, 192
collective distribution, 30
collective experience, 101–2
collective leadership, 1, 67, 70, 119–21
Collins, J., 18, 198
Collinson, David, 5, 126, 189–99
Collinson, Margaret, 5, 189–99
common assessment framework (CAF), 246–7
commonality of purpose, 72
community leadership, 196, 216
competitive advantage, 105, 108
complex organisations, 41, 67, 73, 86,
    231, 281
complexity theory, 103–6, 112
concertive action, 30

conflict, 5, 30
    management of, 89, 165, 237
    sources of, 43–4
    of values, 38, 46–8, 72
Conger, J.A., 68
congruence as an attribute of leadership,
    56, 59–60
connectivity, 22, 19, 21
Connolly, M., 228–9
consultative leadership, 74, 192
context-setting, 68
contextual factors, 4, 145–50
    manipulation of, 148–55
    in the public sector, 151
contextualisation in the curriculum, 164
contingency theories, 78–9
contingent rewards, 77
controllers, leaders as, 11–12, 14–16, 22–23
cooperation, 6, 68, 106, 265
    in communities, 190, 278
coordinated distribution, 30
Copperman, J., 58–9, 62
Courtney, N., 74
Craig, J., 275
Crawford, M., 59
creative insubordination, 48–9
Cruse, P., 57
cultural competency, 68, 70
cultural diversity, 38, 40, 46
cultural-historical activity theory
    (CHAT), 241

Daniels, H., 241
Dao de Jing, 70–1
Darling-Hammond, L., 284
Davies, Barbara J., 83–94
Davies, Brent, 4, 83–94
Deal, T., 88
decentralisation of power, 31, 34–5, 175,
    179, 183
decision-making, 4, 7, 26–8, 42, 73, 97,
    111, 125–6
    collective forms of, 258, 272, 279
    complex forms of, 251
    decentralisation of, 175
    in education, 32, 43, 47, 60, 153,
        193–5, 279
    models of, 100
    student involvement in, 35
decontextualised theories of leadership, 156

delegation, 261, 271–2, 274
  and direction, 5, 17, 192–4
  of power, 133, 147–51
democracy, 41, 175, 220
  in education, 7, 27, 31, 278–9
  forms of, 27–8, 32, 278
  and leadership, 27, 30, 35, 55, 57, 272–3,
    278–80
democratic leadership in schools, 27, 35
Denhardt B., 60–1
Denhardt V., 60–1
Denis, Jean-Louis, 4, 115–26
Denmark, 3, 31–2, 171
Department for Children, Schools and Families
  (DCSF), 57, 276
Department for Education and Skills (DfES),
  159, 241
design views of strategy, 96–9
development and learning, 26
Dewey, J., 27
dialectic nature of leadership, 4–5, 75, 116,
  118–9, 124–5, 190, 199
dilemma situations, 45–6
  avoidance of, 48
  interpersonal and intra-personal, 47
  interpretation of, 48–9
  sources of, 46–7
Dill, D., 182
directive leadership, 26, 78, 168
disadvantaged groups, 206–7
discourse
  and identity, 108–9
  implications for management, 109–11
  and influence, 108
  and legitimacy, 108–9
  and power, 109
  and rationality, 108
  as strategy, 97, 107–8
disempowerment, 5, 150
dispersed leadership, 3, 23, 17, 18, 20
disruptive emotions, 56, 61
dissent, 5, 191
  within school management, 163, 165, 170
distributed expertise, 242–3, 247
distributed leadership, 191, 261
  and education, 26, 270–2, 275, 279
  forms of, 30
  and hierarchical power, 272–3
  and leadership, 29–30, 171, 193,
    199, 233–4

distributed leadership *cont.*
  and networks, 7, 269, 273, 279
  support of, 261, 263, 265
diversity, 5, 201–3
  cultural, 38, 40, 46
  definition of, 202
  goals for, 203–4
  and leadership, 204–9
  policies relating to, 209–10
  of students, 2
division of labour, 121, 246–7, 273
Dowding, K., 229
due process, 45
dynamic connectedness, 57
dynamic leadership, 118–20

e-leadership, 73–4
Eacott, S., 85
eco-ethics, 21
eco-leadership, 3, 22–23, 18–21
economic competitiveness, 173, 176
economic functions of education, 40, 50
Edison Learning (company), 278
education
  leaders in, 150–3
  purpose of, 39–40, 50
  standardisation of, 287
educational accountability, 177–83
  contradictions in, 183
  in higher education, 181–3
  outcomes-based forms of, 178–80
  sanctions for underperformance, 179
educational evaluation, 174
Edwards, Anne, 6, 240–51
effective leadership, 79, 190–2
Eisenhardt, Kathy, 103
embeddedness, 145–6
emergent capabilities, 20
emergent change, 58
emergent strategy, 21, 87, 92
emotional competence, 56–7
emotional intelligence, 3, 12, 52, 58, 61
  and affective leadership, 62
  appraisal of, 55
  critiques of, 55–6
  definition of, 53
  evolution of, 52–3
  and integrated working, 61–2
  key theories of, 54
  models of, 53–5

emotional labour, 58–60
emotional regulation, 59
emotional and social competency inventory, 55
empathy, 53, 55, 58, 60
employees
    empowerment of, 35, 76
    involvement of, 272
Engeström, Y., 243
England, 178, 256–7, 260–1, 265
environmental ambiguity, 2
ethical dimensions of leadership, 2, 3, 20,
        38–42, 44–6, 68–9
    and social justice, 224
ethical posturing, 45–6
Etzioni, A., 12, 228–9, 234–5
Evangelou, M., 251
Evans, D., 57
Evans, K., 209
Evans, P., 170–1
Every Child Matters (*ECM*) agenda, 223
evolutionary change, 78
evolutionary theory, 103, 105
experimentation, 106
extended intelligence concept of, 242
extra-system organisations, 134

Fairhurst, G., 199
Faulkner, W., 132
Feller, Irwin, 5, 173–85
Fineman, S., 56, 60
Fink, D., 256
Finland, 256, 258, 260–1, 265
Fitzgerald, T., 272
followership, 191
Forsyth, D.R., 73
Four I's of transformational leadership, 58
Fourth way of educational change, 283–8
Frank, K.A., 138
Frost, D., 171
functional benefits of strategic ideas, 105
Fullan, M., 54, 254–5, 279
further education colleges
    external engagement by, 196–7
    hierarchical levels in, 192
    leadership in, 189–99
    monitoring of, 190

Gardner, H., 176
Geertz, Clifford, 101
Gemeinschaft-Gesellschaft continuum, 28

Gemmill, G., 192
Genady, M., 170–1
gender categorisation, 203
General Certificate of Secondary Education
        (GCSE) 162, 169
George, J.M., 58
Giddens, A., 134, 147, 171
Gini, A., 68
Giroux, H., 161
globalisation, 1, 3, 19, 38, 43, 154–5, 173–4
Glover, J., 70
Goffee, R., 195
Goldring, E., 26
Goldsmith, J., 272
Goleman, Daniel, 52–7, 59, 61
Gomez, Louis M., 131–42
Google, 106
Gove, Michael, 276
government policy, 57, 242
    for education, 169–70, 270, 274, 276, 283
    for health, 152
Grandey, A.A., 58
Gratton, L., 86, 89
Green, S.E., 108
Greenfield, W. 26
Greenleaf, R., 18 77
Gronn, P., 30, 199, 206, 271
group-centred leadership, 67, 73
group dynamics, 232–3, 236
groupthink, 76
Gudykunst, W., 206–7
Gunter, H., 229, 243–4, 272
Gurin, P., 206

Hallinger, P., 25
Hambrick, D.C., 120
Hamel, G., 88
Hargreaves, Andy, 7, 256, 274, 283–8
Hargreaves, David, 273, 276, 278–9
Harris, Alma, 34, 217, 269–72, 278
Hartley, D., 241–2, 250
Hatcher, Richard, 6, 269–80
heads of department, 33–5
health service leaders, 150–5
Heck, R., 25
Heider, J.L., 70–1
Heifetz, Ronald, 69
Held, Sam, 3, 52–62
hero leaders, 2, 5, 171, 190–2, 198, 215; *see
    also* post-heroic leadership

Heron, J., 56
heterarchy, 272–4
Hickman, G.R., 4, 67–80
hierarchical leadership, 7, 90, 272–3
high schools, 133–4
Higham, R., 275–6
higher education systems, 173, 189
    accountability in, 181–3
    reform of, 176
Hill, R., 277–9
Hochschild, A., 59–60
Hodgkinson, C., 39, 48
Hodgson, R.C., 120
holism, 20–1
Holtham, C., 74
homogeneity, 17, 20, 41, 191, 219
Hooijberg, R., 88
Hopkins, David, 6, 253–66
Howe, D., 59
Hoyle, E., 229
human capital, 4, 131, 136–41
Humphrey, R.H., 59–60
Hunt, J.G., 75
Hutchins, E., 242
hybrid leadership, 2

idealised influence, 58, 75
idealised preferences, 14
identity, 108–9
ideological functions of education,
    40, 50
Iles, P., 207
imperfect copying, 104, 107
inactive leadership, 77
inauthentic leadership, 76–7
inclusion, 5, 201
    definition of, 202
    and leadership, 204–9
    policies relating to, 209–10
individualised consideration, 58, 76
individualism, 12, 57
influence, 229, 237
    definition of, 228
    and discourse, 108
    social, 58
    sources of, 43–4
    see also idealised influence
innovation, 97, 106, 110
Innovations Unit, 227
innovative thinking, 79

inspirational motivation, 58, 75
instructional leadership, 39, 133
integrated working, 61–2
intellectual stimulation, 58, 75
interconnectedness of leader and group, 71
International Education Association
    (IEA), 176
International Successful Principal Project, 31
Internet, 38, 101
interpersonal dilemmas, 47
interprofessional work, 6, 241–4
intra-personal dilemmas, 47
invisible leadership, 72–3, 80
involvement, types of, 234
Iszatt-White, M., 56, 58–9

Jackson, L., 230
James, C., 228–9
Janis, J., 76
Japan, 182
Jessop, B., 273
Johnson, Gerry, 4, 96–111
Jones, G., 195

K-12 education, 173, 185
    accountability in, 177–80, 183
    reform of, 176
Kahai, S.S., 74
Kaiser, R., 199
Kanter, R.M., 132
Katz, J.H., 204–5
Kaur Hayers, P., 207
Kelley, Robert, 68
Kelly, Michael P., 6, 227–38, 274–5
Kenya, 178
Key Stage strategies, 162
Kincheloe, J.L., 216–17
Kirkpatrick, S.A., 89
Klijn, E.-H., 274
Knights, D., 279
knowledge-based economy, 154, 176
Kofman, F., 254
Kouzes, J.M., 191–2

laissez-faire leadership, 77–8
Lakomski, G., 206
Langley, Ann, 115–26
Lao Tzu, 70–1
lateral influence, 68
Latour, B., 135

leaders
  agency of, 146, 171
  contextual influences on, 145–50
  embeddedness of, 145–6
  expanding influence of, 149
  span of control, 146
leadership
  achievement-oriented, 78
  adaptive forms of, 68–70, 254
  as an art, 60–1
  authentic forms of, 44, 59, 77
  blended forms of, 5, 192, 194, 198–9
  capacity for, 255, 260, 262
  collaborative forms of, 62, 192
  collective, 120–1
  and communication, 29–30
  concept of, 30, 80
  consultative styles of, 192
  decontextualised theories of, 156
  dialectic nature of, 4–5, 75, 116, 118–9,
    124–5, 190, 199
  discourses of, 11–21, 22–3,107–8
  and diversity, 204–9
  dynamic, 118–20
  effectiveness of, 79, 190–2
  ethical dimensions of, 2, 3, 20, 38–42, 44–6,
    68–9, 224
  and inclusion, 204–9
  and management, 60, 167–70
  micro-practices of, 118, 122
  narcissistic form of, 167–8, 171
  practices, 3, 6–7, 116, 118–25, 122, 134–5
  as a science, 60–1
  shared forms of, 29, 34–5, 58, 68,
    171, 191
  situated, 121–4
  skills, 57
  sources of influence and conflict in, 43–4
  styles of, 57
  as a tag, 68
  theories of, 3, 11–21, 22–3, 58, 60, 67–80
  in urban contexts, 215–24
  values of, 3, 40–2, 44–5
  within communities, 28–9
Leadership on the Front-line project, 218–21
learning by doing, 87
Learning How to Learn project, 159, 163
learning in and for inter-professional work
    (LIW), 242
learning journeys, 162–6

learning strategies within the curriculum, 164
learning walk, 140
legitimacy, 97, 229–30
  of authority, 97, 122, 239
  definition of, 228
  and discourse, 108–9
  of management, 107
Leithwood, K., 25–6, 270
Lewis, N., 55–6
liberal democracy, 27–8
Lindblom, Charles, 100
Lipsky, M., 175
Literacy and Numeracy Strategies, 160, 165,
    169–70
Litvin, D.R., 202
local authorities, 153, 231–2, 260, 279
local education agencies (LEAs), 133
local initiatives, instigation of, 151
Locke, E.A., 55, 89
Louis, K.S., 27
Lubienski, C., 278
Lucio, M.M., 271
Lumby, Jacky, 5, 201–10
Lundvall, B.-A., 243
Lunt, Ingrid, 240–51

MacBeath, J., 5, 159–72, 234
McCall, M., 202
Maccoby, M., 167
MacCulloch, T., 56
MacIntyre, Alasdair, 11
McKelvey, Bill, 104
McKimm, J., 3, 52–62
management
  legitimacy of, 107
  theories of, 60, 100
management arrangements, development of,
    152
management-by-exception, 77
marketisation of public services, 146, 154
Martinez, R.O., 209
May, A., 19
Mayer, J., 52, 54–5, 57, 61
Mayer-Salovey-Caruso emotional intelligence
    test (MSCEIT), 55
meetings, patterns of, 33–4
Meindl, J., 190–1
mental models, 90, 100
Mesler, Leigh, 131–42
messianic, leaders, 12–15, 17, 20, 22–23

'messy' organisations, 126
meta-values, 45, 47, 50
micro-practices of leadership, 118, 122
Middleton, D., 243
Midgley, G., 242, 247
Miller, F.A., 204–5
Mintzberg, Henry, 55, 87, 89, 112, 190
Moore, Tessa A., 6, 227–38, 274–5
Moos, Leif, 3, 25–36, 171
moral dilemmas, 46, 49; *see also* suspended
    morality
moral dimensions of leadership, 2, 3, 20, 40–2,
    44–5, 50, 90
  and social justice, 224
Morrison, T., 57
motivation, 53, 194
  inspirational, 58
Mulford, B., 26
multinational corporations, 17, 20

Nagda, B.R.A., 206
Nanus, B., 88–9
narcissistic leadership, 17, 167–8, 171
National Center for Educational Statistics
    (NCES), 176
National College for School Leadership
    (NCSL), 227–8, 235, 274, 276
National Curriculum, 258, 270
national education systems, 176–7
National Health Service (NHS), 14
National Leaders of Education, 257
National Workplace Bullying Advice
    Line, 270
neo-liberalism, 20, 276
Netherlands, 256
Networked Learning Communities (NLC)
    programme, 227–8, 231–5, 273–5
networks, 227–38
  advantages and disadvantages of, 231
  in a marketised system, 276–8
  and power, 6, 235–7, 273–5
  system leaders in, 275–6
new public management (NPM), 146, 152, 154,
    174–5, 178, 185
New Zealand, 175
Newman, M.A., 60
Nixon, J., 247, 250
No Child Left Behind Act (US, 2001), 177, 179
normative power, 229, 235–6
Norte, E., 208

Nowotny, J., 243
Nystrom, P.C., 76

Oakley, J., 192
Office for Standards in Education(Ofsted),
    159–62, 166–7, 169–71, 180, 244, 270
  and further education colleges, 190
  and inclusion, 204
O'Leary, D., 275
'omniscient narrator' concept, 161
open-systems perspectives, 20
order-generating rules, 106
organic organisations, 230
Organisation for Economic Co-operation and
    Development (OECD), 174, 256, 262
  co-operation agreements, 257
  Improving School Leadership project, 256
  and social exclusion, 240–1
organisational change models, 4, 72, 84
organisational culture, 70, 101–2, 109
organisational effectiveness, 3
organisational routines, 131, 139–41
organisational vision, 151–2
organisations
  boundaries in, 2, 16, 20, 106, 134
  form and nature of, 98
  goals of, 6, 68, 73, 75, 92, 119, 147,
      149, 151
  interaction and cooperation in, 106
outcomes-based accountability, 178–80

parents
  collaborative relationships with, 163
  role in education, 27
participative leadership, 78
participatory bureaucracy, 271
participatory democracy, 28, 32
path-goal theory, 78–9
Pearce, C.L., 68
peer influence, 68
people-oriented work, 55, 59, 62
perfect knowledge, 100
performance measurement, 175
  and accountability, 174–6
  contradictions in, 184–5
  in education, 173–4, 184
  systems of, 176–7
performance objectives, 79, 175
performative aspects of resources, 135
Perkins, D., 161

Pettigrew, A.M., 120
Pinnington, A., 19
planning, 21, 30, 34, 79, 208, 234
    strategic, 50, 83–4, 86–8, 93, 96, 99,
        109, 112
Poder, Paul, 35
policies
    for diversity, 209–10
    implementation of, 132, 135, 138, 142
    as oppressive, 160–1
    in school contexts, 161–6
    selective response to, 152
    supportive, 160
policy environments, 5, 159–60
policy-making, 133–4, 136–7, 139–42
Pont, Beatriz, 6, 253–66
Poole, M.S., 132
Portugal, 256
Posner, B.Z., 191–2
post-heroic leadership 5, 18–19,
        190–2, 198
power, 29
    definition of, 228
    and discourse, 109
    and involvement, 232–3
    loss of, 233–4
    in a marketised system, 276–8
    and networks, 273–5
    and partnerships, 235–7
    shared, 233–4
practice theory, 115
Prahalad, C.K., 88
Preedy, Margaret, 1–7
primary care trusts (PCTs), 151–5
Primary Strategy Learning Networks (PSLNs),
        227–8, 231–4, 236, 274–5
professional culture, 149–53
professional knowledge, privatisation
        of, 278
professional networks, 133
professionalism, 153, 255, 258, 284–5, 288
    principles of, 285
Programme for International Student
        Assessment (PISA), 176
prototypes, 100
public policy, 137–8, 142, 175, 294
public sector
    accountability in, 174
    competition in, 175–6
    leadership in, 5, 150–4

public services, marketisation of, 146, 154
Purkey, S.C., 133

Quality Assurance Agency (QAA), 190
queer theory, 203

Rainwater, K., 70
Raising Achievement Transforming Learning
        project, 274
rational choice, 97
rationality, 97, 99, 102
    and discourse, 108
    see also bounded rationality
received wisdom, 106
regulatory framework for schools,
        270, 273–4
relational agency, 243, 250–1
relational trust, 138
relationship management, 53
remunerative power, 229, 235
response-focused regulation, 59
resources, 135–6
    allocation of, 50, 148–9, 151–4, 258
    and curricular domains, 141–2
    in the form of human and social capital,
        4, 131, 136–41
    rationalisation of, 260
    for system leadership, 260, 264
Reynolds, D., 26
Reynolds, M., 202, 205
Ribbins, P., 234
Riggio, R.E., 76
Riley, Kathryn A., 215–24
risk-taking culture, 92
Robinson, S., 270
Roche, K., 48
role boundaries, 248
Room, G., 240
Rose, N., 12
Rouleau, Linda, 115–26
Russell, I., 139
Rutherford, D., 230
Ryan, Katherine E., 5, 173–85

Saarni, C., 56, 61
Salovey, P., 52, 54–5, 57, 61
sanctions for underperformance, 179
Sao Paolo University, 177
satellite broadcasting, 101
Schneider, B.L., 138

Schneider, M., 68
Schön, D., 170
school leadership, 272
  co-operation in, 263
  democracy in, 278–80
  reforms of, 26
school practice
  and policy environments, 159–60, 170
  validation of, 162
school self-evaluation (SSE), 180–1
schools
  accountability of, 27, 177–81
  autonomy of, 1, 92, 275, 277, 283 and
      capitalism, 269, 279
  communities in, 29
  core purpose of, 27–8
  leadership in, 25–6, 150–3, 165, 167–70
  public policy for, 137
  reform of, 138
  regulatory framework for, 274
  sanctions for underperformance, 179
  self-improving, 273, 276, 278
  socio-economic status of, 136
Schratz, M., 169
Seholes, Kevan, 96–111
selective attention, 100
self-accountability, 72
self-actualisation, 12
self-awareness, 53, 56
self-improving schools, 273, 276, 278
self-managing teams, 34
self-regulation, 20–1, 53
Senge, Peter, 161, 254
senior management teams (SMTs), 33–4
Sergiovanni, T.J., 28, 88
servant leadership, 18, 77
Shapiro, J., 42
shared leadership, 29, 34–5, 58, 68, 171, 191
shared power, 233–4
shareholder value, 21
Shields, C., 205
Shirley, Dennis, 7, 283–8
short-term objectives, 84, 91–2, 94
silo management structure, 153
Simon, Herbert, 100
situated leadership, 121–4
Skelcher, C., 274
Smircich, L., 19
Smith, M.S., 133
Smith, S., 175

social awareness, 53
social capital, 4, 131, 137–41
social change, 154
social constructivism, 30
social democracy, 28
social deprivation, 217–18, 220
social exclusion, 240–1, 249–50
social influence, 58
social intelligence, 52
social justice, 45, 224
social networks, 55, 139
social skills, 40, 53
socio-economic status of schools, 136
sociological functions of education, 40
Somers, M., 68
Sorenson, G.J. , 72
Sørhaug, T., 29
Southworth, G., 26
span of control, 146
special educational needs coordinators
    (SENCOs), 245
Specialist Schools and Academies Trust
    (SSAT), 257, 274
Spicer, A., 109
Spillane, James P., 4, 30, 131–42
spiritual leadership, 18–19
spontaneous collaboration, 30
Stace, D., 74
stakeholders, 4, 46, 49, 117–18, 146, 196,
    230, 238
  expectations of, 99
  external, 1, 33–4, 96
Stalker, G.M., 228, 230
Stamou, Eleni, 240–51
standardised test scores, 39
standardisation of education, 287
standards, raising of 6, 171, 227,
    237, 277
standards agenda 269–70
Starbuck, W.H., 76
Stefkovich, J.A., 42
Stevenson, H., 269
Stevenson, O., 61
Stier, J., 207
Stone, D., 206
strategic alignment, 73, 105, 259
strategic change, 93, 110
strategic drift, 103
strategic health authorities (SHAs), 154
strategic influence, 89–90

strategic leadership, 3–4, 74–5, 83–94
  and talent development, 90–1
  taxonomy of, 85
strategic management, 108
strategic measures of success, 93–4
strategic planning, 50, 83–4, 86–8, 93, 96, 99,
  109, 112
strategic positioning, 98
strategic vision, 151–2
strategy, 96–111
  as design, 97–8
  as discourse, 97, 107–9
  as experience, 100–3
  selection of, 105
  as variety, 105–7
strategy development, 107
structural properties of social systems, 147
structuration process, 147
student involvement, 35
student outcomes, 26
students' best interests, 47
succession planning, 90
'superheads', 26
supportive leadership, 78
suspended morality, 48
Sveningsson, S., 115, 121
Sweden, 276–7
Swidler, A., 136
system leadership, 6, 253–6
  benefits of, 259–60
  in networks, 275–6
  and professional development, 264
  recruiting for, 263–4
  resources for, 260, 264
  sustainability of, 261–2
systematic analysis, 97
systems theory, 30, 254

Taber, T., 79
tags, concept of, 68–9
'taming the wild' concept, 161
Tao leadership, 70–1
Tapscott, D., 67
task-relations-and-change model, 79
taxonomy of control, 12
teacher quality, 136–7
teaching assistants, 243, 245
Teaching and Learning Research
  Programme, 242

teaching strategy, child-centred view of, 164
teaching within communities, 28–9
team leadership, 73–4
technology as a management resource,
  131, 140–1
therapists, leaders as, 12, 14–15, 17, 22–23
Third Way of educational change, 283–8
Thompson, G.F., 274
Thompson, P., 271
Thorndike, E.L., 52
Tomlinson, Michael, 5, 145–56
Tourish, D., 19
trait model of emotional intelligence, 53
transactional leadership, 77–8
transformational leadership, 14, 58, 60, 75–8
transnational approaches to leadership, 5
Trehan, K., 202, 205

Ubuntu leadership, 71–2
unethical actions, 38, 46
United Kingdom
  Coalition government (formed 2010),
    276–7, 279
  Labour government (1997–2010),
    270, 276
United States
  Department of Education, 183
  educational accountability in, 178
university leaders, 151–2
urban leadership, 6, 215–24
Uruguay, 180

valuation processes, 45
value audit processes, 48–9
values, concept of, 40–2, 44–5
variety views of strategy, 96, 103
  implications for management, 105–7
  importance of, 103–4
virtual teams, 74

Waddington, K., 58–9, 61
Wallace, Mike, 5, 145–56
Weick, Karl, 131, 134
welfare managers, 245–51
Wenglinsky, H., 141
West, M., 229, 237
Western, Simon, 11–21, 60
Westley, F., 88
Wheatley, M., 57

Whittington, Richard, 96–112
Wholey, J.S., 184
'wilding the tame' concept, 161
Wilkinson, A., 271–2
Williams, A.D., 67
Willmott, H., 279
Wise, Christine, 1–7

Woodruffe, C., 55
Wright, N., 270

Yarker, P., 243
Yukl, G., 58, 75, 79

Zhao, Y., 138